The Origins of Modern Feminism

THE ORIGINS OF MODERN FEMINISM: WOMEN IN BRITAIN, FRANCE AND THE UNITED STATES 1780–1860

Jane Rendall

LYCEUM
BOOKS, INC.

59 E. Van Buren
Chicago, IL 60605

© Jane Rendall 1985

Published by
Lyceum Books, Inc.
59 E. Van Buren
Chicago, IL 60605

Printed and bound in Hong Kong

Library of Congress Cataloging–in–Publication Data
Rendall, Jane, 1945–
The origins of modern feminism: women in Britain, France, and the
United States, 1780–1860/Jane Rendall.
   p.   cm.
Includes bibliographical references. (p.   ).
ISBN 0–925065–39–0: $19.95
1. Feminism—Great Britain—History—19th century.   2. Feminism
–France—History—19th century.   3. Feminism—United States–
–History—19th century.   I. Title
HQ1596.R39   1990
305.42′0941′09034—dc20   90–667
                                                          CI

Contents

List of Plates   vii

General Editor's Preface   ix

Acknowledgements   x

INTRODUCTION   1

1 THE ENLIGHTENMENT AND THE NATURE OF
  WOMEN   7

2 FEMINISM AND REPUBLICANISM:
  'REPUBLICAN MOTHERHOOD'   33
  Republican possibilities   34
  Conservative reaction   66

3 EVANGELICALISM AND THE POWER OF
  WOMEN   73
  Evangelical themes   74
  Revivalism and the organisation of women   77
  Millenarianism   101

4 EDUCATING HEARTS AND MINDS   108
  The case for 'maternal education'   109
  The training of teachers   125
  The education of the majority   140

5 WORK AND ORGANISATION   150
  Women's work in the early nineteenth century: changes
    and continuities   151
  Women workers and organisation   161
  The new industrial society: factory labour and domestic
    service   170
  New demands and new jobs   183

6 DOMESTIC QUESTIONS 189
Domestic myths and domestic realities 191
Women and community protest 200
Middle-class domesticity and its boundaries 206
Challenges to domesticity: individual and collective 215

7 POLITICS, PHILANTHROPY AND THE PUBLIC
SPHERE 231
Crowds, radicalism and revolution 232
Political issues: class, slavery and race 243
Moral reform and philanthropy 254

8 THE FEMINIST CASE 276
Three writers 277
Feminist practice: defeat and difficulties in France 291
The United States: feminism and the current of reform 300
Great Britain: feminist politics and the politics of class 307

CONCLUSION 321

Abbreviations 325

Notes and References 326

Notes to Plates 362

Bibliography 364

Index 369

List of Plates

1. A British satire on the Parisian women's march to Versailles in October 1789. British Library print
2. The conservative Edmund Burke, scourged by radicals. British Library print
3. Millet, *The Angelus* (1855–7)
4. The monthly meeting of the women Quakers of Houndsditch, 1843. From the *Illustrated London News*, 10 June 1843
5. 'The Scotch Cottage of Glenburnie'. British Library print
6. Daumier, *The Washerwomen of the Quai d'Anjou* (1850–2)
7. Women powerloom weavers in 1844. From the *Illustrated London News*, 18 May 1844
8. Delacroix, *Liberty Guiding the People* (1830)
9. Attack on the workhouse at Stockport, 1842. From the *Illustrated London News*, 20 August 1842
10. A coarse satire on the Female Reform Soceties of 1819. British Library print
11. Peterloo, showing a woman carrying the banner of the Manchester Female Reform Society on the platform with Henry Hunt. British Library print
12. 'Bravo, Bravo, that's even finer than Jeanne Deroin's last speech', from Daumier's series, *The Women Socialists* (1849)

The author and publishers wish to acknowledge the following illustration sources:
The Trustees of the British Museum – 1, 2, 5, 10, 11; The Mansell Collection – 3, 8; The Brotherton Library, University of Leeds – 4, 6, 7, 9, 12.

General Editor's Preface

SINCE the Second World War there has been a massive expansion in the study of economic and social history generating, and fuelled by, new journals, new academic series and societies. The expansion of research has given rise to new debates and ferocious controversies. This series proposes to take up some of the current issues in historical debate and explore them in a comparative framework.

Historians, of course, are principally concerned with unique events, and they can be inclined to wrap themselves in the isolating greatcoats of their 'country' and their 'period'. It is at least arguable, however, that a comparison of events, or a comparison of the way in which different societies coped with a similar problem – war, industrialisation, population growth and so forth – can reveal new perspectives and new questions. The authors of the volumes in this series have each taken an issue to explore in such a comparative framework. The books are not designed to be path-breaking monographs, though most will contain a degree of new research. The intention is, by exploring problems across national boundaries, to encourage students in tertiary education, in sixth-forms, and hopefully also the more general reader, to think critically about aspects of past developments. No author can maintain strict objectivity; nor can he or she provide definitive answers to all the questions which they explore. If the authors generate discussion and increase perception, then their task is well done.

CLIVE EMSLEY

Acknowledgements

For the opportunity to write this book I should like to thank, in particular, Clive Emsley, the editor of this series, who has offered both patience and constructive criticism throughout, and whose comments on the final manuscript were most valuable. My own interest in comparative history has emerged particularly from the experience of teaching a comparative course on the 'Condition of Women' in the History Department at the University of York over the last ten years, as the map of women's history was transformed. I should like to thank all those colleagues who have shared in its teaching and the many students who have taken part in it. Without their enthusiasm, their arguments and their stimulation, this book would never have been written. I should like especially to thank my colleagues Joanna de Groot and James McMillan who have read and commented upon the manuscript. But the final product is, of course, my own responsibility.

The librarians of the University of York and of the Fawcett Library have been of great assistance in the preparation of this work. Individuals in the British Library have done their best to mitigate the considerable frustrations of a system which keeps all nineteenth-century books about nineteenth-century women on deposit at Woolwich.

I thank Adam Middleton for his invaluable support, especially in the final, frantic stages of preparation. Lastly, I can only acknowledge an immeasurable debt to the women's movement today.

JANE RENDALL

Introduction

IN a sense the title of this book is anachronistic. The English word 'feminism' was not in use within this period. The French word *féminisme* was coined by the Utopian socialist, Charles Fourier, and used only by him. The first recorded use of the term in English, derived from the French, was in 1894, according to the 1933 *Supplement* to the *Oxford English Dictionary*. The relevant volume of the *Dictionary* itself was written from 1894 to 1897 and does not contain the accepted modern meaning of the term.[1] Twentieth-century historians have found the word an essential tool for analysis, and it is a term which may have many nuances of meaning. Gerda Lerner has distinguished between movements for 'woman's rights', in the sense of civil and political equality, and 'woman's emancipation', in the sense of a broader striving for 'freedom from oppressive restrictions imposed by sex; self-determination; autonomy'.[2] I have here used the latter description, using the word 'feminist' to describe women who claimed for themselves the right to define their own place in society, and a few men who sympathised with that claim. Yet it should be stressed that the women described here did not necessarily believe that implied an equality of roles between men and women. They lived and wrote before the impact of Karl Marx was felt, and they interpreted the word 'equality' in terms of moral and rational worth, not in terms of an equality of labour. Such aspirations, of course, were not entirely new; they are to be found, for instance, among seventeenth-century feminists, as well as in the fifteenth-century writer, Christine de Pisan.

I have therefore used the term 'modern feminism' to describe the way in which women came, in the period from the late eighteenth to the mid-nineteenth century, to associate together, perhaps at first for different reasons, and then to recognise and to assert their common interests as women. There has, in the historical literature, been much concentration on the lives and writings of individual feminists, male and female. Though this is vital, so too are the conditions of feminist practice and the social context in which such practice becomes possible. By such practice, I mean the association of women together for a feminist purpose: the ability of women to address other women, and men, in public: and the organisation of a range of activities, campaigns and writing, around the claims of women to determine different areas of their lives. Here I have tried to concentrate less on the careers of individual women, so that there is relatively little, for instance, on Frances Wright, on Anna Wheeler, or even on Florence Nightingale, and more on the historical context which allowed some, often very few, women to come together and assert in their lives and in their actions the values of self-determination and autonomy.

In looking at this context I have chosen to begin this account in the age of the American and French Revolutions, since the 1790s mark a very clear increase in feminist thinking, which must be viewed against the background of the Enlightenment. In ending around 1860, I have taken a point when, in Britain, the *English Woman's Journal* and its associated societies were already launched, and when John Stuart Mill was drafting his *Subjection of Women*. In the United States, the end of the ante-bellum period is a useful moment at which to consider the character and achievements of the feminist movement before the outbreak of the Civil War. In France, the first decade of the Second Empire reveals the weakness of a movement defeated after 1848, and the continuing debate between feminists and their male opponents which takes place from 1858 to 1860 usefully indicates the degree of hostility which French feminists had to counter. Overall by the end of the period, there did exist both a public awareness of the question of women's rights and women's future role and, it will be argued, some sense of the emergence of an international movement among feminists themselves. Yet it still has to be stressed that the numbers of women involved were very small, and their ideas still regarded as extreme and isolated.

There are, however, problems to be encountered in understanding the nineteenth-century world of women, and its relationship to the origins of feminism. In what sense is it possible to describe that world, to enter into a 'woman's culture' which may of its nature seem conservative, moralistic, even itself authoritarian? How far can we relate the firmly held commitment of, say, 'conservative' women like Hannah More or Catherine Beecher, to improve women's condition, to the emergence of a feminist movement concerned to challenge male power? It is not, I think, possible to evaluate the work of nineteenth-

concerned w/ cond. of autonomy
means of challenge: motherhood, language
of religion

INTRODUCTION   3

century feminists without entering sympathetically into such language and such writing. It is very difficult to discard twentieth-
century assumptions about equality, and to understand that the
assertion of an 'equality in difference' could mean a radical step
forward, a claim to the political rights from which women had been
automatically excluded for so long. Stress on the latent moral
superiority of women could bring with it the basis for a new
confidence, a new energy, a new assertion of women's potential
power. Belief in the equality and, at the same time, the complementarity of the different qualities of men and women, could provide the
means for a radical assertion of feminist practice, as the French
feminists of 1848 were to show. Increasingly, the worlds of men and
women were separated in the nineteenth century, a separation based
on the growing division between the home and the place of work.
Within that primarily domestic world, women could and did create a
culture which was not entirely an imposed one, which contained
within it the possibilities of assertion. Here, I am concerned with the
ways in which that assertion could become the assertion of autonomy.
It will be suggested that from discussion of such themes as the need to
improve women's education, the demand for the expansion of
women's employment, the case for the reform of the marriage laws,
came statements and actions which went beyond the limits of their
separate world, into a different debate.

At the same time it is important to remember that the only model
available to women to state their public demands was the political
language of men. We can only understand the importance of the
demand for citizenship if we remember that long tradition of
European thought, based on the classical education from which
women were firmly excluded, which entrenched the notion of the
classical republic and the virtuous citizen at the heart of political
debate. These themes offer the key to the claims made by women in
the 1790s. They had to challenge the view that citizenship was
possible only for male heads of households, excluding the dependent
of all kinds. The means for that challenge, came, eventually, from two
sources: from the republican notion of the increasing and moralising
domestic power of motherhood, and from the feminised language of
evangelicalism. As political conflicts shifted their ground, so too did
the language of feminism, though not as rapidly as is often thought.
The case made by socialist feminists in the 1830s was to draw upon
and to secularise the theme of the moral and regenerating power of

woman. The liberal case of the 1850s was to hark back to the republican ideal of virtue through citizenship. Feminist arguments had to combine both the demands that arose from the perceived needs of women, and the contemporary language of the male political world.

The starting point for women lay in the assumption that their lives and their future had to be seen in the context of their family roles. For them, in reality, there was no future outside the confines either of the family into which they were born or the one which they might themselves create, or, in default of either, the household which they might serve, as servant or governess. Demographers today accept that throughout most of western Europe and the United States, the 'conjugal' family group, of husband, wife and four or five children, with servants, lodgers or apprentices where appropriate, represented the normal and conventional framework of life, at least from the sixteenth century onwards.[3] There were some exceptions to this in a few areas of southern France where the co-residence of households of the same generation still existed at the beginning of this period. In material terms, there was virtually no employment for middle-class women outside marriage – with the exception of poorly paid teaching and, for a few, writing. For the working-class woman, there was little prospect of a 'living wage' for an adult single woman, outside domestic service in another household. A demographic pattern of late marriage, at the age of 24 or 25 for women, meant a long period of waiting. That time might be spent, for working women, partly in aiding the parental family, partly in saving for a future household of their own. Middle-class women might need to wait until capital, or training, or experience, was acquired, on which a future household could be based. High rates of fertility, and a short life expectancy, could mean that much of a woman's twenties, thirties and forties might be dominated by bearing children and caring for them. In an age where mechanical means of contraception were lacking, though family limitation was by no means unknown, the possibilities of choice were indeed limited.

In legal terms, women's very existence depended on their family roles. In Britain, single women over the age of 21 were legal persons. Married women, however, under the provisions of the common law, had no civil existence: they owned no personal property, they could neither sue nor be sued, they could not divorce their husbands, or claim any rights over their children. Wealthy women might have their property protected by a legal trust: but in the interests of their parental family, rather than their own. In colonial America, legal patterns largely followed English practice, though there is evidence, especially in New England, of some moderation of the harshness of the common law. In pre-revolutionary France, there were wide variations in the law and custom of marriage, and the status of women. In the area governed by customary law, broadly the north and centre of France, there was a similar pattern of the community of goods held by husband and wife, with the husband exercising the rights of ownership. In the Midi, where the inheritance of Roman law was still fundamentally important, a wife might have some rights over her property, both the dowry brought to marriage, and her personal belongings. The rights of both husband and wife over the property brought to the marriage – including, particularly, the wife's dowry – were normally established before marriage by means of the marriage contract.[4] Marriage, for all classes, in all three societies, remained an economic institution, for the mutual support, even survival, of all members of the family.

There is, of course, a continuing debate about changing expectations of family life, and about the extent to which the eighteenth century, or indeed earlier periods, saw the growth of 'affective individualism', or a 'romantic revolution'.[5] One aspect of this, it has been suggested, is the growth of the ideal of the 'companionate marriage', with consequences that are relevant to the position of women. My own view is that among sections of the middle and upper classes there may indeed have been some cultural shifts, which stressed the emotional bonds of family members, and more intense expectations of the rewards of family life. But this is in no way intended to suggest any absence of affection between husbands and wives, parents and children, in different classes or in earlier periods. It may indeed rather reflect the time that material security afforded to explore the pleasures of domestic life, and the wider diffusion of literature of all kinds in the eighteenth century. But what is important is that the character of family life was determined by a variety of material considerations, as well as by such elusive cultural shifts: the extent to which marriages were chosen, not arranged; the extent to which family property arrangements might dictate marriage; the nature and the sources of the family income to be relied upon; the kind of domestic labour, paid and unpaid, undertaken on behalf of the household by women. All these could profoundly affect the shape of the family and the situation of women within it: and the possibility of expanding their lives beyond domestic horizons. Twentieth-century assumptions about the separation of home from work may blind us to factors determining the relative strength or weakness of women within domestic life, and the interaction of domestic and public concerns.

My aim here has been to look at the origins of association among women in a comparative way, drawing on the experience of three western societies which shared many common roots, but which, at the same time, experienced urban and industrial changes in the course of the first half of the nineteenth century in very different ways. Religious and cultural contrasts helped to shape the character of women's movements in these three societies. I am aware that this is an ambitious project, even a premature one. Yet it is important that the demands which women made in the mid-nineteenth century should be understood against the background of the political, social and economic life of that world, if we are to understand more clearly the roots of women's continuing subordination in the late twentieth century. So I have tried to offer a comparative discussion, relying primarily on secondary literature rather than on original research. It will be obvious how much I have relied upon the work of a number of distinguished scholars in the field of women's history. It would be invidious to name authors. But I have been prompted to a comparative view partly by the excellence and sophistication of approach of a number of American historians of American women's lives in this period, and I have been helped by several works of considerable distinction published over the last few years on women in Britain. I have also benefited greatly from the questions raised about the character of French feminism by both French- and English-speaking historians of the nineteenth- and early twentieth-century movements. I am sure that they will be able to recognise this dependence and I hope that they will accept this inadequate acknowledgement.

1. The Enlightenment and the Nature of Women

FROM the late seventeenth to the late eighteenth centuries, the intellectual climate of western Europe came to be dominated by a mood of optimism about the potential of individual human reason and the possibility of understanding the natural environment of humanity: this mood of optimism came to be known as the Enlightenment. In Britain, the work of John Locke and of Isaac Newton in the 1680s and 1690s set the scene for a century of expanding horizons, as the belief grew that the laws which governed the physical and moral worlds could be understood and set out just as Newton had done in his work on gravity. In the process, men like John Locke, and, in France, Voltaire, Diderot and d'Alembert, challenged the authority of the Church and the literal interpretation of the Bible, asserting rather the right of the individual to enjoy freedom of speech, of conscience and of religion. That could be extended further, to assert, as did Jean-Jacques Rousseau in the *Social Contract* (1762) and Thomas Paine in *The Rights of Man* (1791–2) that individuals had political rights as citizens, to a democratic voice in their government.

It is often assumed that concern about the rights of women springs from the eighteenth-century Enlightenment, from the assertion of individual natural rights in a period of revolutionary political thinking. When Mary Wollstonecraft wrote her *Vindication of the Rights of Woman* in 1792, she seemed to be applying the arguments of the *Rights of Man* to the situation of women. Yet the heritage of the Enlightenment to feminists and their opponents is an extraordinarily confusing one.[1] The writers on natural law of the seventeenth and eighteenth centuries were to offer a clearly secular and contractual model of family relationships, one which directly challenged assumptions of divinely ordered patriarchy within the family, though this was of course quite incidental to their major work. In their political analyses of state and society, writers such as John Locke, Montesquieu and Voltaire occasionally touched upon the position of women and condemned aspects of their legal or social situation. But, more fundamentally, the preoccupation of eighteenth-century writers with the problem of knowledge, with the nature of human psychology, with the study of the passions, meant more detailed exploration of the differences between the sexes, and much more explicit discussion of how far such differences were innate, how far they were moulded by the environment. As the writers of western Europe embarked upon the history of social institutions, employing material from the past history of Europe, and the situation of contemporary peoples in different parts of the world, they came to justify the position of women and the development of the family in western European commercial civilisation as appropriate to the highest form of social development yet reached. Few writers of the Enlightenment took a deep interest in the relationship between the sexes, and yet the implications of their work were fundamental. The position of women in western Europe was analysed in new terms: it was to be justified by reference to what was natural for their sex, rather than divinely ordained and, at the same time, set into a particular historical framework. These terms were to dictate the grounds of debate for feminists and their opponents in the nineteenth century.

The belief that the divinely ordered patriarchal relationships of the family offered a model for political society itself was attacked by a number of political writers from the late seventeenth and early eighteenth centuries. Although the relationship between the family and the wider institutions of society had been extensively treated by many political writers from Plato onwards, the seventeenth century had seen a careful elaboration of patriarchal thinking, best known in the work by Sir Robert Filmer, *Patriarcha* (1680).[2] In the course of this debate, political thinkers and natural lawyers were to reflect on relationships within the family, not only between parents and children, but between husbands and wives, mothers and children. Though this was in no way their primary concern, the implications were important.

In Britain, patriarchal political theory developed together with that which was used most successfully to assault it: contractual political theory. Both raised questions about the origins of political authority. Where Filmer argued that monarchy was a natural institution, to be traced back to the Biblical account of Eden, to the sovereignty over his family given to Adam, the best known of his contractualist opponents, John Locke, also returned to the origin of government, which for him lay in the state of nature, and to the place of family relationships within that original state of nature.[3] Locke clearly distinguished between the power of parents and political authority. Marriage was a contractual relationship in which, although the male's superior ability might give him the right to manage joint affairs, it gave no absolute sovereignty. Locke countered Filmer's use of the fifth commandment by assuming that parental authority implied the rights of the mother as well as those of the father over their children. The obligations of parents to their children arose from natural law, for family relationships were natural, in a sense that political authority, which sprang from the voluntary entry of citizens into political society, was not. Family relationships were a part of that natural law which could be perceived by reason, which laid down a network of mutual obligations for all family members, which existed within the state of nature, before entry into political society might take place. A husband and father might have authority over wife, children and dependants, but it was limited by natural law and by the terms of the contract involved. Though Locke did try to meet the argument that no such state of nature had ever existed, in pointing to contemporary primitive societies, his argument was neither historical nor anthropological, but a hypothetical reconstruction. Even so, the attack on the political relevance of the family was vital: it implied the separation of political and social worlds. The attack on patriarchy had two results. The family was no longer a relevant political symbol, a model of authority, but a part of the pre-political fabric of society, of a web of natural relationships; within the family the authority of the patriarch was itself deemed to be no longer absolute but limited in a variety of ways.

There was of course a much wider tradition of writing with reference to the natural law, that law which asserted 'that this or that thing ought to be done, because from right reason it is concluded, that the same is necessary for the preservation of society among men'.[4] Natural law, to writers of very different political views such as John Locke and Samuel von Pufendorf, the conservative German professor of Heidelberg, writing in the late seventeenth century, and the English clergyman William Wollaston and the Scottish moralist Francis Hutcheson, writing in the early eighteenth century, provided a means of analysing the obligations and the rights of individuals by virtue of their simple humanity, quite apart from local and particular legal systems. Here was one way of analysing *social* institutions, with reference not to the Scriptures or to the Church or to customary or Roman law, but to the universal experience of living in society. Writing about natural law has a long and complex history which cannot be considered here, but which may be related to medieval political theory, and to the work of the great sixteenth-century Dutch international lawyer, Hugo Grotius. Writers of the Enlightenment throughout Europe looked in particular to the work of Samuel von Pufendorf, who in his *De Jure Naturae et Gentium* (1672) and *De officio hominis et civis* (1673) described a law of nature based on 'the accurate contemplation of our natural condition and propensions', a general and systematic view of the social world. It was not a secular creed, since the assumption was that the laws of nature were essentially God-given, yet related to one part of human experience only: life on earth. Pufendorf does not have a great deal to say about the relationship of men and women, or about the institution of the family. Yet in his chapter on matrimony, quoting Grotius, he described it as 'the chief representation of the social life'.[5] To fulfil the natural needs of mankind, marriage had been ordained both for mutual delight, and as a proper arrangement for the bringing up of children. A contract was essential to marriage, a contract expressing the mutual duties of fidelity and cohabitation. The wife should agree to obey her husband 'in matters relating to their mutual state and to their household'. Yet at the same time the husband had no essential or natural right to the power of life or death over his wife, to inflict any grievous punishment on her, or to dispose of her goods or lands: these matters were left to the contract or to local laws. In societies where the right of paternity was clearly established, the main parental authority over children should be exercised by the father, though in his absence by the mother. Such arguments do not suggest any very radical questioning of the structure of family relationships. Yet the same framework was employed by more liberal writers. Locke, in his *Two Treatises*, had argued that although it will usually be the case that from his better knowledge and education the husband will play the leading role, it need not necessarily always be so. And his challenge to patriarchal authority within the family had rested upon his view that such claims essentially denied the natural right of a mother to authority over her own children, a right which the father should share.[6] Discussion of the family as a natural institution, meeting the needs of different individuals who contracted with each other, could lead to further consideration of the rights of different members of the family.

In the early eighteenth century some writers, such as William Wollaston in England, and Francis Hutcheson in Scotland, while following Pufendorf's essential outlines, offered a less authoritarian view. In his *Religion of Nature Delineated* (1724) Wollaston remarked that he had deliberately refrained from discussion of the authority of husband over wife 'because I think it has been carried much too high'. Both husband and wife were to be governed by reason – and if the man's reason were stronger or his experience greater, then deference by the woman would follow, but such an outcome would depend on the circumstances.[7] Francis Hutcheson, who gave a long and interesting chapter to 'Rights and duties in the state of marriage' in his *System of Moral Philosophy* (1755), explores further and makes much more explicit the ways in which marriage fulfilled 'the intention of nature'. Marriage was of course inspired by the reproductive instinct, yet Providence had so ordained it that sexual desire was naturally incited and accompanied by 'the esteem of virtue and wisdom, the desire and love of innocence of manners, complacence, confidence, and the tenderest goodwill',[8] almost obscuring the more brutal aspects of that desire. Hutcheson stressed the reciprocal responsibilities of marriage, as 'a state of equal partnership or friendship', in which nature offered no foundation for the exercise of authority by one partner over another. Men might have superior strength in body or mind, and prevail by means of those qualities; yet that was by no means universally true, and in the case of disputes, arbitration might be a final resort. Broadly he suggested that domestic affairs seemed to be divided into two spheres, one fitted for each sex, into which the other should seldom interfere. Hutcheson denounced the 'tyrannical and unmanly powers' given to husbands by the laws of certain nations, and suggested that parental powers too should belong to both parents. Hutcheson was effectively widening the grounds of the argument, resting his analyses of the natural order on a detailed exploration of the passions and affections which men and women fulfilled in marriage. For him, the relationship rested upon 'the motives of mutual good liking', and 'the tender sentiments and affections', and in this followed the designs of Providence for a happy companionate marriage undertaken both to rear and educate children and for the mutual happiness of both parties. In this view of the 'natural' relationship, he stressed the emotional bonds of marriage, in which 'all the tenderest joys of life' were to be found. This analysis of the legal and psychological bonds of marriage led Hutcheson to challenge authoritarian views of the relationship to an unusual degree for Enlightenment writers; though male dominance could still be justified on the grounds of the likely practical inequalities between men and women.

Writers on natural law on the Continent did not on the whole move to a more liberal position with respect to the law governing marriage, though one of the more popular translators of Pufendorf, Jean Barbeyrac, went further than Pufendorf had done in stressing the contractual nature of the relationship, suggesting that possibly the length of the marriage might be laid down in the original contract.[9] Few major writers took up the cause before the later eighteenth century. The interest of Voltaire in the legal restraints of marriage and in the need for divorce legislation, for example, seems to have been directed rather against the control of marriage by the Catholic Church, as one element in his anti-clerical crusade. In his *Dictionnaire Philosophique* (1764) he praised the practice of divorce in Roman and early Christian states, and some Protestant countries of Europe, yet more for its greater social utility rather than from any particular sympathy with the condition of women. There are few signs of any real challenge to the legal and social inferiority of women to be found in the *Encyclopédie*, or in the writings of Voltaire and his associates, though there are some signs of humanitarian sympathy.[10]

The writings of natural lawyers had opened up new possibilities in the analysis of the family, yet changing attitudes in the eighteenth century were to come about not from the language of political theory but from discussion of the role women were fitted for by nature, understood through the study of psychology and history. A central theme of the writing of the Enlightenment was the significance of the observation of human nature itself, of the need to chart more clearly human understanding, beliefs and passions. Writers from John Locke onwards strove for a clear description of the ways in which the human mind functioned and how it governed human behaviour. The study of human nature was seen as an essential prerequisite to the study of man in society, and it was to be grounded on the empirical study of human behaviour, from which its laws might be constructed, a procedure crudely grounded on the Newtonian model. John Locke had suggested in his *Essay concerning Human Understanding* (1689) that the human mind was a 'tabula rasa', a blank sheet upon which ideas would be imprinted through the sensations received from the external world, ideas which might then be reflected upon and combined. If 'the dictates of right reason' could no longer be consistently accepted as a guide to moral conduct, it seemed increasingly important to consider the limits of human reason, to gain a fuller picture of the motivations underlying human behaviour, to chart more effectively the irrational side of men's nature. This project could also be extended, sometimes directly, sometimes by implication only, to considering the extent to which sexual differences in behaviour were held to be innate, biologically determined, and how far they were moulded by the environment in which women lived – and, too, how far the different nature of women was equated with their greater irrationality.

Though clearly the representation of male and female qualities was nothing new, the systematic analysis of human nature which is such a feature of the Enlightenment was a secular one and one which claimed the authority of science – for that reason its importance went beyond treatments of femininity and female stereotypes to be found in literature, in satire and in prescriptive manuals of the past. One outstanding attempt at a definitive human psychology in the eighteenth century was of course that of David Hume. For Hume, in the *Treatise of Human Nature* (1739), human actions and affections sprang from human passions, whether direct or indirect, calm or violent: 'reason is and ought to be the slave of our passions'. In particular, the instinct of sympathy played an important part in the process of moral judgement. For Hume justice was not simply perceived by 'right reason', but was an 'artificial' virtue, based on convention and on the common understanding by men of the advantages to be derived from security and protection to property afforded by governments. Justice was defined with exclusive reference to the public, property-owning sphere of life, and counterposed to the 'natural' virtues which brought with them pleasurable sensations – virtues such as 'meekness, beneficence, charity, generosity, clemency, moderation'. Such virtues arose naturally, originally from our affections for those closest to us and, through the feeling of sympathy, were extended more widely because of their effect on the general good of society.[11]

Hume is not concerned with an analysis of the difference between the sexes, though at one or two points he hints at such a comparison.

In analysing the development of a sense of justice, he based his argument on the need to preserve property through the proper organisation of the public sphere, with governments as the preservers of contractual obligations, security and inheritance. The parallel virtue in women was chastity, also an artificial virtue, arising from the need to secure assurance of the legitimacy of children: 'from this trivial and anatomical observation is deriv'd that vast difference between the education and duties of the two sexes'.[12] To secure their fidelity, a particular restraint was imposed upon women, a sense of reputation, and shame at its loss. Through their education, such a sense was deeply internalised and extended not only to women of childbearing age, but to those beyond it. Some understanding of the original motives underlying such restraints was implied in the lesser degree of censure to which men were subject for breaches of chastity. Hume offered little insight into the ways in which the natural instincts of men and women differed; but it is interesting that in his description of the sense of compassion, he suggested that this should be seen as a secondary principle derived from the general principle of sympathy:

> Add to this, that pity depends, in a great measure on the continuity and even sight of the object; which is a proof, that 'tis derived from the imagination. Not to mention that women and children are most subject to pity, as being most guided by that faculty.[13]

There may be a suggestion here that women and children were most guided by sympathy, that power of empathising with the feelings of others which is at the source of moral approbation for Hume. The determinism of Hume was to influence much eighteenth-century writing about human society that claimed to be based on a full understanding of human nature and of the limitations on the freedom of the will. For the relationship between the sexes, the implications were fundamental: the lesson was that that relationship was built upon the natural instincts of men and women, and justified by the conventions and customs of all societies, for the universality of those natural instincts was stressed by Hume.

Others, of course, followed Hume in their charting of human psychology and the mechanisms of sympathy. The *philosophes* of France, in their treatment of sexual differences also stressed the natural differences between men and women; and their discussion of these differences is in many ways more striking than their occasional nods in the direction of legal or political improvement in the condition of women. Montesquieu, for example, in his early work the *Persian Letters* (1721) raised the question of whether women should, by their nature, be subordinate, and offers a gesture towards the ideal of independence in the final letter, as Roxane, from the harem, writes: 'I have rewritten your laws after the laws of nature, and my spirit has ever sustained itself in independence'.[14] Yet at the same time Montesquieu throughout his work showed a profound contempt for female qualities, incorporating the dual view of women as weak, gentle and soft on the one hand, and on the other as frivolous, vain and irrational.[15] In the *Dictionnaire Philosophique*, the energy with which Voltaire calls for improvement in the treatment of women through the introduction of divorce may be contrasted with his very clear suggestions in the articles 'Homme' and 'Femme', that women, physically and mentally weaker than men, had in all societies restricted themselves to the domestic sphere, excluded from the heaviest manual labour. Yet that seclusion meant that women had played no part in the world of wars, atrocities, crime, and that they had preserved a moral advantage through their natural inferiority.[16]

Perhaps the best known French writers in this respect were Rousseau and Diderot, both of whom contributed much to the eighteenth-century view of the 'natural' woman. The impact of Rousseau's work was complex and interesting, and has been the subject of much scrutiny; the Sophie of *Emile* (1762) and the Julie of *La Nouvelle Héloïse* (1761) appear to offer contradictory models, if taken at face value. Neither can be seen in isolation from Rousseau's political arguments, since he was attempting to establish what the natural qualities of women were in the natural state of mankind. In the *Discourse on the origin of inequality* (1755) Rousseau had countered Locke's argument for the existence of the monogamous family in the state of nature by portraying that state as one where sexual relations were governed only by sexual appetites, where no guarantees of paternity existed. But in the stage of society which followed that, with the coming of private property, the existence of the self-sufficient rural family implied the sexual division of labour and the government of the family by the man, justified by the need to establish paternity. There was then a contrast between the original condition of women, with similar sexual needs to men, and that condition which Rousseau also terms a 'natural' one which arises from the following stage of society.

Rousseau continued to define the 'natural' woman with reference to this stage; in the *Letter to D'Alembert* (1758) he argued that the development of certain qualities in women, whether innate or not, must be in the general interest of society:

> If the timidity, chasteness and modesty which are proper to them are social inventions, it is in society's interest that women acquire these qualities; they must be cultivated in women, and any woman who disdains them offends good morals.[17]

Although, when discussing the education of Emile, Rousseau emphasised the importance of environment and education in corrupting the natural instincts of the child, for Sophie there was no such critique, for her innate female qualities were seen in relation only to her future social role. Female characteristics – shame, modesty, the desire to please, even duplicity and cunning, her practical qualities of mind – were all to be cultivated with one function in mind, to fit Sophie for her role as Emile's partner, complementary to him within that rural patriarchal family, a secluded, modest, wife and mother. Rousseau saw the natural qualities of women as including their cunning, weakness, superficiality, deceitfulness and vanity, and he feared the corrupting influence which women might wield over men; as he suggested, it was through female influence that the corrupt and decadent artificiality of city life might corrode the natural man. Yet, in its right setting, female influence might improve and uplift, as when Julie, in *La Nouvelle Héloïse*, put her duty above the passion which she felt for her lover, and became the inspiration of her household, the perfect wife and mistress of a household run along the lines which Rousseau advocated: in a rural setting, segregated from the world, devoted to the natural values. Yet for Julie such values involved a constant struggle against all her sexual instincts. And, in the last resort, Rousseau offered no solution to that duality, that constant struggle for women: there was no alternative for Julie but to obey her parents, to take the man qualified to be her husband and her children's father. Sophie, by contrast, failed when transported to the corruptions of city life, succumbing to seduction, that sin for which in Rousseau's eyes there was no redemption.[18] Rousseau's view of women's nature therefore incorporated both distrust of their moral weakness, their innate qualities, their liability to sexual failure, and also expectations of women as a potential source of moral strength, *if* they could repress their weaker selves, *if* they could live under the appropriate conditions for fulfilling that potential. The family which Rousseau saw as ideal was, therefore, partly a natural institution, founded on feeling, distinguished from all other institutions, and partly a social construction, in which the authority of men over women was founded both on women's weakness and on the necessity of guaranteeing paternity, in the interests of society as a whole. The equality and freedom which the republic of the *Social Contract* (1760) offered to its citizens did not apply to women.

Surprisingly, many contemporary women writers found much to admire in Rousseau: his message for them was not the misogynistic one which twentieth-century interpreters have found. In particular, the influence of the household of *La Nouvelle Héloïse* can be traced in a number of works written on the education of girls in the second half of the eighteenth century. The theme of the moral regeneration of the citizen through the influence of the family became an extremely powerful one; and it was this theme, rather than the artificiality and weakness of Sophie, which constituted Rousseau's appeal to these writers. In the 1770s the works of Mme de Montbart, of Bernardin de St Pierre, of Mme Roland, all stressed the importance of the education of girls for motherhood, a motherhood which would entail the close and personal rearing of their young children, the moral inspiration of their families, and the development of close and emotional bonds between mothers and daughters in particular.[19] Sons were to be raised as good citizens, girls with a view to their future responsibilities as mothers. This is illustrated in particular in the popular work by Mme de Genlis, *Adèle et Théodore* (1782), in which Rousseau's educational principles were applied to the upbringing of Adèle and Théodore, the son and daughter of the Baroness d'Almane. Mme de Genlis' major criticisms of Rousseau lie in the view which he takes of women's innate weaknesses; for her, these should be subject to precisely the same moral judgement and correction as any other failings. A daughter's disposition to vanity, or to artifice, should be corrected like any other fault, since it was due not to ineradicable female weakness, but to the corruptions of the world. In Mme de Genlis' work, the Baroness withdrew from society to devote herself to the care of her children in rural seclusion, to practise the simple educational ideals of drawing out children's natural qualities. The task of education was still to apply discipline; yet it was to be carefully adapted to character and to disposition. Such a plan was especially the task of a mother, though as Théodore grew older his father played a major role. Adèle herself was to be trained not only in practical domestic duties, and in the elementary knowledge of a number of fields of study, but also in motherhood, through the care of a small girl, through which 'she experiences already the pleasures of a good mother'.[20]

Catherine Macaulay expressed precisely the same criticisms of Rousseau in her *Letters on Education* (1790), which may be read as a commentary on Rousseau's educational ideals. For Catherine Macaulay, education had to be understood in the light of the sensational philosophy of John Locke and his successors, in which the influence of the environment, and the power of the association of ideas in the mind, created the culture of 'that artificial being, a social man'.[21] She defended the idea of domestic education, but for her the same rules were to be applied to girls as to boys, apart from physical exercise. For her the rules of morality were to be the same for both sexes, for all rational creatures; such vices as were regarded as peculiarly female by Rousseau were rather the product of women's situation and education. She analysed the way in which Rousseau, while rejecting innate ideas as a part of the human mind, had nevertheless drawn attention to the ignorance, the vanity and the cunning of women, as an element in his argument for masculine superiority. Though women's physical inferiority might have been a cause of their subordination in the past, it need no longer be so, as men saw the advantages of relaxing their tyranny. The education given to women was indeed just that which would most corrupt and debilitate them, with the effects suggested by Rousseau as innately female. Only education based on immutable moral rules for both men and women could bring about a more rational society, in which women no longer needed to rely on their personal charms to attract a husband and masculine protection.[22]

A different kind of exploration of women's nature is to be found in the work of the editor of the *Encyclopédie*, Diderot. In his brief essay *Sur les femmes* (1772), Diderot criticised the work of Antoine Thomas, *Essai sur le caractère, les moeurs, et l'esprit des femmes* (1772), for its coldness and impartiality. Diderot wrote rather of the hardships which women underwent: neglect in infancy, the anxieties of adolescence, the tyranny of marriage, the pains of childbearing, the contempt of legal systems. What was needed was an understanding of the violence of women's emotions, the passions they were capable of and of the influence of their reproductive systems upon their capacity' for religious fanaticism. Incapable of abstract thought, even of understanding in any depth the conceptions of justice and of virtue, they remained savages at heart, in spite of the veneer of civilisation. In his *Supplément au voyage de Bougainville* (1772, published 1796), Diderot contrasted the innocence of the natural savage with the corruptness of sexual relationships in the civilised world. There, in that mythical Tahiti, women and men might freely engage in sexual relationships, as long as they did so in the happy expectation of children, for in that society only motherhood secured their high status to women. Sterile women wore a black veil, menstruating women a grey veil. This analysis of an idyllic community, released from sexual repression, in which women, like men, were free to follow their inclinations, was based on a view of women's nature which found its primary fulfilment in motherhood.[23] In France Diderot brought his own daughter up on the most traditional lines, departing from them only to ensure that she knew something of her own biology and of the processes of childbirth.[24] For Diderot, women's nature was fundamentally different from that of men, intimately related to their reproductive processes, they were both more passionate and more unpredictable than men, not subject to rational control and ultimately mysterious. Diderot, like Rousseau, offers no easy solutions for the fulfilment of women's nature; the contrast between the innocence and happiness of the women of Tahiti and those of his own world was striking, yet, nevertheless, the pressures to conformity of the civilised society should not be resisted, for only by conforming to convention could women secure a degree of contentment.

Other *philosophes* were also concerned to explore the implications of the sensational philosophy, to consider the effect of women's conditioning by their environment, and to speculate on the political possibilities for change. The Baron d'Holbach wrote seriously about the corrupting effects upon women of the educational, legal and political restraints imposed upon them, restraints which developed within them vanity, pride, deceitfulness, coquetry – all the vices of which Rousseau accused them.[25] Rather, he suggested, the tyranny of legislation and the absence of serious moral education for them left women of all classes a prey to such faults. D'Holbach showed a clear political understanding of the ways in which women were oppressed in his society, yet at the same time the changes he proposed were limited ones for 'because of the weakness of their powers, women are not capable of abstract knowledge, of the profound studies which suit men'.[26] Women should rather be encouraged to develop their own best qualities, those of the heart and moral feelings, while also fitting themselves, by patience, industry, frugality and piety, to be the wives and mothers of citizens. These were the objects to which a future legislator should turn his attention, and here again is the recurring image of domesticity as an instrument for the moral regeneration of society. The only writer to accept the full implications of the sensational philosophy in this respect was the *philosophe* d'Helvétius, materialist and atheist, who took it as axiomatic that all knowledge was derived from sense-impressions, and that all faculties of the mind were dependent on that of sensation. He argued therefore that only external factors, such as education, were responsible for the differences between men, and also between men and women who were otherwise naturally equal. He suggested that all children, girls as well as boys, should be removed from the care of their parents, and conditioned in a public educational system, where society could train individuals according to its needs. A further implication of the sensational philosophy was that for mankind the greatest good was reducible to the greatest pleasure to be achieved by the senses, and for Helvétius this was undoubtedly sexual pleasure. Such pleasure was considered exclusively from the male point of view, implying that women should make available for the purposes of the state the sexual rewards they could offer men.[27] The confusion and complexity of these analyses suggests the different strands of the debate: a belief in the corrupting nature of contemporary society for women, and in political change to overcome it, might nevertheless coexist with a belief in the true qualities of women's nature, to be realised only in their proper and domestic setting. Though the optimism and egalitarianism implicit in the sensational philosophy was recognised by a few, its potential radicalism remained to be explored.

Thus, in England and in France, writers of this period were still preoccupied with the balance to be achieved between the qualities of the natural woman, and the restraints that might be imposed both by the individual herself, and by the prevailing conventions of society. Such tensions may be seen in the rise of the sentimental novel in England, which at its most serious, as for example in the work of the Scottish novelist Henry Mackenzie, offered a Humean analysis of the psychology of the hero or heroine, depicting their feelings and emotions without judgement, as a psychological reality. Mackenzie's novel *Julia de Roubigné* (1777) has been compared to *La Nouvelle Héloïse*; its plot is very similar, as the heroine, though in love with another, marries a different man from honourable motives. The difference lies in the outcome: the characters do not achieve happiness, though they are all morally admirable, because they follow convention rather than their own instincts.[28] The sentimental movement in literature is perhaps best known by the reaction which it aroused. Conservative moralists were obviously shocked by the implication that men and women might challenge accepted patterns of social behaviour with impunity to achieve happiness; feminists noted the implication that men and women were governed by their passions, and the further implication that women by nature were more at the mercy of their own feelings and instincts. The battleground for feminists in the next decades was to lie not only on a political front but also within the field of human psychology. The search for the natural woman was to dictate the grounds of the debate, since it offered a new rationale for subordination, and also a new conception of the role which women might play for which their instincts fitted them, in a new social and political order.

There was, however, another way of evaluating the proper position of women. In the secular and critical spirit of the Enlightenment, the hypothetical thesis of the state of nature which Locke, Hobbes and others had advanced to justify a political viewpoint was subjected to continuing analysis. Increasingly, by the middle of the century, such a thesis was simply untenable. Rather, writers were increasingly aware of the new geographical worlds around them, of a variety of different societies and a range of social institutions, which could be studied and which no longer fitted the classical or the Christian modes of analysis. The Indians of North America, the Chinese, the Hindus and Muslims of India, the societies of northern and western Africa: slowly such societies were reported, analysed and made use of, in early attempts to grasp the history of that most fundamental social institution, the human family. In the *Spirit of the Laws* (1749), Montesquieu's aim, to discover the laws that governed human societies, 'the necessary relations arising from the nature of things', led him to describe, comparatively, the condition of women and family relationships. His approach was a dual one in this as in all other aspects of the work. He wished both to consider how the principles that inspired the three major types of government – virtue in a republic, honour in a monarchy, and fear in despotic governments – and how the physical conditions of different societies – climate, geography and size – affected the condition of women. His brief treatment of the application of the principles of government to family life is predictable. In republics, women living simply, without luxury, were restrained by the manners of a society, not by its laws, and in consequence were secluded, virtuous and chaste – so much so that he writes of the Greek cities 'in this respect hardly any people were ever known to have had a better or wiser policy'.[29] In a monarchy, on the other hand, women lived in considerable freedom, assuming a spirit of liberty, called to court through the distinction of ranks, yet subject to vanity and corruption by luxury. In a despotism, women were in a state 'of the most rigorous servitude', in close confinement. At the same time, in Book XVI, Montesquieu argues that climatic and physical conditions also have an important effect on the treatment of women. In hot climates, where women matured very young, 'their reason . . . never accompanies their beauty', and they ought therefore to be in a state of dependence. In temperate climates, women tended to mature later, to be more knowledgeable at the age of marriage, and to preserve their charms better, so that a kind of equality tended to be suited to these climates, as well as the institution of monogamy:

> Nature, which has distinguished men by their reason and bodily strength, has set no other bounds to their power than those of this strength and reason. It has given charms to women, and ordained that their ascendant over man shall end with these charms: but in hot countries these are found only at the beginning and never in the progress of life.[30]

Only climatic conditions could render polygamy tolerable; in itself it was of no service to either sex, yet it could still serve a utilitarian purpose, since the slavery of women conformed to the spirit of a despotic government, and the liberty that women enjoyed in a monarchy would cause anarchy to an eastern government. The argument faces difficulties: if the influence of climate had consequences contrary to the natural laws governing the relationship of the sexes, then civil laws should 'oppose the nature of the climate' as in Patan in India where the influence of climate violated the natural shame of women at incontinence, and 'the wanton desires of the women are so outrageous that the men are obliged to make use of a certain apparel to shelter them from their designs'.[31] Montesquieu praises the naturally good manners of women in northern countries, where 'all their passions are calm' and the conversation of women embellished society generally, Ideally, Montesquieu clearly admired the condition of women in a republic, the unattainable embodiment of frugality, chastity and virtue. In practice, he was left evaluating the dangers and the advantages of the relative liberty enjoyed by women in a monarchy, a freedom which might allow women's natural weaknesses to develop. And as a fantastic contrast to his discussion of the family in temperate northern climates, Montesquieu initiated a lengthy European fascination with the 'oriental despotism' of the family, the model of absolute and patriarchal authority in a distant setting, against which European practice might be measured.

In his discussion of the condition of women, Montesquieu mostly compared static societies, though he did discuss the changes in the condition of women which followed the transition in Rome from republic to empire, changes which followed the dissolution of old republican manners, bringing luxury and, inseparably, public incontinence. He did not consider the development of the history of the family in an organised way, though his three-fold division of family types was to be extremely influential. Other French and Scottish writers were, however, to elaborate universally applicable theories of history, based on the different stages through which, it was held, all societies and their institutions passed. The development of family life and of the condition of women could be understood only in relation to such an evolutionary view of society, at the apex of which was to be contemporary, commercial, western European society. In France Turgot and Helvétius, in Scotland, Adam Smith, Adam Ferguson, William Robertson and John Millar, all, in the process of exploring the history of their own civilisation, devoted attention to the history of the family and the condition of women; and their arguments contributed much to that complacently Whiggish position on the history of the family which was becoming orthodox by the end of the eighteenth century. Adam Smith, delivering his lectures on jurisprudence in the 1760s, was also elaborating the view that human society passed through four stages in its development – savage, pastoral, agricultural and commercial – and that such stages were fundamentally defined by their mode of subsistence, which also clearly determined all aspects, social and political, of the life of that society.[32] The influence of Montesquieu here is obvious and so also is the significance of the contemporary work on American Indian societies. The early study of the Abbe Lafitau, *Moeurs des sauvages amériquains comparées aux moeurs des premiers tems* (1724), offered important guidance to these historians, since it suggested that contemporary American societies could be regarded as a kind of living model of the earliest stages of human society. No longer would it be necessary to hypothesise from a state of nature. Historians could compare the levels reached by different societies, and could use both contemporary and historical materials to construct an evolutionary ladder based on the four-stages theory, in which the highest point was their own commercial civilisation, the lowest the primitive world of the American Indians. Analysis of family relationships, and of the condition of women, was to play a larger part in this historical enterprise than in more conventional political histories, for the family was an essential part of the social and economic fabric of these different societies. And new evidence was, for these writers as for Montesquieu, raising the challenging possibilities of different kinds of family organisation: the matrilineal descent of the Iroquois, the collective marriages of Eastern Iran, the polyandry of the Nairs of the Malabar coast, all these challenged the simple assumptions that the monogamous family alone was that which accorded with the law of nature. Awareness of the wide variation in the condition of women in such different societies was to lead to a new kind of justification of the position held by women in the contemporary western world.

Adam Ferguson and William Robertson both wrote of the early human family, with particular reference to the American Indians. They noted that among Indian tribes, the women laboured together in the fields, and had responsibility both for domestic cares and for all the property of the household. Ferguson wrote of the pattern of matrilineal descent, with men moving to their wives' families on marriage, yet argued that such a pattern did not indicate a high status for women: 'it is a servitude and a continual toil, where no honours are; and those whose province it is, are in fact the slaves and the helots of their country.'[33] He saw women's domestic labour in this context as a form of slavery, though one which was softened by affection, and which delayed the coming of formal slavery. This theme, of women in primitive societies as burdened by labour, was one which was to be more fully explored and emphasised. William Robertson, in his

History of America (1777), was to stress even more strongly the superiority of the contemporary world in this respect: 'That women are indebted to the refinements of polished manners for a happy change in their state, is a point which can admit of no doubt. To despise and to degrade the female sex, is the characteristic of the savage state in every part of the globe.'[34]

The most thorough treatment of this theme, and one of the most interesting of all eighteenth-century historical studies of the condition of women, is to be found in John Millar's *Origin of the Distinction of Ranks* (1771, revised 1779). In a lengthy chapter, 'Of the Rank and Condition of Women in Different Ages', Millar traced the evolution of the family, and of women's position within it, indicating how that progression had led to changes in patterns of human behaviour, from the narrow horizons of savage society to the refined and polished culture of the modern world, assuming always 'a natural progress from ignorance to knowledge, and from rude to civilized manners'.[35] Such progress followed a uniform pattern, though it might vary for particular national reasons. Millar, treating of different varieties of subordination, began his work with a consideration of the position of women, since:

> Of all our passions, it should seem that those which unite the sexes are most easily affected by the peculiar circumstances in which we are placed, and most liable to be affected by the power of habit and education. Upon this account they exhibit the most wonderful variety of appearances, and in different ages and countries, have produced the greatest diversity of manners and customs.[36]

In the savage state, the difficulties of achieving a mere subsistence, and the absence of private property, meant very little time for, or interest in, the rapidly satisfied passion of sex, and certainly no acquaintance with 'those artificial rules of decency and decorum'.[37] The savage was moved by simple, natural instincts, analogous to those of animals; yet the association of the sexes might last longer than those of the animal kingdom, because of the length of the dependency of childhood, and the arrival of new children. The advantages of marriage increasingly became apparent, though they tended to be undertaken without any regard for personal preference, but through family negotiations. Such savages still had little respect for chastity among women. Women were normally treated as servants or slaves, constantly labouring in agricultural or domestic work, while their husbands, if not engaged in war or hunting, might remain idle at home. Millar charted the kinds of submission which husbands expected from their wives – their lack of access to property, their purchase with the bride-price – in all savage nations, still existing in some. Yet he noted that however shocking this picture was, it might be seen as one not unsuited to the condition in which such savage societies were placed. He noted one exception, that in some countries where marriage was not fully established, a woman who continued to live by herself though having sexual intercourse with several men would be at the head of her own household with authority over her children, and thereby raised to a position of rank and dignity. This happened among the Lycians, among some Indian tribes and among the Nairs, where the practice of a woman taking several husbands is cited by Millar as being entirely inconsistent with 'the views and manners of a civilized nation'.[38]

The depressing condition of women in most savage nations meant that their condition could only improve, and Millar charts the means of improvement as:

> every circumstance which tends to create more attention to the pleasures of sex, and to increase the value of those occupations that are suited to the female character; by the cultivation of the arts of life; by the advancement of opulence; and by the gradual refinement of taste and manners.[39]

Therefore in a pastoral society the acquisition of property, of cattle and sheep, led to inequality and subordination, and hence to a reserve and checking of familiarity, and to an increase in delicacy and modesty among women. Even modern notions of pastoral life, though exaggerated, might, according to Millar, in favourable circumstances fairly represent the shepherd state. Such a development was heightened with the introduction of settled agriculture and of property in land, though the treatment of women by men might not necessarily be improved. Yet, from the particular circumstances of the invasions of Europe by barbarians, and the military spirit which governed Europe for so many centuries, were to grow the distinctive institutions of chivalry, 'productive of the utmost purity of manners, and of great respect and veneration for the female sex':[40] the legacy of the chivalric spirit remained important. In modern Europe, however, Millar saw economic developments as the cause of a steady improvement in the condition of women. As men's interests ceased to be entirely military, and as some degree of refinement was achieved, then increasingly greater value might be placed on female accomplishments and virtues.

> In this situation, the women become neither the slaves, nor the idols of the other sex, but the friends and companions. The wife obtains that rank and station which appears most agreeable to reason, being suited to her character and talents. Loaded by nature with the first and most immediate concern in rearing and maintaining the children, she is endowed with such dispositions as fit her for the discharge of this important duty, and is at the same time particularly qualified for all such employments as require skill and dexterity more than strength, which are so necessary in the interior management of the family. Possessed of peculiar delicacy and sensibility, whether derived from original constitutions, or from her way of life, she is capable of securing the esteem and affection of her husband, by dividing his cares, by sharing his joys, and by soothing his misfortunes.[41]

Millar suggests that women have an important role to play in eighteenth-century society, for which they should be properly educated. If they are engaged in their proper duties, they are less likely to be swayed by the attractions of society, and more likely to give their attention to their family, improving and cultivating the feelings of the heart, employing themselves in useful domestic (and this, of course, included industrial) occupations. There were, however, limits to the advantages of economic improvement, since great opulence might lead to great liberty for women which, exempting them from labour, might leave them to the pleasures of society, ex)osing them to the dangers of licentiousness, diminishing the di;nity of women, 'rendering them only subservient to the purposes of animal enjoyment'.[42] Again the industry and virtue of women of the Greek and Roman republics were contrasted with the rapid decadence of the Roman empire. Millar's domestic ideal was placed very clearly within its historical context; it was relevant to a society in which the growth of commerce and of manufactures was improving the standard of living of the population and, against this background, he suggests that women's work within the family and in domestic manufacture was valued as never before. At this particular stage of economic growth, this particular model of family life would enable the best parts of women's nature to be most fully developed. Millar's combination of psychological and historical arguments, justifying the superiority of the domestic ideal as he conceived it over all other forms of family relationships, and his conception of the progressive improvements in the condition of women, were to remain extremely influential, under various guises, throughout the first part of the nineteenth century.

Many of the themes of the eighteenth-century debate about the nature of women were drawn together in the work of Antoine Thomas, *Essai sur le caractère, les moeurs et l'esprit des femmes*, to which Diderot was to reply. For Thomas, women everywhere were adored and oppressed, both by their own weaknesses and by society. In savage societies women were ruled by force everywhere, since in the East they were subject to despotism, and even in temperate climates, though they were not deprived of liberty they were placed in a state of dependence and subject to surveillance. Again in Thomas's work there is also a note of nostalgia for the households of Greece and ancient Rome. Republican women were strong, austere, frugal, devoted to their domestic duties and uncorrupted by luxury. He too noted the impact both of Christianity and of that spirit of chivalry which emerged in medieval Europe. Thomas directly posed the question of whether the differences between men and women were fundamentally those of nature, or created by their environment, with respect to four different kinds of talent: philosophical, imaginative, those related to memory, and those of morality. He believed that women were by nature incapable of the hard and disciplined intellectual approach required for the philosopher; as for imaginative art, women's fancy might be active, yet they were hardly able to depict through art the strong and violent passions, though they might excel in the delicate and tender. Both men and women might in theory be capable of the exercise of memory necessary for scholarship, yet in practice women would lack the patience for the long, hard studies required to pursue learning: and as for their moral and political talents, what was needed in government was a knowledge of character, a broad judgement and comprehensive understanding, for which women were unlikely to have the understanding or natural ability. Nevertheless, Thomas suggested, such an approach still failed to analyse the particular strengths of women. Women were more likely to display the religious virtues, to show greater sensibility and flexibility, feeling more and reasoning less than men; in the domestic virtues, so closely linked to those of religion, and in compassion and benevolence, qualities related to the emotions rather than to the reason, women excelled. They were less likely to display the qualities of true friendship and of patriotism, less likely to understand the true meaning of justice or the active nature of courage. Women were led by their feelings, and incapable of exercising the kind of detached judgement required of those who played their part in public life, though they might show great courage in the passive sense. For Thomas contemporary France was a world in which the lightness, the pervasive gallantry, and the false pleasures of society meant that women were viewed only as accomplished ornaments. Even so, there were women deserving of admiration:

> And so there are mothers who dare to be mothers. In some homes one may find Beauty, busy with the tenderest cares of nature, and in turn pressing in her arms or to her breast the son whom she nourishes with her milk, while her husband silently divides his tender glances between son and mother.[43]

If only such examples might recapture past virtues, then women would recover their empire and the interior life of the family be greatly enhanced, though the life of society might suffer. In Thomas's work both his view of history and his analysis of sexual differences led him to call for a return to the ways of nature, a natural order which for him was exemplified most clearly in the domestic ideal of republican nostalgia. Its relevance to contemporary France was that woman might regain respect in a corrupt world by fulfilling her natural duties, duties most clearly seen in her maternal role, duties in accord with her proper sentiments and feelings, enabling her to fulfil her true moral potential.

Thomas's work went through a number of editions and, in England, two translations.[44] One translator, William Russell, added to the work much material from Adam Ferguson, John Millar and William Robertson on the early history of women, and also an essay on the progress of women in British society in the eighteenth century, contrasting the learned ladies of the beginning of that century with the contemporary corruption, to be compared to that of France, brought about by wealth and by commerce. However, Thomas's work was also extensively used in the lengthy, anecdotal and confused *History of Women, from the earliest antiquity to the present time* (1782), by William Alexander. Alexander also looked back to the high position of women among the Germanic tribes and in the age of chivalry, contrasting this with the deteriorating situation of women in contemporary Britain, and the unchanging state of women of the East. In his portrait of 'barbarian' women he located an early domestic idyll:

> We see their women placing no small share of female excellence in the exercise of the domestic, and still more in that of the conjugal virtues. We discover that their mothers had early instilled into their minds that modesty, which more than any other ornament adorned, and that frugality and industry which maintained and supported them, though little assisted by their pen, and still less by the fruitfulness of their country. Their employment was not only to take care of, and manage all the domestic concerns of the family, but also to provide whatever could be obtained by peaceful industry; for their husbands, unwilling to concern themselves in anything but war and hunting, left everything else to the conduct and direction of their wives.[45]

As the influence of the barbarians was felt in western Europe after the invasions of the Roman empire, so 'nature resumed her feelings, and instigated women again to apply themselves to the task of suckling and rearing their own children'.[46] Alexander, drawing on material from Thomas and from Millar, also traced the different stages in the history of the condition of women, suggesting that the differences between the two sexes became increasingly marked as civilisation advanced; and that in Europe, where public affairs were directed by men, their discoveries had been much more favourable to the growth of civilisation than the unchanging societies of the American Indians and of Africa, where so much more was left to women.[47] Yet women should not be seen as inferior, but as naturally marked out for a separate sphere of life, a sphere which needed to be more clearly defined. A similar discussion is to be found in John Bennett's *Strictures on Female Education, chiefly as it relates to the culture of the heart, in Four Essays* (1787), which despite its title used much historical material from Millar and Thomas, Montesquieu and Robertson, in giving an account of the poor position of women in previous uncivilised ages.

feeling rather than reason
imaginative rather than analytical
good moral qualities

THE ENLIGHTENMENT AND THE NATURE OF WOMEN   31

While the general condition of society might account for such a situation, Bennett was concerned with the contemporary degradation and neglect of womanhood. Like Millar, he found that the best situation for women was to be found in a civilised but not an opulent world, where in a degree of domestic seclusion women might themselves find fulfilment, and help to bring about a moral improvement:

> When does she [woman] appear to so much advantage, as when, surrounded in her nursery by a train of prattlers, she is holding forth the moral page for the instruction of one, and pouring out the milk of health to invigorate the frame and constitution of another. . . . Such a maternal culture, such a revolution in the sentiments and conduct of that sex, would be attended with the happiest advantages.[48]

Following Thomas, Bennett saw women as lacking intellectual strength, yet superior above all in the qualities of the heart, best exercised in domestic solitude, for 'whatever undomesticates a woman, so far unmakes her, as to all the valuable purposes of her existence'.[49]

Enlightenment writers elaborated a view of women's nature as governed more by feeling than by reason, particularly subject to the impact of sensations from the outside world, imaginative rather than analytical, and possessed of distinctive moral qualities which could be fulfilled only in the right setting. Writers like Voltaire and Diderot did show awareness of the oppressiveness of the legislative codes of western Europe towards women, of the subjection of women to their husbands, of the economic fragility of women's situation, of the condition of prostitutes. Yet the remedies proposed were limited, such as the introduction of divorce legislation; few before Condorcet were prepared to contemplate the possibility of extending political rights to women. The improvement of women's situation was to come through a new evaluation of their domestic role, through which they would contribute to the moral regeneration of society. The arguments of historians about the development of the condition of women were in effect two-pronged, incorporating a selective nostalgia with more general assumptions about a continuing progress in the treatment and status of women. Montesquieu and Rousseau shared admiration for the position of women in the ancient republics; English and

Scottish writers, while agreeing, also superimposed their own view of the high place of women among the Germanic tribes. The natural instincts of women were, in both these contexts, equated with simplicity, domesticity and the frugal care of the household. Yet at the same time, by the late eighteenth century the notion was gaining ground that women's condition had steadily improved as the economy of western Europe advanced. Though nostalgia for a mythical past might be a source of inspiration and exhortation, it appeared to many, like John Millar, that the situation of women was better than ever before. As long as luxury and decadence were not allowed to appeal to the worst side of women's nature, then there would be hope for the future, in the increasingly clear definition of the sphere allotted to women. In America and in France, by the end of the eighteenth century, the rhetoric of republican motherhood was to take on a much more positive meaning. The domestic sphere was no longer to be merely the backcloth to public and social life, but to have a positive educational and inspirational function. A woman's position was no longer to be merely that of the passive partner, and the practical organiser of the household; her nature would allow her, in the right setting, to uplift and to regenerate the spirit of her society. While a new status might, in this setting, be ascribed to woman, the boundaries both of her nature and of her domestic role were increasingly more tightly defined – and it was these boundaries which nineteenth-century feminists were to challenge. The assertion of the positive nature of domesticity both focused attention on the situation of women and restricted it.

2. Feminism and Republicanism: 'Republican Motherhood'

IN the history of feminism, the 1790s is often seen as a critical decade. Although earlier women writers – Christine de Pisan, Mary Astell, 'Sophia' – had written effectively and movingly of the condition of women, and suggested that educational reforms, in particular, might improve their situation, it was only in the context of a world in which revolutions in America and in France opened up the possibilities of reshaping the social as well as the political order that radical changes in the relationship between the sexes began to seem feasible. The best known feminist of the late eighteenth century was of course Mary Wollstonecraft; earlier Judith Sargent Murray had written of a new role for women in the new American republic, and in the rapidly changing political scene in France after 1789, Olympe de Gouges, Etta Palm d'Aelders, Claire Lacombe, Pauline Léon and others were to draw attention to the rights of women. The philosophy of natural rights, embodied both in the American Declaration of Independence and in the French Declaration of the Rights of Man, seemed relevant to women. A small number of women, of nerve and intelligence, were to explore the implication of those natural rights for women, both politically and in their personal lives. And a small number of men were also drawn to speculate on the possibilities of social change. Yet, as so many later historians have remarked with varying degrees of complacency, these feminists of the 1790s seemed to achieve little, to attract more ridicule than followers. In England and in America, the conservative reaction against Mary Wollstonecraft made her name an impossible one to follow for some generations; in France, even before the conservative reaction of Thermidor, the leaders of the revolution themselves turned against the feminists. But it can be argued that the defeat was by no means a total one, and that the issues raised by feminists were not lost to view. In the age of revolutions, it was suggested, positive reforms were needed to establish the natural rights of women: legal changes in the position of married women, divorce reform, improvements in women's education, in the treatment of women as workers and, perhaps, political recognition. All these concerns were related by feminists to their central acceptance of the immensely important role which women played within their families, their situation as mothers. Mary Wollstonecraft's view of 'the indispensable duty of a mother' was echoed in Judith Sargent Murray's practical advice to her readers, and Etta d'Aelders' rhetorical *Appel aux françoises* (1791).[1] For the writers associated with the radicalism of the 1790s in Britain, France or America, the part which women would play in the new society would be inextricably linked to their task of raising new citizens. For them it was a task whose status should be fully recognised, deserving a voice in the political arena. What distinguished the feminist view was that that task should be undertaken by women, freely, rationally, with independence, as their contribution to the new and transformed world of the republic. These conditions for 'republican motherhood' were hardly to be met. Yet feminist support for the improved status of women as mothers remained one important element in the nineteenth-century re-evaluation of the appropriate spheres for the sexes; and the boundaries between feminists and conservatives, in their treatment of family roles, are not always easy to recognise. Briefly, however, in the 1780s and 1790s, the ideal of 'republican motherhood' seemed to offer a way of uniting public and private responsibilities for women, and dominated the feminist arguments of that decade.

REPUBLICAN POSSIBILITIES

Historians of the American Revolution have recently considered the ways in which the war for independence, and the founding of the new republic, affected women's experiences and aspirations.[2] Naturally, their practical experiences were very diverse, yet in some way or another the lives of the great majority of women were changed: Northern or Southern, black or white, patriot or loyalist. As the political arguments between Britain and the colonies grew fiercer, in the 1760s and 1770s, women were necessarily drawn into the debate, even though they were regarded as incapable of independent political judgement. Yet as purchasers for their households, and as producers too, they had to play a part in economic warfare, in the successive boycotts of goods from Britain. Female patriots were especially involved, for instance, in the boycott of tea and other goods which the British government taxed in 1767. Groups of women responded with enthusiasm, and some even formalised their agreement to abstain from the use of tea. In 1774 a group of 51 North Carolinan women signed an agreement to adhere to the resolutions of the provincial congress on non-importation policies, and to do all in their power to support 'the public good'.[3] The meeting was derided by the British as the 'Edenton Ladies Tea Party' – and yet it represented a serious political initiative by women themselves. As shopkeepers, too, women would be called upon to observe non-importation agreements. Women bore the brunt of appeals for a greatly expanded cloth production for the needs of the army. In the South this would be the work of female slaves. In the North the normal household tasks of spinning and weaving took on a different political significance. Newspapers were now covering spinning bees, seen as examples of female patriotism, christening those who took part 'Daughters of Liberty'.[4]

By the outbreak of war, it was clear that many women were taking an active and informed interest in the progress of public events, and that a few, such as Mercy Otis Warren, dramatist and historian, sister to James Otis the patriot, were speculating on the right of women to address themselves to major political questions: 'As every domestic enjoyment depends on the decision of the mighty contest, who can be an unconcerned and silent spectator?' she wrote to a friend in 1774.[5] She felt that women's duties to their families positively required them to take a political interest. Other women felt similarly, though they have expressed their views only in their private correspondence. Political awareness might still be confined within the domestic sphere, yet that sphere itself was taking on a new political significance. With the outbreak of the revolutionary war, many women were to face new responsibilities, especially in the absence of their men. If their area was occupied by British troops, they could be subject to forced billeting, and even to political attack. Many women, both on the loyalist and on the patriot side, were forced to define their own political position, even though they were formally regarded as outside the political nation. Some women found that their only access to government lay in the humble petition. The petitions of distressed widows, whose husbands had died in the Continental armies, emphasised their own feeling of political support and sacrifice for the republic. But these petitions, on the whole, received little attention and had little effect. The most organised form of political action by women in the course of the war was the fund-raising drive organised in Philadelphia and New Jersey in 1780, initiated by a broadside from a Philadelphian, Esther de Berdt Reed, *The Sentiments of an American Woman*. In this she defended the right of women to contribute to the revolutionary cause, recalling the 'heroines of antiquity, who have rendered their sex illustrious'. The meeting of Philadelphia women that followed this publication organised a highly successively drive for funds, and embarked on correspondence with women in other towns and counties, most effectively in New Jersey, Maryland and Virginia. The purpose of the movement was to some extent deflected by General Washington's insistence that the considerable funds collected should be used to make shirts, providing ample opportunity for condescension towards the aims of the Ladies Association.[6] Some individual women, of course, took a far more active part in events, directly aiding prisoners to escape, and carrying messages or spying on behalf of revolutionary or loyalist forces, but these were atypical. Most significant was the inescapable infusion of political partisanship into domestic life. Friendships, even marriages, could be strained and broken by strongly held political differences.

Republican rhetoric might of course be thought to hold implications for the position of women yet the leaders of the revolution were on the whole unwilling to contemplate the natural rights of women. However, the legal situation of married women, governed by English common law, whereby the wife's identity was legally entirely subordinated to that of her husband, was questioned in the course of the revolution. Women, though not required to take the oath of loyalty to the republic, could certainly commit treason, even though they were not full citizens; but a married women leaving the republic to join her loyalist husband was not normally treated as a traitor, though her husband was. However, a number of treason statutes passed in different states allowed wives to preserve their own property interests in their husbands' estates, which were forfeit, if they made their own political commitment clear. In 1779 the Massachusetts legislature promised to protect a wife's property rights if she remained in America, declared herself separated from her husband, and proclaimed her loyalty to the republic. But under this statute, if a wife joined her husband, it would be assumed that she had made her own political decision, and she would suffer the consequences. Therefore the political duties of married women to their country, distinct from their obedience to their husbands, were under some circumstances acknowledged. Some lawyers argued that married women had a political responsibility to influence their husbands, and that if they failed to do so they should suffer the legal penalties with them.[7] The case of Florence Cooke is worth considering. After her Tory husband was exiled and his property confiscated, Florence Cooke, in 1783, petitioned the General Assembly of South Carolina:

> She is informed that herself is deprived of her right of Dower, and her child a Daughter of Twelve years of age, of all future claim on the inheritance of her father. This law she humbly thinks the more severe as her Child received early & strong impressions of real attachment to the liberty of her Native Country; with a confirmed aversion to her enemies; principally inculcated by yr Petitr who if Providence had blessed her with a number of sons, would have thought herself happily engaged in employing all the influence & care of a Mother, to render them fit for the defence and support of their country.[8]

Her claim is based on her own patriotism and her maternal responsibilities.

To some, the freedom to pursue life, liberty and happiness seemed to involve also the right to divorce, to be free of any unhappy marriage. Divorce statutes passed by colonial assemblies had been contrary to the law of England, and liable to veto; in 1773 such an act, passed by Pennsylvania, was disallowed by the Privy Council, and so, in a minor way, became part of the constitutional conflict. Before the Revolution divorce was legal only in New England states, and was most frequently used in Connecticut, where women clearly made more use of the law than men. In Connecticut, the disruptions of the war meant that the court met less frequently and there were fewer divorces in those years, though a marked increase afterwards. Only in Pennsylvania was a new divorce law adopted as a result of independence. In 1785 the Pennsylvania Assembly claimed the right to regulate divorce for itself. Elsewhere, divorce required a private bill in the state legislature.[9] Only one state, after the Revolution, made a gesture towards the political recognition of women, and that was an accidental one. In 1790 New Jersey adopted an election law explicitly referring to voters as 'he or she'. The state constitution of 1776 had defined voters as 'all free inhabitants' and it appears that during the 1780s women took advantage of this vagueness and claimed the right to vote in local elections. The 1790 statute simply legitimised the situation and fully established female suffrage.[10]

These minor legislative changes offered little hope to women whose political awareness had been roused. Those who reflected seriously on the position of women in the new American republic did not take women's public standing as their starting point. Rather, a writer such as Judith Sargent Murray used the texts of the Enlightenment and of republicanism to return to virtue as the key principle of the republic, and to stress increasingly the greater potential of women for virtue, and their fitness for the task of instilling virtue into new generations of republican Americans. Judith Sargent Murray, of Gloucester, Massachusetts, who married first a sea captain, and then the Universalist minister John Murray, wrote as early as 1779 an essay 'On the Equality of the Sexes', published in the *Massachusetts Magazine* in 1790. She continued to write plays, poems, and in the 1790s a series of essays entitled *The Gleaner*, also published in the *Massachusetts Magazine*. In 'On the Equality of the Sexes' she wrote of the honour that should be attached to the position of wife and mother:

> A sensible and informed woman – companionable and serious – possessing also a facility of temper and united to a congenial mind – blest with competency – and rearing to maturity a promising family of children – Surely the wide globe cannot produce a scene more truly interesting.[11]

Such a future could imply real equality. She denied that women were inherently less capable than men. Using the historical material of Antoine Thomas's *Essai sur le caractère, les moeurs et l'esprit des femmes*, she pointed to the degraded condition of women in the savage state, the unduly elevated reverence for womanhood in the age of chivalry, and argued that as nations progressed the potential of women was better understood, for they were capable of mastering 'any attainment within the reach of *masculine exertion*'.[12] Though she accepted Thomas's argument that women might be inferior in reason and judgement, this was, she believed, only because of their inferior education and their lack of opportunity to develop their own talents. Foreseeing a new age, in England, France and America, she looked

forward in her essays to that female independence suggested by Mary
Wollstonecraft. Women should cease to regard marriage as the
highest good and ultimate goal – but they would only be able to make
a deliberate and rational choice if they were educated and equipped to
live independently. Girls needed to acquire self-respect, to 'reverence
themselves'. In describing the ideal education given to the fictional
Margaretta by the wise Mrs Vigilius, Murray emphasised that a
liberal, wide-ranging education would give women the ability to
reflect and to reason, qualities necessary both for women to exploit
their talents to the full and for the mistress of a household. In the story
of the contrasted sisters, Helen and Penelope, Helen is portrayed as
acquiring only ornamental accomplishments and fashionable manners, Penelope as earning a modest independence through her
competence as a seamstress.[13] Useful skills, self-respect, and independence of mind should be the aims of female education in the
republic, so that marriage might become a free choice rather than a
necessity. Murray was clear that she did not desire to 'unsex' women,
for she too believed them to be superior in the feelings of the heart, in
their possession of maternal affection; and she too quoted that
passage, already given above from Thomas's essay, which portrayed
the suckling mother.[14] The new model of republican womanhood
united the higher capacity for virtue and feeling with the rational and
competent independence which Judith Sargent Murray looked for.

Many of the points made by Murray were also made by other
reformers of female education, notably that leading citizen of
Philadelphia, Benjamin Rush. In his essays 'Of the modes of
education proper in a republic', and 'Thoughts upon female education, accommodated to the present state of society, manners and
government in the United States of America', Rush argued that
unless women too were involved in the republican education of their
sons, it would not succeed:

> To qualify our women for this purpose, they should not only be
> instructed in the usual branches of female education, but they
> should be taught the principles of liberty and government; and the
> obligations of patriotism should be inculcated upon them.[15]

Rush, like Murray, contrasted the accomplishments, the habit of
novel-reading, the reliance on servants, which were typical of
women's education in aristocratic, decadent, European societies,

with the useful, rational and principled education more appropriate to a republic. The difference between them lay in their starting points. For Rush female education in a republic was significant for what it might achieve for the men and the children of that republic, not as a means of fulfilment for women themselves. He sketched the content of a curriculum designed to fit girls to educate their children, to be agreeable companions, conduct any necessary business, instil the spirit of patriotism, and run their homes frugally and modestly.[16] Such duties did not necessarily imply increased autonomy or independence for women, though the worth of their contribution was recognised.

These issues were again explored in essays written in the 1790s (partially published only in 1798, and the final section posthumously in 1815), by Charles Brockden Brown, novelist and man of letters. In *Alcuin: a dialogue*, Brown offered a fierce denunciation of the exclusion of women from political society. In the dialogue, the middle-aged widow, Mrs Carter, pointed out to the schoolmaster, Alcuin, what his platitudes about the high position of women in their society concealed:

> While I am conscious of being an intelligent and moral being; while I see myself denied, in so many cases, the exercise of my own discretion; incapable of separate property; subject, in all periods of my life, to the will of another, on whose bounty I am made to depend for food, raiment, and shelter: when I see myself, in my relation to society, regarded merely as a beast, or an insect; passed over, in the distribution of public duties, as absolutely nothing, by those who disdain to assign the least apology for their injustice – what though politicians say I am nothing, it is impossible I should assent to their opinion, as long as I am conscious of willing and moving.[17]

And the case for women participating in political life, against that 'act of odious injustice' which excluded the whole sex, was put. Alcuin himself was forced to retreat from his early unthinking acceptance of the concept of equality, and his prejudices against such a public role for women revealed. Mrs Carter pointed also to the injustice of assuming that because she opposed the contemporary bondage of women to husbands and fathers, she was necessarily an enemy to marriage, a 'champion of sensuality'. Her view of the current state of marriage was that as an institution it was a sacred one, but that 'iniquitous laws', had made it a 'compact of slavery', depriving women of their property and subjecting them to their husband's authority. She was prepared to defend divorce as a means of freeing women from that kind of constraint, transforming marriage into her ideal of a 'union founded on free and mutual consent'. She poked fun at those makers of constitutions who pretended to pursue liberty and equality, yet excluded the young, the poor, the black, the non-resident and all women.

Historians of American women of the later eighteenth century have suggested, from the evidence of correspondence, diaries and manuscripts, that there were signs of a greater freedom in the choice of marriage partners, and a move towards more egalitarian relationships within the family in these years. For example, there is evidence that the decision to limit the size of the family was being taken jointly.[18] Recent studies of divorce records suggests the possibility that women in particular had rising expectations of marriage and were determined to secure that personal satisfaction which they expected.[19] It is of course extremely difficult and controversial to try to estimate such shifts in behaviour; but it has been forcefully argued that the study of the private world of women of the more literate part of the American community does offer glimpses of such a development, co-existing with more traditional patterns of behaviour. The direct influence of revolutionary republicanism was to be brief, and has to be seen in the context of other major social and economic changes affecting women. Broadly speaking, a white, educated American woman had by 1800 'only a modicum more control over her destiny than her uneducated grandmother . . . in 1750', and her position in society had been subject to much clearer definition than before. The boundaries of domesticity, the public expectations of women's role within the family, were now unmistakable. The language of natural rights had proved much less powerful than the republican conception of womanhood.[20]

More positively, the major legacy of such a conception lay in the expansion of women's education through the female academies of the new republic, expanding fast from the 1790s. Most of these were cast along the lines indicated by Benjamin Rush, stressing academic subjects to a greater degree than earlier schools. In Philadelphia, Boston, New Haven, New York, new academies were founded in the 1780s and many others in the following decade. They were as likely to be situated in small towns as in large cities. These academies often had a stronger financial basis than previous one-woman schools, and were clearly more likely to last. Increasingly, in the new republic, parents were taking for granted the necessity of educating their daughters, and learning was recognised as a permissible goal for girls. Some academy graduates of these years went on to teach or to found new academies – some, like Lydia Maria Child, Prudence Crandall and Zilpah Grant, were to be active participants in the debates on women's role in early nineteenth-century America. Many lesser known students were to go on to teach at the elementary level, especially in the North, as new town schools and charity schools were established. Though teaching might be seen as an acceptable profession for women, if only temporarily, the academies still saw it as their primary duty to train wives and mothers for the new republic: but such education could carry with it other consequences.[21]

In France too the language of republicanism and the political turmoil after 1789 had their effects on the position of women. There the case for endowing women with those natural rights which formed the basis of the Declaration of Rights was put by a leading *philosophe* and supporter of the revolution, the Marquis de Condorcet.[22] Condorcet was clearly reflecting about the nature of women's position in society before 1785, since in his unpublished notes on a speech to the French Academy, he made it clear that he regarded women's position in society as an important determinant of the civilisation of that society. Their education had given them no opportunity to display their potential.[23] At the same time Condorcet was also engaged on his *Essai sur la constitution et des fonctions des assemblées provinciales*, finally published in 1788, in which the issue of a public political role for women was raised. He criticised the regulations for the voting qualifications for these assemblies. Women owning property which would qualify men to vote should be able to nominate a representative; other women should be able to join in the nomination of a delegate to the next level of the elections. In the same work he showed himself seriously concerned about social issues which affected women. In particular he drew attention to the condition of prostitutes and the severity of their treatment by the law and society. He argued that only public elementary education for girls and boys could improve the level of manners and morals in their society.[24] In 1787, in *Lettres d'un bourgeois de New Haven à un citoyen de Virginie*, the case made earlier was expanded. Women as rational creatures and as moral beings should be able to exercise political rights. The oppressive laws existing everywhere against them were sufficient proof that men had very different interests in mind as legislators. Women, who paid taxes, who were entitled to exercise their own free will, had a right to be full citizens, to vote and hold public office. Their talents deserved recognition, in the interests of society, since apart from the temporary disability of pregnancy, there were few differences between the sexes which were not the result of faulty education. Men should take the opportunity of distinguishing a republic from unfree states by admitting half the human race to citizenship.[25] After the outbreak of the revolution Condorcet's views became more radical and more specific. He pointed out how men had come to take for granted the violation of the natural rights of women, and asked whether any proof existed that the natural rights of the sexes should be different. The arguments used against women's rights could be turned against many men: that they lacked genius, that they were uneducated, that they had no time to acquire a rational and enlightened political outlook. There was no reason why political rights should distract women from their domestic duties; they were better fitted to care for young children, but such work no more disqualified them than did a man's profession. Women, properly educated, inspired too by their feeling for republican liberty, could be full citizens. And if their circumstances were inappropriate for the holding of public office, then the voters should decide that, rather than the law exclude them. Condorcet's case is firmly based on a philosophy of natural, individual rights, and on the view that the difference between the sexes was primarily due to education and environment.[26]

Yet the question of political rights for women was not one which surfaced in the *cahiers* which expressed the diverse grievances of the three legal orders, nobility, clergy and third estate, before the summoning of the States-General in France.[27] Many *cahiers* in fact called for the maintenance of the Salic law, which banned inheritance to the throne of France through the female line. Some showed considerable concern for the situation of poor women. The need for greater care for young mothers, for better facilities and improved training for midwives, whose ignorance was denounced, was noted in some *cahiers* from areas of rural France. The system of *déclaration de grossesses* by which a public declaration of pregnancy was required, was denounced as contributing to the shame of illegitimacy. Greater assistance to working women was also suggested, through more professional instruction, as in spinning schools, or in the creation of *ateliers* as centres for the production and sale of work, or the creation of *béguinages* or communities of single women working together, perhaps on needlework. Few female corporations were able to draw up *cahiers*, though two from the florists and dressmakers of Paris exist, concerned primarily with preserving their own position in the Parisian markets.[28] Clergy and members of the third estate called for stern measures against prostitution, only one *cahier* suggesting the establishment of refuges for those giving up that life. What is most striking is the general recognition of the need for improved elementary education, not only for boys but also for girls, though not all give education the same priority. That of the Parisian third estate, for instance, envisaged a master and mistress in every parish for all children of both sexes. The mistress would be required to pass an examination.[29] Most *cahiers*, however, envisaged education as conducted by the religious orders, and very few referred to secondary education. The proposals of the *cahiers* on the whole reflected, where women's situation was referred to at all, benevolent and charitable purposes, rather than any interest in the political rights of women. Only the third estate of Châtellerault (Poitou) called for citizens of both sexes and all ages to have an equal share in the appointing of deputies and the debates of the assembly.[30]

Nevertheless, in the outburst of pamphleteering and political literature of 1788 and 1789, a few feminist notes were sounded, and not only by the Marquis de Condorcet. Some pamphlets were written in the form of unofficial *cahiers*, or petitions, though there is a problem of discriminating the erotic or merely flippant writings from those expressing genuine sentiment. Pamphlets such as the *Requête des dames à l'assemblée nationale* (1789) combined apparent calls for political rights with a satirical tone. But the political challenge did arouse women writers. The *Cahier des doléances et réclamations des femmes* (1789) par Mme B.B. . . . described her own conversion to feminism, called for a better education for women to fulfil their true potential and, pointing to the enfranchisement of common men and to the freeing of black slaves, asked if the nation would be silent on the rights of women? This pamphlet was republished as the *Cahiers des doléances et réclamations des Femmes de la département de la Charente*, by Marie de Vuigneras. Like other such works it was frequently reprinted, notably in the *Etrennes Nationale des Dames*.[31] There were, too, pleas from groups of working women. The *Pétitions des femmes du Tiers-Etat au Roi*

(1789) urged the king to assist their demands for a better education to gain themselves proper trades, to prevent their being forced into convents or on to the streets. They asked too for men to be excluded from women's trades. In September 1789, a Mme Rigal published her speech to a group of women artists and silversmiths, in which she had called for women to display virtue and self-sacrifice in the national interest, to sacrifice money and adornment to prevent national bankruptcy.[32] The best known feminist of the early years of the revolution was to be Olympe de Gouges, or Marie Gouze. In 1788 and 1789 her works called for the emancipation of women for the greater good of the nation as a whole. In *Le cri du sage par une femme* (1789) she pointed out the valuable and conciliatory role which women could play in assemblies. And in *Le bonheur primitif* (1789) she, like others, called for the urgent summoning of the States-General. A playwright and publicist, she was a convinced royalist, yet one who was also convinced of the need for a national regeneration, a transformation in which the maternal role of woman would play a critical part. One of her pamphlets, the *Lettre au peuple, au projet d'une caisse patriotique* (1788), called for the voluntary contributions of women to the financial support of the new state.[33] Another writer, Sophie Rémi de Courtenai de la Fosse Ronde, claimed the right of women as of men to propose radical solutions to the problems facing France, and particularly the problems of poverty, in her *Argument des Pauvres aux Etats Generaux*.[34] Serious proposals were also put for legal reforms, and especially for divorce. Divorce was advocated by a number of writers, mainly male, who following the ideas of the *philosophes* advocated reform and improvement in family relationships, and the ending of clerical authority in this sphere, as did, for example, the author of the *Réflexions d'un bon citoyen en faveur du divorce* (1789), and the Comte d'Antraigues in his *Observations sur le divorce* (1789).[35] The author of the *Griefs et plaintes des femmes mal mariées* (1789), whether male or female, went further in denouncing the absolute authority exercised by husbands in marriage, and saw divorce as a means to ending that authority.[36]

Such arguments suggest that the language of revolution was beginning to excite speculation about the position of women; though this of course must not be exaggerated. The *cahiers* in which such issues were mentioned, the pamphlets and brochures on this subject, were insignificant in number. The issues were, however, also to be raised in a small part of the rapidly growing newspaper press. The

Etrennes Nationales des Dames, besides republishing pamphlets of interest to its readers, commented on the events of 1789 in a militant style. The October days had proved the courage of women:

> We are suffering more than the men, who with their declaration of rights leave us in a state of inferiority, or, to tell the truth, of the slavery in which they have kept us for so long. If there are husbands sufficiently *aristocratic* in their homes to oppose a division of patriotic duties and honours, we shall use against them the weapons which they have employed with so much success.[37]

The journal demanded the representation of women in the National Assembly and the Commune of Paris, and called for the establishment of divorce and greater equality in sexual affairs. Little is known of the women involved in this journal, apart from Marie de Vuigneras, from the Charente. From January 1790 there was also the *Véritable Ami de la reine ou Journal des Dames*, politically moderate, offering reports of political events, clearly concerned also with the role of mothers in preserving through the family the manners and morality of the nation, a theme which was similarly stressed in Mme Mouret's petitions to the National Assembly to support her educational schemes.[38]

Thus in the early stages of the revolution there were articulate women and men prepared to address themselves both to specific reforming measures that would benefit the lot of women and to the more general theme of the situation of women in revolutionary France. The conditions of the revolution were in effect also to bring working women into the political area. In the crowded *quartiers* of Paris, at the heart of the political debates, women were to prove themselves active. They had traditionally played a leading role in economic protests, closely aware as they were of the level of bread prices, and the immediate problems of subsistence. As the revolutionary press stimulated debate, as political discussion spread in the public places of Paris – in cafés and markets as well as, later, in clubs and societies – women could not be unaware either of the immediate economic issues or of the changing political situation. As in America, the language of revolution and of citizenship was becoming more familiar even to the illiterate. While writers such as Olympe de Gouges and Marie de Vuigneras were looking for the regeneration of the nation through new political institutions and the greater involvement of women, so the working women of Paris, affected by the high price of grain in the autumn of 1789, and by the decline in the luxury trades and the need for services, were learning to give new political labels to their old concerns. By July, women who went in almost daily processions to thank the patron saint of Paris for sparing the city in that month, also went to the *Hôtel de Ville* to present Lafayette, of the National Guard, with a bouquet or a loaf of bread. And in the days of October, on 5 October, it was the Parisian women who called for Lafayette to lead them in the march to Versailles to demand bread from the king and the National Assembly; with the support of the National Guard, they were able to demonstrate their political feelings. They also roused observers to use all those epithets – 'furies', 'harlots', 'shrews' – which were to be so frequently applied to women entering into political action of all kinds (Plate 1). Whether, in October 1789 'women were beginning to transform themselves into *citoyennes*' is perhaps arguable.[39] Yet clearly what was changing was the target for such women's actions – no longer the city and the magistrates of Paris, but the king and the established deputies of the Assembly.

Over the next two years, 1790 and 1791, there was relatively little popular protest, though radical middle-class women, especially, continued to press for specific reforms, and to use the press to advance their case. They began to gather together in clubs, and to formulate their case more effectively. They began to petition the National Assembly directly. As early as November 1789, the Assembly received the *Motions en faveur du sexe*, which, considering the best ways of achieving happiness and equality for women, denounced the dowry system and called for women to be able to take up better kinds of employment then reserved for men but within women's capacity. 'Feeling for the wrongs of all my sex has penetrated to the depth of my heart', declared the writer, and the remedies were economic, allowing women a genuine alternative to marriage.[40] In March 1790 Mme Mouret presented her scheme for the improvement of women's education to the Assembly, and followed that in June 1790 by presenting to the Commune of Paris a project for a 'Confédération des Dames' to take an oath to bring up their children as good patriots, loyal to nation, law and king. And in September 1791 she made an offer to the National Assembly to educate freely twenty-four orphan girls, whose fathers had fallen for their country and later asked for the grant of a former convent for this purpose.[41] In July 1790 a group of women from Beaune protested to the Assembly against the refusal of the municipality to allow them to take the civic oath on 14 July, 'as women citizens, wives, and mothers'.[42] In April 1792 Etta Palm d'Aelders, a Dutchwoman prominent in these early years, asked the Assembly to consider the state of degradation to which women were reduced as far as political rights were concerned, and called for full recognition of their natural rights; her demands were put in the context of a historical review of the situation of women, as evidence of their equal potential with men. To achieve the full participation of women in the Revolution, she listed four essential demands: that girls should be given education; that they be declared of age at 21; that political liberty and equality of rights should be common to both sexes; and that divorce be permitted.[43] Most of these pleas were met with condescension and hostility in successive Assemblies, though the discussion of divorce received some sympathy from deputies. In February 1792, for example, Lequinio, a deputy from Morbihan, in calling for divorce as a means of regenerating the nation, denounced the slavery in which women were held and suggested that it was time for the revolution to do something for the liberty of women.[44] But there was no serious consideration of female suffrage when the constitution of 1791 was debated.

Nevertheless in these years women were clearly finding new opportunities for involvement in clubs and societies, some of which were ready to admit women and discuss issues with which they were concerned. One of the earliest was the 'Cercle social', founded in January 1790, where by November of that year, Etta Palm d'Aelders was speaking in public on the revolution's treatment of women.[45] From that November also, the new and genuinely popular 'Société Fraternelle des patriotes de l'un et l'autre sexe' admitted women to full membership and as officers and, in March 1791, became the 'Société fraternelle des patriotes des deux sexes'. Other sociétés fraternelles were founded, and followed its lead, throughout the Parisian sections, and it was in these societies most of all that women were initiated into public life.[46] Three women members of the 'Société fraternelle', d'Aelders, Théroigne de Méricourt and Pauline Léon, were active as feminists in the last years of the constitutional monarchy. D'Aelders wrote of the natural rights of women, as well as speaking in the National Assembly and in societies. In her speech to the 'Cercle' of 30 December 1790, she called for 'a second revolution in our customs', and denounced those unjust laws which allowed wives and mothers only a secondary existence, and transformed their duties into slavery, while they continued nevertheless to carry the burden of the preservation of virtue. If women were to fight for a new constitution, then men should give them justice and education, and see them as voluntary companions. The idea of eternal subordination could no more be true of French women than of French men after July 1789. She saw clearly male prejudices still at odds 'with revolutionary principles and natural rights for women'.[47] In March 1791 she went further, to call for associations throughout the 83 departments which women should join to unite themselves in patriotic societies with the new government. These women *amies de la vérité* could help to point out enemies of the revolution but also concern themselves with aid to poor women, the supervision of charity schools, the employment of wet nurses, and other benevolent works affecting women.[48] She denounced, too, that provision of the *code de police*, presented to the Assembly by the Constitutional Committee, Article XIII, which allowed a husband to accuse his wife of adultery and imposed a punishment of up to two years imprisonment, without any reciprocal rights for the wife. She called for the powers of husband and wife to be equal and separate, for morals to be reformed through 'moral education' for girls. Her stand was taken first on 'equality of rights, without discrimination of sex'.[49] D'Aelders continued to work to set up schools and workshops for poor girls, and to be an associate of the Cordeliers, throughout 1792, but, increasingly under political suspicion, she left for Holland in January 1793.

Théroigne de Méricourt, who had taken part in the October march to Versailles, was also a member of the 'Société fraternelle'. She had tried in early 1790 to found an ephemeral political society, and had encouraged women to form a militia company in February 1792. But her political moderation and her association with the Girondin political group led to her receiving a flogging from Jacobin women in March 1793; the beating appears to have contributed to her later mental illness. Pauline Léon was to be one of the few women activists from the early years who survived to take a full part in the events of 1793. A chocolate-maker, she rapidly became a member of the 'Société fraternelle', and in March 1791 petitioned the National Assembly for women to have the right to bear arms.[50]

The involvement of women in political clubs was not confined to Paris. Certainly throughout the provinces, from 1790, groups of women had come together to support the revolution, to celebrate 14

July, and to offer their services to the local authority. One of the oldest was the 'Club des femmes de Dijon', already in existence in 1789. In Breteuil, a group of young women founded the 'Soeurs de la Constitution' in August 1790, and thoughout small and large towns in France groups of women participated, formally or informally, in such celebrations. However, such involvement in many ways represented a largely supportive role, and sometimes also a direct continuation of the charitable and philanthropic work undertaken before the revolution by aristocratic and clerical authorities. The women involved in such societies tended to come from the reasonably well-educated and middle-class provincial supporters of the revolution and to combine their patriotic and philanthropic work in such societies.[51]

But the best known individual feminist of these years was not a member of such clubs. It was Olympe de Gouges who, in *Les Droits de la Femme* (1791), most clearly expressed the direct application of the philosophy of natural rights to the position of women. A monarchist, whose work was addressed to the queen, her political beliefs were confused and quite untypical of other feminists. For her, the Constitution was entirely silent on women's rights, ignoring that principle which for her came first, that: 'Woman is born free and lives equal to man in her rights. Social distinctions can be based on the common utility'.[52] *Les Droits de la Femme* called for complete equality for men and women in all public spheres, freedom of thought and communication for all, equality in all the obligations of citizenship, and in the right to own property. Improved education, a more rational marriage contract, protection against seducers, and the regulation of prostitution, were all measures which, she suggested, would enhance the standing of women. De Gouges was guillotined for her royalism in 1793.

In the course of 1792, as the military situation in France deteriorated, the militant Jacobin and Girondin leadership gained ground, and increasing support from the people of Paris. Politically active women like Théroigne de Méricourt and Etta Palm d'Aelders at first played a part in this though they were too closely identified with the Girondins to survive, since after the fall of the monarchy on 10 August the Girondins lost credit. In this critical year economic hardship at a time of inflation led also to the greater involvement of the women of Paris in political action. As the Paris sections became increasingly influential, though still directed by men, their leaders were drawn to a much greater extent from the popular classes: so the influence of Parisian women was strengthened, in the sections and in the societies. The *citoyennes* of Paris sent deputations to the commune, called for debates and action on the hoarding of and speculation in grain. They also clearly acted as initiators and leaders of collective protest, in attacks on warehouses and bakers' shops. For a brief period that threat to order won Parisian women some political influence.

It was at this point of the greatest potential influence that the most important female society of the revolution, the 'Club des citoyennes républicaines révolutionnaires' was founded, to unite the issues that concerned Parisian women, and the specific grievances of the feminists, from February to October 1793.[53] Their leaders included Pauline Léon, and the actress Claire Lacombe, both of whom had been active Jacobins but were now linked to a group to the left of the Jacobins, the *enragés*. The women, after the foundation of the Club, pressed the Jacobin Montagnards for economic action, for the introduction of price controls and the regulation of supplies. They supported the Montagnards in their battle with the Girondins, but after the fall of that group were rapidly disillusioned. By September 1793 their support for the *enragé* and *sans-culottes* demands, and their influence, were at their height. As the price controls were established, and the Terror set up, so the Club succeeded in bringing pressure on the Convention to pass a law on 21 September 1793 compelling all women to wear the tricoloured cockade in public. In so doing they roused the hostility of many Parisian women, and there were public confrontations between market women and members of the Club over the wearing of the cockade and the maintenance of price controls, which the market women disliked. Police reports also noted the dangers to public order of: 'these enemies of public tranquillity [who] flatter the pride of women, seeking to persuade them that they have as many rights as men in the government of their country.'[54] The Club and its members had misjudged their support; *sans-culottes* leaders had little liking for the life style of the feminist aims of women like Claire Lacombe or Pauline Léon, and the leaders of the revolution were, by autumn, sufficiently politically secure to put into practice their fundamental hostility to the involvement of women in politics. On 30 October Montagnard leaders struck a blow both against the *enragés* and against female disruptiveness by outlawing all women's clubs and associations, and reminding women that their life lay within the home. That defeat marked the end of formal women's organisations in the revolution, though women continued to petition the Convention, and to attend political societies and clubs. The proclamation to women indicated clearly what was expected of them in the new republic:

> Women! do you want to be republicans? Love, follow and teach the laws which recall your husbands and children to the exercise of their rights; honour the great deeds that may be done for your country, to show that they will be done for you; be simple in your dress, hardworking in your home; never go to popular assemblies with the wish to speak there, but so that your presence may sometimes encourage your children.[55]

The exciting political atmosphere of the years 1789 to 1793 had clearly brought some women to the point of claiming political rights for themselves in the language of the Enlightenment. Yet the rise and eventual defeat of the *sociétés fraternelles* and the 'Club des citoyennes républicaines révolutionnaires' was by no means the complete story of the politicisation of women in the course of the revolution. In the provinces the character of women's associations was changing. From early 1792 onwards their awareness of the worsening economic situation and their involvement in the war effort dominated their concerns. Societies worked to raise money, clothes and bandages for the armies; and they led attempts to stabilise prices. One of the most active was the 'Club des Amies de la Liberté et de l'Egalité' at Besançon. There they called for the shutting of local convents, for the enforcement of laws against aristocrats and demanded that all teachers should have their pupils learn by heart the Declaration of the Rights of Man. That club was probably the only provincial one to have addressed to the Convention the demand that women should vote in primary assemblies. In the same town the 'Société des femmes républicaines de Besançon' raised very considerable supplies of money and clothes for the armies.[56] In September 1792, women in Lyons drew up a tariff of prices for all necessary household goods and occupied a number of shops.[57] Such activities were common throughout France, though the defeat of the 'Club des citoyennes républicaines révolutionnaires' certainly had some repercussions outside Paris. In Rouen for example the municipality forbade a group of women to form a women's club, following the decree of the Convention in November 1793.[58] The attitude of the government increasingly coupled with economic realities, was to bring a rapid decline in such movements throughout France, even before the overthrow of the Jacobins and the coming of the Thermidorian government.

There had, of course, been recognition of some aspects of the feminist case. Discussions of divorce, and the divorce legislation of September 1792, had seemed to go some way to meet this demand. In the course of the debate in that month, M. Aubert-Dubayet had declared resoundingly that women should not be enslaved to men, and that although women's interest seemed to have escaped the notice of legislators up till then, the time had come, through divorce, to help those sacrificed to the despotism of fathers and the faithlessness of husbands.[59] The divorce legislation did in fact treat men and women equally, and provided for divorce by mutual consent. Other reforms offered help to women: inheritance laws gave male and female children equal rights. Women acquired majority at 21, could contract debts, act as witnesses in civil acts, acquired as married women some say in the disposal of their property and had some authority over their children acknowledged.[60] But even before the defeat of 1793, little had been done for that cause which all active women united in supporting, the improvement of women's education; numerous projects for a national system of education for boys and girls were considered, but nothing achieved. Also the public role of women was given virtually no consideration: the suffrage issue was dismissed, and even the right to take a civic oath, as token of citizenship, was regarded as doubtful.

After the feminist defeat, one of the most interesting pieces of writing in the revolutionary aftermath came from Charles Theremin, whose *De la condition des femmes dans les républiques* (An VII, 1799) derived directly from the tradition of enlightened republicanism. Theremin, like John Millar, Turgot and Condorcet, viewed the changing position of women in its historical context, correlating the improvements that had taken place with the development of civilisation. Since a republic was a more perfect government than a monarchy, the question should be faced – how should the situation of women within a republic be improved? He explicitly disagreed with William Godwin that in a future state the sexual instinct would play little part, and believed rather that in a future world, as humanity became more civilised, the pleasures of love would grow stronger.[61] He agreed that happiness came in the course of the fullest development of one's physical and moral faculties, through the widest possible range of activities – yet women were imprisoned within such a narrow sphere of life as to make this degree of self-development impossible, though as distinct rational and moral beings they should have that opportunity. Women were equally responsible for their souls, subject to the same moral laws; the physical differences between men and women should still allow women their own independence. He suggested that changes would come about only through the transformation of male attitudes, in a true republic. In such a society, the degrading dependence of existing marriage laws, the frivolity and vanity characteristic of monarchy would disappear, and legislation guaranteeing full citizenship for women, bringing them education and work, should be introduced, when women's natural qualities would begin to appear. Only in minor respects, such as the introduction of divorce, had the French Republic met these requirements, since in other ways women were treated almost worse than in a monarchy. For Theremin, there could be no justification for attempting to return to the austerity and frugality of manners of the Greek and Roman republics, which appeared to offer a model. He followed Turgot in suggesting that the last economic stage of society, in which agriculture was combined with industry, depended on the consumption of its members, unlike the old agricultural and militaristic ancient world.[62] In the modern economy, in which full employment was more useful than unnecessary privation, women too should be able to work and support themselves. Yet in all this Theremin rejected any wide political role for women. It would not be necessary for them to vote, since husband and wife formed one political person – and it followed that women could not exercise sovereignty. He tried, perhaps a little desperately, to suggest the right ways of attaching women to the republic. They might take part in family tribunals, even in juries and national festivals. Through better public education, enabling them to realise their potential, perhaps in future they might become true citizens, yet one is left with the feeling that Theremin's elaboration of the republican theme ends on a particularly timid note in that he balked at the prospect of following his arguments through to their logical conclusion. He portrayed the loss of those hopes which Condorcet had expressed 'in the shipwreck of liberal ideas', the defeat of the revolution, and he could offer little better prospect for the future in France, in this late attempt to construct a view of 'republican womanhood'.[63]

It was from Great Britain, which did not experience a major political upheaval in the late eighteenth century, that the best known feminist writer of these years emerged. Mary Wollstonecraft's *Vindication of the Rights of Woman* was to be a key document for feminists and anti-feminists, not only in Britain but in the new United States and in Europe, and her name was to be identified, notoriously, with the feminist case. In Britain such views were to emerge from those who dissented from the established political and religious order, who associated themselves with an English radical movement which dated from the 1760s and the dissenters' fight for religious toleration. Yet the nature of the case put forward was rather different from those already considered, in France and America. In the relatively stable political situation in Britain, there were few new opportunities to raise in public debate the question of women's political rights or to suggest legislative changes which might improve their situation, such as divorce, or the revision of married women's property rights. The acceleration in writing about women's condition in the 1790s, by both feminists and anti-feminists, was certainly prompted by the new political challenge coming from France and the response of British radicalism to that challenge. But students of the democratic radical movement in Britain in the 1790s have traced no female societies or clubs comparable, for instance, to the 'Club des citoyennes républicaines révolutionnaires'.[64] The arguments about the personal and public role of women were confined to the literary field, and to a relatively small circle of women and men who through their imaginative and political writing reflected on the means by which women might secure a greater degree of autonomy. In so doing they not only took account of the rights which, it had been suggested, women might exercise, but also contributed to the continuing eighteenth-century debate about women's nature.[65]

Mary Wollstonecraft's own life story has frequently been related.[66] Faced with the need to earn her living and eventually to help support her family, she had worked as a companion, a governess and a schoolteacher before coming to London in 1787 to live by her writing and join the liberal and radical circle of intellectuals around Joseph Johnson, who had already published her *Thoughts on the Education of Daughters* (1787). It included William Godwin, the novelist and playwright Thomas Holcroft, Joseph Priestley and Elizabeth Inchbald, the actress and playwright. It was a group inspired by belief in the possibility of moral progress for humanity, through the use of reason to overcome the forces of privilege and prejudice, the oppression and injustice which they saw around them. For the next three years, Mary Wollstonecraft worked as a journalist and translator in London, benefiting from her new friendships and with them closely watching events in France. She, like others, felt inspired to answer the work of Edmund Burke, *Reflections on the Revolution in France* (1790), in her first political pamphlet, *Vindication of the Rights of Men* (1791). In this she denounced the existing state of society in England and the condition of the great majority of the population, as well as strongly attacking Burke himself. Not entirely successful, it was still an important step in her own political development. The *Vindication of the Rights of Woman* was to be written the following year: it united her new political awareness of the deprivation of rights suffered by the great mass of the population, and her understanding of the conflicting arguments about the nature of women, and their particular, specific claims to autonomy.

To understand the *Vindication* fully, it is important to understand the nature of these claims, and the context in which they were explored. In the best sentimental novels of the 1760s and 1770s, emotions and feelings were portrayed realistically as natural and irresistible, and the sympathies or passions of the hero or heroine were vindicated; such novels had much to say about the subjective life of the individual, much less about action. The Jacobin writers of the 1790s were, too, to find the novel a fundamental weapon in the spreading of their ideas. But they distrusted that stress on the feelings and the passions. Elizabeth Inchbald, Thomas Holcroft, Robert Bage: all, like Mary Wollstonecraft, were concerned that such a deterministic view of human action was a morally dangerous one, reinforcing passivity rather than the individual rational will; and they noted that it had especial dangers for women, since it reinforced the already powerful social influences making for female submissiveness, against self-assertion and individuality. At the centre of this group was William Godwin who, in his *Political Justice* (1793) was to denounce the sentimental view and to argue that men were slaves neither of their own passions nor of their environment, but that their best hope lay in the conscious and deliberate use of reason, in 'the perfectly voluntary state'.[67] Jacobin novelists, like some conservative ones, were therefore to stress the importance of controlling the passions through reason, by education and the acquisition of disciplined habits; and it can sometimes be difficult to distinguish between the Jacobin and conservative positions. But for the Jacobins, the argument had to be conducted on two fronts: against the determinism of the sentimentalists, on the one hand, and on the other, against Rousseau's case for the inferiority of the 'natural' woman, the cunning, frivolous, vain and weak Sophie. Mary Wollstonecraft was to attack that double standard, and to plead for virtue in women to be recognised as having the same root as in men: the exercise of reason and of understanding, gained through the control of the passions. The rationality of woman had to be acknowledged, since only through the exercise of her reason, in that self-discipline, could autonomous status be achieved.

There are a number of novels by members of this circle which illustrate the speculation and discussion about women's role which must have been familiar to Mary Wollstonecraft. These novels were seen as having a didactic purpose, uniting the beliefs that environment and education moulded character while, at the same time, that progress could be achieved through the conscious use of individual reason. Elizabeth Inchbald's *A Simple Story* (1791), contrasted the disastrously undisciplined upbringing of the beautiful and sympathetic Miss Milner with the cloistered and careful education given her daughter. Once married, Miss Milner is to succumb, out of boredom and vanity, to the advances of a lover, and to destroy her formerly happy life. Her daughter, put to the severest of tests by an exceptionally despotic father, nevertheless proves the moral worth of her training. There is of course much more to the novel, yet there was no doubt that its fundamental theme was conveyed in the final sentence: 'the best legacy that any father can give his daughter is: A PROPER EDUCATION'. Charlotte Smith, another popular woman writer with some connections with Godwin's circle, also touched upon this theme in a number of her novels. In *Emmeline* (1788) the good judgement and clear understanding of the orphaned and vulnerable Emmeline is contrasted with the wild passions of the young man Delamere, brought up with all that indulgence usually given to such young men, the eldest sons of aristocratic families, 'accustomed from his infancy to the most boundless indulgences'. In a later novel, *The Young Philosopher* (1798), Charlotte Smith was to show more openly her sympathy for Mary Wollstonecraft, whose talents she praised in her Preface. In this, the young Medora, brought up as a 'child of nature' without prudery, coquetry or fear, eventually finds happiness with George Delmont, educated as a philosopher by an enlightened mother,

against the background of the spreading political message of the
American and French Revolutions.

Neither of these women writers went much further than reflecting
on the failure to educate women so as to meet the challenge of their
personal lives, though both united political liberalism with some
realisation of the hardships, both personal and economic, suffered by
women in their society. Such a realisation can also be found in the
work of Thomas Holcroft, an old associate of Godwin's and active in
the radical movement, and the provincial Jacobin novelist Robert
Bage. Holcroft's *Anna St Ives* (1792) attempted both 'to teach fortitude
to females' and to exemplify the principles on which William Godwin
was to base his *Political Justice*. And in the philosophical discussions
between the virtuous hero and heroine, Frank Henley and Anna St
Ives, reform or abolition of marriage as a civil institution was clearly
seen as one important element in that future state of society they
aspired towards:

> Of all the regulations which were ever suggested to the mistaken
> tyranny of selfishness, none perhaps to this day have surpassed the
> despotism of those which undertake to bind not only body to body
> but soul to soul, to all futurity, in despite of every possible change
> which our vices and our virtues might effect, or however numerous
> the secret corporal or mental imperfections might prove which a
> more intimate acquaintance should bring to light![69]

For Anna St Ives, the commands of reason alone were to be obeyed,
not those of husbands or fathers: 'reason and not relationship alone
can give authority'.[69] Yet these were visions of the future, and in the
contemporary world Anna St Ives and Frank Henley acknowledged
the need for laws to protect women. This analysis of marriage
followed that of Godwin in *Political Justice*, where though he deals with
the subject only briefly, marriage, like other social institutions, was
seen as a monopoly and a fraudulent one. In a future state marriage
would be the free choice of two partners, for as long as that choice
should last, and would enable the two partners to follow their rational
inclinations, neither tyrannising over the other.[70] In his *Hermsprong*
(1796), Robert Bage, the Jacobin novelist from Derby, clearly parallels
public and domestic tyranny; though there is little direct reference to the
French Revolution the allusions are clear. The domestic oppression of
Lord Grondale is challenged by his lively and frank heroine, Maria

Fluart, and contrasted with the conventional submissiveness of Caroline Campinet, who though a well-educated and rational young woman, still accepts her father's authority and the limitations placed upon her sex. The issue here was clearly defined as one of autonomy, not only subjectively, in attempts to control the passions, but in terms of positive action against those who rule. Bage's frankness in sexual matters and his challenge to the social hierarchy are reflected not in philosophical discussions as in Holcroft's work, but in his character-isation. But, writing in 1796, he had clearly been influenced by Mary Wollstonecraft, and criticised the contemporary state of education for women, lamenting their waste of intellectual energy where they too might have learnt to be 'beings of reason'.[71]

In their novels, neither Mary Wollstonecraft nor Mary Hays, the two most recognised feminists of the 1790s, was successfully to achieve portrayal of an independent and rational heroine. Yet the *Wrongs of Woman* (1797) contains much material of great interest. In this, the heroine, Maria, denounces the legal, economic and personal despotism that might be exercised by men in marriage, and the sexual hypocrisy of the double standard. She portrays vividly the experi-ences of the servant-girl, Jemima, first as a servant and then as a prostitute, reflecting on the impossibility of women earning their own living in such an oppressive society. Yet Maria throughout is a passionate and observant victim of the injustices of the world, suffering a series of increasingly destructive blows, claiming the right, too, to follow her own passions in her love for her fellow prisoner, Henry Darnford. Similarly Mary Hays, who was an associate and friend of Mary Wollstonecraft and William Godwin, and also a feminist writer, though a less successful one, wrote in her *Memoirs of Emma Courtney* (1796) of a heroine who, inspired by philosophical ideas, and by Rousseauist views of passion, offered her love to Augustus Harley, the man she desired. The novel was the subject of contemporary ribald ridicule. It was, however, clearly based on the premise that there was 'something strangely wrong in the constitu-tions of society', and that as men began to think and reason, an increasingly wide degree of freedom might be achieved.[72]

The novel was one much employed way of reflecting upon the personal and economic tensions which women might suffer. But the achievement of Mary Wollstonecraft in her major work, the *Vindica-tion of the Rights of Woman*, is that while incorporating these themes she stepped beyond the mere assertion of the *moral* autonomy of women, to make a clearly political statement.[73] Her analysis dealt fully with the arguments of the conservative prescriptive writers on education: Rousseau, Dr James Gregory, George Fordyce. Beyond that, she looked to the possibility of 'a female revolution in manners', with profound public implications; her apprehension of such a transformation shared the millenial aspirations of republicans in France and in America – yet for Mary Wollstonecraft such aspirations did not arise from the greater good of the republic, but from the need to develop the potential of women themselves.

It must be remembered, of course, that underlying the *Vindication* is Mary Wollstonecraft's profound religious belief in the work of the Creator, that Divine Providence who has through the gift of reason enabled men to pursue and to achieve virtue. That gift in women had been distorted and neglected, and the purpose of regaining it could only be to develop their potential for equality in virtue. A central issue was therefore Mary Wollstonecraft's assertion that there were no 'sexual virtues', no virtues predominantly belonging to one sex or the other. Virtue could have 'only one eternal standard', or it would be a relative ideal. Such qualities as courage should not be seen as primarily masculine, counterposed to the insipidity of gentleness in women. Even if – and this was left open – women might not be able to attain to the same degree of virtue as men, yet their virtues were the same in kind, and women were, equally with men, full moral agents. Even modesty and chastity were appropriate qualities for both sexes.[74] In this argument, Wollstonecraft clearly pointed to the conflicts imposed upon women by the Rousseauist view of education, which saw women as destined only to please men, both through the arts of pleasing, through sensibility and passivity, and through obedience and the practice of the domestic arts. Neither his view of the good wife and mother, nor of the cherished and coquettish mistress allowed scope for women to be autonomous beings, capable of defining by the use of their reason their own potential and aims, and of controlling the emotions and passions, subduing them in the pursuit of virtue. Nevertheless for Mary Wollstonecraft the achievements of such equality had to be dependent on the domestic and the political environment, for 'as sound politics diffuse liberty, mankind, including woman, will become more wise and virtuous'.[75]

She accepted the common contemporary view that the education and the expectations of women in the world around her had corrupted and degraded the sex. She shared the common acceptance of the sensational theory of knowledge. For her, ideas, which impinged from the external world through the sensations of the individual, were experienced in order, and through that order, and the work of the understanding, each individual had his or her own habitual associations, or patterns, of ideas, a 'habitual slavery to first impressions' which Wollstonecraft argued had more effect on women than on men.[76] Women were imbued with the sense of their femaleness from early childhood, and as they grew older were still not accorded full adulthood: in such a situation they were too open to receive easy associations of ideas, and to be carried away by their feelings, while having no routine business in the day to distract them. Such a wide view of the process of education meant that Mary Wollstonecraft was considering not only education itself but the whole domestic environment, as others, particularly Catherine Macaulay, had done earlier. From the beginning the aim of education should be the training of the understanding:

> the most perfect education, in my opinion, is such an exercise of the understanding as is best calculated to strengthen the body and form the heart. Or, in other words, to enable the individual to attain such habits of virtue as will render it independent.[77]

Such a task was clearly not merely a question of education in the home, since all had to be shaped largely by the manners and customs of their own society. What had happened to women was that from their earliest years, their education had disregarded the use of their reason and their judgement. Taught that theirs was the province of the feelings and the heart, never trained in the powers of analysis and generalisation, a sexual character was imposed upon their personalities from the very earliest years. Always the cultivation of the understanding was subordinated to frivolous accomplishments, accomplishments designed merely to make women pleasing to men without any thought for their future work or their needs as individuals. Such emphasis on beauty brought vanity and corruption; such inattention to health and exercise a ridiculous degree of delicacy. Such expectations were rapidly internalised by women themselves:

> Women are everywhere in this deplorable state; for, in order to preserve their innocence, as ignorance is courteously termed, truth is hidden from them, and they are made to assume an artificial

character before their faculties have acquired any strength. Taught from their infancy that beauty is woman's sceptre, the mind shapes itself to the body, and roaming round its gilt cage, only seeks to adore its prison.[78]

Women found their senses inflamed, 'the passions . . . pampered', while their judgement was left unformed, wavering and inconsistent.

Clearly the question which Mary Wollstonecraft still had to confront was that of the social context in which women's potential might be equal to that of men, which did not necessarily imply that she would be called to exercise it in the same duties or sphere of life. There is no doubt that she saw the domestic sphere as that in which women would most likely excel, and that for which they should be trained, though they should also be able to meet all eventualities in a self-reliant way. The husband and wife who were both necessary to, and independent of each other, because each fulfilled their necessary duties, with a minimum of wealth, were in an ideal position; then a woman might fulfil her nature as a mother, nursing her children, inspired by a rational though not an excessive or passionate affection for them. The 'peculiar destination' of women was indeed to take the responsibility for rearing and caring for children; to do this, they should be carefully educated with a view to such duties rather than to pleasure. But the 'simple grandeur' of 'dignified domestic happiness' could not be achieved until the ignorance and folly of women themselves had been corrected.[79] To achieve that, it was essential that women should not only be able to undertake the challenging task of caring for, and rearing children, but also that they should where necessary be equal to the challenge of independence. Mary Wollstonecraft considered the fate of a woman trained to please and to be obedient, whose husband dies; left to herself, she cannot face these responsibilities, is unable to educate her children, and either falls prey to some man after her money or becomes discontented and merely indulgent. If she had been taught the arts of coquetry, as Rousseau had advocated, she might give an example of folly, perhaps vice, to her daughters. A woman of good understanding in the same situation might be raised to heroism by her misfortune, repress her own natural inclinations, forget her sex and all ideas of pleasing men, and give herself entirely to her maternal duties. It was a call for the rejection of passion, for constant and watchful self-discipline.[80]

So far, there were echoes of many other writers on similar subjects, of the Jacobin novelists, and even of the domestic happiness of *La Nouvelle Héloïse*. Yet Mary Wollstonecraft was distinguished by her constant emphasis not merely on a woman's duty to society, but on her duty to herself: 'Speaking of women at large, their first duty is to themselves as rational creatures, and the next, in point of importance, as citizens, is that, which includes so many, of a mother.'[81] But for the possibility of that independence to be real, Mary Wollstonecraft envisaged changes in the political and social order, changes which would mean husband and wife were equal in their importance as citizens, and in the degree of protection afforded them by the state. Women were no longer to be merely dependent on a husband's income, but to be given protection by the civil laws. And though she was prepared for ridicule Mary Wollstonecraft suggested, too, the possibility of representation for women 'of a superior cast'. But as things were they had no more reason to grumble than all those mechanics who had no vote and yet paid their taxes. What women needed was activity of some kind, whether, as for the majority, as wives and mothers, or for some, by carrying on a trade or business, as physicians, or midwives, or other suitable occupation. If properly educated, women would not be faced with the choice of marriage, or the most menial of employments, or prostitution:

How many women thus waste life away the prey of discontent, who might have practised as physicians, regulated a farm, managed a shop, and stood erect, supported by their own industry, instead of hanging their heads, surcharged with the dew of sensibility that consumes the beauty to which it at first gave lustre?[82]

Such suggestions were clearly most relevant for the middle-class woman, and Wollstonecraft in her Preface made it clear that she paid particular attention to such women 'because they appear to be in the most natural state': that is, less tainted by the corruption of the aristocracy and the degradation of the daily grind of the poor. She does not deal with the means of relieving poor women, though she does show much sympathy for their situation, and her scheme for national, public education did envisage that at an elementary level, all, rich or poor, boys and girls, should be educated together. Nevertheless she did not lose sight of the broader context: women might achieve virtue only through exercising independence, and they could do that only in a society which had ceased to respect the privileges of wealth and beauty. Men too were oppressed by riches and inherited honours, yet women were still more degraded because they had no way left to them, as men still did, to stretch and test their own powers. Only liberty and self-reliance could do that.[83]

It was undoubtedly a radical republican analysis, using the language of republicanism and good citizenship; yet her most important theme was that women were to be good citizens and good mothers as part, primarily, of their duty to themselves, though they could do that only in the context of wider changes. That was the originality of Mary Wollstonecraft's analysis. And one of the most impressive themes of her career was the extent to which she attempted to maintain that ideal of self-reliance in her private life. Even after her unhappy relationship with the American, Gilbert Imlay, whom she met in Paris, she was determined that her association with William Godwin, with whom she renewed her acquaintance in 1796, should meet the views they both held about marriage. They maintained their individual independence by separate residences, and went through a marriage ceremony reluctantly, only on discovering her pregnancy. And in her professional career as a writer and journalist, she rejected that condescension which was too often showed to women writers. She rebuked Mary Hays, who was, she thought, trying to take advantage of that humility thought suitable for her sex, bolstering her own confidence with the support of great names: 'Rest on yourself – if your essays have merit they will stand alone, if not, the shouldering up of Dr this or that will not long keep them from falling to the ground.'[84] In her last work, her novel *The Wrongs of Woman*, she was determined to show 'the wrongs of different classes of women equally oppressive, though from the difference of education equally various'. The situation of Maria in that novel was significant, because for her 'the matrimonial despotism of heart and conduct' was the key to women's oppression in all spheres of life, the 'particular wrongs of women; because they degrade the mind'.[85] Such concerns are frequently lost if Mary Wollstonecraft is seen as primarily interested in the middle-class woman. Her language was still that of the republican, and her ideal for women, as for men, was of moral fulfilment through active participation in all spheres of life as a full citizen. The virtues she looked for were civic virtues, and her achievement was to call for women to exercise autonomy, in unifying public and private commitments.

There were of course other feminist critics who drew their material from the Jacobin inspiration. Mary Hays, the friend of Wollstonecraft and Godwin, was not only a novelist but also wrote the *Appeal to the Men of Great Britain on behalf of Women*, probably mostly written before the *Vindication*, but published only in 1798. In her *Letters and Essays* (1793) Mary Hays made it clear how much she admired and wished to follow the lead of her friend. She too called for an end to sexual virtues, for 'it is time for degraded woman to assert her right to reason in this general diffusion of light and knowledge'.[86] Rational education, and a respect for judgement and firmness in women were essential. In the *Appeal* Mary Hays attempts to argue against the scriptural case for the subjection of women, and to put a rational case for equality. She saw no evidence from the teaching of Jesus to justify the authority of men over women.[87] Many of her arguments are very similar to those of Mary Wollstonecraft. She looked at the contrasting images men form of women, as coquettes or as drudges, and she called for gradual emancipation and reformation through education, a reformation which would lead to the revision of laws that bore so harshly upon women, and to a redistribution of wealth. Yet she shrank from some of the consequences of the arguments. Though women were to be companions and equals to men, nevertheless: 'delicacy as well as common sense points out objections so very striking to women taking any active part in popular assemblies' and similar delicacy would apparently prevent women wanting physicians and surgeons of their own sex (which for Mary Hays would be 'like an emetic').[88] Domestic commitments had to come first. In her later works, in a long writing career, Mary Hays was to return to the feminist cause; but in the immediate aftermath of bitter personal attacks following the publication of *Emma Courtney* and the *Appeal*, she shifted to safer historical ground, in her *Female Biography* (1803).

Support for the cause could come from unexpected quarters. That strange figure, James Lawrence, wrote in his *Essay on the Nair system of gallantry and inheritance* . . . (1800?) of his support for Mary Wollstonecraft's view of the equal rights of women. Women's education had never allowed their potential to be developed. The answer to the oppressive authority exercised by men was to end the institution of monogamous marriage, to adopt one more akin to the matrilineal system of the Nairs of Western India. Men and women might enjoy sexual freedom; women, as mothers, keeping their children, uncontrolled by men, passing on their property to their children as their heirs. 'As long as marriage continues a profession, love will continue a trade'.[89] Yet the different occupations of the two sexes would divide them; in Lawrence's discussion women remained marked out for the domestic duties for which their education should prepare them. Such a system, he suggested, would bring happiness, equality and also a healthy and growing population, since it would encourage the birth of children. Such an interpretation of the benefits of sexual freedom was reminiscent of Diderot's *Supplément au voyage au Bougainville*, and was reiterated again in Lawrence's novel *The Empire of the Nairs; or, the Rights of Women. An Utopian romance* (1811), and again in the company of the Saint-Simonians, in Paris in the 1830s. His stress on sexual freedom, atypical though it was, points to a theme which proved disastrous for many of the feminists of the revolutionary decades.

CONSERVATIVE REACTION

The conservative reaction to the feminist arguments of the 1780s and 1790s was, in England, France and America, a powerful one. With the conservative victory, following the federalist and constitutionalist success in the United States, Thermidor in France, and Pitt's repression in England, and the polarisation of opinions on social as well as political issues, those arguments were to be brutally suppressed. In spite of the political appeal of the theme of republican motherhood, reaction to further claims for female autonomy was swift and vicious. This was perhaps least marked in the newly independent states of America. Yet even there, though the case for better education for women might be accepted, the radical politics of a Mary Wollstonecraft were not. Among many other critics, for example, Benjamin Silliman, a teacher at Yale, in *Letters of Shahcoolen . . .* (1802), condemned her demand for total equality, her ideal of the renovation of the female character, her introduction of women into the 'camp, rostrum, cabinet'.[90] Her writing of matters that should better be veiled was a sign of her own coarseness; her pleas for the seduced and dishonoured should be seen in the light of her own lewd behaviour. It was her critique of the existing marriage bond which gave such a weapon to her enemies, and enabled them to condemn her degraded purposes. The consequences of such views, Silliman thundered, would be the abolition of all social virtues, with women held in common, in a return to the savage state, in which women had been viewed merely as beasts of burden and instruments of pleasure. The ridicule of Mary Wollstonecraft was popular and easy, especially after the publication of William Godwin's frank *Memoirs of Mary Wollstonecraft* (1798). Another American schoolmaster, Timothy Dwight, labelled her as 'female philosopher' and as 'strumpet' in a political satire running for eight instalments in the *Mercury and New England Palladium* in 1801–2.[91] In spite of her own clearly stated moral purposes, Wollstonecraft's life seemed to associate female learning and presumption with a dangerously free sexuality.

Politically, the independence of the new American republic brought with it no immediate prospects for change and, in the course of the 1780s and 1790s, conservative voices surfaced against even the most modest proposals to improve the situation of women. Even in Connecticut, where divorce laws were well established, the frequency of divorce in the post-war years led a group of Congregational ministers to campaign for a tightening up of the law, to save the declining moral standards of the young republic.[92] As the legal complications relating to the confiscation of loyalist property continued to work their way through the American courts, the doctrine of coverture continued to be discussed. In an important case in Massachusetts in 1805 Federalist judges and Federalist lawyers argued that married women could not be regarded as guilty of crimes performed jointly by husband and wife, since the wife was subject to her husband:

> Was she to be considered as criminal because she permitted her husband to elect his own and her place of residence? Because she did not, in violation of her marriage vows, rebel against the will of her husband?[93]

There were no signs that the brief revolutionary breach in the subordination of married women to their husbands had any lasting effect at all. Even that accidental victory in the winning of the vote for women in New Jersey was to come to an end. New Jersey critics in the 1790s vehemently attacked women as unfit for the privilege, and after a fraudulent referendum in 1807, women and black voters were made the scapegoats and disfranchised.[94] In general neither political party of the republic, Federalist or Republican, took a very consistent line, though hostility to feminist claims seems to have been particularly marked in Federalist circles and Federalist newspapers. The legacy of the American Revolution to women is therefore ambiguous and controversial. The language of natural rights and republicanism did provide a vocabulary and a means of rousing women's political interests and, perhaps, might be applied and extended to their own situation. Yet the role for women which came to be seen as their best service to the republic, that of motherhood, while recognised as valuable and patriotic, was still essentially private and domestic. The tentative steps into public political life left no mark, and the boundaries of domestic life were to be even more closely defined, though it was acknowledged that women needed better preparation and education for such a life.

In France the end to feminist aspirations came more brutally. Olympe de Gouges, Etta Palm d'Aelders and Théroigne de Méricourt had fallen not so much for their feminist views as for their association with different political groupings. The 'Club des citoyennes républicaines révolutionnaires' suffered also from the association of its leaders with the *enragés*; in crushing it, the National Convention took the opportunity to make quite explicit its opposition to women's societies, and women's participation in political life. In November 1793, as has been outlined above, women's societies and clubs were outlawed, and the grounds for this were quite clear: women's nature unfitted them for political action:

> The private functions for which women are destined by their very nature are related to the general order of society; this social order results from the differences between man and woman. Each sex is called to the kind of occupation which is fitting for it; its action is circumscribed within this circle which it cannot break through, because nature, which has imposed these limits on man, commands imperiously and receives no law. . . .
>
> What character is suitable for woman? Morals and even nature have assigned her functions to her. To begin educating men, to prepare children's minds and hearts for public virtues, to direct them early in life towards the good, to elevate their souls, to educate them in the political cult of liberty: such are their functions, after household cares.[95]

Condemned in the Convention and in the Paris Commune, the protests of the women's clubs received little sympathy. Women continued to participate in mixed clubs and the sections of Paris, but their status remained unclear. Together with other *enragés* Claire Lacombe and Pauline Léon were arrested in April 1794, and no other women emerged to speak for their cause, especially after the coming to power of the Thermidorian government in July 1794.

By 1794 the effects of wartime inflation and of the decay of luxury trades were affecting women in the working population throughout the country. The lifting of price controls in December 1794, and the disastrous harvests of that year, brought hunger, disease and starvation, with the brunt borne by women within their families. The situation was aggravated by the failure of revolutionary governments to provide any kind of replacement for the Church's system of poor relief. In this harsh economic climate women were to be prominent in the popular insurrections of Germinal and Prairial, in the spring of 1795. In the Prairial days, women led an invasion of the Assembly, demanding a fair price for bread, the Constitution of 1793, and their rights.[96] As a result, the following day women were excluded from the galleries of the Assembly and could watch only if accompanied by a male citizen; on the next day they were banned from meeting in the streets in groups of more than five.[97] In the aftermath, tribunals were set up which effectively identified and imprisoned male and female leaders of the popular movements. These events represented the last of the revolutionary *journées*. After 1795 women throughout France were struggling to survive in the harshest of conditions; undoubtedly many saw their best recourse in the authority and stability of the Catholic Church, compared to the famine and the war for which revolutionary governments could be blamed.[98]

What remained, if only briefly, as signs of the revolutionary legacy in France, were the legislative improvements in the position of women. Inheritance laws guaranteed male and female children equal rights. Women were given new rights in civil law, to contract debts and be witnesses; married women had a greater share in the administration of their property and of control over their children. Yet all this remained only until the new Napoleonic Civil Code was introduced in 1803, when almost all these gains were lost. Women did retain the principle of equal inheritance, but the subordination and obedience owed by a wife to her husband were very precisely spelt out in that Code. It preserved the institution of divorce, though on very much less favourable terms for women, and even that was abolished in 1816 immediately after the Restoration.[99] The association between feminism and the revolution had brought women very few benefits.

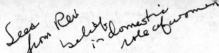
Revolutionary leaders had failed to accept the arguments of Condorcet, and had no sympathy for the claims of women to participate in public life. So, in France, from these contradictory attitudes towards the nature of women debated in the eighteenth century, there was to come, in the early nineteenth century, from conservatives and republicans alike, a belief in the primarily domestic role of woman, for which she was best fitted by her nature, through which she could best serve the state and society. The dominance of that view, together with the taint of revolutionary politics, was to make the task of feminist writers in France over the next fifty years a particularly difficult one.

In England also, the discrediting of Mary Wollstonecraft and her circle was to play a not insignificant part in determining the tone and direction of future feminist writing. Conservative opponents used every possible weapon, and the most potent was obviously Mary Wollstonecraft's private life, as illustrated by Godwin's *Memoirs*, seen as an affront to conventional opinion. She was described, in one conservative poem, *The Unsex'd Females* (1798), as 'ripe for every species of licentiousness'.[100] The *Anti-Jacobin Review* lost no opportunity: 'Here we must observe, that Mary's theory that it is the right of women to indulge their inclinations with every man they like is so far from being new that it is as old as prostitution'. And the *Review* also published, in 1801, the vicious poem, the 'Vision of Liberty':

> Whilom this dame the Rights of Women writ,
> That is the title to her book she places,
> Exhorting bashful womankind to quiet
> All foolish modesty and coy grimaces;
> And name their backsides as it were their faces;
> Such licence loose-tongued liberty adores,
> What adds the female speech exceeding graces;
> Lucky the maid that on her volume pores,
> A scripture, archly framed, for propagating w-----s.[101]

The vehemence was extended – to Mary Hays, to Helen Maria Williams, to Elizabeth Inchbald and others. But Mary Wollstonecraft's own life provided such excellent material that it remained the focus of criticism at such a level for many years. Even more influential, perhaps, than the public press, was the literary mood after the mid-1790s. After the Jacobin novel, a school of conservative novelists clearly emerges. Most direct were the comments of

Elizabeth Hamilton, in her *Memoirs of Modern Philosophers* (1800) in which some praise was given to Mary Wollstonecraft, and to her attack on Rousseau's double moral standards, but much more space given to the caricature of a feminist, Bridgetina Botherim. Bridgetina plays a key, if secondary role in the novel. Humourless, ugly, absurd, conversing in abstractions rather than paying attention to real human needs and feelings, she is an interesting example of the qualities attributed to feminists; and her ideas had the disastrous effect of allowing the much more beautiful, if emotionally vulnerable, Julia to be seduced, swept away, and eventually abandoned to prostitution. The lessons of her folly were forcibly hammered home to the miserable and pathetic Bridgetina. Less directly, there was a powerful conservative argument which may be traced in much of the literary work of the early nineteenth century. The work of minor novelists, such as Elizabeth Hamilton, Jane West, Charles Lucas and Robert Bisset, suggests how close was the identification between sensibility and a dangerous social and sexual radicalism. Though radical writers such as Elizabeth Inchbald had themselves condemned excessive sensibility, the restraints they proposed were to be autonomous, through the use of reason and not imposed by the conventions and hierarchies of society. For Jane West, for example, in her *Tale of the Times* (1799), the mistake of the heroine was identified with the potentially catastrophic principles of revolution:

> Should it therefore be told to future ages, that the capricious dissolubility (if not the absolute nullity) of the nuptial tie and the annihilation of parental authority are among the blasphemies uttered by the moral instructors of these times . . . they would not ascribe the annihilation of thrones and altars to the arms of France, but to those principles which, by dissolving domestic confidence, and undermining private worth, paved the way for universal confusion.[102]

And the work of a much greater writer, Jane Austen, can only be understood within this conservative context. There was a political message to *Sense and Sensibility* (first draft 1795, published 1811); a lesson to be learnt from the condemnation of the theatrical performance of *Lovers Vows* (translated by Elizabeth Inchbald) in *Mansfield Park* (1814). The novel became a counter-revolutionary force, as domestic life also came to have a new political content.

In England there were no practical consequences, no legal changes affecting women, or any legacy of political association dating from the 1790s. The effective discrediting of Mary Wollstonecraft and the association of feminism and free love were to prove serious obstacles in the future. Yet the *Vindication* had clearly stated, in the language of republicanism, the case for an autonomous life for women, in a world in which proper respect would be given to their experience and self-respect. The prospects for that case in 1800, in France, Britain and America looked bleak. Yet though the political claims of women had received so little support, that re-evaluation of women's social worth, seen in the ideal of republican motherhood, was to remain important, as the boundaries of domestic life continued to be defined and explored, in these differing societies.

3. Evangelicalism and the Power of Women

THE religious revivalism of the late eighteenth and early nineteenth centuries had profound implications for the position of women, most evidently in Protestant countries. Evangelicalism was to infuse the prescriptive works, the models for conduct, even transform the popular novel with a dynamic Christianity, a theology no longer arid or rational, but relevant to the emotional life of home and family. Leaders of the movement, from William Wilberforce in England to Charles Grandison Finney in the United States, preached a religion of the heart: and the qualities of the reborn Christian, as opposed to the merely nominal Christian, were qualities that have been described as quintessentially female. Such a Christian was humble and submissive, self-denying, obedient and passive, for evangelical discipline and upbringing was based on the breaking of the will and the denial of self. That profound sense of human depravity which was a part of the evangelical code meant repression, denial of the flesh and the unceasing quest after purity. Only when the self had been destroyed could the crusade to regenerate a sinful world have meaning. So, whether as a part of the established church or nonconformist sect, or in the popular revivalist meeting, the dynamic evangelistic Christianity of the nineteenth century was to have a complex and ambiguous effect on the position of women: exalting what were seen as their essential qualities, defining their own sphere more clearly, offering a limited but positive role within the movement itself. Movements of religious renewal were by no means confined to Protestant countries; the 'feminisation' of religion was widely observed across Europe in the nineteenth century. The contrasts between such movements are most relevant to any discussion of the origins of feminist activity. It is possible also to compare those messianic movements of the period in which the female principle was exalted to new heights, as the most extreme exploration of such a theme, sacrilegious to the orthodox.[1]

man's innate sinfulness

EVANGELICAL THEMES

The evangelicalism of the early nineteenth century, of whatever denomination, rested on a profound sense of man's innate sinfulness, on the possibility of salvation through the conversion and rebirth of the individual, and on the necessity for the repression and renunciation of the self, through self-discipline constantly exercised in the framework of the family within the Christian community. With it came a sense of mission, a drive to regenerate and save a corrupt and vicious world. The interaction of religious and theological changes with changing views of women's role is an immensely difficult cultural problem. However, historians have begun to examine certain ways in which evangelical religion was 'feminised' in the nineteenth century. Certainly some common trends are apparent in the United States and in Britain, though both must equally be seen within their own national context. Evangelical literature was to pay particular attention to the role of women in society, an attention which steadily grew, as more women writers identified themselves with the cause. Undoubtedly the individualistic act of conversion, the constant watchfulness which women, like men, had to keep over their own souls, reasserted in a fundamental way the principle of religious equality; yet that was joined by a redefinition of the sphere of woman within religion. Women increasingly found within their church or sect a means of associating with other women, whether in the prayer meeting or the charitable organisation. And their new moral strength gave them an acceptable way of asserting their own standards in the creation of the home as a refuge from the harshness of the market economy, or against a specifically male morality – the double standard of sexual behaviour, the culture of the pub or club.

The appeal of evangelicalism was to the heart; it protested against the 'nominal Christianity' of those who, while professing to believe, were content with rational proofs of the existence of God, with leading an unexceptionable life, with the acceptance of worldly standards. The movement called for battle by the converted against sin in all its manifold forms, by those who, suffused with the conviction of righteousness, were prepared to enter that everlasting warfare. To this battle, whether against the luxuries of the rich and worldly, or the drunkenness and vice of the frontier, the qualities ascribed to womanhood were essential. Women, assumed to be more emotional and affectionate than men, were increasingly assumed to be potentially closer to God. The prescriptive literature of the period emphasises that latent moral superiority, in terms which suggest women's greater power to embody the evangelical appeal. In Britain that belief is apparent in the works of the leaders of evangelicalism within the Church of England, William Wilberforce and Hannah More, for whom women were: 'the medium of our intercourse with the heavenly world, the faithful repositories of the religious principle for the benefit of the present and of the rising generation'. Providence had so divided the role of the sexes, that men in the public sphere, daily encountering the concerns and temptations of worldly life, should be sustained by that 'more favourable disposition to religion in the female sex'.[2] So too in New England in 1810 the Rev. Joseph Buckminster asked his congregation if it was surprising that 'the most fond and faithful votaries of such a religion should be found among a sex, destined by their very constitution to the exercise of the passive, the quiet, the secret, the gentle and humble virtues?'[3] Later evangelical writers on the role of women began from the fundamental starting point. For Sarah Lewis, in *Woman's Mission*, published in 1839, the essential quality on which women's moral worth depended was their 'renunciation of self' embodied, in its most perfect form, in maternal love:

By entrusting to woman a revelation of himself, God has pointed out whom he intends for his missionaries upon earth, – the disseminators of his spirit, the diffusers of his word. Let men enjoy in peace and triumph the intellectual kingdom which is theirs, and which, doubtless, was intended for them; let us participate in its privileges without desiring to share its domination. The moral world is ours, – ours by position; ours by qualification; ours by the very indication of God himself, who has deigned to put in woman's heart the only feeling . . . which affords the faintest representation of his most unextinguishable love to us, his erring and strayed children.[4]

Those qualities which, as we have seen, it had become commonplace in the eighteenth century to see as 'naturally' female were enhanced and given dynamic qualities by the Christian message of the early nineteenth century.

Politically such a message was conservative; socially its effects were ambiguous and contradictory. A distinctive feature of much early nineteenth-century evangelical writing on the family was the stress on a divinely ordained 'domestic constitution', which unlike civil governments, reflected unchanging divine purpose in the relationships of its constituent parts: husband, wife, children, servants. One of the most quoted Biblical texts in these works is that of Ephesians, v. 22:

> Wives, submit yourselves unto your own husbands, as unto the Lord. For the husband is the head of the wife, even as Christ is the head of the Church: and he is the saviour of the body. Therefore as the church is subject unto Christ, so let the wives be to their own husbands in every thing.[5]

The implications of that text were fully expounded by such a well-known evangelical leader as the Birmingham Independent minister, John Angell James, covering all aspects of domestic life. For him, most of all, the wife and mother '*must* be *a keeper at home* to fulfil her duties'. Yet he too noted the predominance of women in religious congregations.[6] The search for models in the women of Scripture confirmed this emphasis on the domestic virtues, in portraits of Rebekah or Hannah or Ruth.[7] Comparison with other religions and civilisations was made to confirm the assumption that Christianity alone had raised woman to her destined and natural place, neither 'tyrannised . . . nor impiously honoured'.[8] Yet at the same time the theology of evangelical Protestantism was shifting away from the harshness of Calvinism, in a direction that was to favour the moral superiority of woman. The central theme of evangelical preaching lay in the depravity of man and the atoning power of Christ's death. On conversion, the individual, overwhelmed by a sense of sin, surrendered to God's mercy, and was 'saved'. But for John Wesley, and many who later followed him, the prospect of salvation was no longer predetermined, but universally available to the woman or man who would continue to demonstrate, of their own free will, their continuing zeal in the faith, and their good works, as well as a moral life. This softening of doctrine brought an emphasis on the humanity of Christ, on his sacrifice in atoning for the sins of the world. His meekness, his humility and his voluntary renunciation were stressed – and Theodore Parker, a New England minister, pointed to the need to recognise female qualities in the person of God.[9] The language of hymns, especially Methodist hymns, was full of such themes as sacrifice, renunciation and submission.[10] Christ became a personal saviour, with whom women especially could identify, and such an identification between the redemptive powers of Christ and the sacrifices demanded and expected of women could lead women to consider their own redemptive powers. Evangelical religion offered them not only a clear definition of their expected sphere but also a very positive, even exalted, role within it.

REVIVALISM AND THE ORGANISATION OF WOMEN

The components of this process of 'feminisation' should be considered both for its effects on the daily lives of women, and for its difficult relationship with the origins of feminist activity. The process was already noted by Elizabeth Hamilton in 1801, when she wrote that:

> Meekness, gentleness, temperance and chastity; that command over the passions which is obtained by frequent self-denial; and that willingness to sacrifice every selfish wish, and every selfish feeling, to the happiness of others, which is the consequence of subdued self-will, and the cultivation of the social and benevolent affections; are considered as female virtues, derogatory to the dignity of the manly character. Nay, further. By this unfortunate association, has religion itself come into disgrace; devotional sentiment is considered as a mere adjunct of female virtue, suitable to the weakness of the female mind, *and for that reason*, disgraceful to the superior wisdom of man.[11]

However, historians have only recently begun to analyse this phenomenon, and most work has been done on the power of religion to shape and give meaning to women's lives in America. It has been suggested that by the early nineteenth century the majority of the Christian faithful in America were women. In the Second Great Awakening, the revival movement lasting from around 1790 to about 1830, Protestant evangelical Christianity emerged as the 'civil religion' of the nation, expressed in a number of different denominations, and with varying theological differences which need not concern us here.[12] In conservative New England, Methodism and infidelity seemed by the 1790s to challenge the established Calvinism of the Congregational and Presbyterian churches. New leaders from within those churches, especially Lyman Beecher and Nathaniel Taylor, organised a revival movement which modified the rigidity of Calvinist doctrine and emphasised the process of conversion; new converts and old reborn members were together brought into a whole network of voluntary associations, directed towards missionary activity and good works: moral reform, temperance associations, Sabbath observance. Such societies, mostly Congregational and Presbyterian, offered a socially conservative but morally redemptive message. Women flocked into such churches and such societies. Female converts in the New England Great Awakening between 1798 and 1826 have been estimated to outnumber male converts by three to two. Young unmarried women made up the largest age and sex grouping in these revivals.[13] Women's associations multiplied rapidly. Prayer groups, mission societies, benevolent reform societies, Sunday School organisations: all clearly derived from the revivalist movement. The large cities and small towns of New England all had their own, spontaneously generated, local associations. The appeal of such movements to women was immense, both because of their fitness for women's qualities, and because, as Harriet Martineau said, 'women pursued religion as an occupation'.[14] The emphasis of evangelical religion was now increasingly on usefulness, both inside and outside the home, fulfilling the requirement of renouncing the self, yet offering opportunities for action that were socially approved, in the company of like-minded women. Ministers encouraged their female members:

We look to you, ladies, to raise the standard of character in our own sex; we look to you to guard and fortify those barriers, which still exist in society, against the encroachments of impudence and licentiousness. We look to you for the continuance of domestic purity, for the revival of domestic religion, for the increase of our charities and the support of what remains of religion in our private habits and publick institutions.[15]

Yet ministers clearly believed also that such associations had clear limits; their contribution could only come through the extension of their domestic role. Women were explicitly forbidden to preach by a number of New England ministers. Their moral influence depended on their remaining in the appropriate sphere, subordinate and dependent on their husbands. But the contradictions inherent in this position were soon apparent.

The core of evangelical religious life was the household and family. The clergy appealed to women's inspiration with increasing intensity, as their own concerns merged with those of the young republic for the best education of citizens, and interest in the process of early childhood learning gained strength. One feature of this interest in New England was the spontaneous foundation of local Maternal Associations, in response to the elevation of the mother's role. Women such as those who formed the Dorchester Maternal Association in 1816 saw their duties as praying and reading together, discussing how best to fulfil their 'highly responsible situation as Mothers and as professing Christians'. Many of the works and magazines published in the 1820s and 1830s were to encourage such associations, which brought women together in activities which were based on their family roles, yet identified their own tasks positively. But increasingly, while women flocked into maternal and moral reform societies in New England and elsewhere, ministers appeared uneasy at these developments, and Cott suggests that by the 1820s and 1830s sermons were beginning to stress the boundaries of women's sphere.[16] The prospect of women preachers had been opposed by ministers in the older churches in an early stage of the revival movement. Any threat to the authority of husbands was perceived as socially dangerous.

By the 1820s the style of revivalism of Charles Grandison Finney gave a new appearance to the Second Great Awakening. Finney conducted a series of revivalistic crusades in western New York, and then brought his campaigns to the eastern cities. He made revivalism a powerful force in American religion and many evangelists of different denominations employed his ideas and style. His own works blended Calvinist, Methodist and Arminian elements. At first eastern leaders such as Lyman Beecher distrusted the enthusiasm and fervour of his meetings, yet by 1831 his reputation was reaching its height and the more orthodox were reconciled. In the wake of these revivals, voluntary societies of all kinds arose on an unprecedented scale, frequently uniting different denominations in the cause of benevolence, moral reform or missionary zeal. The part which women played in these events was significant. Women had been known to preach in western New York before Finney's arrival, had taken a key part in Methodist meetings, and had been accustomed to pray aloud in Presbyterian churches. Among the Baptists, some women itinerant preachers, such as Martha Howell, who had travelled through the Whitestown districts attracting the wrath of male ministers, and Clarissa Danforth, 'the sensational preacher of this decade', according to one Baptist historian, of Wethersfield, Connecticut, and later of western New York, were extremely successful. In Finney's revivals, they were expected to pray aloud individually and in small meetings; it was expected that both men and women would express themselves. But Finney and others soon found that they had to defend this practice against New England opposition. And in Utica a tract published in 1823 on 'Female Influence' by the Presbyterian Utica Tract Society denied women the right to lead prayers, but invited them to expand their influence throughout society in other, more acceptable, ways. Apart from Quaker women, and some frontier missionaries, women preachers faced considerable hostility, both from the more 'established' churches, and, more generally, from public opinion. The Utica tract clearly expressed the orthodox evangelical, though not always the revivalist's, position on this.[17]

Nevertheless, the influence of women in the progress of the movement in western New York, the Burned Over District, was critical. Finney himself first went to upper New York State as an agent of the Utica Female Missionary Society. It was the women of Utica who were responsible for that dynamic eruption of religious enthusiasm, in their careful preparation and continuing missionary endeavours. Mary Ryan's detailed study of the town of Utica, at the heart of the revivals, has suggested that women were in the majority in each church, and in every revival as converts, making up between 52 and 72 per cent of converts at each revival btween 1814 and 1838, and 62 to 65 per cent of church membership.[18] A study of kinship networks also suggests that women were instrumental in conversions among their own kin. While such women were not actively demanding a public role, they appear nevertheless to have dominated the progress of the movement. The evidence makes it likely that it was the influence of mothers converted in the first revival of 1814 which was later responsible for the conversion of their children. Again the most public example of such efforts lay in the Female Missionary Society and the Maternal Association, both of Utica, the second succeeding the first. Ryan's detailed study of this town suggested that, answering to the revivalist call as their own opportunity for employment decreased with the decline of domestic and household manufactures, the young women of Utica became wives and mothers and also dedicated evangelists, dominating the religious concerns of their own children; but they were evangelists also in the cause of 'Christian Motherhood', as the Maternal Association and the *Mothers Magazine* of Utica emphasised their task as 'the private guardians of American souls'.[19] Both Cott and Ryan in their studies of New England and Utica respectively make out a strong case for a close relationship between the economic changes affecting these areas, with the decline of household manufacturing, and the strength of women's involvement in these religious movements.

Finney's revivals had a profound and dramatic effect not only in rural areas but also in the eastern cities. From the beginning of the Second Great Awakening, revivalism had spread in these cities, and church membership had grown rapidly in the most populated areas of the United States. Numerous missionary societies were founded specifically to spread the word, the duty of all those who experienced conversion and grace. Such missions were directed not only to the remote frontier but also to the poor of the cities, through the new tools of evangelical communication: Bible societies, tract distribution and the establishment of Sunday Schools. In 1816 the inhabitants of New York, for example, founded three separate organisations to bring religious faith to the poor of the city: the Young Men's Missionary Society of New York, the New York Evangelical Missionary Society and the Female Missionary Society for the Poor of New York. Their efforts were directed both towards the unconverted frontier and to the poor of their city; the latter responsibility led members of the Female Missionary Society to the active organisation of systematic visiting through the wards of the city, discovering the religious and, perhaps, the material needs of the poor. The objectives of such visits were limited, since the slum poor were still identified as vicious and irreligious, and beyond saving, though missionaries might still reach and save the children of the poor. These societies did not last beyond the mid-1820s, yet their importance foreshadowed later developments. As the tone of evangelist preaching shifted, increasingly stressing the power of man's free will, the availability of salvation to all men, so the responsibility of the individual Christian to bring about the moral reformation of fellow humans increased. The character of the missionary societies of New York changed significantly in these years. From passively distributing Bibles and tracts, they came to exercise a more active oversight, becoming 'a society to carry the Gospel by the living voice', as well as the written word 'to every creature'.[20] The work of Finney was a major element in this change, since in his revivals from 1829 onwards, Finney called upon New Yorkers to go through the streets seeking converts. The number of tract distributors, male and female, grew tenfold from 50 at first to 500 in 1830, and in his second revival, from 1834–5, over 1000 laymen and women were engaged in this work. The relevance of this was to lie in its direct impact on female organisation. In the spring of 1834 a group of New York women, under Finney's inspiration, founded the New York Female Moral Reform Society. The work of this society, which will be dealt with later, was to illustrate how far the consequences of the evangelical revival could broaden the horizons of women, even in appealing to the prostitutes and fallen women of New York City, even to directly challenging the double standard of sexual morality. The range of associations in the field of philanthropic and reforming activity undertaken by women in this period will be examined later: yet clearly evangelical religion could provide women, in rural New England, in small towns and large cities, with new means of expressing themselves, fulfilling the inspirational duties given to them, and associating together. And such associations, originally entirely religious in their purpose, could move to a more secular orientation, could begin to confront social and political problems.

The effect of evangelicalism is perhaps most easily traced in the northern and middle states, yet it played a vital role in the southern United States also. There, at an earlier point, the revival movement rapidly took on a more dramatic and emotional shape; indeed, in the South it is difficult to differentiate the end of the First Great Awakening from the coming of the Second, since Methodist missions continued to develop from the 1760s to the 1790s. But historians have generally seen the growth of camp meetings from the late 1780s as injecting a new spirit of intensity into southern religious life. Much of the South was still very sparsely settled and much of it still had the characteristics of a frontier society. Given the absence of other institutions, of educational facilities and of cities, the churches played an even more vital role in focusing social life in the South than in the North. Camp meetings might provide a first social focus outside the household, where men, women and children might join together, to form churches and associate isolated neighbours. One historian of women's role on the frontier has nevertheless written that 'The one public event that women claimed as their own was the religious meeting' and recorded that it was women who were most likely to play a leading role there, though often in the face of male mockery.[21] Baptists and Methodists were the dominant denominations, though Presbyterians and even Episcopalians showed themselves in the later years as open to the same force of religious revivalism. Other smaller groups, such as the Disciples of Christ, were to flourish in frontier conditions. Evidently, as in the North, the appeal of evangelicalism to women was profound, and there were particular factors affecting the response of southern women. As elsewhere, it gave them the opportunity to associate together. There too, they formed the majority of Church members, and before the end of the eighteenth century were organising their own prayer groups and, after the revivals of 1802, were founding local education and aid societies.[22] It is not yet possible to estimate how the impetus, membership and objectives of those societies compared with those of the North – yet it would seem that the emphasis of such groups was to a much greater extent on the achievement of a personal morality. The evangelical injunction was to benevolence and usefulness, yet the extension of such ideals beyond family prayers and the maintenance of family religion could immediately force southern women to face the relationship between slavery and Christianity.

The religious development of Angelina Grimké, an early feminist abolitionist from a well-to-do South Carolina family, is an interesting one. Undergoing a religious conversion at an early age, partly due to her dissatisfaction with the Episcopalian Church, she joined the Presbyterians:

> The Presbyterians, I think, enjoy so many privileges, that, on this account, I would wish to be one. They have their monthly prayer-meetings, Bible-classes, weekly prayer-meetings, morning and evening . . . .[23]

She absorbed herself in these activities, teaching a large Sunday School, and organising an inter-denominational prayer meeting for women. Yet rapidly she came to protest even to the elders of the Presbyterian Church against the morality of accepting the institution of slavery. She was rapidly expelled from that Church and became a Quaker, soon leaving South Carolina for Philadelphia. Such determination, in a woman whose life was to exemplify progress from the ideals of a dynamic Christianity to a fervent belief in the equality of the sexes, was of course quite atypical. Yet southern women, inspired by the grace of conversion, did become committed to the improvement of the condition of black slaves, as did Anne Randolph Meade, who educated her slaves, condemned the sexual exploitation of black women, and was committed to the colonisation of Liberia.[24] Her benevolence was exceptional, but as such still acceptable, since occasional charitable activities were unlikely materially to affect the relationship between slaves and slaveowners. Evangelicals might acquire moral credit, but no further obligations. Virginia Cary, in her *Letters on Female Character*, published in Virginia in 1830, wrote of slavery as 'a fearful evil; a canker in the bud of our national prosperity; a bitter drop in the cup of domestic felicity' but her conservative emphasis on female subordination allowed her to do little more than suggest that the task of white women slaveowners should be the mitigation of the grievances of slaves through kindly treatment, and the prevention of harmful and degrading effects in their own family circle.[25]

The majority of white men and women in the South owned no slaves, but were still likely to be involved in the evangelical reaction to slavery. In particular, southern white women joined in the mission to slaves after 1830.[26] That mission aimed to carry the message of evangelical Christianity, a message stressing content with one's existing station in life, and the necessity of individual salvation and the conquest of the sinful self. To achieve this, it looked for the conversion of the black population, to be maintained through education, a family system and church discipline. Yet at the same time, southern evangelicals were also drafting a justification of slaveholding: first, as a thing indifferent to salvation and, secondly, as part of a social system ordained by God, because of the sinfulness of man. Some of the cruder preachers were to compare the inferiority of slave to owner with that of wife and husband; enforced subordination could be and was defended on such grounds. The impulse to benevolence therefore did not grow as rapidly as in the North. There were signs that women were thought less trustworthy on issues relating to slavery, more inclined to be sympathetic, misled by their natures, distrustful of white male licentiousness. But southern women, fundamentally powerless, in fact achieved little, and though a network of women's associations continued to exist, their interests failed to expand to those in the North. The evangelical ideal of womanhood spread rather in the notion of the 'southern lady', one which was remote from the lives of the great majority of white southern women.

The message of the southern evangelical movement was a vital one for the black people of the South also. The Methodists and Baptists from the beginning of their revivals and missions in the South saw their task also as the conversion of slaves, and from the 1780s to around 1830 evangelical black churches grew in strength under the leadership of both white and black preachers. After 1830, and Nat Turner's revolt, southern states were hostile to any independent form of black leadership, and independent black churches in any numbers existed only in northern cities. For slaves, a Gospel based on individual autonomy and responsibility to God clearly immediately presented contradictions – how could the chattel property of another man be free to observe the laws of Christian morality in, for example, sexual morality and family life? The missionary message was frequently not that of salvation through zeal in the faith and good works, but rather the simple one of good behaviour, obedience, and resignation. They also preached the virtues of family life, unreal though such preaching was. Yet black churches, under black leadership, where they grew up, were virtually the only tolerated black institutions, in North or South: and their part in nineteenth-century black culture was immensely significant, combining both a distinctive adaptation to white evangelicalism and African religious survivals. Women, like men, found within these churches a faith that offered some explanation of their daily lives, some way of expressing, if only through song, their feelings as slaves. There were black women preachers too, though evidence of them is scarce. A British traveller, John Melish, visiting a Methodist meeting in Georgia in 1807–8, heard of a most effective preacher in Dorothy Ripley.[27] The preacher 'Elizabeth', born into slavery in Maryland in 1766, travelled throughout the country for many years after receiving her freedom at the age of 30, preaching in the face of hostility and disbelief from her audience. So too did Jarena Lee, born free, converted in 1805 at the age of 22 by Richard Allen, the leader of the African Methodist Episcopal Church movement, of which she was described as the first female preacher. Lee defended the right of women to preach against the conservative inclinations of Allen:

If the man may preach, because the Saviour died for him, why not the woman? seeing he died for her also. Is he not a whole Saviour, instead of a half one? as those who hold it wrong for a woman to preach, would seem to make it appear.

Did not Mary *first* preach the risen Saviour, and is not the doctrine of the resurrection the very climax of Christianity – hangs not all our hope on this, as argued by St Paul? Then did not Mary, a woman, preach the gospel? for she preached the resurrection of the crucified son of God.[28]

Such preaching and such churches offered black women, like black men, some form of solidarity and an imagery of redemption and deliverance. And some women, like 'Elizabeth' and Jarena Lee did through their preaching express the oppression of slavery.

The extent to which a clear pattern of family relationships formed an essential part of the evangelical message can be seen in the confrontation between missionaries and American Indians in the early nineteenth century. For these missionaries, the conversion of the Indians was not a question of religious conviction, but the bringing of the whole Christian civilisation to the heathen peoples of the Indian tribes. An essential part of that civilisation was the proper relationship of the sexes, and missionaries laboured hard to transform male and female sex roles among the tribes, to make Indian men into farmers, and Indian women into housewives and mothers. The directors of a Protestant Episcopal Church's missionary society declared that the condition of women was indeed one of the chief dividing lines between barbarism and civilisation:

It is a fact too glaring to be denied, that in no country, either in ancient times or modern, where the sound of the gospel is not heard, is woman placed in a grade which renders her a rational companion, or possessed of rights secured to her by equal law.[29]

They were not particularly successful in their aims, but the importance which they attached to the proper role of the sexes does suggest the strength of that prevalent view, of the high status of women in 'civilised' Protestant countries. It was the implications of that status which women were themselves exploring.

The Second Great Awakening in America took place simultaneously with and in some respects following the Evangelical movement in Britain. The effect of that movement on the position of women in Britain has been much less studied, and yet it would seem to form an essential element in that 'Victorian' conception of womanhood which has become all too familiar a term of abuse, without being subjected to more detailed analysis. The term 'evangelicalism' is usually taken to refer to that group within the Church of England which from the 1780s worked for the 'reformation of manners' in England from within that Church. Yet it may also, particularly in the context with which we are here concerned, have a broader application. Here it will be used, by analogy with the American practice, to cover those, Arminians or moderate Calvinists, Methodists, Anglicans, Baptists and others, who were committed to the experience of spiritual rebirth, the discipline of the self, and a continuing commitment to spread the word of God.[30] In England that message was discernible from the 1730s in the 'methodistical' movement within the Church of England, a movement which rapidly acquired its own separate impetus and identity, though many who shared its aims remained within the Church. The revivalism of Wesley and George Whitefield, from the 1740s onwards, brought that evangelical spirit to a much wider audience. Throughout the second half of the eighteenth century Methodist ministers and lay preachers held out the prospect of salvation through conversion and the Methodist discipline; they were gradually organised into a church divided into circuits, governed by the Methodist Conference, held together by Wesley's leadership, yet still formally not outside the Church of England until after his death in 1795. By then, though its appeal was vital, membership was still comparatively small, around 80,000, and the real period of expansion was to come in the next decades, especially in the northern industrial cities, until by 1851 there were some half a million Methodists. By then, however, Methodism had itself become a more rigid organisation, and the frequent secessions, of whom the largest was that of the Primitive Methodists, witnessed the need to maintain the original spirit of the evangelical movement felt by some. Wesley had seen his original mission as for the poor and the working population of the cities – though in practice much early Methodist work was undertaken in rural areas. By the early nineteenth century Wesleyan Methodism evidently had a strong appeal for the lower middle classes and offered a clear route to 'respectability'. But Primitive Methodism, led by individual preachers at camp meetings, originated in Staffordshire and their greatest successes remained in rural areas.

While, throughout the eighteenth century, Anglican churchmen, such as Henry Venn of Huddersfield, sympathised with the aims and vitality of the Methodist movement, the evangelical movement within the Church of England initially took a very different form. Men such as Venn had, like their Methodist colleagues, devoted themselves to the preaching of the gospel to the rural and urban poor. But the leaders of the strong, early nineteenth-century movement within the Church of England were to be those individuals who gathered around the leadership of William Wilberforce, whose work, *A Practical View of the Prevailing Religious System of Professed Christians in the upper and middle classes in this country contrasted with real Christianity* (1797), and whose fervour against slavery, provided much early inspiration. Their message lay to the upper and middling classes, for the moral reformation of their own worldly and complacent society. The poor were present in their works, to be converted and materially aided, but as much for the spiritual improvements of their betters as for their own needs. The achievements of these evangelicals in their own declared sphere were considerable. Many observers testified to the change in manners of the ruling classes of Victorian society, and many historians have acknowledged the impact of evangelical doctrine on all aspects of Anglican life. Under the initially small but powerful leadership of the Clapham Sect this movement was to dominate developments in the Church of England until the 1830s. Allied to evangelical Methodism, and to increasingly similar developments in other nonconforming Churches, evangelical religion was to be one of the most powerful forces shaping Victorian life, touching all levels of society and profoundly affecting expectations of family life. Many questions still remain to be asked about its effect on the situation of women in the early nineteenth century, and much research still remains to be done. As yet, for example, there is only scattered, though suggestive, evidence as to the extent of 'feminisation' among different denominations in Britain.[31]

The works of the earliest generation of Anglican Evangelical writers certainly suggest that the role of women in the movement was fundamental from the beginning. Their vital role within the household and family was clearly identified by such writers as Hannah More and the Rev. Thomas Gisborne, as was the part that women of the upper and middle classes should be playing in reforming the manners of society. In an early work, *Essays on various subjects principally designed for young ladies* (1777), More denounced the defective state of female education, in which so little attention was given to the cultivation of the heart, so much to the acquisition of accomplishments. Girls were not sufficiently prepared at an early stage to receive religion as they should, or to regulate their passions, or to sacrifice their opinions, to acquire a properly submissive temper. While she joined a chorus denouncing the current state of women's education, More did so from a clearly evangelical perspective. In 1799 in her *Strictures on Female Education*, she expounded on the responsibilities of women for the strengthening of religious principles and the educating of children within the family. The early forming of proper habits among children, in preparation for the hoped for spiritual rebirth from the original depravity with which they were born, was her primary task. More discounted what she saw as the 'impious' discussion of 'rights' for women. The natural propensities of women were the best indications of God's intentions for the two sexes:

A woman sees the world, as it were, from a little elevation in her own garden, whence she makes an exact survey of home scenes, but takes not in that wider range of distant prospects which he, who stands on a loftier eminence, commands.[32]

For More: 'The chief end to be proposed in cultivating the understanding of women is to qualify her for the practical purposes of life'.[33] More put her search for the ideal evangelical woman into fictional form when her *Coelebs in Search of a Wife* was published in 1808, describing at tedious length a search concluded only with the discovery of Lucilla Stanley, brought up along admirable principles, educated, but inconspicuously, indifferent to worldly pleasures, withdrawn in her rural retreat, committed to philanthropy and charity along lines which enabled the poor to help themselves, ready to take her place in an evangelical gentleman's Christian household. This constant obligation to usefulness and service for women, defined and limited by the domestic sphere, was preached to the well to do of early nineteenth-century England from the pulpits of the Church and from the prescriptive works of More and similar writers.

The Rev. Thomas Gisborne, an Anglican evangelical, followed his *Enquiries into the Duties of Men in the Higher and Middle Classes of Society* (1794) by *An Enquiry into the Duties of the Female Sex* (1797) in which he considered the best use which women might make of their practical energies. For Gisborne, the effect of the female character was of most importance in three outstanding ways. First, a woman's task was to contribute daily and hourly to the comfort of all those around her in the domestic circle, in all circumstances; secondly, to form and improve the manners and conduct of the opposite sex by her society and example; and thirdly, to model the human mind in its early stages of growth, caring for girls, especially, until they became women. The further aim of supreme importance, the achievement of everlasting life, required attention to these three areas of life, the tasks defining woman's lot. For the young and single there was the need to find 'serious and instructive occupations', such as serious reading, the performance of domestic duties and philanthropy, as well as healthy exercise. But to Gisborne what was of prime concern was that: 'Home is the centre round which the influence of every married woman is principally accumulated'.[34] Methodical employment in those duties was the best armour against metropolitan temptations and those vices to which women were prone. Gisborne's view was a narrower one than that of either More or Mrs Sarah Trimmer, whose *Oeconomy of Charity* (1797) rested equally on that assumption of the need for women to be useful, to discipline themselves through regular and methodical tasks. Again, she appealed to 'persons in the middling state of life' to help to heal that conflict between the different classes of society so prejudicial to the nation, by supplementing public charity by private benevolence. Women could best assist in, for example, the development of Sunday Schools:

> What more suited to the tenderness which is allowed to be natural to our sex? Can a woman, accustomed to the exercise of maternal affection towards her own beloved offspring, be indifferent to the happiness of poor children, who have no means of learning their duty but what these schools afford?[35]

The experience of mothers would be invaluable especially in the education of girls. For the single woman, such work would offer opportunities for exercising qualities lost in their private lives. And for young girls, the task would both improve their characters and maintain their own Christian commitment, and help to train the servants of the future. Such work could be expanded into the visitation of the poor, and the discovery of their material wants, especially those of women in childbirth, and into the establishment of houses for industry for poor girls.

The methods of the Anglican Evangelicals were similar to and often preceded the Second Great Awakening in the United States – the

British and Foreign Bible Society, for example, was founded in 1803 with the aim, simply, of distributing Bibles. But the earliest methods of evangelical propaganda were the tract and the school, and More herself was a zealous worker in both these causes. Her combination of religious commitment, political conservatism and female philanthropy was directed towards the lower classes in her *Cheap Repository Tracts* starting in 1795, which offered simple stories, poems and prayers, and to the poor the prospect of salvation combined with industry, resignation and humility to their betters. Most of all, More played an important part in popularising the Sunday School, both as a medium of instruction and, as Sarah Trimmer had advocated, a sphere in which women of the middle classes could fulfil their need to be useful. By 1800 she had established over a dozen day and Sunday Schools in the Mendip Hills where she lived, and her example was rapidly followed by other leading Anglican evangelical women and more slowly in many parishes of the Church of England. Their object, however, was not primarily educational, but religious, with Hannah More committed to the teaching of reading but not of writing.[36]

Other denominations also shared the same commitment to the spreading of the evangelical message, though not necessarily the same social attitudes. The expansion of evangelicalism, cutting across denominational boundaries, was in many ways the most significant factor in the religious map of Britain in the early nineteenth century. The example of Anglicanism and Methodism had its effect on the old dissenting congregations, and in the early nineteenth century evangelical theology was battling against the older Calvinism within Congregationalist and Baptist churches. In 1832 the group of churches brought together in the Baptist Union defined itself as a union 'who agree in the sentiments usually denominated evangelical'. Quakers too were split between those who retained their belief in a quietist religion, in the Inner Light, and those advocating an evangelical approach. Within all these churches, there were of course still many schisms and many variants. There still remained, most notably within the Unitarians, the legacy of eighteenth-century 'rational' religion, and the Unitarians, as will be seen, made a quite distinctive contribution to the development of feminist thinking in Britain.

Nonconformist denominations, Methodists and others, were to come to share the essential elements of the Anglican view of women's role in society: but the starting point, for popular revivalist movements, was a different one. Within such movements, in their early years, women might play a leading role as preachers. The notion of women speaking in public was treated with some horror by Anglican conservative and prescriptive writers. M. A. Stodart, the evangelical editor of the *Christian Lady's Magazine*, for instance, denounced the notion of women as preachers as contrary to the injunctions of St Paul and the Apostles.[37] But among eighteenth-century Methodists the practice was common. It was approved, with qualifications, by John Wesley, who wrote, after many doubts, that women in exceptional circumstances when inspired by the word of God, might speak in public.[38] Mary Fletcher Bosanquet, one of the earliest women preachers, accustomed to speaking to large gatherings of several thousands in the open air, echoed that view when she wrote in 1803: 'I do look on the call of women as an *extra* – not an *ordinary* call; therefore I strove and do *strive now* so as to act, not out of custom, but only when I have a clear leading thereto, and this leading may and will differ at different parts of our lives, but to follow the cloud is the thing I aim at, and the soul feels a peace and comfort in so doing for "where the spirit of the Lord is, there is liberty".'[39] In the great Methodist revival of West Yorkshire in 1792–6, an intinerant woman preacher, Ann Cutler, played a dominant role in the early years, as the course of the revival clearly followed her own mass meetings and her progress around the Yorkshire circuits. John Baxter has suggested that the background of this revival should be seen as the economic dislocation and unemployment of these war years, a time when women were especially vulnerable and receptive to the appeal of revivalist religion. However, by 1803 the Methodist Conference had imposed a clear ban on women preachers, with this exception, that if a woman felt an *extraordinary* call, 'she should, in general, address her *own sex*, and *those only*'.[40] The ban was to remain official throughout the nineteenth century though a number of women in the decades following defied it, such as Mary Barritt, who after her marriage to the preacher Zechariah Taft continued to act as an additional itinerant preacher in the circuits which her husband travelled.[41] The foundation of the Primitive Methodists by Hugh Bourne in Staffordshire took place at least in part in defence of the ministry of women, in creating: 'a preaching establishment where the female shall have full liberty to exercise her talents in persuading sinners to fly to Christ'. Bourne, in his tract *Remarks on the Ministry of Women* (1808), defended that ministry with reference to Joel II.28: 'And your sons and your daughters shall prophesy'. Prophesying was interpreted by him to include both preaching and the higher duty of looking to the future.[42]

Among the Primitive Methodists over 40 women preachers have been identified, though the real number must be many more. They played no administrative role, and received lesser allowances. The last woman itinerant preacher, Elizabeth Bultitude, retired in 1862, though many women continued to preach locally. In the rather similar sect of the Bible Christians of Cornwall, similarly, women were admitted as preachers from the beginning. Between 1819 and 1861, when the last woman itinerant preacher was accepted, there were 71 itinerant female preachers among the Bible Christians, touring not only Devon and Cornwall, but the whole of the south of England – though they never held any supervisory position within the sect.[43] The same pattern must have been true of other new revivalist sects, though not of the older dissenting congregations. As such sects became more structured, more established, the role of women preachers declined, as it had done in Wesleyan Methodism. Even among the Quakers the position of women was challenged. In the early nineteenth century, women ministers, that is, those who spoke in Meetings, significantly outnumbered men – Quaker practice strongly influenced Hugh Bourne. Yet the influential and evangelical Beaconite Quakers were to reject the ministry of women. The most influential woman preacher of the period, the elderly Sarah Lynes Grubb, was a strong defender of the traditional theology of the Light Within, for as a quietist minister she believed that her words were literally inspired by God, as she acted merely as a passive human mouthpiece.[44] Perhaps, speculatively, the evidence so far suggests that the advance of evangelicalism from revivalism to organisation brought a shift away from the potential power of the woman prophet or priest – who might passively be permitted to convey God's words – towards the limited, but active and practical tasks of the domestic sphere, broadly interpreted.[45]

Much more typical of the spread of evangelicalism in Britain was the participation by women in a whole range of religious activities: distributing tracts and Bibles, teaching in Sunday Schools, fundraising and forming voluntary associations. Such activities were not merely confined to well-to-do Anglicans: Sunday Schools, for instance, were also 'the creation of poor and humble weavers, blacksmiths and shoemakers'.[46] Some of the earliest Sunday Schools were founded before More's work began. Catherine Cappe, then an Anglican, later a Unitarian, taught poor children to read on Sundays at Bedale in the 1760s and the Methodist Hannah Ball of High Wycombe, Sophia Cooke of a village near Gloucester, and a number of other men and women all began Sunday Schools in the decades before the 1780s. In the late eighteenth century a number of interdenominational schools were set up, and at the same time working people themselves began to take the initiative. In spite of much detailed work on the Sunday School movement we have no very clear picture of the participation of women in the teaching and organisation of these schools; yet their role was clearly a very important, if not a leading one. As the numbers of such schools grew, and as the interdenominational schools patronised by the middle classes collapsed, so the need for more teachers grew. There were simply not enough young women of the kind envisaged by Trimmer and More. By 1839 the *Sunday School Magazine* reported that: 'The bulk of our teachers, as well as our scholars, belong to the lower – some of the best of them to the lowest – classes of society'. The evidence suggests that these teachers were both men and women, many including former pupils. The Sunday School, dominated by laymen and women, was an important force in the organisation of working-class religion and an indication of achievement. The radical Chartist, James Watson, said of his mother that she: 'although poor was intelligent, as proof of which I may state that she was a teacher in one of the Sunday Schools of the town'.[47]

The desire to spread the faith was most obviously illustrated in the distribution of tracts and Bibles. The British and Foreign Bible Society had by 1819 about 350 female associations with about 10,000 women regularly employed in their work, frequently supplanting and performing much more effectively the work of male auxiliary societies. The participation of women in such activities was strongly defended by one of the leading figures of the Bible Society, C. S. Dudley, against conservative critics. Their work would neither disrupt their domestic duties nor bring them unduly into the public eye, but give them an opportunity rather to cultivate 'the best feelings of the heart'. Their example should be 'the Marys and Priscillas, the Tryphenas and Tryphosas of early times', for the Bible formed 'the charter of the female sex against degradation and oppression'.[48] A few individual women's societies formed spontaneously. The Aberdeen Female Servants Society for the promotion of the Scriptures was founded in 1809, and by 1811 had 110 members. By 1811 the first Ladies Bible Society in direct contact with the national organisation was founded in Westminster with a committee of 48 women. It became too large, and by 1815 had divided its members into thirteen

districts covering the neighbourhood of Westminster. Over the next
few years the movement spread very rapidly throughout the country,
with an extensive network of Ladies Associations developing, supervised by local male-run branches. In 1817 the first Ladies Auxiliary
Branch Society was formed in Liverpool and soon supervised ten local
Ladies Associations, because of: 'the great inefficiency of gentlemen
in a plan professing to embrace the distribution of the Bible through
every part of a numerous, poor and ever-varying population'. By the
end of the first year over 20,000 home visits had been carried out by
the collectors of the Association, it claimed, and by 1821 Liverpool
had nearly 700 collectors.[49] Liverpool's example was followed by
many other areas. Within these associations and branch societies,
though the help of men was frequently sought at the outset, women
formed the committee and held the offices of the society. The time
which they had available, and the funds which they succeeded in
collecting, were quite invaluable to the association, and in this the
history of the Bible Society was typical of most. The historian of the
Church Missionary Society wrote that in the early years the society
had been largely dependent on women for the collection of funds.[50]

The Bible Society was only one of a whole range of new voluntary
associations appearing in this period, with both religious and
philanthropic aims. In Britain it has been suggested by F. K.
Prochaska that between 1790 and 1830 some 130 new organisations
were established. By then there were many thousands of provincial
ladies' auxiliaries. Where the membership of such societies has been
studied, it is clear that the proportion of women members was rising
significantly in this period. Prochaska's study of twenty such societies
suggested that women subscribers in the Church Missionary Society
rose from 12 per cent in 1801 to 29 per cent in 1829, in the Society for
promoting Christianity among the Jews from 12 to 27 per cent from
1809 to 1813, and in the major tract societies, the Society for
Promoting Christian Knowledge, the Bible Society, the Religious
Tract Society and the Prayer Book and Homily Society, percentages
increased from 10 to 20 per cent (1790–1817), from 12 to 23 per cent
(1805–17), from 11 to 24 per cent (1801–29) and from 10 to 20 per cent
(1814–30) respectively. Evidence suggests too that the financial
contribution made by women was in proportion to their numbers. As
well as increasing participation in mixed charities, the period also saw
'an explosion of female societies . . . in which ladies committees made
policy'.[51] The form and activities of such societies will be considered

later. Not all this activity was undertaken by evangelicals: Quakers, High Church Anglicans and others also participated. But the expansion of evangelicalism across the denominations in early nineteenth-century Britain, and in particular the outlook of evangelical Arminianism, with its stress on individual agency and on good works, was one important element in the creation of a new role for women of the upper, middling and 'respectable' classes. Evangelicalism contributed much to the ideal of domesticity, yet its implications were not entirely constraining. There are many suggestive similarities here between Britain and the United States, though some developments cannot be paralleled. For instance, the attempt to import Maternal Associations failed.[52] But, similarly, as they spread the word, women were drawn to organise together, and from the earliest years, through visiting the poor were drawn towards benevolence, especially towards their own sex. By the 1850s, Ellen Ranyard's Biblewomen in London, from distributing Bibles, were led to offer aid and assistance, especially in household management, to poor women.[53]

There are important contrasts to be drawn between the pattern of events in Britain and America on the one hand, and in France on the other. In France a revival of religious commitment and piety was already evident in the Napoleonic period, a revival with clear-cut political implications. Conservatives had seen in the events of the French Revolution the consequences of rationalism and indifference, and as a response they turned increasingly towards the authority of the Church. For the poor, especially for women, the Church too seemed to offer the only hope both of material assistance and of spiritual consolation for their hardships. Aristocratic émigrés in exile, and those of conservative temper in France, began before 1814 to build new Catholic associations, dedicated to the restoration of the Bourbons and to the elaboration of new conservative social doctrine. A part of that doctrine was to be the conservative Catholic and pious family. Such an image is found in the writings of leading conservative political theorists of the day.[54] In the years of the Restoration that old analogy between the government of society and the government of the family was to be restated in all its force by Joseph de Maistre and even more notably by Louis de Bonald. In his pamphlet, *Du divorce* (1801) and later in his speeches in the Chamber of Deputies, de Bonald made it clear that for him divorce was to be equated with democracy, as the disrupting of divinely ordained authority, an authority which was single:

In domestic society, or the family, man holds power, and that power is indivisible; and in that public or general society called the state, man should hold power, a power always indivisible, in spite of appearances to the contrary. . . .[55]

The key to the regeneration of society lay not only in the rightful ordering of the public sphere, but in return to the proper domestic relations of the family, governed by paternal power. So the 'domestic constitution' reappears in another, more authoritarian, setting. De Bonald and the royalists were successful in securing the abolition of divorce in France in 1816. It has been suggested that changes in the manners of the French aristocracy, not so dissimilar from those taking place in the Victorian upper classes in this period, may have had a consciously political context. Condemnation of religious scepticism could lead many, even the most worldly of noblewomen, to experience religious conversion, and from there be drawn from frivolity to the life of a devoted wife and mother: like the Marquise de la Tour du Pin, who left her record of these changes in her life.[56]

The Catholic revival thus certainly shared some of the characteristics of Protestant evangelicalism. Orders of missionary priests undertook evangelistic missions throughout France, which were undoubtedly successful. There was a growth both of religious and of charitable societies. The 'Société pour la Propagation de la Foi', a purely lay organisation, had as its objective the defence of the Church through the publication of Catholic works, from liberal and anti-clerical onslaughts.[57] It is clear too that the process of 'feminisation' was at work in Catholic France as well as in Protestant countries. The Restoration certainly saw a marked growth in the number of religious congregations of women in France, a growth which continued steadily throughout the century. Such foundations might begin as individual initiatives by groups of women, perhaps in isolated towns or areas, coming together to live the contemplative life, or to educate or nurse those in need, though always under the supervision of the parish and later of the diocesan clergy.[58] In a number of specific studies, historians have noted the different orientation of men and women to religious practice. In Paris, the bourgeoisie studied by Adeline Daumard was predominantly rationalist in outlook, yet religious belief, if it was significant, was transmitted by women at all levels of the bourgeoisie. The evidence of their wills suggested the much greater part which it held in their lives than in those of their

husbands and fathers, though even so, in Paris, the extent of such
faith should not be overestimated before the religious revival of the
mid-1830s.[59] In Lille in the 1840s, Mme Louis Josson, wife of a
prominent government official, founded the 'Archiconfrèrie des
mères chrétiennes', for women despairing over the defection of their
husbands and sons from the Church, who might come together to
pray. Bonnie Smith's detailed examination of the religious faith of the
well-to-do bourgeois women of Lille suggests that these women found
in the Church a way of life, a symbolism and a series of rituals 'in
perfect harmony with the domestic way of life'. Their husbands,
however, the leading politicians, businessmen and intellectuals of the
Nord, were increasingly to see such faith as reactionary and
anachronistic.[60] In her study of the French peasantry, Martine
Segalen has pointed to male disaffection with the Church, especially
when after 1830 it ceased to be mandatory for households to attend
Mass together. It was the woman within the peasant family who
mediated between the Church and the family, taking care of the
religious education of children, faithfully attending Sunday Mass,
carrying out her necessary religious obligations. And Segalen emphasises how Millet's painting, the *Angelus*, completed between 1855 and
1857 (Plate 4), 'underlines the feminisation of religious life' – it was
the woman who prayed, who spoke directly to God.[61] A study of the
Church and the workers in nineteenth-century Lyons found that the
Church had a significant hold over working-class women. A republican weaver commented in the 1850s that the church provided them
with both charity and sociability, and that many women 'preferred
the church that helped them to live and raise their families to their
own husbands'.[62] Hostile critics of the left, like Jules Michelet, were to
attack the political influence of women, however indirect, for this very
reason, arguing that the influence of priests and church drove a wedge
into the very heart of domestic life, challenging that male authority
which republicans and anti-clericals as well as Catholics upheld in
France.[63] It is interesting that an English reviewer of Michelet's book,
in *Blackwood's Review* in 1845, suggested that the answer was for men
to re-establish companionship with their wives, through leading
religious duties in the household, 'a re-establishment of patriarchal
piety' which was for the reviewer one of the great strengths of
Protestantism.[64]

In France as elsewhere, this religious strength led to the expansion
of all kinds of associations: sodalities, prayer groups, charities with a

religious foundation. Yet Catholic women, in their devotions, gave themselves not so much to missionary activity, to the spreading of faith, as to the pursuit of their own devotions, embodied in a theology which was of direct relevance to domesticity. Smith has pointed to the ways in which: 'in their devotions the women of the Nord selected those features of Catholicism that emphasised trial and fragility'. Their consciousness of their own sufferings as women, in childbirth and sickness, is revealed in their devotion to the Sacred Heart, representing the sufferings of Christ, Mary the Mother of Sorrows, and Saint Monica the burdened mother of Saint Augustine. Above all, Mary embodied the image of the reproductive woman. Women might, as they did at all their meetings, pray to Mary and the saints for intercession and exhibit their devotion, to try to atone for their sinfulness and the sins of the world. Nevertheless sin, evil and poverty remained inevitable on earth: whatever the possibilities of energy and organisation in a secular world, Catholic women were resigned to their impotence, still guided by the laws of the Church, not those of man or of science. Smith has put it:

> As commercialism posed an alternative standard, or as democracy sought to substitute the law of man for the laws of God, the women of the Nord became arch supporters of the rule of the Father, be he embodied in the Church itself or in his surrogate, the King.[65]

Among the peasantry too the only societies to which women had access were religious, normally based on particular devotions and, modelled on male brotherhoods, known as *confrèries*. But organised societies were rarer than informal devotions or celebrations normally reflecting the particular concerns of women. In some regions, devotion to Saint Agatha, the patron saint of wives, mothers and nurses, was popular and married women would attend Mass together, then share a meal – 'They sing songs, and celebrate women's special qualities. . . .'[66]

So while such associations could and did provide a basis for expanding charitable activity, they were based not on the pursuit of individual salvation by individual means but on the collective devotion of women within the context of hierarchical Church authority. Voluntary lay associations could not in this context be seen as a force for radical change, rather for intercession and for palliation.

It is interesting that of the three most notable works on the education of women published in the Restoration, all were by women leaning towards liberalism both in politics and in religion. The educational advice of these books, *Lettres de famille sur l'éducation* (1824) by Mme Guizot, a deist, *Essai sur l'éducation des femmes* (1824) by Mme de Rémusat, the wife of a leading liberal politician, and *Education progressive, ou étude du cours de la vie* (1828–38) by Mme Necker de Saussure, will be discussed later. But all three books employed a mixture of philosophy and psychology, stressing the training of the will and of the reason, so that girls should follow the moral law, should come to accept their domestic responsibilities, not merely out of blind faith or obedience, but because they recognised the necessity. Mme Necker de Saussure, the Protestant, emphasised more strongly than the others family worship, religious education within the household, and the wider philanthropic duties of women. Perhaps then within the Restoration, advocating an improvement in the status of women was linked to political and religious dissent, however moderate its form.

It would be useful to know how far the Réveil, or religious revival, among the French Protestant community from 1817, affected the participation of women in associations and in charities. Inspired by events in England and in Geneva, this was an eventful time for the French Protestant community. Missionary societies, educational and Sunday School societies, tract societies, all grew up at this time, yet we have only a few glimpses as to the way in which these affected French Protestant women. For example, Mme Mallet, from a well-established and patrician Protestant family, is known to have confronted local Catholic authorities in her continued distribution of tracts and Bibles at Mont-Dore in the department of Puy-de-Dôme, in the face of prohibitions; in this she was joined by her woman friends and relatives. The picture here in this community must surely be one in which useful and charitable works for men and for women were strongly stressed, as they were in Britain. This contrast between Catholic and Protestant faiths has suggested that both experienced 'feminisation' in the nineteenth century: perhaps to understand this we need to look more closely at the changing relationships between public and private lives which affected all these societies, at all levels. Yet there is also a further contrast in the individualism inherent in the Protestant experience of salvation, and the more positive Protestant evaluation of women's domestic and religious role which, it might be suggested, brought women to take a more active part in sects and churches, in religious and charitable activity outside the home, in the formation of voluntary associations. For Catholics the possibility of such initiatives was limited by their own theology, and by the role allotted to them by an established and hierarchical Church.[67]

MILLENARIANISM

Within the principal evangelical groupings, women's spiritual mission had been exalted, though their domestic role had been clearly delineated. And as, from the 1780s onwards, there was a clear growth in millenarianism, the belief that a time would come in the not so far distant future when Christ and the saints would reign on earth, so women prophets began to appear in significant numbers. Such beliefs had always been present among small groups, in Britain in particular from the seventeenth century onwards, but the pace clearly quickened after 1780. Such prophets and prophetesses were known to John Wesley, and perhaps Methodist doctrines were encouraging to popular enthusiastic religion. As has been suggested, it was accepted that the Spirit might speak through men or women; and in certain though by no means all of these sectarian movements, historians have discerned a 'sturdy feminism'.[68] The number of female leaders in the period from the 1770s to the 1840s is striking, and women were equally prominent among the membership.

One of the earliest was Mother Ann Lee, a young woman once one of George Whitefield's Methodist audience, who in 1758 joined a group of ex-Quakers, who met together united by millenarian beliefs. By 1770 she proclaimed herself the new female messiah, and asserted her own leadership within the sect. In 1774 she left for New York with a group of followers, where, though facing initial difficulties, they succeeded in attracting converts, largely from those already 'awakened' in New York State and New England. By the end of the eighteenth century there were eleven Shaker communities, though Mother Ann Lee had died in 1784, and the sect continued to grow in the first half of the nineteenth century, profiting from evangelical revivals and expanding its communities, with a majority of members clearly women. A Scottish contemporary, Mrs Luckie Buchan, living in Ayrshire, began in the 1770s to seek for perfection through attending 'fellowship meetings'. After hearing a sermon by the Rev.

Hugh White, a seceder from the orthodox Presbyterian Church of Scotland, she began to correspond with him. He proclaimed her the 'Woman clothed with the Sun' forecast in Revelation 12, a saint and a mystic who would dispel the darkness of the rule of Satan on earth. They faced much local persecution, but built a community based on the acknowledgement of the divinity of the Friend Mother, and the prospect of a second coming at any time. Another prophetess, Jemima Wilkinson, daughter of a Quaker farmer of Rhode Island, like Ann Lee spent her early religious life among the Quakers, but after her conversion in 1777 preached with great effect among the Quakers and the 'awakened' of Rhode Island, Connecticut and Pennsylvania. She herself did not claim divinity, or the status of a prophet, but the name of Public Universal Friend, believing herself to be inspired by a new spirit, a messenger from Christ, destined to proclaim salvation for all. In 1788 she founded the community of New Jerusalem in that haven of popular evangelicalism and millenarian movements, western New York State, the Burned Over District.

The best known prophetess of the period was of course Joanna Southcott. A farmer's daughter from Devon who had worked as a domestic servant and upholsteress, she became involved with Methodism around 1780, and later, in 1792, joined the Methodist society in Exeter. Yet in that year she had a strange visitation calling her to act as a prophetess. She received no support from Methodists or Dissenters, but her mission was considerably helped by a number of sympathetic Anglican clergyman. She wrote many pamphlets to explain her continuing visions, and other Southcottian congregations formed throughout the country. She claimed that all she spoke and wrote was inspired by the Spirit, and that she herself was that same woman foretold in Revelations, who would defeat Satan. She had a sizeable following at her death in 1814 of around 20,000 officially 'sealed' believers, and many more followers, from a similar social background and geographical distribution to Methodism. Harrison has estimated that women outnumbered men by 63 to 36 per cent.[69]

What these women, and many others more obscure and unrecognised, shared was undoubtedly a religious enthusiasm which embodied the particular mission of woman. Mrs Sarah Flaxmer, interpreting the military defeats of 1795 in the light of the apocalyptic prophecies of Revelations 12, looked to the Apocrypha I Esdras 4, where the powers of women over men were listed. Mrs Luckie Buchan claimed that she too was the woman of Revelations 12, and also the third person of the Godhead, with Christ, the second person, as her elder brother. And Joanna Southcott too identified herself with the woman of Revelation, and the bride of the Lamb in the nineteenth chapter of that book:

A woman Satan chose at first, to bring on man the fall;
A woman God has chose at last, for to restore us all.
As by a woman death must come, so life must come the same,
And they that eat the fruit she gives, may bless God's holy name[70]

So woman was to be redeemed, and finally to bring about the deliverance of man through childbearing. The imagery of divine marriage is very strong among these prophetesses, as it was, though often less explicitly, among more 'respectable' denominations. Such imagery, frequently sexual and erotic, could be coupled with a deeply felt asceticism in sexual matters in this world. Mother Ann Lee's own experience of marriage and childbirth had proved a tragic one, since she lost four young children in childbirth. Denial of sexuality was central to the Shaker creed and commitment to a Shaker community meant celibacy. But in such a community it was also clear that women were to have equality of rights in the running of their affairs, derived from the clear intention of God in the Bible, and 'the manifestation of Christ in the female'.[71] Jemima Wilkinson in her community also strongly advocated celibacy, though not as inflexibly as the Shakers. Experimentalism could, however, take other forms. The members of Luckie Buchan's community gave up their married status, denounced the bonds of matrimony and intended to bring up their children in common.

Such millenarianism was by no means a Protestant preserve. In France, Suzette Labrousse, from Périgord, who until 1790 had lived the life of a pious recluse, began to prophesy that the changes brought about by the revolution in France would bring with them the moral and spiritual renovation of the country. As she journeyed across France, on foot, towards Rome, she addressed meetings both inside and outside churches, in spite of attempts to prohibit her, as a woman, speaking. But her modest piety, and her limited claims, meant that she built no following for herself. The elderly Catherine Théot, born in 1716 into a peasant background, who possibly remained illiterate, won a reputation for piety throughout her life, though in 1779 she, with a few followers, was arrested for repeatedly speaking in church against the preachers. In Paris, in 1793, she clearly came to attract a small following, as she preached that the French Revolution was a part of God's own plan for his true Church. Her language became increasingly millenarian, looking forward to the Second Coming, and she, like Joanna Southcott, saw herself as: 'a New Eve, who will deliver us from the iniquity into which the first Eve led us by her disobedience'.[72] Clarke Garrett has traced the roots of such movements in France to a variety of sources – popular piety, Jansenist offshoots, interest in occultism – but has argued that millenarian doctrines were less widely accepted or asserted there than in England at the end of the eighteenth century.

There was in fact no clear dividing line separating the followers of such leaders from the members of other revivalist sects. The appeal of such millenarianism cannot be explained simply in terms of the individual psychology of the leaders. Explanations of its strength at this time have dwelt on the particular deprivation of the classes to which it undoubtedly appealed: artisans, tradesmen, the lower middle classes. But the relevance of women's experience should also be stressed, though it is difficult to do more than to speculate, whether, as has been suggested with regard to the Burned Over District, and even West Yorkshire, the decline in domestic production and economic dislocation were affecting particular groups of women. Perhaps women were protesting not only at the social deprivations which they suffered together with their men, but also at their own domestic and sexual subordination. The concern of communities such as New Jerusalem or the Shakers, to reorder the domestic, and, even more, the sexual and family relationships of members, would suggest so. The appeal of enthusiastic religion to women could, under certain circumstances, bring a radical challenge to social and sexual orthodoxies.

In the future such a challenge was to be taken up rather by secular communitarian movements than by the heirs of the millenarians. The language and drama of millenarianism mainly, though not entirely, associated with militantly evangelical Protestantism, were employed to express that vision of the future which might alone sustain those threatened in a period of social change. The boundary between religious and secular aspirations was to prove a narrow one. In the 1830s and 1840s several groups straddled that uneasy borderline, incorporating the notion of the female messiah, of Woman-Power, The group of disciples of Henri de Saint-Simon, who gathered together in the late 1820s in France, around Prosper Enfantin, held a mystical creed, which aimed to reconcile the dualism of Christianity, of the spirit and the flesh, through the moral and intellectual regeneration of humanity. One key to this regeneration lay in the emancipation of women, to be granted independence, and to be equal and complementary to men. The new social unit was to be the 'couple' in which the qualities of men and women would complement each other. And the sign of the future millenium was to be the coming of *la femme messie*, the Woman Messiah. In this confused semi-religious millenarianism, the improvement of women's condition was constantly emphasised – so too were the undefined but mystical qualities of Woman as Mother. The creed was to provide an important route to feminism for a number of women, though at the same time these doctrines, and the notion of the *femme libre* or 'free woman' was to drown the movement in ridicule by 1834.[73]

In Britain links between Southcottianism and the socialism of Robert Owen was formed by James Elishama Smith, editor of the newspaper *The Crisis*, who had spent two years among a Southcottian faction, the Christian Israelites, from 1830–2. After quarrelling with Owen in 1834, he founded his own newspaper, *The Shepherd*. In both papers he put forward his own Doctrine of the Woman, amalgamating, he claimed, mystical and secular prophecies for the coming of the great female messiah. Smith had also been influenced by the Saint-Simonians and became one of their chief English promoters. The last important group combining these roots was to be the Communist Church of 1841 to 1849, the work of Goodwyn and Catherine Barmby, Chartist and Owenite. There was a considerable overlap between the Communist Church and Owenism, though at its height the Church could claim around twelve separate branches. Like Smith they saw Southcott as exemplifying the mission of woman. Both Goodwyn and Catherine Barmby went on to develop a notion of the androgynous personality, one which would in the future transcend and combine the qualities of maleness and femaleness:

> Grace be to those in whom woman-nature . . . and man-nature are at present equilibriated and active. We hail them as true priests of humanity, as the veritable social apostles.[74]

It was a radical critique and one which was to lead the Barmbys to campaign in the future directly for the political and social emancipation of woman.

Women's role then, as defined by evangelicalism, combined a central domestic focus with a high evaluation of women's moral worth, of their positive and unique qualities, and their mission in the world. There was, of course, contradiction and ambiguity here, and in the exploration of such ambiguities the domestic focus was to be expanded until it became unrecognisable. There were also those resistant to or untouched by the forces of evangelicalism. In Britain and in the United States, mainly in New England, small but influential and well-to-do Unitarian communities were shaped from those congregations who wished to preserve something of the rationalist and egalitarian outlook of the eighteenth century. But even Unitarianism, in the early nineteenth century, was to be split between those who, like William Johnson Fox, editor of the *Monthly Repository*, looked to that rationalism, and men like James Martineau, brother of Harriet, and William Ellery Channing of Boston, who were committed to a liberal, non-sectarian, pietism. Unitarianism was to provide, perhaps because of its very distance from other congregations, an important route to feminism, and a source of egalitarian views about the relationship between the sexes. The conservatism of many evangelical ministers might and indeed did drive many women from the more inflexible denominations towards Unitarianism. One historian, Ann Douglas, has argued that the influence of women within American Unitarianism was substantially to change the outlook of the Unitarian leadership, and to 'feminise' its doctrines.[75]

Reaction could, however, take more extreme forms, in the complete rejection of Christian principles. Emma Martin, born into a lower middle-class Bristol family, was converted into a Particular Baptist congregation in 1829 at the age of 17, and became a tract distributor, collector and worker in the evangelical cause. After a not too successful period of her life, in which she ran a school, broadened her educational horizons and experienced an unhappy marriage, in 1839 she heard a socialist lecturer speak and challenged his views of the Bible. Over the next few months, she was converted by secularist arguments, and in the 1840s became a leading lecturer, travelling throughout the country, in the cause of Owenite socialism and of freethought. Like other lecturers in the cause, male and female, she denounced the part played by clerical and religious orthodoxy in enforcing the dependence of women, 'the football of society thankful for its kicking'.[76] Martin was to use all the available methods of the evangelist in her career as a lecturer and campaigner, debating with ministers, facing many hostile audiences. For her, the dynamism of evangelicalism was translated into a secular and co-operative creed.

The legacy of dynamic, evangelical, religious belief, which offered a re-evaluation of women's domestic and moral status, is therefore a very complex one to trace, with both conservative and radical possibilities for the situation of women. In its language and imagery, in the individual experience of conversion, in the religious life of the family, and through association with other women outside the family, the religious revivalism of the early nineteenth century offered an important framework through which the changing situation of women could be expressed.

4. Educating Hearts and Minds

In the early nineteenth century, educationalists, whether evangelical, rationalist or romantic, in their approach were united in stressing certain common themes which would prove to be of great significance for women's education. In England, France and the United States, speculation about child development, drawing on the diverse inheritances of Locke and Rousseau, and on the work of such contemporary writers as Pestalozzi, emphasised the role of family and parents, and especially mothers, in imprinting good and moral lessons upon the child in infancy, in drawing out what was best in the child's nature. So 'maternal education', or the task of the mother as educator and as socialiser became the focus for much important work. In particular, mothers were required to turn their attention to the next generation of educators, their daughters. Such a theme clearly formed one part of that enhancement of the domestic sphere which was such a feature of the early nineteenth century. Some women, and some men, interested in the quality of women's education, were to carry the argument further: was women's education to be undertaken only in the interest of later generations, or were those generations better served by first concentrating on women themselves? What could women achieve, through self-culture and self-improvement? The emphasis had shifted by mid-century, as education for middle-class girls came to be seen as much in the light of its links with future employment. Without an improvement in the quality of secondary education, no such employment or financial independence could be contemplated and, for feminists, such an improvement was an essential prerequisite to all further changes. Working-class girls, whose illiteracy rate remained high throughout this period, did in Britain share in the expansion of grant-aided elementary education, and of cheap private schooling, together with the development of teacher-training institutions. As yet, such education was nowhere compulsory. In Britain, at its best, it could provide higher standards than the middle-class girl was likely to receive. The opportunities were nevertheless likely to be widest for the white American girl, though immense regional and social variations did still exist. But in general, discussion of the nature and quality of women's education, at all levels, did lead to more general reflection on the status and degree of independence which women might hope to enjoy, and led also to further action.

THE CASE FOR 'MATERNAL EDUCATION'

Almost all writers on women's education at the beginning of the nineteenth century were agreed on its deficiencies. They could agree in denouncing the poor quality of basic education and the attention paid to ornamental accomplishments and superficial learning, as had the most orthodox of eighteenth-century preceptors, Dr John Gregory, in his *A Father's Legacy to his Daughters* (1774), and Mrs Hester Chapone, in *Letters on the Improvement of the Mind* (1773). The same can be said of Benjamin Rush, Mary Wollstonecraft and Mme de Genlis. More important was the extensive attention now being paid to the purpose and method of the education of women, at least in educational theory. The reasons for such attention were various and some have already been traced. Evangelical writers were profoundly concerned with the upbringing of children from their earliest years. Republicans and revolutionaries of the 1790s had seen the education of women as the key to the rearing of future generations of citizens. Liberal and 'enlightened' writers were concerned to investigate the insights of Locke and Rousseau, and to develop further their philosophical understanding of the process of education. In the early nineteenth century all these approaches had certain themes in common: education as a preparation for motherhood, the social importance of motherhood, the vital importance of nurturing and training in the early years of childhood, the emphasis on the relationship between mothers and daughters.

Two writers of a rather similar, liberal outlook, whose works were influential in Britain, France and the United States in these years, were Maria Edgeworth, with her father the author of *Practical Education* (1798), and also a novelist, and Elizabeth Hamilton, whose best known educational work was perhaps the *Letters on the Elementary*

Principles of Education (1801), but who was also a not unsuccessful novelist. Maria Edgeworth's earlier *Letters for Literary Ladies* (1795) was, however, focused most specifically on the question of education for women. In these *Letters*, Edgeworth expounded the case for women's education, not as a champion of 'rights for women' but to enlighten their judgement, to cultivate their understanding, to enable them to occupy their time independently, and above all to increase domestic happiness and the attractions of home and family.[1] It is a modest argument, yet one for a wide-ranging education, intended to counter any implication of the natural inferiority of women's minds. Already in Edgeworth there is apparent a recognition of the necessity for women to make in practice as well as in theory informed moral judgements, to discriminate rationally and to enter 'that inner life of continuous discrimination and ethical choice' which was so relevant for women.[2] In *Practical Education* the Edgeworths showed their detailed concern for the upbringing of young children from the earliest years, an upbringing which, drawing on Rousseau and other educators, should above all be a gradual process of cultivating the moral instincts of the child, not just memory or academic prowess. Children would learn best in a happy home, treated with kindness, where parents were concerned to guide and channel their natural feelings and affections, at the child's own pace, while at the same time offering a moral example and training in good principles. The Edgeworths' educational philosophy was child-centred, based on the home and parents, directed especially towards the mother.[3] However, Maria Edgeworth drew on an optimism about human potential, and a belief in individual capacity for moral judgement, which left little room in her printed works for the teaching of revealed religion, and for this she was much criticised by contemporaries.[4] In spite of this, her educational writings, and her novels and short stories, many of which had early education as their theme, continued to have a wide appeal and circulation and she personally maintained many contacts with educationalists and liberal philosophers in Britain, France, Switzerland and elsewhere.

The Scotswoman Elizabeth Hamilton wrote from a rather different viewpoint, as a profoundly Christian, if not evangelical, moralist, and her hostility to the radicalism and feminism of the 1790s has already been noted. Her links were with the intellectual circles of Edinburgh and the philosophy of common sense, as expounded by Dugald Stewart, who was Professor of Moral Philosophy there. Though less

well known in England, the common-sense philosophy, ultimately
derived from the felt need to counter the philosophical scepticism of
David Hume, in its popularised form argued for the existence of an
irreducible and innate moral sense in every human being, on
philosophical as well as religious grounds. It was a mainstay of much
ethical and philosophical teaching in the universities of France and
the United States in this period, offering an acceptable, conventional,
secular morality. At the same time, Hamilton was also increasingly
interested in new educational theories, and in the psychology of
childhood. She saw a new field of investigation opening up for women,
one particularly suited to their domestic lives and their duties as
mothers.[5] It was mothers above all who bore the responsibility for
those first critical impressions received by infant minds. And
Hamilton aimed to rouse mothers from the 'lethargy of quiescent
indolence' to exert those faculties with which they were endowed.
Like Maria Edgeworth she wished to encourage education through
children's natural interest and curiosity, while guiding their feelings
and developing their moral principles. Such principles were to be
founded on the Christian religion, but on 'a rational and practical
assent to the truths of the Gospel', rather than on 'creeds, catechisms
and homilies'.[6] Neither Edgeworth nor Hamilton challenged the
primarily domestic, subordinate position of women, yet within their
work there are clear indications of a desire for greater recognition of
women's worth, of a proper valuation of their lives, for, as Hamilton
argued:

> Nor can I, perhaps, plead the cause of my sex more effectively,
> than by explaining the influence of early education; and thus
> rendering it evident to every unprejudiced mind, that if women
> were so educated as to qualify them for the proper performance of
> this momentous duty, it would do more towards the progressive
> improvement of the species, than all the discoveries of science and
> the researches of philosophy.[7]

Both Edgeworth and Hamilton also contributed to the further
development of the novel of education, in which the key to the plot
might lie in the effectiveness of education in enabling the heroine to
achieve self-mastery, a rational control of her emotions. Susan
Ferrier's *Marriage* (1818) contrasted the different upbringing given to
two separated sisters: the whole theme of the novel was the effect of

childhood training on character. Edgeworth's later novels, like *Belinda* (1801), *Patronage* (1814) and *Tales of Fashionable Life* (1809–12), though not necessarily her best, served to popularise her educational ideas. Hamilton, in *The Cottagers of Glenburnie* (1808) (Plate 5), extended the theme of education and instruction to the domestic life of the Scottish village, and to a class not previously treated in such novels. Such novels were to become increasingly popular.[8]

However, in the course of these decades, discussion about the purpose of women's education came to be suffused with the overriding evangelical imperative. From the 1770s Hannah More had argued that in spite of some improvements in female education, not enough attention was paid to the heart and the temper, nor were girls sufficiently prepared at an early age for the reception of serious religious truths. In her *Strictures on Female Education* (1799) she went further in exhorting women of rank to encourage useful and principled education for women. The chief end of such education should be 'to qualify them for the practical purposes of life'. Serious study could accustom women to industry and labour, yet it should always be regarded as for 'home consumption rather than foreign export'.[9] Better education could improve women's understanding, yet its objectives should be rather to look towards another world. In spite of exhortations to action, the impression left by More's educational philosophy is of the denial of women's equality, in understanding and judgement:

> An early habitual restraint is particularly important to the future character and happiness of women. A judicious unrelaxing, but steady and gentle curb on their tempers and passions can alone ensure their place and establish their principles. . . . They should, when very young, be inured to contradiction. . . .
>
> Girls should be led to distrust their own judgement; they should learn not to murmur at expostulation; they should be accustomed to expect and to endure opposition.[10]

More, who believed in the doctrine of original sin, and was criticised for its place in her educational theory by both Edgeworth and Hamilton, took a much less positive view of the task of mothers than they did. Though the role of parents was exalted, and the task of the mother critical, the aim was not to nurture the best and most natural instincts of the child, but to require obedience and submission in preparation for conversion – and these qualities were evidently required most of all from girls. There is plenty of evidence of the effect of evangelical religious belief on family life in this period. The autobiographies of the novelists 'Charlotte Elizabeth' and Elizabeth Missing Sewell, as well as the better known Brontë family history, suggest the introspection, the suffering and the emotionalism of the strictly evangelical upbringing, which must have been shared by many middle-class children.[11] But to suggest from this evidence 'a nineteenth century reversal' or 'a reassertion of patriarchal authority in the early nineteenth century', as Lawrence Stone argues, is to mistake the dominant trend. For that narrow message of Hannah More's, based on a firm and orthodox conviction of the original depravity of children, rapidly seems to soften in the prescriptive literature addressed to women, perhaps as Calvinist orthodoxies gave place to a greater stress on the free will of the individual in the achievement of salvation. In Sarah Lewis' *Woman's Mission* (1839) the evangelistic impulse was clear, with women as the instruments of God's purpose. They were to be educated not in accomplishments or academic subjects, but to develop their consciences, their hearts and their affections, to fit them not for a brief period of irresponsibility, but for the whole of their married lives. Lewis combined constant emphasis on the need for self-renunciation with the duty of women to instil into their children, especially their sons, by teaching and by example, 'exalted notions of the female character'.[12]

As religious renewal moved through the different denominations of early nineteenth-century England, reaching even High Church Anglicans, so doctrinal issues might recede into the background, but the theme of a strongly Christian and maternal education remained a prevalent one. It could be found in a whole range of minor but extremely popular literary works. Catherine Sinclair's *Modern Accomplishments: or, the March of Mind* (1836) followed the same theme as Susan Ferrier, contrasting the education of twin sisters, one inspired by a truly religious aunt, the other brought up in materialistic and worldly surroundings. The Jewish novelist, Grace Aguilar, whose *Home Influence: A Tale for Mothers and Daughters* (1847) was to go through 41 editions before 1905, addressed herself to 'the education of the HEART, believing that of infinitely greater importance than the mere instruction of the MIND', and similarly contrasted the upbringing of two sisters whose future was to be determined by the early influences they experienced.[13] In spite of doctrinal differences, the works of Charlotte M. Yonge contained the same emphasis on the education of the heart and conscience in domestic settings, the same concern for sacrifice and self-denial, especially in women. Such novels, denouncing the vices of luxury and mere ornamental accomplishments, suggested the practical, useful and essentially moral education necessary to the future mother of children. It was, of course, a theme which clearly met the needs of the family life of the expanding middle and lower middle classes. Yet it could also seem quite impracticable. Where was such education initially to be acquired? In practice, in spite of current denunciations of boarding-school education, many middle-class (though not upper middle or aristocratic) parents sent their daughters to school for at least a brief period. Anna Elizabeth Pendered's *Remarks on Female Education, with an application of its principles to the regulation of schools* (1827), though tediously longwinded, both recognised the strength of the case for domestic education and pointed to its limitations. Education at home meant reliance on a poorly educated mother or governess, its quality entirely dependent on parental influence. Schools, when well administered, could similarly offer truly religious principles and an education which could fit girls not only for their maternal role, but as future governesses or teachers.[14] It was an argument which was to be important in the future.

Nevertheless the evangelical ideal did not go unchallenged even in the early years of the nineteenth century. Sydney Smith, the Whig clergyman, favoured a substantial improvement in the quality of education of the 50,000 or so women who suffered from too much leisure, both for their own sakes and the sake of society in general.[15] But critics in these years mainly came from old dissent, from those nonconformist denominations which had retained a rationalist, liberal outlook, looking back to Catherine Macaulay's insistence on an equality of education in almost all spheres. Richard Wright in 1799 in his 'Letters on Women' in the Unitarian *Universalist's Miscellany* defended the right of women to a liberal education. Their training for domestic life might be compared to that of men for a trade or profession, but should not unfit them for general intellectual and cultural activity.[16] The *Monthly Repository*, also Unitarian, under the editorship first of Robert Aspland then of W. J. Fox, was a consistent source for the radical case. In 1815, it took a favourable view of the egalitarian arguments in John Morell's *Reasons for the classical education of both sexes* (1814). In 1821 it opposed Henry

Brougham's education bill not only because it made few concessions to dissenters, but also because it did not provide for the education of girls.[17] So the way was prepared for the substantial contributions of Harriet Martineau and Mary Leman Grimstone. In 1822 Martineau's article 'On Female Education' aimed not to claim equality in the powers of mind of the two sexes, but to put the case for an education for women which gave much greater scope for the development of their potential, since it was impossible to know how far the relative achievements of the two sexes depended on the differences in their early training. When women's talents were given freer play, they might prove comparable to men's, perhaps making up in perseverance what was lacking in enterprise. Martineau hoped to create 'a race of enlightened mothers' and 'rational companions' for men. Yet the education which she proposed was wide-ranging, covering history, natural philosophy and the philosophy of mind, together with modern languages. Such an education would not, she argued, detract from domestic duties or feminine qualities, but rather would lead to the appropriate powers of mind and judgement, informed by Christian humility.[18] Ten years later came a radical call for reform from William Bridges Adams. 'On the Condition of Women in England' (1833), denounced the education received by women at all levels of society, for: 'Women must be regarded and treated as the equals of men, in order to work the improvement of man himself'. His argument was not for female legislators, but for women to be educated to do work more vital than men's, in the rearing of children. In the same volume of the *Repository* the anonymous author of 'On female education and occupations' put forward a plea for a more solid education for women, both for domestic duties and to provide the foundation for more varied employment for those who did not marry: many branches of trade and commerce could be thrown open to women. The plea was a passionate one:

> If woman is inferior to man, it is not in nature, but in degree, reason and virtue must be the same in both; if their duties are different in some respects, they are still human duties, and their foundation and end must be the same.[19]

Discussion in the magazine over the next few years was continued by Mary Leman Grimstone, who both in the *Repository* and in the Owenite paper, the *New Moral World*, denounced the image of women created by men, and perpetuated by women's education: passive, vapid, uninquiring, yet amiable. While not arguing for political rights for women, she did not admit their incapacity for such public work once properly educated. Her 'Sketches of Domestic Life', brief portraits of stereotypes of womanhood, were inspired by a similar spirit. In one sketch, for example, she described the woman who cultivated insipidity, attracting a man who believed in the submission of women. Yet the right kind of education would allow women to provide for themselves, marrying when they wished.[20] The anonymous author of 'Infant Education' in the *Repository* in 1836 praised the new infant schools for offering 'an entirely new province for cultivation, that of the heart and moral feelings, which was previously utterly unknown to scholastic instruction' and then continued to denounce the unequal moralities expected of men and women, especially the sacrifices demanded of women, as 'one of the fundamental principles of human nature, the selfish principle . . . is forced down', and they sink into a 'regrettable nothingness' of purely domestic concerns.[21] The *Repository* had a notable record in this field, though its radicalism did affront much Unitarian opinion. But after Fox's editorship ceased in 1836, Martineau, Grimstone and Adams continued to advance their cause elsewhere, notably in the radical press, and the magazine rapidly declined.

It will have been seen that the argument for the potential equality of women, given educational opportunity, could arise from a concern for the education of mothers, and that emphasis was often a matter of degree. Evangelicals, liberals and radicals were frequently not far apart. The case for the proper education of mothers did continue to be put frequently. Harriet Martineau, for example, in her *Household Education* (1849) examined the educational processes of the household, for young and old, the aim of which should be to strengthen and exercise all the powers given to each individual. In the course of much practical advice, she denounced the nonsense talked about women's education. To maintain a proper household, women needed the best possible education, for most ignorant women were consistently the worst housekeepers. Every girl's potential should be fully exploited, especially since not every woman would be supported by a husband or a father. Such views were echoed from many sides.[22] But the further step that could be taken from these arguments had been stated most clearly by Margaret Mylne in a lengthy review essay in the *Westminster Review* in 1841, when she suggested that the case for the improvement of the education of wives and mothers was now won. Yet why should women be seen only in relation to others:

> The prejudices of sex have a tendency to make women be regarded oftener in the dependent and subordinate position in which they appear in relation to man, than as possessing, in common with him, a moral, rational, responsible, and, therefore, independent existence of their own.[23]

As Mylne said, writers like Sarah Lewis, the author of *Woman's Mission*, overlooked the 'moral independence' of women, in their stress on sacrifice and on dependence. So the argument moved a step further: were women to be educated only for others, or for themselves?

The tensions in this debate were to be found elsewhere, and notably in the correspondence columns of the Owenite journal, the *New Moral World*. Owen himself had rejected the role of parents as educators of their children, yet for correspondents the issue clearly still remained an important one. Mary Leman Grimstone, in her article in the *New Moral World* in February 1835, 'Female Education', noted a new moral courage arising among women, an assertion of their equal moral status and equal intelligence. While she did not undervalue devotion, a life of martyrdom and dependence was no life for any human being.[24] 'Kate' (Catherine Watkins, later Barmby), in her 'Appeal to Woman' in August 1835, argued that the future improvement of society, for which Owenites were planning, would depend on the acquisition of useful knowledge by women.[25] Subsequently a number of articles suggested that women needed to learn especially the importance of the early years of childhood, the significance of early ideas and impressions, the basis of maternal care – in spite of the views of Owen himself.[26] In 1839 'Marianne B.', 'Anna' and 'A Lover of Truth' all called for much more attention to be given to the education of women, for no proper comparison of the abilities of the two sexes was possible while women remained so ignorant. Yet they differed as to whether such education should be directed towards the benefit of future generations, or whether it could take place only when women were freed from domestic drudgery.[27] In 1840 John Goodwyn Barmby recorded his visit to the school of Levi-Alvarès in Paris, where the education of daughters by their mothers was practised, and noted how much was derived from the ideas of Pestalozzi and his stress on the formation of the female character.[28] The issues were here clearly stated. 'J' in January 1843, writing on the 'Emancipation of Women' described how those seeking to improve women's position had emphasised influence rather than power. Only in a rationalist context could the range of prejudices and superstitions affecting that position be confronted and women's claims to serious occupation be considered.[29] The arguments of 'M.A.S.' were even clearer. Women would do well to proceed to their *mental* emancipation before they moved to the regeneration of society, the abolition of the marriage bonds. Such a movement must come from below, from women's own determination. Only education, 'the great equaliser', could lead women to 'equality of rights and reciprocity of duties'. Her call was for women themselves to take action. In doing so she roused the hostility of Owen himself: for Owen, women could not change unless their external circumstances did, effected by better educated men. 'M.A.S.' was clear in her response: while self-culture was not of itself sufficient to change women's condition, it was a necessary pre-requisite.[30] Throughout 1845, contributors 'Syrtis', 'Homo' and 'Stata' continued to review the issues, with 'Syrtis' echoing the call of 'M.A.S.'.[31] Owenite papers therefore gave much space to the issue, reflecting the interest among correspondents. And, interestingly, that debate in the *New Moral World*, between advocates of female influence and female autonomy, offered a curious parallel to the debates of the respectable press.

This emphasis on education for motherhood is one which can be paralleled in France and in the United States in this period. Its universality is an important element in changing notions of woman-hood. Clearly there was much international correspondence and much mutual interest in the development of educational ideas. The work of Maria Edgeworth and Elizabeth Hamilton was much admired in France and in the United States. American, French and English writers were all interested in the achievements of the Swiss educator Pestalozzi, and by the 1830s of the German Friedrich Froebel. In the United States, as in England, theological orthodoxy could present problems to those concerned to advance educational psychology and to advocate the vital role of mothers. In the 'republican' context of the United States, the new educational theory had both to reject 'fashionable' and 'aristocratic' tendencies, and to incorporate Protestant evangelical values, while gradually departing from that strong Calvinist inheritance which stressed infant depravity and salvation by grace alone. Leading clergymen of New England, such as Lyman Beecher and Theodore Parker, were already by the 1820s denying the full impact of the doctrine of infant depravity. Here, as in England, conservative writers on domestic education who were committed to its religious purpose, and progressive or romantic educationalists, for whom childhood was a state of innocence, shared a common commitment to the vital importance of the early years of infancy and childhood. By the 1840s a leading Unitarian, Horace Bushnell, had formulated an ideal of Christian nurture which, accepting infancy as a separate stage of life, stressed the gradual development and acquisition of grace by children, through the nurturing process.[32] Well before this, however, educationalists began to explore how domestic life might best be reformed and women enabled to fulfil their mission within the home. As in England, that mission could justify the improvement of female education at all levels, and could also raise that question already asked by Judith Sargent Murray – must women always expect education for the sake of others?

In the first twenty years of the nineteenth century, American ministers were coming to accept the view that mothers were more important than fathers in shaping the characters of their children, and that childrearing was primarily the task of women. In these decades, the case made in the aftermath of the Revolution found new force. Ministers preached the need for better education for women 'as beings, who are to be wives and mothers, the first and most important guardians and instructors of the rising generation, as being endued [sic] with reason and designed for immortality.'[33] Educational reform journals, of which a number were founded in these years, spread the arguments. So did ministers and laymen who identified themselves with the cause of women's education. For example, the Rev. J. S. C. Abbott, of Worcester, Massachusetts, who, especially concerned with the cause of domestic reform as a Calvinist who believed that 'maternal influence, more than anything else, forms the future character', wrote *The Mother at Home* (1830). His brother, the Rev. Jacob Abbott, a Congregationalist, produced a handbook, *The Little Philosopher, or the Infant School at Home* (1830), designed for the instruction of young children at home. A number of ministers, while retaining something of an older, sterner outlook, were prepared to consider some of the practical ends of education recommended in progressive educational literature, as in the text *Domestic Education* (1840) by the Rev. Heman Humphrey, Congregationalist and

President of Amherst College, and in *Fireside Education* (1838) by a layman, Samuel Goodrich, who published children's books. The initiative did not come only from ministers. A leading politician of New York State, De Witt Clinton, consistently championed the cause of women's education, since 'our first and best impressions are derived from maternal impressions'.[34]

Some women wrote rather as educational reformers. Emma Willard, Almira Phelps and Catherine Beecher were all New Englanders ready to identify themselves with the cause of domestic reform and women's education. Their concrete achievements will be considered later but it is clear that their first inspiration lay in the cause of domestic reform. In 1819 Emma Willard, proposing her *Address to the Public; particularly to the Members of the Legislature of New York, proposing a plan for improving Female Education*, to Governor Clinton of New York, made clear the social function of women's education:

> were the interests of male education alone to be consulted, that of females becomes of sufficient importance to engage the public attention. Would we rear the human plant to its perfection, we must fertilize the soil which produces it. If it acquires its bent and texture upon a barren plain, it will avail comparatively little should it be afterwards transported to a garden.[35]

Almira Phelps worked with her sister, Emma Willard, and taught with her. In her articles and books, including *The Female Student, or Lectures to Young Ladies on Female Education* (1836), her emphasis was similar to that of her sisters: 'Is not the character of the future men of our republic, to depend on the mothers we are now educating?'[36] The two sisters translated Mme Necker de Saussure's *Progressive Education*, published in Boston in 1835, and as an appendix Phelps, following the advice of the author, printed her own journal on the development of her own child, 'Observations upon an infant, during its first year'. There were of course other well known American educators, aware of the work of Rousseau and Pestalozzi, of British and French writers, in this period. Bronson Alcott, the Transcendentalist and father of Louisa Alcott, and the Peabody sisters of Boston, who were later to found the first American kindergarten, both wrote of the role of women in caring for their infants, suggesting that, as Alcott wrote 'it was the great purpose of Pestalozzi, to inspire mothers with a just sense of their value in the scale of being'.[37] Such domestic reformers could show how evangelical assumptions might fuse with progressive educational ideas, to create a new and more elevated role for mothers. Lydia Child offered a popular distillation in her *Mother's Book* (1831), suggesting that wherever possible a mother should take entire care of her own child, guiding it both by her example and by her nurturing.[38]

Catherine Beecher, daughter of the New England minister, Lyman Beecher, wrote on women's education from the mid-1820s, having already founded her Hartford Female Seminary, and offered a more sophisticated argument. In her article in the *American Journal of Education* for 1827, she not only criticised education in accomplishments but emphasised that 'a lady should study, not to *shine*, but to *act*'. A course of study very similar to that undertaken by men in public institutions was needed to allow women's understanding to develop. In 1829 these plans were further expanded in her essay, *Suggestions respecting improvements in education*, which stressed not only intellectual improvements, but also 'the correction of the disposition, the regulation of the social feelings, the formation of the conscience, and the direction of the moral character and habits'. This emphasis on moral training represented, her biographer has suggested, 'a new alliance between evangelical morality and feminine refinement'.[39] For Beecher, brought up, though not unquestioningly, on evangelical lines, was interested not only in the truths of Christianity, but also in philosophy and psychology, and in 1831 published her *Elements of Mental and Moral Philosophy*. The dominant influence in American philosophy in these years was the common-sense philosophy of Scotland. This, rooted in human psychology, seemed to offer to Beecher, as it had done to Hamilton and Edgeworth, a morality rooted in the individual conscience, but one which assumed that the conscience, the disposition, the temper, of individuals required nurturing and training.[40] Such a secular philosophy assured her of the existence of those norms of morality, those common-sense precepts, latent in all individuals – and, by implication, needing the care and guardianship of women as mothers. In her work she stressed two tests of moral character, both especially applicable to women: the individual's striving for purity, and their behaviour in their family circle. Such tests surely indirectly indicated the moral superiority of women. Her philosophy was linked to her educational programme. Here and in her later writings of the 1830s, she developed her theme of 'moral instruction', and her belief in the essential task of character formation – it was to be women's role to sacrifice themselves in the interests of society to perform these tasks.[41] There was no doubt, in the United States, that allocation of such responsibilities to women had a very positive impact on the movement for women's education. What is striking, however, is that, in the United States, so many of the writers on the education of mothers were themselves actively engaged in founding and teaching in schools for girls – the same was not true in Britain or in France.

In France, the notion of the mother as educator dominated both prescriptive literature for women and educational literature directed to girls. Such manuals as those of Mme Necker de Saussure, Mme de Rémusat and Mme Guizot already mentioned, saw a mother's duty both as the nurturing of her infants and young children and the complete oversight of the education of her daughters. A number of journals and magazines addressed specifically to women followed their lead. These writers all, in different ways, at odds with the dominant conservatism of Restoration France, shared the view that mothers should attempt to nurture and to train the will and reason of their daughters, so that they might follow the laws of morality of their own free will. Such arguments had a good deal in common with those of Catherine Beecher, in that they appealed not only to ecclesiastical authority, but to the latent moral feelings of the individual, offering a secular rationale for morality. Indeed the Scottish common-sense philosophy had much appeal for the liberals of the Restoration, as did the educational works of Edgeworth and Hamilton.[42]

Nevertheless such writers might well differ as to the amount of liberty and the degree of independent judgement to be permitted to girls, given their inevitably domestic future. In Mme Guizot's *Lettres de Famille*, Mme Attilly, the most authoritative correspondent, suggested that girls should not be allowed to develop certain faculties, political, intellectual, artistic, to their full potential, for fear of arousing ambitions which could not be fulfilled. And while a greater degree of liberty could be allowed to very young girls, as they learned and grew older, they should be made aware of the limitations of their freedom, to see them as necessary, a part of God's will with which they could identify.[43] For Mme Necker de Saussure it was less necessary to be so cautious in the arousing of girls' intellectual ambitions, more relevant to consider their possibly wider duties, their future if unmarried. While never losing sight of the centrality of women's maternal concerns, Mme Necker de Saussure believed the number of unmarried women to be increasing, and in any case thought it desirable to delay marriage for a while. Therefore other spheres of activity for women needed to be considered, especially philanthropic and charitable work, for which women were particularly fitted. And 'the task of teaching was made for women'. The care of small children, in the *salles d'asiles*, or nursery schools, interest in the welfare of working women, involvement in missionary work – all these were occupations suitable for women, to which their education should also be directed. The most obvious field in which women might exercise such talents lay in the education of poor children, who needed the right sort of books and instruction.[44] Even though some men, approving the philanthropic motive, might dislike these activities as suggesting a greater desire for independence, such action alone might help to revive and regenerate society.[45] In the later years of life, higher intellectual pleasures might be taken up – botany, natural history, psychology, history – yet they should be solitary studies, not undertaken with any thought of authorship.[46] The three writers are united in their view of the mother as educator of her daughters, within the well-ordered household. But Mme Necker de Saussure, the Protestant, writing some ten years later, offered the broadest concept of what that education should be.

Perhaps the most dramatic and exaggerated case for 'maternal education' was made by Louis Aimé-Martin, in his *Education des mères de famille ou de la civilisation du genre humain par les femmes* (1834). The work was extraordinarily influential throughout Europe and the United States. Among many other works, Sarah Lewis's *Woman's Mission* derived direct inspiration from it. For Aimé-Martin, education should focus upon 'maternal influence – an influence which is exerted on the heart, which through the heart may direct the mind, and which in order to save and regenerate the world, only requires to be properly directed'.[47] Maternal love, part of the divine law of nature, was to be the instrument by which women might take up their civilising mission. The work is written in religious, even millenarian tones, suffused with a vague and unspecific evangelism. But there are more precise recommendations. Interestingly, he writes not only of the well to do, but of the women of the peasantry. Regeneration must come from the countryside, in which women were still brutally treated, as drudges and beasts of burden. Universal primary education in the countryside for girls would transform their lives and their society, even though contemporary legislators, as in the new law on primary education of 1833, might ignore the question. Yet 'teaching young girls will make a school out of every house!' Such schools would establish the superiority of women and enable them to exert their civilising influence. They would allow women to leave hard agricultural work and return to the occupations proper to their sex. Such a move would not necessarily be unprofitable, for spinning, dairy work and similar occupations, would help rural society.[48] Reform and regeneration would come through the moral education of women, not from their higher education or from violation of the natural laws governing the division of labour of the sexes.

As elsewhere, the theme of maternal education featured in a number of periodicals for women by the 1830s, ranging from the Conservative and Catholic to those influenced by Saint-Simonian views. The Catholic case, put by Madelaine Sirey in *La Mère de Famille*, published from 1833, was one which differed significantly from the conservative publicists of the Restoration, responding to a new concern for better educational methods. The magazine, an early example of Christian feminism, was interested in such issues as the teaching methods of Pestalozzi, the importance of physical education for girls, the need for more teacher training colleges for women: all were reviewed in the light of developing the role that women could play within the family.[49] *Le Journal des Femmes*, published from 1832 to 1838, described by Evelyne Sullerot as 'very middle class, moderately Catholic and relatively feminist', claimed to be written 'by women, for women', though most of all it was run by its founder, Fanny Richomme. Sullerot has identified some fourteen women who wrote for this journal, as well as some better known contributors such as George Sand and Delphine Gay, mainly from the aristocracy and upper middle classes, solidly Christian, but also interested in the expansion of opportunities for women and in education as a means to that end. The first article of the first number was entitled 'Progrès de l'instruction chez les femmes du xixe siècle', and contrasted the ignorance of women in previous centuries with the ability of women in the nineteenth-century Christian family to instruct and enlighten themselves on their duties as wives and mothers. The journal called for two particular reforms: for the establishment of schools for infants under 6, and for the instruction of women as teachers. Fanny Richomme and others visited and reported on a number of private institutions undertaking this work. The journal was imbued with the notion of improving women's condition, in the context of Christian morality and a domestic future.[50] The inspiration of the editor of the

Conseiller des Femmes, of Lyons, published in 1833, and followed by the *Mosaique Lyonnais*, was rather different. Eugénie Niboyet had been an active Saint-Simonian in 1831 but returned to the Protestant 'Société de la morale chrétienne' shortly afterwards. Her journal promised to deal with questions of education for girls, at all levels, covering hygiene, psychology, domestic economy, theatre and fashions. The theme of education, both to improve the understanding of middle-class women and in the discussion of establishing schools for poor children, was strongly stressed. Her discussion won her the commendation of Mme Necker de Saussure, with whom she was largely in agreement.[51]

THE TRAINING OF TEACHERS

In France, in England and in the United States, the case for education for motherhood was by the 1830s and 1840s largely made out, and winning increasing support. But the grounds of the debate were gradually shifting. While the theme of 'maternal education' continued to be of fundamental importance, so was the evident need of women to support themselves. The most natural progression was to suggest that women should be trained for employment in that capacity nearest the maternal role: as a teacher of children. The result of this was to be new initiatives in the foundation of schools and colleges for girls of the middle classes. This was not, of course, a new argument. Mary Wollstonecraft had foreseen the need for better instruction for women to take up employment as teachers, whether as governesses or in the public schools she envisaged.[52] Priscilla Wakefield, writing in 1798, had called for a college for the education of young women as governesses, to offer a way for young women to support themselves, and allow girls to be educated by well-qualified teachers of their own sex.[53] The task of educating others was not of course the only possible employment for which girls might be prepared – but to observers in the early nineteenth century it was by far the most appropriate and realistic possibility. The suggestion also met national needs, as will be seen.

Thus public attention gradually turned towards the quality of education which young women destined to become, if only temporarily, future teachers would receive. In New England, young women, normally daughters of local farm families, tended to be hired to teach summer sessions of local primary schools, often merely reading and sewing, though male teachers were hired for the winter. As such schools, and the new academies founded after the Revolution, multiplied, the demand for women teachers grew and was placed on a more formal basis. A number of the women who pioneered the new academies stressed that they had a dual function, both to prepare for domestic life, and to spread the ability and qualifications to teach. Academies multiplied, initially on the eastern seaboard, but soon sending their pupils to found others in the West and South. The best known of these were the school of Catherine Fiske, at Keene, New Hampshire, founded in 1814, Troy Seminary, established by Emma Willard in 1821, the Adams Academy, Derry, New Hampshire, run by Zilpah Grant, George Emerson's school at Boston, dating from 1823, the Ipswich Female Seminary, run from 1828 by Zilpah Grant and Mary Lyon, Catherine Beecher's school at Hartford, Connecticut, from 1823 and Mary Lyon's Mount Holyoke College, opened in 1837.[54] It is clear that this generation of women, committed to the advancement of the education of girls, saw the need to train teachers as a vital part of their work. Co-educational Oberlin College, founded in Ohio in 1833, strongly under the influence of the evangelist Charles Grandison Finney, took a much more restricted view of the purposes of the education of women, seeing their students very much as future ministers' wives. Though, at the same time, attempts were made in some cities to create public secondary schools – in Worcester, Massachusetts in 1824, in Boston and New York in 1826 – the movement made slow progress before the Civil War. The initiative lay with the private academies. The distinctive work of Emma Willard, as a missionary for the cause of women's higher education, has been recognised. Her case was rejected by the New York State Legislature, and her plans for Troy Female Seminary went ahead independently. The prominent role of mathematics in the curriculum, the examination requirements, and the training of teachers (though not her primary purpose) all set the school apart from existing seminaries. So too did Willard's preparation of school textbooks, and her deliberate attempts to encourage the growth of similar academies elsewhere in the United States. As at Troy, the school founded at Ipswich by Mary Lyon and Zilpah Grant needed first to train its own teachers, then to award its diploma to those who might be regarded as qualified to teach elsewhere. Mary Lyon drew up plans in 1832 for a New England Seminary for Teachers, but found insufficient enthusiasm at Ipswich or at Amherst to sustain it. So, in 1834, she left Ipswich and by 1836 had planned her own future college, Mount Holyoke Female Seminary, which aimed to educate middle-class girls more cheaply than elsewhere, since they themselves were to do much of the domestic work of the college. The new seminary was to prove very successful, having by Mary Lyon's death in 1849 educated some 1200 girls. Teaching was clearly the immediate destination of most of those who left. Mary Lyon's own religious faith was clearly a major inspiration for the school, and missionary work was also an alternative future career for such girls.[55]

The seminary movement spread rapidly to the South and West of the United States. As an example of this progress, the development of Jacksonville Female Academy, in Illinois, might be taken. The academy originated from a meeting of men favourable to such a project, and opened in 1833, under Sarah Crocker, recommended to the town by Mary Lyon. Two years later, having married, she was replaced by Emily Price, recommended by Zilpah Grant, and from then onwards the school became a major centre of influence. A Ladies Educational Society was formed in the town, with the object of aiding the preparation of young women for teaching.[56] Between 1830 and 1860, as far as official views of state legislatures were concerned, the female seminary provided the answer to the secondary education of women, the basis on which in the future both high schools and women's colleges would build.

Perhaps the best known missionary for the seminary movement was Catherine Beecher. Her experience at Hartford Female Seminary gave her experience and the confidence necessary for educational leadership. She had not only taken a leading place in Hartford society, but also led a religious revival, in 1826. What had been a private school was turned into a large female seminary with the backing of the community, as she herself was turning from Calvinist orthodoxy to a more secular morality, based on common-sense principles. Catherine Beecher, more clearly than Emma Willard, campaigned for teaching as a profession to be dominated by women, who both in their domestic *and* in their educational roles, were to provide the means for the regeneration of a nation. Her view of the moral superiority and maternal instincts of women, together with her understanding of the needs of single women, led her to believe that they could meet the demands of an expanding population for improved education, for all its citizens, at secondary and at elementary levels. Besides, she believed, and put into practice, that frontier America might be the place to test her view of education. In her *Essay on the Education of Female Teachers* (1835), she put forward 'a detailed plan for shaping a national morality', one which called for a body of women teachers to civilise the newly settled areas of the United States, to teach as they were best fitted to do. Yet her own plans to found a seminary in Cincinnati failed for insufficient support. Only in the early 1840s did she again take up the task of missionary for women teachers, and 'the elevation of my sex by the opening of a profession for them as educators of the young'. In a series of addresses she elaborated the future for Protestant women as the carriers of a new morality. Women of all classes were called upon to play their part in the West:

> Soon her influence in the village will create a demand for new labourers, and then she will summon from among her friends at home, the nurse for the young and sick. Soon, in all parts of our country, in each neglected village or new settlement, the Christian female teacher will quietly take her station, collecting the ignorant children around her, teaching them habits of neatness, order and thrift; opening the book of knowledge, inspiring the principles of morality, and awakening the hope of immortality.[57]

She toured, spoke at public meetings, and organised groups of missionary teachers for the West. Her plans in effect coincided with a shift already just becoming apparent. Women already by the 1840s outnumbered male teachers. In Massachusetts, women teachers increased from 56 to 78 per cent of the teaching force from 1834 to 1860. And throughout the United States women were cheaper to employ, and more easily available. Sentiment, evangelism and economic reality joined to feminise the profession of teacher, and to hasten the emergence of formal training schools for such teachers. Others besides Beecher had already written of the need for such schools. Samuel Reed Hall, Principal of his Model School at Concord, Vermont, in 1829 published *Lectures to Female Teachers* and, in 1837, presided over the Homes Plymouth Academy, a seminary for male and female teachers. There were a number of other enterprising men running private institutions for the training of teachers. But the first state-sponsored normal school came with the foundation in Massachusetts in 1839 of three schools, one exclusively for women students over 16 for a course lasting three years. Others followed, at Albany in 1844, at Philadelphia in 1848, and New Britain, Connecticut, in 1853. In 1853 a petition was forwarded to Congress for the setting aside of three or four million acres of land to endow one normal school for female teachers in every state of the Union 'because in the influence of intelligent and pure-minded women lies the moral power which gives safety and permanence to our institutions, and true glory to our sex'.[58]

In Britain, the strength of the early nineteenth-century movement for the improvement of women's secondary education came not so much from the reform and development of female academies, but initially from a concern for the qualifications of governesses, and of the new elementary school teachers. By the 1820s the inadequacy of the preparation given to governesses was clearly apparent. A few girls' schools offered academic subjects within the curriculum. One of the best known, Abbey House School, Reading, attended by Jane Austen and Caroline Lamb, included French, Latin, some Greek and Italian, history, literature and geography in the curriculum. Margaret Bryan gave lectures both on astronomy and on mathematics in her schools in Blackheath and Hyde Park Corner from 1795 to 1815. But the majority of such schools were small, private establishments, often run rather as an 'extended family unit' than as an academy. Most probably took less than thirty girls, some as few as seven or eight. The proprietor of such schools could well find herself playing a quasi-maternal role. The Schools' Inquiry Commission of the 1860s estimated that there were around 500 such establishments; we have no earlier evidence on this. But clearly there was no expansion of academies with high standards and expectations in Britain in the early decades of the nineteenth century as there was in the United States.[59] Perhaps the strength and prosperity of the English middle and upper classes, together with the availability of young women for employment, contributed to the importance, not of the independent school teacher, but of the dependent governess. In 1833, in an anonymous article in the *Monthly Repository*, Macaulay and Wollstonecraft were recalled, and the argument put that new channels of employment should be found for properly instructed single women.[60] Mary Leman Grimstone, in the same journal, and in *Tait's Edinburgh Magazine*, pursued that argument:

> For those women whom early widowhood, or other causes, consign to celibacy, I see not why civil offices should not be open,

especially chairs of science in colleges endowed for their education
of their own sex. Why should moral philosophy come with less
power from the lips of woman than of man? Why may she not fill a
professorship of poetry as well as he?[61]

An anonymous article in the *Metropolitan Magazine* in 1838, 'An
Outline of the Grievances of Women', put the case for a college whose
curriculum would include the mathematical and physical sciences,
metaphysics, astronomy and mechanics. And the author called for
women to organise themselves into associations to demand a
woman's college, foreseeing 'associations of determined and enlightened women springing up in every town and village'.[62] The domestic
arguments for the improvement in women's education nevertheless
remained the most widely accepted. Yet the progress of the debate
can be traced in the writings of Anna Jameson, writer and essayist
who, in 1832, put the case for a reform to fit women for 'their future
destination as the *mothers and nurses* of legislators and statesmen'. Ten
years later, her opinion had clearly shifted. After her visit to Canada,
recorded in *Winter Studies and Summer Rambles* (1838), she had
contrasted the condition of Indian women, not with the middle-class
ideal of womanhood, but with the reality of life for the women of the
labouring classes in Britain, domestic servants, sweated and factory
workers, and prostitutes. And she posed the novel suggestion that:
'Her [woman's] condition is decided by the share she takes in
providing for her own subsistence and the well-being of society as a
productive labourer'. In an article published in 1843, in the wake of
revelations about the working conditions of women and children in
mines and factories, she pointed out how rarely women were
considered as they truly were, as labourers. In a further essay, 'On the
relative social position of mothers and governesses', the anomalous
situation of the educated yet dependent governess was discussed. So
too were the difficulties facing a college for governesses: were they to
teach merely what would be useful, what would gain employment, or
rather to offer education for its own sake, to widen the aspirations and
the horizons of young women?[63]

The general quality of the education afforded to governesses was
agreed to be exceptionally low. Public debate on this contributed both
to that specific issue and, more generally, to the broader question of
secondary and even higher education for women. Some women wrote
simply from their own experience of the problems of the unqualified,

forced into the profession of governess or teacher. Pendered's *Remarks on Female Education*, in 1827, had been directed to those forced to make their own living through the foundation of schools. R. Mudie's *The Complete Governess* (1826), a popular book which went through many editions, pointed to the complete absence of suitable textbooks for the governess, whether she was educating future mothers or those who might need to support themselves.[64] The changes in the climate of opinion were, however, registered most uncompromisingly in Marion Reid's *A Plea for Women* (1843) which pointed out the complete lack of any colleges of secondary or higher learning for women. In this, and in Anne Richelieu Lamb's *Can Woman Regenerate Society?* (1844), there is a distinctive question, one which returns to the notes of Mary Wollstonecraft. Education should not be merely a means to domestic happiness, to salvation, or to employment: 'the true reason for the culture of any human being is to be found in the benefit which that being derives from cultivation'.[65] Education was to be not a means but an end in itself for the individual woman, for her self-culture and fulfilment.

In reality, of course, the beginnings of any more formal development of secondary and higher education for women were elementary and limited, with concern for the education of governesses paralleled by the growing importance nationally of acquiring qualified teachers for the expanding elementary schools. The project of a college for governesses was first brought forward by the Hon. Amelia Murray, a friend of Anna Jameson, as well as maid of honour to the queen, who had attempted to interest the College of Preceptors in the proposal and, separately, by the Governesses' Benevolent Institution, founded in 1843, which had rapidly found it necessary to involve itself in the qualifications of governesses. The projects were combined by 1846, and attracted the assistance of a group of intellectuals, most notably the Christian Socialists, F. D. Maurice and Charles Kingsley. Maurice, a Professor at King's College, London, strongly interested in the education of girls, helped in 1847 to organise a series of courses by nine lecturers connected with King's. Lady Visitors were also to attend the lectures, which were open not only to governesses but to all 'ladies'. Examinations followed, though standards were more those of a secondary school than of a university. By 1848 Queen's College was established in Harley Street. Within six months of its foundation, Bedford College too was established, through the initiative of a wealthy widow, the Unitarian Mrs Elizabeth Reid, who had initiated a series of lectures in her house in 1847 and, from then onwards, hoped to see her foundation achieve university status as Bedford College. She hoped that the organisation of her college would be entrusted primarily to women; though this proved to be impossible, women retained a much greater share in the administration of Bedford College than at Queen's, which remained firmly under masculine control.[66] In spite of all their limitations, the education offered at these colleges was to be vital to many leading figures in the Victorian feminist movement. Among the original students at Queen's College were Adelaide Procter, founding member of the Langham Place circle, Sophia Jex-Blake, the medical pioneer, and Julia Wedgwood, an early lecturer at Girton College. There were also two well-known pioneers of education for middle-class girls: Frances Mary Buss, who attended evening classes at Queen's College, was, in 1850, to found the North London Collegiate School for Girls; and Dorothea Beale, pupil and then tutor at Queen's College, was to transform Cheltenham Ladies College. Barbara Leigh Smith, who dominated the campaign for legal reform in the 1850s, attended some of the first classes at Bedford College.

Clearly by the 1840s the climate of opinion had shifted towards recognition of the extremely poor standard of education offered to middle-class girls. One exception to these poor standards, however, lay in the quality of the new institutions set up to train teachers for the new elementary schools. In the early nineteenth century, schools for working-class children were either private, or dame schools, or Sunday Schools, or monitorial schools. The latter were founded by the National Society for Promoting the Education of the Poor in 1811, and the British and Foreign Schools Society, in the Dissenting interest, in 1814. Leading members of these societies had been much concerned as to the educational standards of their teachers, and had set up small training departments attached to schools, as in Joseph Lancaster's Borough Road school, and the National Society's Central School, before the 1830s. The new movement for infant education equally realised the necessity of trained teachers, and in spite of objections to women teachers from Samuel Wilderspin, the pioneer of infant teaching, most instruction in these schools was by women. The most successful of these early colleges was in fact the Home and Colonial Training College, founded in London by the Home and Colonial Infant School society, an Evangelical foundation. Over the next ten years the College trained 1443 teachers, mainly single women, in a course gradually extended to last six months. A number of other small model schools were set up, to teach potential teachers by example, though not by academic or formal instruction. But as a result of the grants made to these societies by the British government after 1839, and on the initiative of Sir James Kay Shuttleworth, a new network of over twenty residential training colleges for men and women was established between 1839 and 1846. Mostly small, they charged fees of around £20 a year, with courses varying considerably, from three months to three years. In 1846 Kay Shuttleworth's new scheme for pupil-teachers offered those who could pass an examination a subsidy of four-fifths of the cost of their training. Between 1849 and 1859, the number of pupil-teachers at work in schools rose from 3580 to 15,224, and over the same period the proportion of females rose from 32 to 46 per cent.[67] Teaching as a profession, then, required a period of studying, followed by examinations and further academic work. Such labour was not initially considered suitable for middle-class girls, though a certificated teacher could earn more money and live in greater independence than a governess could expect.

The pupil-teacher scheme was clearly directed towards bright working-class girls. Yet detailed study of one college, Whitelands College, Putney, has shown that early recruitment did not necessarily bear this out. Entrants to Whitelands, opened in 1841, came from very diverse backgrounds, including ex-domestic servants, the daughters of artisans, clerks and the lower middle classes, together with girls from professional families. Some were paid for by patrons, others paid for themselves. There were no fixed age limits, since women might come in their mid-20s or later for training. In these early years the colleges appear to have been flexible in structure. And, even more important, academic standards were initially low, and middle-class girls lacking a sound educational background were less likely to feel inferior than later in the century. In 1851, for instance, some 10 per cent of students at Whitelands were from a professional background, and just over 50 per cent from the lower middle classes. Over the next ten years, the intake of girls from working-class homes had considerably increased, and the proportion of those with professional backgrounds reduced to around 3 per cent. The rate of applications in the 1840s perhaps suggests the nature of the demand for better secondary education among women.[68]

This demand was of course related to the possibility of future careers as governesses or teachers, but not entirely so. There were protests at the assumption that the destination of unemployed young women must necessarily be the teaching profession. Lady Ellis commented on a plan for a governesses' institution for the daughters of ministers:

> It is contrary to all observation and experience to suppose, that all persons are calculated to obtain the means of subsistence by being taught to teach. There are other pursuits of a noble and elevating character which the female mind is capable of comprehending if the means are afforded of so doing. The limited view of female power and usefulness which we have just alluded to, operates very prejudicially with regard to the happiness of young females who have a certain position in society; and who are nevertheless, compelled by narrow circumstances to have recourse to daily exertion for support.[69]

She suggested that it would be more valuable to nurture the individual talents which women might have than to concentrate so narrowly upon teaching. By the 1850s, the situation of the governess, poorly paid, undereducated, in an overstocked market, could be reviewed in relation to other possible employment for women. Charitable solutions were mere palliatives for the governess problem. What was needed were higher standards of education, judged by examinations, certificates, diplomas, relevant to other kinds of occupation. Sarah Austin, Barbara Leigh Smith and Harriet Martineau, as well as the *English Woman's Journal*, all saw the evil clearly:

> The evil is plain enough. The remedies seem to be equally clear; to sustain and improve the modern tests of the quality of educators; and to open broad and new ways for the industrial exertions of women; or at least to take care that such as open naturally are not arbitrarily closed.[70]

The *English Woman's Journal*, the first feminist journal in Britain, founded in 1858, strongly advocated the improvement of women's education, not only to make women better wives and mothers, or to make them better qualified governesses or simply to improve their minds, but so that they could take up some kind of independent employment, as the range of occupations open to middle-class women widened. To do this, they needed both a reasonable standard of general education and specifically vocational training. The first article of the first number called for women to turn away from the overstocked market for governesses, towards new occupations. Education alone could offer a degree of financial independence, and do away with 'the taint diffused through the female character *by the consciousness of dependence on marriage for the means of existence*'.[71] Such employment could include, for instance, medical work for women: work which was of course seen as especially suitable for women, yet posed in an acute form the question of admittance to institutions of higher education, of specialised training. The determined Elizabeth Blackwell, the first woman to receive a medical qualification, graduated from Geneva College, New York, in 1849, and in 1859 lectured in Britain on the medical profession for women, attracting to her lectures Elizabeth Garrett, who in 1860 entered the Middlesex Hospital for her training.[72] It was also in 1860 that Barbara Leigh Smith pointed to the startling disparity between the education provided in the state system and the education received by middle-class girls: what was needed was a proper system of inspection and examinations. And in that year, Emily Davies also entered the argument, writing to her local Newcastle paper on the need to broaden the occupations of women. It was to be Davies who would secure admission for women to university examinations from 1863, and eventually, though the possibility seemed distant in 1860, pioneer admission to higher education.[73]

The debate on women's education in France was to take a revealingly different course. There too the state was drawn into the question of regulating the education of girls, primarily through its control of teaching qualifications, and there too the issue was complicated by religious issues, notably the relationship between the Catholic Church and the state. Before 1860, the question of secular secondary education for girls was not taken very seriously, although for the Church such education could appear as one route towards the rechristianisation of the leaders of French society. Therefore when the question did surface, there was to be a significant political dimension to the discussion. The legacy of the French Revolution had not been an encouraging one. Revolutionary legislators, shutting down the convents of France, the main source of education outside the home for bourgeois and aristocratic girls, had stated their belief in the essentially domestic future of women, for whom primary, but not secondary, education should be provided. This division, an important one, was to exclude girls from any participation in state secondary education in the first part of the nineteenth century.[74]

This period saw constant rivalry between the education offered by the religious orders, who returned revitalised and grew steadily in number after 1815, and the private lay schools, the *pensionnats* and the *cours*. There is no doubt that, for girls of the middling and higher ranks of society, the only ones with any chance of secondary education, the religious orders were to be the dominant force. New foundations, the order of the nuns of the Sacré-Coeur, whose schools spread rapidly after 1815, the teaching orders of Saint Clotilde from 1821, and the Assumption, from 1839, were all, by the years of the July monarchy, devoted to the teaching of girls from the highest social classes. The quality of such education was likely to vary greatly, but would probably include some polite accomplishments, some acknowledgement of domestic responsibilities, and would certainly exclude any classical learning. Such convents were more likely than their pre-revolutionary predecessors to be aware of the worldly future of their pupils. And Catholic views of education were by no means unchanging. From Mme de Rémusat to Bishop Dupanloup, liberal Catholics denounced the frivolity of women's education, and defended their right to serious instruction, the better to qualify them for their future role in society, but, as far as is known to little effect.

Such convents undoubtedly outnumbered lay schools. The earliest estimate of any reliability, in the 1840s, suggested that lay secondary schools of any academic pretensions were centred on Paris, and a few exceptional departments, such as Seine-Inférieure and Loire-Inférieure. In 1844–5 there were some 253 *pensionnats*, boarding schools run by mistresses, in Paris, with just over 13,000 pupils; at the same time, some 30 convents in Paris could offer some form of secondary education.[75] Such a picture was, however, quite untypical of the rest of France. Most reports suggest that lay schools laid considerable stress on accomplishments rather than academic learning, partly, at least, because parents of the middle and lower bourgeoisie believed that these were likely to provide better qualifications for the future teacher or governess. The best chance of further education of some intellectual content came not in these boarding schools but in the *cours*. These were uniquely French, almost entirely Parisian, courses run normally by men, attended by young women, probably with their mothers, which seemed to incorporate both the principle of 'maternal education' and the possibility of developing more advanced instruction. Such courses were held one day a week, when pupils were questioned on their work, undertaken during the week under their mothers' supervision. The educational philosophy underlying such courses looked back to Rousseau and to Pestalozzi. Some, however, emphasised the potential intelligence of young women, and introduced, for example, elements of scientific work into the classroom. Such *cours* became fashionable in the July monarchy and in the 1840s some 2000 young women were attending these courses in Paris, and small numbers in other cities. They were to last until the end of the century. The teaching of women at the highest levels that existed, in the *pensionnats* and in the *cours*, remained very largely male-dominated, in spite of the importance of the theme of 'maternal education'. Strong prejudices still faced the woman teacher in France.

Nevertheless, it was to be through the regulation of the qualifications for women teachers that the state was to take any part in secondary education in this period. Napoleon had patronised Mme de Campan, left without resources by the revolution, who founded schools for the daughters of holders in the Légion d'Honneur. Her proposal for central inspection of girls' secondary schools was, however, never treated seriously, though it foreshadowed a continuing concern of French legislators. The Restoration government of 1820, less interested in secondary education for girls than in the extension of primary education, passed an ordinance providing for a very simple examination for all mistresses and teachers in *pensionnats*, from which members of religious orders were exempt, and for women inspectors. Unfortunately, subsequent evidence suggests that this legislation was quietly ignored throughout most of France. The important law of 1833, providing primary education throughout the country for boys, ignored the question of women teachers' education; yet it was rapidly becoming a matter of public interest. An ordinance of 1836 at last gave some legal recognition to all girls' schools, prescribing the appropriate curriculum and examinations for primary and secondary levels. Examinations were to be run by the Sorbonne, and members of religious orders were exempt from those at primary level, but not at secondary. In 1837, on the initiative of the prefect of the Seine (the department which included Paris), a new decree prescribed two different kinds of secondary schools for girls, the *pension*, whose teaching was basic, and the *institution* which offered a much wider range of subjects. The distinction was similar to that made for boys' schools in 1808. So, in Paris, such examinations were set by the *Hôtel de Ville*. But this applied only to one department, and was optional in others, and also only to boarding schools. In 1844 the same department made a reality of the provisions for inspection, appointing three women, two with long teaching experience, as inspectors. Clearly by the end of the 1830s a potential pattern of examinations for aspiring teachers had emerged. Few women sat the secondary examinations of the Sorbonne; in 1846, 17 passed, from 21 candidates. But far more sat the simpler examination of the *Hôtel de Ville*, clearly not only for teaching purposes, since in 1845 there were 777 candidates.[76] By the eve of 1848, the case was being made, by the prefect of the Seine, and in the journal of David Levi-Alvarès, leader of the *cours* movement, that some kind of *baccalauréat* for women should be introduced. The new qualifications were obviously serving not only a professional but an educational purpose.

Still, though teaching was almost the only career open to middle-class women, the prospects were extremely poor, even as an assistant mistress in a Paris boarding school, and worse in the provinces. The prestige of the visiting male professor offered little scope to the poorly educated mistress, while prejudices against women in secondary school teaching remained strong. In 1845, Louise Dauriat, who had written in the Saint-Simonian *Tribune des Femmes* in the 1830s, attacked Levi-Alvarès for his continued argument that at a secondary level 'the education of a woman is complete and serious only in so far as it has been undertaken by an enlightened man'.[77] Some institutions, especially one or two of the *cours*, aimed directly at the training of young women for these examinations. The need, both for such institutions and for improved examinations which aimed not merely to train the memory but to nourish girls' intelligence, was clearly perceived. In the 1840s Josephine Bachellery, mistress of a successful Parisian *pensionnat*, campaigned forcefully both for the introduction of training colleges and for a national plan for girls' education, incorporating 'lycées ou collèges de femmes'. For women teachers, regulation and control by the state could offer them a degree of material security and recognition, which appeared infinitely more desirable than the vulnerability of the private institution.

The aftermath of 1848 was a disappointment for liberals and republicans who had hoped for much from the revolution. The new minister of education, Hippolyte Carnot, made a good start in opening the courses of the *collège de France* to women, and drafting a bill for girls' primary education, but this progress was not continued. The 'loi Falloux', of 1850, revising all previous legislation, provided for girls' schools in all communes with over 800 inhabitants, but only if resources allowed. It gave legal recognition only to primary schools for girls and confirmed the exemption of members of religious orders from qualifying examinations. This was naturally followed in 1853 by the abolition of the higher examinations set by the *Hôtel de Ville*. It was not surprising that in the 1850s the *pensionnats*, in the wake of economic crisis and revolution, suffered badly, and the schools of religious orders grew in popularity. But the *cours* gained in strength, and Françoise Mayeur has commented on the continuing appeal of that theme of 'maternal education', inherited ultimately from the *philosophes*.[78] Yet the demand for qualifications, at least for teaching at primary level, continued, and by the 1850s some of the *cours* had specifically become training institutions for teaching examinations, as had some of the religious schools, though the numbers cannot be precisely judged. But only with great difficulty did Julie-Victoire Daubié succeed in becoming the first woman to obtain the *baccalauréat* in 1861, from the reluctant authorities of Lyons.

The contrast between events in France and in the United States and Britain is a revealing one. The political defeat of 1848 delayed the expansion of the state's role in women's education at all levels, until, in practice, the 1880s. But the effect of these political differences was complex. Both reforming anti-clerical republicans, such as Jules Simon, interested in women's education by the 1840s and 1850s, and a liberal Catholic such as Bishop Dupanloup shared a fundamental commitment to the primarily domestic future and responsibilities of women.[79] Women's education was still merely a weapon in the continuing battle between Church and state for the minds of French citizens. The French bourgeoisie, locked into that battle, traditionalist in their social views, never gave sufficient backing to the campaign for improvement. The strength of the centralised French state meant that voluntarist, spontaneous growth of secondary schools and colleges, so much a part of American, and later British, developments, never gained sufficient momentum. There was little available space or support in France for women to explore, for their own sake, the ambiguities and implications of the domestic sphere, as women like Catherine Beecher, Harriet Martineau and many others, had been able to do elsewhere.

THE EDUCATION OF THE MAJORITY

Of course, for the great majority of girls in France, Britain and the United States, such aspirations towards secondary education were entirely irrelevant. For all three countries, much work still remains to be done in the history of mass elementary education, in evaluating the particular experience of girls. Clearly, in Britain, eighteenth-century provision at an elementary level for girls lagged behind that for boys, and continued to do so: literacy rates show a clear differential throughout the period. Most historians agree that literacy rates were rising for both men and women in the first threequarters of the eighteenth century. But even by the 1780s one historian has estimated that 68 per cent of men, but only 39 per cent of women, in England could sign the marriage register. The extent to which industrialisation affected literacy levels is a highly controversial area: but there is considerable agreement that literacy may, in certain areas, in the early stages of industrial development before about 1830, have fallen for both men and women. T. W. Laqueur suggests that in Manchester, for instance, female literacy may have fallen from around 29 per cent in the 1750s to only 19 per cent in 1810–20: other historians have confirmed that the average literacy rate of the textile labour force of Lancashire fell rapidly between these years.[80] Literacy was not a prerequisite for the new labour force. On the other hand, in stable small and middling towns, and in the country, in areas which did not experience rapid social changes, literacy rates probably continued slowly but steadily to increase. After the 1830s that rise continued, though again with regional variations and considerable differences between the sexes. In 1844, national figures for those unable even to sign the marriage register were 37 per cent for men, 48 per cent for women. In the south-eastern counties the same figures were 31 and 38 per cent, in the north-west 39 and 67 per cent.[81]

Yet bare literacy rates based on marriage registers tell us very little about the likely experience of education for girls. In the late eighteenth century opportunities were largely limited to private or 'adventure' schools, small dame schools, and charitable or industrial schools. From the 1780s, evangelical initiatives did expand the number of schools available to the poor, whether charitable day schools or Sunday Schools. In their commitment to the idea of the uniqueness of childhood, the necessity of literacy sufficient to read the Bible, and of a moral reformation led by the upper and middle classes, pioneers like Hannah More and Robert Raikes did indicate a new kind of concern for education, a concern shared by very many working people themselves.[82] However, what emerges in the foundations of women like Sarah Trimmer and Catherine Cappe is a dual purpose, that girls should have the ability to read the Scriptures and that they should be able to maintain themselves in the proper kind of employment. Carding and spinning wool, knitting stockings and needlework, were all recommended by Sarah Trimmer in her proposals for schools of industry. Such employment was deemed far more appropriate than work in agriculture or any kind of work outside the home. The aims of such schools were to make 'good working servants, wives, and mothers'.[83] It is clear from the Reports of the Society for Bettering the Condition of the Poor, that a range of charity schools established by benefactors in this period were intended to serve this aim. At Chester, for example, two schools were reported as thriving, where, for two years, girls were taught to read, attended Church, and for the rest of their time learnt to knit and sew. The schools were linked with the Sunday Schools of Chester, since the best behaved girls were apparently elected from the Sunday Schools into the few places available: 'This has a powerful and extensive effect in improving the morals and behaviour of all the girls in the Sunday Schools, and with them of almost all the female children in Chester.'[84]

Such provisions seem to have changed little from the kind of education offered to poor girls in the eighteenth century. Yet it was becoming clear, even in Chester, that the teaching and charitable resources available were unequal to the task and, also, that the prospects of employment in domestic industry were decreasing. Still, perhaps especially for girls, the legacy of the charity schools and their orientation to the domestic future of girls was to have a profound effect on nineteenth-century educational provision. Elementary education was of course developed rapidly in the early nineteenth century, on the basis of the monitorial system of Andrew Bell and Joseph Lancaster. Denominational rivalry led to the foundation of two voluntary societies, the National Society for promoting the Education of the Poor in the Principles of the Church of England, in 1811, and the British and Foreign Schools Society in 1814, with the backing of Nonconformist opinion, supporting non-denominational schools. These societies dominated educational provisions in England and Wales for the next thirty years. While the number of these schools grew rapidly the quality of education offered was often very limited indeed, and for girls, in particular, they might mark little advance on the charity schools. In Spitalfields, the close relationship between the education offered by the new schools of the British Society, and the charitable concerns of local and City evangelical and Quaker philanthropists has been well documented. There, at Hackney Road Girls School, the curriculum was basically reading, writing and needlework, and more intangibly, training in morality and in industry.[85] Similarly, in the National Society's schools at Kennington, a public statement of 1825 referred to 'the progress of the children in useful knowledge, and that of the girls in industrious work'.[86] There the girls spent four afternoons a week on needlework, while the boys did more arithmetic and reading. A price list for the girls' work was issued to families in the neighbourhood. In 1839, with the establishment of the Education Committee of the Privy Council, under the influence of Sir James Kay Shuttleworth, state machinery for the inspection of these schools was introduced, and inspectors indicated, in a number of reports, the lack of success of the monitorial schools, both in teaching elementary skills and in moral and religious education. Their reports also indicated the differences in the achievement of boys and girls. The Rev. Baptist Noel summarised his findings in 1840:

> In some of the girls' schools very few of the children could write, and the writing was very bad; while even in the boys' schools, where more attention is paid to this important art, there were very few boys . . . who had attained to a running hand without the use of lines. In several of the girls' schools the children do not learn arithmetic at all.[87]

The attendance patterns of boys and girls varied with local employment prospects, and the need for girls, especially, to help at home. A study of Mitcham National School in the 1830s suggests that boys were more likely to leave school early to enter employment, and girls to remain at school longer, and to enter domestic service: but the number of girls attending the school overall was less – between 1830 and 1839 400 boys and 290 girls attended.[88] In industrial areas, where both boys and girls were employed very young, the half-time system was introduced effectively only after 1845, when, if lucky, children might receive a few hours education daily.

From the 1830s education provision was slowly improving, as the state played a greater part, financially and through inspectors, in the establishment of training colleges. New schools for different disadvantaged groups grew up: ragged, workhouse, prison and factory schools. And the rejection by working-class people of the charity ethos surrounding so many schools, and their choice of the best accessible education for their children, did help to raise standards. Charity did give place to education. But the consequences of that transition for girls remain to be traced. In England, unlike France, girls did share, even if to a lesser extent, in the benefits of expanding elementary education from the beginning, and the state did not formally discriminate between girls and boys. But the quality of the education received by girls was undoubtedly different. Women's literacy did remain lower, and girls were more likely to attend inferior schools, such as local dame schools.[89] Even in the National and British schools there were clearly differences in the curricula for girls and for boys, as suggested above. Arithmetic was never as important for girls, and they were unlikely to be taught algebra, geometry or further mathematics in the higher classes. The Birmingham mistress of a National School, observed by Baptist Noel, who 'thought girls should not learn beyond compound addition in arithmetic', and taught them no more, reflected contemporary views.[90] Needlework and knitting remained of great importance. In the 1851 census of education, a much higher proportion of girls than boys were said to be receiving 'industrial instruction', by which was usually meant needlework. From 1846 onwards the Education Committee of the Privy Council encouraged schools to make provision for instructing girls in domestic economy, through, for example, a school wash-house. Although domestic subjects were not formally introduced into the school curriculum until the 1860s, there is no doubt that the ground was already laid.[91] And there was, within this period, an important shift of emphasis. For example in Leeds, the Industrial School, founded by 'benevolent ladies' in 1802, taught reading, writing, knitting and sewing to girls who were 'proper objects of charity' to prepare them for domestic service. In 1852, some equally benevolent ladies founded the Leeds Factory Girls' Sewing School, open to all, in the evenings, to teach the same subjects, to prepare girls for being wives and mothers.[92] Education, for working-class girls, was no longer perceived as being for industry or for employment, but for that future as wife and mother which the middle classes saw as being so inevitable and so exclusive.

Many working-class women did demand a better education. Owenite discussions of women's education clearly reveal understanding, both of the obstacles girls faced in their existing society and of male attitudes towards such demands. In the Owenite and Chartist movements of the 1830s and 1840s, educational classes for women were uniformly popular. Such education might be seen within a domestic context: 'Woman, especially, stands in need of education, inasmuch as she is one of the great instruments by which the people themselves are to be educated. She is, indeed, the great Teacher'.[93] But the case could also be made out for women's own sake, as by these East London female Chartists:

> Sisters, we have hitherto been considered inferior to men in powers of intellect, and truly the want of education has made us appear so; but we much doubt whether this would have been the case had we possessed the same opportunities of acquiring a proper education which the other sex has enjoyed. Let us endeavour to remove this approach, by embracing every opportunity of cultivating and improving our minds.[94]

Similarly, when Owenite leaders attacked Mechanics Institutes for failing to admit women, they might do so on the grounds that 'young women should be taught the duties of housewifery'. But Owenite women might themselves organise, as the Ladies Class of the London Al branch did in 1844, as a self-governing class with a wide curriculum, including some political and economic subjects, addressed by some of the leading women speakers.[95] Yet ambiguities and uncertainties remained. In 1858 Fanny Hertz spoke to the National Association for the Promotion of the Social Sciences of the women's classes in the Mechanics Institutes of Bradford and Huddersfield, firmly rejecting the view that education for such women was for a purpose, to make better wives and mothers. Yet her discussion and argument wound to the conclusion that such successful ventures would produce 'suitable and worthy helpmates for educated and intelligent working men'.[96]

Nevertheless by the 1850s the debate on women's education in Britain at all levels was clearly transformed. It is not always a simple matter to disentangle these levels. The emergence of elementary school teaching as a new occupation for women, and the range of interest from the Chartist and Owenite movements, suggest an active demand for better education from women of respectable working-class and lower middle-class backgrounds.

The *English Woman's Journal* demanded practical and vocational education for women of all classes, directed towards their future employment. Education was a necessary prerequisite to the improvement of the condition of women of all classes. Yet neither Chartists, nor Martineau, nor Hertz could rid themselves of a sense of the necessarily different nature of women's education, in their understanding of the probable destiny of women. The debate reached a much broader audience socially than is often suggested: though there were still very many for whom such issues were totally irrelevant. The young girls, London street traders, interviewed by Henry Mayhew in 1849–50 for the *Morning Chronicle* identified themselves as workers, not as children. For them, no school or educational process delayed or rationalised the coming of the harsh world of domestic responsibilities and casual work.[97]

In the United States there is much evidence to suggest that among the white population, literacy rates and attendance rates were considerably higher than in either Britain or France by the 1850s. However, local patterns of education for the majority of children differed considerably. By that time an American public school system had clearly emerged from the republican commitment to education, though the pace with which different states, left to their own devices by the federal constitution, advanced in this area varied greatly. In New York, grants to voluntary societies had by 1814 clearly come under state superintendence, and a three-tiered system for the organisation of schools by towns was created. In Massachusetts, the cause of state control of town schools and a more systematic organisation was won with the creation of the Massachusetts board of education in 1837, and the first compulsory attendance law in 1852. Southern states in general lagged behind these examples. But new mid-western states were likely to develop a comprehensive system of elementary education at the same time as secondary and higher education. In this confused situation, the differences between public and private schools were by no means always clear; and certain denominations, notably the Roman Catholic Church, fought hard to preserve their own schooling systems. The case for public schooling was made in strong political terms by the 1840s, and was irresistible.[98]

Again, however, the particular effect of this on girls remains to be explored. Female literacy does appear to have increased dramatically in New England between 1790 and 1850. Historians of Massachusetts have suggested 'a decided surge in school provision' for girls in small and middling towns throughout the late eighteenth and early nineteenth centuries, both in private and town-supported schools. With the shift to co-educational, public elementary education, access, for such groups as those young daughters of New England farms who made up the first generation of Lowell workers, and the daughters of the shoemakers of Lynn, was likely to be straightforward.[99] But among the children of Lowell millhands, who grew up in the town, daughters were more likely to leave school early than sons, before the age of 13, and the daughters of immigrant, mainly Irish families, were much more likely to leave very young than those of native-born families. The demand for child workers, the lower incomes of immigrant families, together with, perhaps, better prospects for boys' employment in the future, meant that girls' education was most likely to be shortened in the family interest.[100] That close relationship between economic and family needs, whatever the availability of educational provision, affecting boys and girls differentially, especially at the lower income levels, must have been not uncommon, as immigration and industrial change affected the structure of the labour force throughout the eastern states. In the mid-West public schooling was far more inclusive of the white population than in the East coast cities. Estimates from one Illinois county, around 1859, suggest that roughly 90 per cent of children between 5 and 15 spent some time in some kind of school, even before a state system was introduced. On the western frontier, provision was clearly patchy and variable, changing rapidly. The situation was again different in the South, where public schools tended to cater for the poorest white children only, and provision was undoubtedly at a much lower level. Only North Carolina developed a state elementary system of any vigour before the Civil War, though voluntary societies and private schools flourished.[101]

At an elementary level, public co-educational provision, more effective at an earlier date, did offer native-born white American girls a very much better start than their European counterparts. Illiteracy rates for white females over 20 in 1860 were 5 per cent in New England, 20 per cent in the South, though the illiteracy rates among immigrant groups were much higher.[102] The Irish Catholic families of Boston and New York and the German Lutherans of Pennsylvania made their own demands. Yet the assumption was still that they could be assimilated and ultimately Americanised. Other barriers, not of culture or class but of race, were impassable. Public school provision did not extend to black children, free or slave. For slave girls, their education, such as it was, would come from their own parents, and perhaps from their participation in religious congregations. Only a very few would manage, through charity or luck, to evade the legislation passed after 1831 by all the slave states against the use of any written materials in the instruction of black people. In 1853 Mrs Margaret Douglass was imprisoned in Norfolk, Virginia, for contravening this law, even though she had done so for religious reasons, and to resign the slaves to their situation. Even for free blacks, the difficulties were enormous. Prudence Crandall, who in 1819 in Connecticut attempted to open a school for black children, found local opinion implacably and violently hostile. More successfully, the white Myrtilla Miner in 1851 braved prosecution to establish a black teachers' college in Washington DC, after herself educating black children in Mississipi. There is very clear evidence of a demand for education among free black people. In 1793 the former slave Lucy Terry Prince boldly defended her people's right to education before the trustees of the new Williams College for Men, on behalf of her son. In the same year, another ex-slave, Katy Ferguson, established a school for black and white children in New York. Other schools existed, organised by blacks in the face of white hostility, in Richmond, Baltimore, Charleston. By the 1850s black churches in most leading cities offered some educational opportunities, in Sunday or day schools; Baltimore's black schools had over 2600 black students in 1860, though the balance between men and women is unknown. Still, before the Civil War, the obstacles that faced black women could be overcome only by a very few.[103]

In France, as has already been suggested, the state did distinguish between the education of boys and girls at an elementary level, since the important law of 1833, establishing a primary school in every commune. Some of its provisions were extended to girls in 1836, but they did not include an obligation on communes to set up a separate girls' school. In fact most village schools were mixed schools, split down the middle of the classroom, and girls did share, to a lesser extent, in the extension of primary education after 1833. By 1847, just over $1\frac{1}{4}$ million girls, compared to just over 2 million boys, were attending such schools.[104] Yet the direction of reform was to create a separate system for girls, and the 'loi Falloux' of 1850, providing for communes with over 800 inhabitants to maintain a separate school for girls if resources allowed, if implemented normally meant a shift from a mixed lay school, to one run by a teaching order. The quality of the teaching in such schools, and the commitment of parents to them, varied enormously. In the countryside, for example, the peasant parents of Marlhes, a village near St-Etienne, were likely to send their children to the village school by the 1840s, but only for a few years, before they reached 13. The literacy levels of such peasants, between 1841 and 1870, based on marriage registers, were still only 55 per cent for women, and 76 per cent for men. In other, more remote areas, evidence suggests much less participation, depending both on local employment patterns and on the demand for children's agricultural employment, especially in the summer. In 1844, in the Pyrenees, in one valley there was little sign of any school enrolment: 'the land is so poor that its people cannot make any sacrifice. The children guard the cattle in the mountains, while the parents work without a stop'.[105] Similarly, in French towns and cities, it was the need for children to work in the family interest that limited their education. In Lille, the absence from the available schools, or the brevity of attendance, of the children of industrial workers, aroused much comment. There literacy rates were, in 1851–6, only 49 per cent for women, 68 per cent for men. In the cities of France by the 1850s the great majority of schools for girls were run by the religious orders: in Roubaix, Elbeuf, Le Creusot, St-Etienne, Lille. By 1863, nationally religious orders taught some 54 per cent of all girl pupils, compared to 22 per cent of boys. Such a difference, probably both in the quality of teaching, since nuns required no qualification, and in separation from the boys' curriculum, must surely have stressed the different kind of education and future offered to girls.[106]

Demand for change in the educational system was fundamental, for all those advocating improvements in women's condition, from the 1780s onwards. The grounds for these arguments might shift: from recognition of the necessity of educating better wives and mothers, to education and training for future employment and, simply, for its own sake. Greater understanding of the disparity between men's and women's education, and its social consequences, was a basic stage in the definition of feminist issues, for women of all classes. It was not surprising that the *English Woman's Journal* chose to begin its first issue, in 1858, with an article on 'The Profession of the Teacher'. For the authors of the journal the immediate priority was to secure access to professional training and to higher education, not yet achieved by 1860. Yet at the same time they went further, to face even more fundamental issues. In an article 'Why boys are cleverer than girls', reflecting on the apparently greater mathematical abilities of boys, the limitations of educational change were raised.[107] Educational institutions which merely mirrored social expectations could not themselves be agencies of change, at any level. The acquisition of formal educational skills, discussed for all three countries in this chapter, did indeed depend on and reflect the varying perceptions of women's future in France, Britain and America, though it also reflected the varying educational provisions of those societies.

5. Work and Organisation

THE effect of complex economic changes on gender roles in this period is extraordinarily difficult to measure. No simple contrast between a traditional, pre-industrial world, and modernised, urban, industrialised societies can do justice to the changing balance between paid and unpaid labour, between domestic work and work undertaken outside the home. Expectations of women's work were undoubtedly shifting: but the question which is of interest here is how far women themselves identified and articulated what was happening, and how far they voiced their own concerns and grievances. In the late eighteenth century, a sexual division of labour was common and accepted at all levels in the three societies here considered. That division had its focus on the primary responsibilities of women: on childbearing and childrearing, and on the necessary work of maintaining the household: cooking, cleaning and washing. But beyond those primary concerns, women might have a range of acceptable tasks which could contribute to the welfare of the household either in cash or in kind. These were such different tasks as communities thought appropriate for women, where labour was in demand: the work of the dairy or the garden, casual agricultural employment, paid domestic industry, including spinning, lacemaking, knitting, or perhaps assistance in a husband's trade or craft, or the running of a small shop. Unmarried young women, leaving home probably either to augment the family income or to accumulate their own dowry, would normally be employed either in another household as a domestic servant, or perhaps as a textile worker in a workshop. The high proportion of unmarried women in the great cities of Paris and London, far exceeding any others in size in these years, suggests the demand for such employment. In the course of the next fifty years, economic changes already in process, especially in Great Britain, were to bring about significant shifts in the nature of women's labour, inside and outside the home. Here, in considering paid labour, women's responses to these changes, and the obstacles facing the association together of women as workers will be discussed. In certain domestic and factory industries, women did organise to improve their condition: but hostility from employers, and sometimes from male colleagues, together with their isolation and divided loyalties, meant lengthy and often unsuccessful struggles. By the 1850s the condition of women workers was a fashionable subject for concern. The conditions of their labour, in factories and in mines, rightly horrified a Victorian public in England. But such a response was ambiguous, coming both from humanitarianism and from the strength of that domestic model of womanhood so prevalent among legislators and shapers of opinion, as well as among the leaders of middle- and working-class movements. Faced with this, middle-class feminists still explored the contradictions of these arguments. They were profoundly concerned with the conditions of women's labour. Their solution was to broaden the very restricted pattern of paid employment to which women were limited, by demanding access to a very much wider range of occupations, which could still be defended as suitable for women, both working-class and middle-class.

WOMEN'S WORK IN THE EARLY NINETEENTH CENTURY: CHANGES AND CONTINUITIES

For some women, the tasks deemed appropriate for them changed little. There was to be little change in the sexual division of labour in agricultural matters for the small rural household at a distance from production for the commercial market. On the moving American frontier, women had since the early colonial days had a full and well-defined burden of labour. They had to produce clothing and furnishings, soap, candles, medicines and the food of the household, from the resources of the farm and the countryside, the domestic garden, the dairy and the hen house, to be cooked or preserved. Where necessary they helped with much of the farm work, especially sowing and planting: though some tasks, such as clearing land, construction, ploughing and hunting, were men's work.[1] The small farmers of the mid-West were, on the whole, not drawn into market production before the Civil War, though the possibilities were always present. In some areas of France, the sexual division of labour between men and women in the peasant household similarly saw no major changes in this period. There too, the work of the household could not be clearly differentiated from the work of the farm. Women carried the full responsibility for fetching the water of the household, and cooking for it. But they might also feed the chickens and the pigs, force-feed geese, milk the cows, and work in the fields where necessary, especially at sowing and harvest time. Regional customs varied, but the overlapping of tasks was the general rule. In the small household, some production for the market might make little difference to the organisation of labour, though on larger farms agricultural changes and employing other workers might alter the situation. Middle-class French observers of peasant life tended to stress the heavy burden of physical labour undertaken by French peasant women, as indicating their inferior status: 'These rough country men have for their womenfolk that profound disdain and despotic contempt typical of all savage people'.[2] As Segalen has indicated, such comments are more revealing of the outlook of the observers than of the real relationship between men and women in the complementary rural households of the nineteenth century, where the organisation of labour was only one of the factors determining the hierarchy of the household.[3]

In other areas, where commercial agriculture depended on larger farms and the employment of labourers, the pattern of women's work might be rather different. Less labour would be expected of farmer's wives, but the demand for female agricultural labour might continue. In Britain, the demand for women's labour followed essentially similar patterns to that for men's, especially at sowing and harvesting time, in the early eighteenth century. But from around 1750, with increasing specialisation, recent evidence suggests that the demand for women's labour fell in areas of intensive grain production, with plenty of available male labour and increasing use of the physically more demanding scythe. In pastoral farming, on the other hand, where women were needed especially in the dairy, the demand remained constant. Work on the land was, for women, dependent on a number of factors: on the local economy, on the season, on womens' individual strength, and on the number of their children, and on the availability of other work. In some areas, for instance, the shortage of male agricultural workers during the Napoleonic Wars could mean that women were employed on unusually heavy work.[4] But by the mid-nineteenth century there is overwhelming evidence of disapproval, at the upper levels of society, of such work for women. Fieldwork would:

almost unsex a woman, in dress, gait, manners, character, making her rough, coarse, clumsy, masculine; . . . it generates a further pregnant social mischief by unfitting or indisposing her for a woman's proper duties at home.[5]

The range of tasks performed by women in the early nineteenth century – gleaning, sowing, weeding, and so on – was in marked contrast to the amount of work performed a century earlier. Opinion had shifted, as the demand for such labour fell, and the coincidence is a striking one, even though there were some important exceptions to the tendency, such as the surviving 'gangs' of women and children workers, in East Anglia. Some contemporary evidence suggests that women themselves may have regretted this forced shift away from a more companionable, outdoor, work.[6] In the United States, the employment of white women as agricultural workers was relatively rare by the early nineteenth century. Lydia Maria Child suggested that such work was done mainly by the daughters of immigrants. In eastern America, such work rapidly came to be seen as degrading and inappropriate for women, though this did not apply to the frontier, or to the responsibility for supervision, on southern plantations as on eastern farms, which many women must have exercised. And farm women might, as in the United States, continue their own contribution to the household economy by the production, for instance, of butter or market-garden produce, for sale at local markets.[7] In France, in some areas of larger landownership, agricultural modernisation may well have created a temporary demand for women as agricultural labourers, though not a lasting one, as one study of a Norman village, Auffray, in the Pays de Caux, suggests.[8]

Though women were clearly involved, in different degrees, in the labour of rural societies in all countries, there is very little evidence of any protest by women, as agricultural workers, at the conditions of their own employment, at least before the 1860s. They were undoubtedly involved in many protest movements, against the enclosures of common land, and in resistance to the clearances of peasants from their lands in the Highlands, and, in France, to attacks on communities' long-accepted communal rights.[9] But such protests should be seen rather as similar to action over the price of bread, or the level of poor relief: as indicating that they shared the grievances and the values of their communities, and their families within those communities. For men and for women, the conditions of agricultural labour in the first half of the nineteenth century did not permit any effective, organised, coming together of individual workers.

For most black women, both slave and free, agricultural labour was central to their lives. Slave women's work was defined in two different ways: firstly, on the plantation, by their owner, and secondly, within their own families and cabins, according to their own customs, inherited and acquired. In field work, the great majority of slaves were likely to spend their time in the hard manual work of the cotton and rice fields, ploughing, hoeing and picking. Some tasks were reserved mainly for men: clearing land, chopping wood and learning skilled artisan trades. The division of labour between the sexes could, however, disappear, in the needs of the small farm or plantation, and also, as, in the cotton fields, planters realised that: 'women can do plowing very well, and full well with the hoes, and equal to men at picking'. By contrast, in their own cabins, 'Blacks maintained a traditional division of labour between the sexes'.[10] It is not clear precisely what these traditions were, since they would have varied between West African societies, and were clearly affected by the demands and assumptions of white masters, and the degree of their survival remains controversial. But where possible, black women helped to provide the family's food and clothes, perhaps working together in washing, spinning, weaving, making soap and candles, growing food on their small patches of land, both for their own families and for the slave community. It has been convincingly suggested that the sexual division of labour within domestic life, in so far as that could exist under the conditions of slavery, could represent a form of assertion, an insistence on human priorities, against a system which viewed men and women workers indiscriminately as labourers for profit. For free black women, there were few options. Most continued to live in the countryside, and many, probably, to do field labour. Many, too, would enter domestic service, as cooks, cleaners, washerwomen and seamstresses.[11]

One of the most important themes in the history of women's work in this period must be the effect of industrial capitalism on women's domestic industry. The effect was to be felt over a lengthy period, and the pace of technological change can be exaggerated. In some processes, such as the spinning of cotton, mechanisation and the shift to factory production brought rapid disruption. In others, such as the weaving of woollens, the effects were only being felt by the end of this period. Similarly it is by no means clear whether any uniform pattern of development, incorporating first household production, then 'proto-industry', or cottage industry, based on the putting out of work by merchant capitalists, and then factory production, can be constructed. The disruption of familiar patterns of paid domestic labour could lead women to protest, to articulate their grievances. But such disruption also caused hardship and difficulty, and probably an overall reduction in the employment available to married women. It was in the cotton factories of Lancashire, of northern France and of New England, that women's unionism was to emerge eventually, though, apart from New England, there are few signs of it in this period. The main alternatives facing women who sought to supplement the household's income still lay within the domestic sphere. Cottage industries were becoming the 'sweated trades' of urban and rural societies alike. And for the majority, there was domestic labour, whether, for the unmarried, as domestic servants, or for married women, casual and irregular work, taking in lodgers, washing, cleaning, childminding, sewing.

Only on the American frontier, in some rural areas of the United States, and in the poorer, remoter areas of England and France, did production purely for household use survive.[12] By the second half of the eighteenth century, commercial organisation of the 'domestic system' in the textile industries was well established, and expanding with particular strength in Britain. It is important to remember the different, interacting, factors that dictated whether outwork remained a viable and profitable part of the organisation of production in particular industries: the available supply of labour and its cost, its regular availability (which might, in turn, depend on agricultural prosperity and changes), the practicability and cost of mechanisation, the ease of transporting materials, the cost of factory rents, and so on. Throughout this period, the pattern of outwork remained an important, often expanding alternative to factory production, which could take a number of forms: work could be done within the home, involving all the family, or women and children, or women only, or a subcontractor might employ all workers together in a small workshop. There was to be no wholesale flight to factory production: outwork was to prove too easy and profitable a way to supply certain sorts of mass consumer demand, especially in clothing, in a newly urbanising world. So the 'cottage industry' of the eighteenth century, often viewed nostalgically, and the needlewomen and the shirtmakers of nineteenth-century Paris, London, Leeds,

Baltimore, New York, were all part of the same profitable way of organising production to meet expanding demands. It was the very existence of such a large pool of cheap, available labour, in married women based mainly at home, that was one of the most critical factors stimulating entrepreneurs to continued to expand outwork to meet demand.[13]

Such outwork was of most importance in the many branches of the clothing and textile trades. The relationship between factory production and outwork in the different branches of textiles is complex: but understanding this can tell us something about the timing of women's protests. Different processes – the preparatory work, the spinning of yarn, the weaving of cloth – were mechanised, first water-powered, then steam-powered, and brought within factories, at a very different pace. As production expanded through the speeding up of single processes, so the demand for outworkers in a different process would grow, to meet the bottlenecks created. Most obviously the mechanisation of the spinning of cotton yarn in Britain, on a large scale from the 1780s onwards, was to bring the most dramatic changes. Where the spinning of yarn – cotton, wool, flax – had been a nearly universal form of employment for women at home, over the next forty years it was virtually to disappear, brought within the factory, and located within specialised regions of production. Even so, the pace was slower for other textiles than for cotton. In Yorkshire, for example, the mechanisation of spinning in worsteds was complete by the 1820s, but, for technical reasons, took another decade in the woollen industry. In France, such changes began for cotton spinning in the north, in Normandy, Picardy and Flanders from the 1790s, and in Alsace rather later, from about 1806. There, in the north domestic spinning continued for considerably longer, though in Alsace it was rapidly ousted, and completely replaced by factory production by the mid-1820s. Similarly, even the most advanced areas of woollen cloth production, in the Norman towns such as Elbeuf, saw the slow introduction of spinning mills from the 1820s onwards, and continuing domestic spinning through the country. Everywhere, the spinning of flax remained largely domestic until the 1830s, when linen spinning mills were introduced, though they did not challenge domestic industry seriously for some years. In the United States, the English example was seriously studied, and from 1790 the spinning mills of Rhode Island and Massachusetts were successful.[14]

These initial developments, in each branch of textile production, were to co-exist with and to feed expanding domestic production, both in preparatory work and, most notably, in weaving. The need for handloom weavers to deal with the expanding production of yarn grew and technical changes lagged behind. In Britain, in Lancashire and other northern towns, and in the Clyde valley, the numbers of cotton handloom weavers grew rapidly, whether in the new cities or in rural areas. Some were specialised and highly skilled, others saw it as a casual, supplementary occupation. But in many areas, women and children formed the majority, fitting in the work according to the level of male employment, with casual agricultural and domestic work. The economic prospects for a time looked good; not until the middle of the 1820s did the powerloom seriously threaten their livelihood. Then for cotton handloom weavers in Britain there was no future, and over the next twenty-five years they disappeared from the industrial scene, their face graphically described by many observers. In the United States, again, the example of Britain was closely followed, in New England and the middle states. Francis Cabot Lowell, who in 1813 founded the first cotton mills for both spinning and weaving in Massachusetts, helped to keep American technical progress close to that of Britain; and the powerloom was, similarly, by the 1820s a serious threat to American domestic weavers in most northern states. In France, the threat was felt more slowly. In the 1860s, in the north of France, handloom weaving was still far more common than the powerloom; but in Alsace, handloom weavers were very much in the minority.

Tragic as the fate of the cotton handloom weavers was, it is important not to see that fate as exemplifying the end of outwork, or domestic production in this period. The mechanisation of the production of other kinds of textiles came much more slowly. In the Yorkshire woollen industry, the powerloom was little used at all before 1840. In France, in the 1860s, even in the major centres of production, in Rheims, Elbeuf, Mazamet, handloom weavers were in the majority. And in other areas of the country, less specialised, mechanisation was to follow even more slowly in the weaving of woollen cloth: in the West Country and East Anglia in Britain, across much of the south in France. Other textiles too were still to be produced in a domestic framework. Linen was badly hit by the competition of cheap cotton – the weaving of linen still remained a rural activity in the 1850s. In France, the great silk industry centred on Lyons remained largely unmechanised for most of this period, and

Lyons' entrepreneurs expanded, rather than contracted, domestic labour, by increasingly putting work out to unskilled rural workers subcontracted to convent workshops employing large numbers of women rather than trust it to the more militant, skilled, artisans of the city.[15]

Other domestic trades, too, saw deliberate expansion, to meet the demand for labour from women and children suffering from the loss of spinning. The rapid growth in England of the strawplaiting industries of Bedfordshire, Hertfordshire and Buckinghamshire, at the end of the eighteenth century, was fostered by philanthropists and parish guardians concerned at the loss of paid domestic spinning. Women and children plaited straw and made hats and bonnets. Hatmaking was gradually to move into small workshops in neighbouring towns, as domestic strawplaiting declined. In the long-established lacemaking industry, which in the late eighteenth century was focused around Nottingham, key inventions, in 1778 and 1808, offered the means of mechanising the making of lace net. But as factory production expanded, much of the final work was put out to outwork on a very extensive scale. Lacefinishing was still regarded, at the end of the nineteenth century, as one of the major sweated trades.[16] In parts of Normandy, similarly, women suffering from the loss of income from spinning were likely to take up the making of gloves, as in the Vexin, for Parisian entrepreneurs, or lacemaking, as in the pays de Bray.[17]

The progress of outwork is most clearly illustrated in the clothing industry, in all three societies. The new mass markets for clothing of all kinds brought the decline of the tailoring craft and its replacement by the subdivision of processes involved in making up garments, and the putting out of these different tasks to homes and workshops. The appalling wages and conditions of work of the needlewomen and slopworkers of London in the 1840s attracted the attention of philanthropists and journalists such as Henry Mayhew of the *Morning Chronicle*. But their numbers continued to grow throughout the major cities of Britain. In France too, the same developments are clear. A study of the Parisian tailoring industry shows that from being an insignificant part of the tailoring workforce in 1828, women came to dominate it numerically by 1848, with the coming of *confection*, the ready-made trade. The great majority of them worked at home.[18] Similarly, in the United States, in the early nineteenth century, the demand for ready-made clothing, especially for the army and navy, and for southern slaves was rapidly recognised, and a clothing industry, centring on New York, Boston and Philadelphia, but spreading far beyond those cities, developed. The coming of the sewing machine was simply to expand such a demand. There too, the tailors, long-established, skilled craftsmen, felt their control of their craft reduced and destroyed by these new forms of organising production. In this sense, outwork was growing rather than declining in these years, stimulated by the availability of cheap and appropriate labour.

Other areas of the industry were subject to the same changes, as, for example, the making of boots and shoes. New mass markets brought a capitalist-based industry relying on a strict division of labour between the skilled and the unskilled, and on a combination of factory production and outwork. In the United States, in Massachusetts around the town of Lynn, by the 1830s, household production had given way to the capitalist-owned central shop, with women doing the handstitching, binding and trimming of shoes, skilled male cutters preparing the leather, and journeymen fastening tops to bottoms. The British trade lagged behind the American, with the industry rather less subdivided before the 1850s and the coming of the sewing machine.[19] In France, the weaving of silk ribbons, which grew very rapidly in the area around St-Etienne in the first thirty years of the nineteenth century, was made possible through its control by the urban *fabricant* or merchant, who distributed specific tasks – cleaning, spinning, dyeing, carding, designing, weaving – to skilled and unskilled workers throughout the countryside.[20] Similarly, glove-making relied in the early nineteenth century on outwork, in Britain based especially on localities in the West Midlands and the South West. An account was given to the Royal Commission on Children's Employment in the 1860s:

the various parts of the glove are given out to be sewn together. The people who do that are wives and daughters of agricultural labourers scattered throughout the neighbouring country. It is purely domestic work. . . . If they live near, they bring in their work as it is finished; if far off, probably someone goes round once a fortnight and collects all that is ready, bringing it in for a small percentage. The girls are taught by their mothers; a girl of 14 becomes very useful, at 16 she will often earn as much as her mother, or even more, because she will not be occupied with household matters so much. There are whole villages of born glove makers; it is quite a hereditary talent.

That account does suggest something of the character and extent of rural outwork in this period, characteristic not just of the glove-making area around Worcester, but of the very similar patterns of organisation in areas of France and the United States. In the Connecticut valley of the United States, for example, new sources of outwork, like the Amherst hat industry, helped to preserve the independence, for a time, of small rural families, while allowing women to accommodate their employment to other household tasks.[21]

One area of outwork which did not fit the 'traditional' view of women's paid activities lay in their employment in the metal trades. In Great Britain this employment was concentrated in the West Midlands. Nailmaking was an expanding outwork trade in the eighteenth century, probably reaching its height around 1830, when it began to meet the competition of machine-made nails. After that it tended to become rather a supplementary source of income for women workers, extending from the Black Country into the country-side, on the margins of urban industry. Chainmaking was, however, expanding from the 1820s and employing more women, though the numbers before 1850 were fairly small, and even then concentrated around Cradley. But the number of small metal and hardware trades, and their subdivisions, were very great: nails, chains, nuts, bolts, screws, files, buckles, stirrups, locks, might all be made at home or in small workshops, by women, though by the middle of the nineteenth century factory production was clearly increasing. In Sheffield women might be employed, at home, or in workshops, on some of the inferior, less skilled, cutlery processes. In other areas of the country they might make watches, pins, or needles.[22] In the United States women seem to have been less likely to engage in this kind of work before mid-century, though they were certainly employed in small numbers as type rubbers in New York and Boston, and as metal polishers. Some too were employed in the jewellery and watchmaking trades.[23] Such domestic industries cer-tainly existed in France, though there is little to suggest whether women participated in them. The role of one woman in a strike of pinmakers in 1831, in the department of the Eure, might suggest so. Certainly they were employed in workshops as burnishers and polishers, and in other more specialised trades. In Paris in 1847, of 2000 workers in the clock and watchmaking trade, there were some 155 women.[24]

WOMEN WORKERS AND ORGANISATION

The picture that emerges of the effects of economic change on domestic industry is a confused one, but does not suggest any catastrophic ending of the system. The early stages of mechanisation would create more work within the home, or could relocate it. Given the expanding population, the availability of the cheap labour of married women and their children provided a powerful incentive to maintain some form of putting out system in the country and in the towns and cities. Here then, it is relevant to consider how women reacted to these changes. Naturally, they affected every member of the family – but the unique position of married women, and their domestic responsibilities, tended to define their availability for employment. At this stage we should consider how far the participation of women in formal and informal associations together, and in disputes related to their work, allowed them to identify their own interests not only as workers, but as women workers. The links between industrialisation and women's industrial and political activity are still barely understood. What can be offered are merely some reflections on this problem. Within this immensely broad spectrum of domestic employment and of outwork, it might be considered that the isolated conditions of work, so unlike factory employment, or larger workshops, and the characteristics of that work (cheapness, lack of skill, irregularity) precluded the association of women together and the growth of unionism. And, of course, the realities of working women's lives need, always, to be borne in mind. For the domestic worker, who might be working some 12–14 hours a day, combining this with work directly for the household, the chances of coming together with others outside the home would be slight, unless moved by the harshest of economic circumstances.

In this context it should be remembered that in Britain, throughout the eighteenth century, female friendly societies had provided one model of organisation for women. Some such societies were mixed, some exclusively female. They could cover sickness benefits, funeral expenses, perhaps lying-in expenses, and also offered the opportunity for social occasions. They might have arisen spontaneously or, initially, from some philanthropic initiative. They were sometimes known also as 'box clubs'. A Manchester society, known as the Blue Bell Society because it met at an inn of that name from September 1795, decided that any member who fell ill, or was unable 'to work at her trade, calling or employ' should receive 5s a week for six months. Women of bad character were not admitted (though an unmarried woman could not receive anything out of the box 'for more than one lying in'). The society held an annual feast. Such a society might be organised and administered entirely by women, but it was not a trade society, since working women from all trades might join.[25] The difficulty of tracing women's participation in early trade unions is complicated by linguistic ambiguities. In Britain, only in 1811 did an Act of Parliament clarify that the word 'journeyman' could be taken to incorporate 'journeywoman'. In practice, it was clear that women might be engaged in similar kinds of work to journeymen, but also that women were at a disadvantage (though there are many local exceptions) in their chances of apprenticeship, and in the likelihood of their being admitted as members of guilds, of craft societies, or of journeymen's combinations. There is evidence that women in some long-established industries might belong to associations. The Worsted Smallware weavers of Manchester, established in 1747, accepted journeywomen as equal members, and so did the Associated Cotton Spinners of Manchester in 1795. In various London trades, among the woollen workers of Yorkshire and the West Country, and the textile industries of the East Midlands, there is scattered evidence of such involvement. Yet one recent study of eighteenth-century trade societies in Britain fails to mention women either as participants in mixed societies, or as founders of their own. C. R. Dobson remarks, too, that:

the most consistently successful bargainers were those with a permanent base for continuous association. This was not necessarily the workplace. . . . The rise of the British trade union movement is intimately linked with that of the public house.[26]

The point is not frivolous. It was not impossible for women to associate as workers in this way, but it was, clearly, rare. That must, surely, relate to the domestic focus of their lives and work, away from any continuous, permanent meeting place. In the United States, similarly, there is no evidence of trades societies among women in the eighteenth century. In France, however, a few long-established female trade associations did exist before the revolution, only to be suppressed, along with all the others, in 1791. But the oldest, and most lasting, tradition of organisation, the *compagnonnage* for travelling journeymen, clearly excluded women.[27]

In the early nineteenth century, the organisation of women workers made only limited advances. Two themes of the period may be noted: the participation of women workers, especially in the textile trades, in brief sporadic movements of protest; the second, the increasing hostility of some skilled male workers, both from the old, threatened crafts, and from the new, skilled, factory-based unions, to the employment of women. Women's protests were to be found both in small-scale craft industries and in the textile trades, and they shared in the reaction of their male colleagues to the introduction of new machinery and to attacks upon their wages and livelihood. One exhaustive study of industrial disputes in France under the July monarchy illustrates this. In Paris, in August 1830, a small group of women working with rabbit fur, in the millinery trade, called a strike against the reduction of their wages by their masters. The new government, immediately after the July Revolution of 1830, supported them. In a period of Luddite attacks on machinery throughout France, in September 1831 women strawcutters in Montmartre demonstrated against the installation of a new machine to do a task which had always been regarded as one for women to do.[28] In April 1834, in Paris, in the aftermath of nationally organised workers' movements in a number of trades, wood engravers forced one workshop to close, after an attempt to reduce wages. Six women were among the eight ringleaders sent briefly to prison.[29] But for the rest of the period, women were recorded primarily as sharing in the response of woollen workers to their deteriorating conditions. Between 1839 and 1847, women shared in a series of spontaneous and isolated strikes among the weavers of leading woollen towns: Lodève, Elbeuf, Mazamet. In 1839, groups of 200 to 300 women attempted to stop strike-breaking workers entering the workplace in Lodève. In 1846, in Elbeuf, 40 women who normally worked at home were sacked on the installation of new machinery. Crowds of several thousand gathered in support, and were dispersed only by rapidly summoned troops. Of the 18 workers of all trades arrested, the only woman was charged with Luddism, the rest with rebellion. Detailed analysis of Lodève has suggested that 'women workers often stood at the forefront of the movement', in a city where collective action of some kind took place almost every year. It was a city where solidarity was strong, already established among woollen workers *before* the coming of mechanisation, in resistance to the *fabricants*.[30] Many instances of involvement in crowd action by women must simply have been unremarked and unrecorded; yet perhaps it is not merely coincidence that those instances of participation in industrial protest which do survive, are those where women may have been assumed to identify with their male artisan colleagues, or with their close-knit communities. The first *société de résistance* formed among women in France is said to have been among the hatters of Paris, who in 1844 organised the 'Société Chapelière de Sainte-Marie' to ask for a tariff of wages. It still existed in 1848.[31]

In Britain, in the early nineteenth century, there are similar glimpses of women's protests, though it remains impossible to estimate the level of their participation. In 1811, for example, women laceworkers of Loughborough showed a 'spirit of combination', organising meetings in their own and neighbouring towns to demand a rise in wages. In the hosiery and ribbon trades of the East Midlands, unions negotiated wages with the connivance of employers, and women workers undoubtedly shared in the benefits, as they did in the processions that paraded around the town.[32] In the great handloom weavers strike of 1808 women weavers were singled out by the comments of *The Times*, as more turbulent and insolent than the men.[33] It is very likely that they also took part in the later Lancashire movement of 1818, and perhaps in the loom-breaking of 1826. In 1820, Buckinghamshire laceworkers paraded around the town of Aylesbury in processions directed against the new machines, with banners 'Support Bobbin Lace', 'Down with the Machine Stuff'.[34] In 1804 the women glovemakers of Worcester, threatened by changes in fashion and 'more disposed to be mutinous' than the men, attacked those wearing silk gloves in the streets of Worcester. Clearly they did not fail to play their part among fellow workers in the distress of 1825, and the unionism of 1833–4.[35] Where such solidarity existed, men and women might clearly be united in industrial protest, especially in times of the greatest hardship.

The national trade union movement of the early 1830s in Britain has been analysed as one which was dominated by the older crafts, although it drew, also, upon a new analysis of the value of labour. It was a short-lived movement, from 1828 to 1834, yet, like the revolutions of 1830 and 1848 in France, it drew attention to some of the specific problems of women workers. Taylor has shown how women's participation in Owenite unionism grew. The co-operative ideal, as a means of redressing the distribution of wealth, attracted workers, including women workers, rapidly. In 1832, a 'Society of Industrious Females' was formed by women to win a better reward for their labours through producing clothing co-operatively and selling it through Robert Owen's Labour Exchange in Grays Inn Road. Other groups of workers made buttons, shoes, gloves. Local co-operative workshops, like those of male and female handloom weavers in Huddersfield in 1832, followed. Once the Grand National Consolidated Trades Union (GNCTU) was formed, in 1834, women workers from many trades joined, forming lodges and associations, both mixed and all-female: lacemakers, bonnetmakers, stockingers, glovemakers, shoebinders. The issues engaging these workers, and the leaders of the movement also, were in many respects new: industrial changes, and changes in the organisation of production, seemed to bring the sexual segregation of labour to a much greater degree than previously, through the use of cheap female labour. In 1834 the question was thrown open, briefly, for debate, in the 'Woman's Page' of The Pioneer, widely read among the working classes. The claim, not only for political or marital equality, but of equality for women at work was made:

> Why, I ask, should women's labour be thus undervalued? Why should the time and the ingenuity of the sex . . . be monopolized by cruel and greedy oppressors, being in the likeness of men, and calling themselves masters? Sisters, let us submit to it no longer . . . unite and assert your just rights![36]

But the delegates of the GNCTU who met in London in February 1834, while supporting women's unionism, had limited their support to all female lodges, and founded the Grand Lodge of Miscellaneous Female Operatives, which clearly saw its purpose as the discussion of 'domestic matters' as well as union business. The letters to the 'Woman's Page', however, revealed a different picture; there were letters from women fully aware of masculine hostility to their organisation, from women who condemned 'the men . . . as bad as their masters', from P.A.S., the straw-bonnetmaker who complained of male invasion of women's jobs, and called for co-operation and association between the sexes as workers.[37]

But 1834 in Britain also saw a major strike by London tailors, which illustrated the struggle between skilled artisans, seeking to preserve their status and control of their trade, and the new methods of organising production. This conflict exemplified the hostility that might exist between such workers and women employed as cheap, unskilled labour, undercutting their respect and their wages. It is one which took place in France and the United States as well, as urban skilled trades gave way to unskilled female competition. Strikes against the dilution of skills and the employment of female labour in the tailoring trade took place in London in 1810, 1814, 1827 and 1830 – but the tailors' position was weakening. In April 1834 they struck again for higher wages, for shorter hours and the abolition of piecework and homework. Contemporaries agreed that this was fundamentally a strike about women outworkers, though they were not openly mentioned. The union, and Owenite supporters, were divided. James Morrison, editor of the *Pioneer*, saw the tailors as having 'declared war against the female tailors', and a letter to the 'Woman's Page' from 'A Woman', a tailoress, declared:

> surely the men might think of a better method of benefiting themselves than that of driving so many industrious women out of employment. Surely, while they loudly complain of oppression, they will not turn oppressors themselves.[38]

The same pattern existed in Paris. There, after 1828, the ready-made trade increasingly took hold. In the 1830s journeymen still identified their problems with their direct employers, the master tailors. By 1848 masters and men were to a degree united in their protests against *confection*, piecework and female labour, though, again, the latter only by implication.[39]

Similar developments can be traced in the United States, where the practice of separate unions was rapidly established. In 1834, for example, women shoebinders of Lynn, Massachusetts, responded to falling piece rates by the foundation of the Female Society of Lynn and Vicinity for the Protection of Female Industry, since they were:

> driven by necessity to seek relief, impressed with the belief that women, as well as men, have certain inalienable rights, among

which is the right at all times of 'peaceably assembling to consult upon the common good'.[40]

The new society had a detailed constitution, and led a successful strike for a new wage scale, in this case actively supported by the men's Cordwainers Union. The society did not last long, but their initiative was followed by, among others, the Female Boot and Shoe Binders Society in Philadelphia in 1836, which struck for better wages along with its male colleagues. The impact of the demand for ready-made clothing was felt acutely in American cities by the 1820s, and it is clear that women workers in the industry were then seeking organisation as a means to relief. In February 1831 a meeting of tailoresses was held in New York, and in June the United Tailoresses Society of New York led its 1600 members out on strike for a new wage scale. Their leader, Sarah Monroe, declared: 'if it is unfashionable for the men to bear oppression in silence, why should it not also become unfashionable with the women?'.[41] The strike was supported by the labour press, but seems to have had little success. In 1833 their lead was followed by the Female Union Society of Tailoresses and Seamstresses in Baltimore, again with little better success. Neither appears to have lasted long. Although there are examples of male union support for such movements, in general in the United States early trade unions, like those elsewhere, fought hard against the subdivision of labour and the reduction of wages involved in the widespread employment of women in a number of trades. In 1819, journeymen tailors of New York went on strike to prevent the hiring of women by master tailors. In 1832 the Typographical Society of Philadelphia denounced a plan to employ women compositors in one printing office.[42] By the middle of the 1830s, the issues, and the alternatives, were openly discussed. One solution was that urged by the 'Journeymen Cigar Makers of Philadelphia', in 1835:

Resolved, that the present low wages hitherto received by the females engaged in cigar making is far below a fair compensation for the labor rendered. Therefore, Resolved that we recommend them in a body to strike with us and thereby make it a mutual interest with both parties to sustain each other in their rights.[43]

The Committee on Female Labour, at the third convention of the National Trades' Union, in 1836, however, argued differently. A report urged that women should enter into separate or mixed unions, so that men might, temporarily, offer their protection and aid. But ultimately such employment should end, and women return to their domestic labours, since 'her efforts to sustain herself and family are actually the same as tying a stone around the neck of her natural protector, Man, and destroying him with the weight she has brought to his assistance'.[44]

Behind this complex pattern of economic change, in which not only technology but the capitalist reorganisation of production threatened old-established skilled crafts, and male dominance within them, lay also a threat to domestic stability and security. In the eighteenth century, as has been suggested, the assumption was that married women would contribute by their labours to the household income: yet their income was not normally seen as the family's primary means of support. For craftsmen and artisans, skilled weavers and tailors, the challenge was not only to their trade, but to their position as the primary provider within the household. One way of responding to this was to stress the proper domestic focus of women's lives. In these years, the boundaries between domestic and working lives were still in the process of definition. So, women's protests and grievances could be voiced on their own behalf, but were as likely to be voiced on behalf of their family or, where close-knit groups of workers were long established, as a part of collective community action. Such women, given current wage levels, felt that they had no choice. Women had to work, and given this, had to defend their wages and conditions as best they might. But the prospect of domestic life supported by a husband's higher earnings was perhaps, an equal, even a better, prospect for the security of the household.

As the dilemma became clearer, some women and men chose to reassert not the domestic values, but forms of co-operation which would meet the needs of women workers, especially women artisans and outworkers. Most notably, the French women socialists of 1848, Desirée Gay, Jeanne Deroin and Pauline Roland, made their concern for the condition of the Parisian working women clear.[45] In the first weeks of the revolution, new associations of women workers were enthusiastically founded, as were those for men. Desirée Gay set up the 'Club fraternel des lingères', the newspaper, the *Voix des Femmes*, an 'Association des femmes à gages', and Parisian midwives the 'Sages-femmes unies'. But there was an immediate problem: whether to co-operate in the immediate relief of hardship among unemployed

Parisian women, or to advance the principle of association. A few women delegates did sit in the Luxembourg Commission, a 'parliament' of delegates from different trades set up in Paris – three leather-workers, three metal polishers, and a representative of the *lingères*. The problems discussed there relating to women were mainly the unfair competition to women's work offered by prisons and convents, and the need to organise in co-operative workshops. There were also proposals to establish better relations between male and female societies in the same trades. In the short term, tailoring workshops were set up by the municipal authorities of Paris for unemployed women, with five women to be elected as delegates from each *arrondissement* to represent their interests. The ex-Saint-Simonian dressmaker and active feminist, Desirée Gay, was elected as a delegate, and workshops were rapidly set up, turning out shirts for the *garde mobile*. They were hierarchically organised and paid on piece-rates. Gay rapidly denounced them in the feminist newspaper, the *Voix des Femmes*, as 'despotism under a new name', and called for women in the Luxembourg to represent their sisters more effectively. For this, she lost her post. Criticisms of the workshops nevertheless continued. The *Voix des Femmes* called for *crèches* to be provided, and for training to be given by skilled working women. Gay called for a new kind of co-operative association, incorporating the responsibilities of women to their families: laundries, restaurants, a library and social rooms should be a necessary part of the co-operative association. The workshops were closed after the June insurrection in Paris. Feminist interest turned towards the independent association of working women. Elisa Lemonnier had helped to set up an 'Association des Couturières' which petitioned the government for aid in June. Desirée Gay and Jeanne Deroin, also an ex-Saint-Simonian and self-taught schoolmistress, established the 'Association Fraternelle des Ouvrières Lingères', a co-operative workshop of 30 working women, in October 1848. Profits were divided into four, a quarter as wages, a quarter as social insurance, and half to increase working capital. The *Opinion des Femmes*, the newspaper which had succeeded the earlier *Voix des Femmes*, appealed to bourgeois women to understand the real requirements of working women, to help in the sale of their goods and the provision of capital. Jeanne Deroin's vision went beyond this: her ideal was for a united federation of associations of men and women workers, and in 1849 she helped to bring together 43 delegates from different associations to discuss this. For her work she was arrested and tried in May 1850 together with Pauline Roland, another feminist, with whom she had helped to found a union for schoolteachers, and a number of male union leaders. Deroin had defended women's right to work against the narrowly domestic and maternal focus of the socialist Pierre Joseph Proudhon, in the polemical battle between the Proudhonian *Le Peuple* and the *Opinion des Femmes*. But she and the other feminists of 1848 all retained from their own experiences and understanding a strong awareness of the double burden of domestic and paid labour which working women performed. Their projects arose from their own experience and knowledge of working conditions.[46]

In the future, the cause of the outworkers and the sweated trades was to become the concern of philanthropists and middle-class socialists, rather than develop its own forms of organisation. This was the case with, for instance, the Tailoresses Industrial Union and its workshops in Philadelphia in 1850, or the New York Co-operative Clothing Store from 1851.[47] The difficulties of organisation for women working at home or in small workshops were insuperable. They represented the lowest levels of the labour force, in common with immigrants and those without status or skill of any kind. Men's participation in the old-established craft trades was declining, and where it remained as, for example, in the printing trades, did so partly as a result of maintained hostility to female employment. Little support from a still barely developing male trade union movement was to be expected, as the interests of the sexes at work seemed increasingly to diverge. Owenism in England and similar forms of co-operative socialism in France had seemed to offer a solution, transiently, to tailors, shoemakers, weavers, hard hit by economic change – but these solutions came to appear visionary. Permanent organisation awaited a more united and stable labour force.

THE NEW INDUSTRIAL SOCIETY: FACTORY LABOUR AND DOMESTIC SERVICE

The role of women in the factories of industrialising nations is much better known and, perhaps, often exaggerated. Women working in large-scale, mechanised factories were, even in Britain and America, a relatively small proportion of the overall labour force in the early nineteenth century, and in France an even smaller group. Yet factory work represented, for many social observers, the essence of the social changes taking place, with the cotton factory as the prime example of the kind of regular, full-time, disciplined labour in which women were employed for the first time. But women had been, and still were, called upon to work in some expanding areas of 'heavy' industry. Such work, especially women's work underground in the coal mines, was in some ways anachronistic, almost part of the domestic system of industry rather than exemplifying any new pattern of work. This employment, although primarily affecting small numbers of women in certain areas in Britain, raises interesting questions about attitudes to women's work in this period. The Mines Act of 1842 represented the first gender-based protective legislation enforced by the state, and was an Act supported both by groups of miners and by sections of employers – but it was primarily the responsibility of the state. Before 1842 women were employed only in certain mines, mainly those of eastern Scotland and Wales and northern England, where they worked mostly in the transport of coal as 'hurriers' rather than directly as hewers of coal. Their employment depended on the type of mining, the availability of labour in the area, and the degree of capitalisation of the mine. Their wages were usually regarded as part of a family wage, especially where the majority worked, in eastern Scotland. Jane Humphries has argued strongly that working men's support for such legislation cannot be interpreted either in terms of fear of female competition, given the existing sexual division of labour, or as the result of patriarchal control within the family, since this was never threatened. Rather, it was the type of work available to women that was attacked, criticised by miners themselves as well as by scandalised politicians. The *Report* of 1842, which set out the horrific conditions of women's work, though intended only to deal with children's labour, stressed not so much the effect of such hard labour on women's maternal roles, as the moral and sexual improprieties of the work, as well as the lack of domestic training received by miners' wives. The state, sharing the interest of employers in a regulated and efficient labour force, and sharing also common cultural assumptions about the 'natural' role of women, was prepared to control the conditions of labour for those who, for the first time, were judged not to be independent agents in the market place. From a different tradition, and from their own experience, miners, possibly affected by evangelical religious beliefs as well, generally supported the change, though they and their families were to be quite seriously financially affected. Some women, especially the younger, stronger women, were not so prepared to accept the financial loss involved, and evasion remained widespread in the 1840s.[48] There was no similar tradition of underground work in French coal mines. Where, as in the mines of the Nord and the Pas-de-Calais, women and girls were to be found as haulers, the practice had been introduced by Belgian miners, and declined, without state intervention, in the course of the Second Empire. Women might still, however, customarily undertake certain kinds of heavy manual labour, such as the women porters of Toulon and Marseilles.[49] In other important and new areas of heavy industry – in iron works, in engineering workshops – women nowhere played a significant part.

Protective legislation, both for women and for children, was, however, very relevant to the new textile factories. Throughout the first half of the nineteenth century, some workshops still continued merely to centralise processes undertaken by hand under one roof. But the first symbol of the new industrial world was of course the spinning mill which went with the new machines for preparatory work such as carding and roving, which in Britain were appearing in Lancashire from the 1780s, and elsewhere, more slowly from the 1790s. The majority of those employed in the early spinning mills were men but children's labour was also much in demand (except in the early worsted mills). But the mechanisation of weaving which was slowly, throughout this period, established in the cotton, woollen and worsted trades, brought women workers, deprived first of spinning, then of handloom weaving, into the factories, which still varied greatly in scale and organisation. There is evidence to suggest that in some early factories the family organisation of labour still persisted, as long as the scale of machinery used permitted. The extent of this is still not clear, however.[50] Increasingly, the mills came to employ young single women, with a minority of poorer, married women, mostly as powerloom weavers, or in the preparatory processes such as carding. The nature of women's employment in these new factories, so far away from the boundaries of domestic life, aroused the passionate, if ambiguous, concern of philanthropists and middle-class legislators and observers. Nevertheless, in spite of often miserable working conditions, such factories were likely to contain the best paid working-class women, the most likely to share in the organisation of their male colleagues.

There are significant differences, however, between the workforces of these early mills, in the three different societies. In the United

States, in the early stages of industrialisation women went from the farms of New England, from parents with a solid stake in the land, to fill the years before their marriage, to send money home to aid the family economy, to earn for their own future education, or for their dowry. For the great majority of these young women, their earnings, though useful and affording some independence, were not a necessity. Thomas Dublin's study of the Hamilton Company's workforce at Lowell suggested that well over 90 per cent of women workers were single, and that the few exceptions were without children. He has commented that such patterns of work and orientation to the family economy, are 'strikingly different' from those found in Europe at the same time.[51] Louise Tilly and Joan Scott have pointed out that in France daughters were sent to work by their families, and frequently turned over all or part of their earnings directly to their family.[52] In England too a daughter's earnings could greatly assist, even play a critical part in, the family economy. Young women dominated the labour force. In the census of 1851 the proportion of married or widowed cotton operatives was 24 per cent in Blackburn, 18 per cent in Burnley, 29 per cent in Preston – on average, around a quarter of the female workforce. Nevertheless, the individual wages of the young woman worker in France or England could still eventually, especially after a time away from home, allow a degree of independence or at least a position of strength within the family. For the minority of married women who worked in the mills, normally from family necessity, when a husband's wages were low or there were no other family members to contribute, assistance from relatives, or lodgers, in childcare and looking after the house was necessary. But the very existence of the mills, and women's employment in them, created large numbers of casual domestic jobs – washing, cleaning, teamaking – more likely to be the married woman's first resort.[53]

The vital question that remains is one which observers and historians have debated, from Engels to Pinchbeck: whether participation in factory production, receiving a regular wage sufficient for subsistence, constantly associating with other workers, provided the most obvious route for working women to attain a degree of independence. The contrary view, that put by Tilly and Scott, is that such labour was undertaken for traditional reasons, in the family interest, and might simply mean residence in closely supervised boarding accommodation, as in Lowell, Massachusetts, or the convents of southern France, where women silk workers lived, rather than achieving any kind of autonomy. The history of women's unionism in the textile trades after mechanisation offers only confused guidance.

In the United States women workers in the New England textile factories did, in the 1830s and 1840s, forge new bonds of solidarity, based on their work experience, their communal living conditions and their reaction to the growing labour movement. Their response, however, was not initially to form a part of a wider trade union movement, but a series of strikes in protest against changing conditions, both in those states where whole families were employed together in the mills, and in those operating the 'Lowell' system. From 1824 to 1836 at least twelve strikes took place in textile factories, in which women were the main participants.[54] Few were successful. The first occurred in 1824 in Pawtucket, Rhode Island, when around 100 female weavers joined with male workers to protest at increased hours and reduced wages, meeting separately from the men. The first all-women strike took place at the Cocheco mill in Dover, New Hampshire, in December 1828 against the attempt to impose a new and exceedingly strict list of regulations. The strikes of the 1830s were to be on a much larger scale. In 1834 some 800 women workers at Lowell 'turned out' or left work to oppose a reduction in piece rates. Many meetings and processions followed, and at one rally the *Boston Evening Transcript* reported: 'We are told that one of the leaders mounted a pump and made a flaming Mary Woolstonecraft [sic] speech on the rights of women and the iniquities of the *"monied* aristocracy" which produced a powerful effect on her auditors, and they determined "to have their own way if they died for it" '.[55]

In their rhetoric the women of Lowell, well educated and from a rural farming background, clearly identified with the revolutionary and republican tradition as 'daughters of freemen'. They defended their economic independence, which seemed threatened: yet behind their defence lay also the assumption that for them such labour was not ultimately necessary for support – they could always return to their parental farms. That strike was followed by a not dissimilar one of 1836, when between a third and a quarter of the workforce came out, revealing much more effective organisation in the Factory Girls Association. Dublin's detailed analyses of these movements suggest the important factors underlying their success: solidarity, a sense of sisterhood functioning rather like the common bonds of a craft among skilled artisans, and their own values of independence and republicanism, which made them respond strongly to threats to their own wellbeing. Circumstances enabled revolutionary rhetoric to survive even within the cotton mills.

These strikes were to give way to a new and more developed labour movement, as the 1840s saw the decline in prosperity of New England agriculture, and an almost permanent agitation directed towards the Ten Hour Day. The factory operatives of Lowell, Manchester, Dover and Waltham were to form the first trade unions of women working in factories, the Female Labour Reform Association, led by such women as Sarah G. Bagley, Huldah Stone and Mehitabel Eastman. Formed in 1845, the new association springing from the campaign for the Ten Hour Day worked with the New England Working Men's Association. Sarah Bagley, in speaking before them, declared:

> For the last half century, it has been deemed a violation of woman's sphere to appear before the public as a speaker, but when our rights are trampled upon, and we appeal, in vain, to legislators, what shall we do but appeal to the people?[56]

She was elected as vice-president of the Working Men's Association. Throughout the 1840s the campaign continued, through petitions and strikes, though it never saw success, since a ten-hour day was not recognised in Massachusetts until 1874. But it has been compared to other campaigns among women, those for moral reform and for the abolition of slavery, in bringing about a unity among women, committed to the same end, and in raising the question of 'woman's sphere'. The periodicals of Lowell, and the speeches of women organisers, reflect this broadening of concerns. 'An Operative' wrote in the *Voice of Industry* in 1847:

> Woman is never thought to be out of her *sphere* at home; in the nursery, in the kitchen, over a hot stove cooking from morning till evening – over a wash-tub, or toiling in a cotton factory 14 hours per day. But let her once step out, plead the cause of right and humanity, plead the wrongs of her slave sister of the South or of the operative of the North, or even attempt to teach the science of Physiology, and a cry is raised against her, '*of out of her sphere*'.[57]

It is interesting that work even in a cotton factory is here equated with womanly duties, though any entry into the public sphere lies outside them. The concern of these textile operatives did stretch beyond their own industry. Sarah Bagley and Eliza Hemingway, another operative, became involved in the movement for consumer co-operatives throughout New England. The Lowell appeal to all working women in America, though the work of such individual leaders and the circulation of the *Voice of Industry*, led to the formation of Female Labour Reform Associations in the other mill towns of New England and western Pennsylvania. In a series of articles in 1845, the *Voice of Industry* publicised the condition of women workers in New York, especially seamstresses, and wrote with interest of the foundation of the Female Industrial Association of New York, which included representatives of almost all the women's trades. Yet by the late 1840s the campaign had lost its impetus, though the Pennsylvania movement retained its militancy, and there the ten-hour day was in fact achieved in 1848. Of course, not all the workers at Lowell shared this outlook. Many of those who wrote in the *Lowell Offering*, the rival to the *Voice of Industry*, did not, and defended both loyalty to one's employer and a subordinate relationship between men and women. The great majority of women in the mills, 85 per cent of Dublin's sample, married, as they must have expected to do, after completing their years of employment.[58]

Nevertheless, factory employment did seem to bring women together, and while challenging their conditions of employment, they also came to challenge the assumed narrowness of women's sphere. Though these women had so far breached convention as to speak before a committee of the Massachusetts state legislature, they sent no delegates to the vital Woman's Rights Convention at Seneca Falls in 1848, and their grievances formed no part of the agenda of that convention. Yet in reading the Declaration of Sentiments issued by the women there, the *Factory Girls' Voice* declared: 'We rejoice in that convention as a significant indication of the tendencies of this age'.[59] It is worth considering why the Lowell experience was so distinctive; and under what conditions such participation in large-scale production could lead to a questioning, a broadening of women's role, if not a radical challenge to it. First, it is clear that the Lowell experience was brief. The new conditions of labour in the New England mills in the 1850s and 1860s did not permit the same kind of organisation. Irish immigration transformed the labour force, as a result both of declining demand from native-born women and of the scale of immigration. The new women employees worked with a higher proportion of men, were more diversified in age, included more married women and younger women living with their families and, of course, they had no alternative economic resources. It would be untrue to say that militancy entirely disappeared: but women's participation in the ten-hours movement of the 1850s was greatly reduced in the rank and file, and entirely gone in the leadership. The strikes of 1859 did, however, include women workers, both native and immigrant. But the older basis for militant unity, among native-born New England women, had gone, though perhaps a rather similar response can be seen from the women shoebinders of Lynn, in their strike against the mechanisation of their industry in 1860.[60]

In the 1830s and 1840s, there can surely be no doubt that, without romanticising the work of these women, the conditions and rewards of labour were far better at Lowell than they were for the weavers of Lancashire or of the Nord. The comparison should be instructive. In Lancashire there were some signs of women's industrial action but also, from the very early stages, a well organised male labour force. There were no parallels to the boarding houses of Lowell for the daughters of Lancashire countrymen who came with their families to Oldham or Preston, possibly, initially, to work together in those family units. Before the 1830s women did occasionally participate in strike action in Lancashire, as in the cotton spinners' strike of 1818, and that of the powerloom weavers which followed it in the same year. But those who had received equal strike pay in that year were nevertheless excluded from the union immediately afterwards.[61] Women were excluded from the associations formed by the skilled male mule spinners, the aristocracy of the mills, most notoriously by the cotton spinners' union founded in 1829 by John Docherty, and afterwards. Lancashire women factory workers took little part in the movements of 1833–4. Though there are a few examples of women participating in union action in these early decades, the shift was to come with the considerable expansion of powerloom weaving which took place between 1830 and 1845, notably in the cotton industry, much more gradually elsewhere. In cotton, and in worsted weaving, women quickly outnumbered men, though not in the woollen trades. In these years, there are some indications of increased industrial activity among women. In 1833 Glasgow women spinners and powerloom weavers combined in an effort to achieve parity with male piece rates, holding a meeting of over 1000 women. Women winders organised unions in Hamilton, Airdrie and Irvine in October 1836.[62]

In May 1833, the *Leeds Mercury* condemned a display of female independence by female combers demanding higher rates. In 1838, women weavers protested against poor pay and warped looms in Bradford, leaving their work at Brand's mill unfinished.[63]

By the 1840s women in factories were more numerous and more prominent in industrial protests. In Stockport, in 1840, women throstle spinners went on strike, as did in April some 4000 powerloom weavers, mainly women. At a mass meeting a Mrs Wrigley is reported to have addressed the 1800 or so women present: 'The women were the majority of the weavers, and if they would stick true to their cause they would succeed'. Yet on the whole they were active in the crowds that appeared in the demonstrations of the 1840s as secondary supporters rather than as principal participants. In the Plug Plot riots of 1842, for example, their presence, in force, in crowds and turn-outs was recorded, but they clearly played no part in the deliberations of their leaders. They might taunt soldiers, police and blacklegs, sing and march; but the representatives of the spinners, the weavers and the cardroom hands who deliberated on future action were all men.[64]

The participation of women in Britain in the ten-hours campaign was again rather different. In Yorkshire, from the beginning, women helped to organise the movement under Richard Oastler's leadership, and 'the tears, the smiles, the songs, the vows of the women and children' are said to have made those meetings unique. But as a campaign its force was directed initially, from 1830, against the long hours worked by children, and the impression left is that women participated rather as the mothers of families than in any attempt to improve their own conditions of work. And the ambiguity of that movement, aiming partly to relieve intolerable conditions of labour, partly at the limitation of the cheap, competitive labour of women and children, is borne out in the indifference, even hostility, of Lancashire women workers to that movement.[65] In the agitation surrounding the Ten Hours Act of 1847, 'Elizabeth' of Todmorden wrote to complain of the 'apathy that is manifested by my sex generally', calling for women to see themselves as workers, and to consider the possibility that shorter hours might be advantageous for them. Male spinners still dominated the movement, though in its aftermath, in 1848–9, women appear to have been prominent in attempting to resist relay and shift systems introduced by employers to evade the legislation. Both men and women workers were, by now, ambiguous as to whether women should identify themselves, as workers, with the union movement, or whether they should see their ultimate goal as withdrawal from the factory.[66] In a dispute in Preston in 1853 women workers, including women delegates of the union, themselves supported the withdrawal of married women from work, and the payment of wages sufficiently high for married men to support their families. But, nevertheless, it was among powerloom weavers, first in Lancashire and on the Clyde, and then in Yorkshire, that women's involvement in trade unions was first to grow. In 1853, the Blackburn Association of Cotton Weavers, Warpers and Winders was the first to negotiate successfully a district price list for weaving. By the 1870s that spirit had spread to Yorkshire: but its results were not to be apparent in the period discussed here. By the 1840s and 1850s the militancy of the dying trades still provided some impetus, as in the Nottingham lacerunners' strike of 1840. Yet most women did not associate together as workers in this period. In an important article Dorothy Thompson has remarked on that retreat from radicalism which is apparent among working-class women in the late 1840s.[67] Unmarried women, working together, with above average wages, were most likely under the right circumstances to defend their own position as workers and to join a union. Married women identified with their families' need, their own position redefined as within an unproductive domestic sphere in the eyes of the state and the dominant classes. They might still join the protests of their husbands or their communities, but they were increasingly more likely to withdraw from that public arena into the daily struggle against the dual burden of paid and unpaid work, in isolation.

In France, the same pattern is even more apparent. In the new factories young women predominated. After the failure of the associations of 1848, the political climate of the 1850s did not permit the formation of trade unions as such, but friendly societies, or *sociétés de secours mutuels* continued to grow. Women's part was, however, small, often because they were deliberately excluded. In 1860, of a total membership of 473,000 just under 70,000 were women. Sometimes the conditions of membership were inferior, as in one Rouen association, where the subscriptions were higher and privileges fewer for women. Some women had consequently formed their own organisations, and in 1860 there were just under 140 such societies, with about 12,000 members, some probably initiated by philanthropists.[68] In the late nineteenth century, there is no doubt that, as elsewhere, women textile workers were to be in the forefront of women's trade union organisation: but there were few signs of this by mid-century. No protective legislation affected women's work in France in this period. Conditions of work might be, as in northern France, similar to those in Britain. But they might also reflect a different, and distinctively paternalist, attitude to the workforce by employers. In Mulhouse, the new city designed for the workers incorporated homes for families and houses set aside as lodgings for single workers, austere dormitories, as Jules Simon describes them. In the silk mills of rural south-eastern France, young girls working away from home might move into 'industrial convents', supervised by nuns, where conditions were strictly regulated by the terms of apprenticeship contracts. By the end of the 1850s some 40,000 young women were employed in these factories.[69] For both political and economic reasons, women workers were unlikely to associate together in mid-nineteenth-century France. There too married women, still engaged in a wide range of domestic and casual occupations, were more likely to identify their interests with those of family or community than the industrial workforce.

Yet, numerically, the most important occupation for women in this period did not lie within the productive sphere at all: domestic service, sometimes including farm service, was the most likely option for young girls on first leaving home in all three societies. In France, England and the United States, domestic service in this period saw a rapid expansion continuing well beyond the 1850s. It was a period of rapid urban growth, of significant and continuing migration from the countryside to the towns, and a rising standard of living among the middle and lower middle classes. The latter was reflected in the number of household manuals published, for servants and for mistresses, and in the constantly increasing demand for servants, both from the wealthiest households looking for special skills – housekeeper, childrens' nurse, parlourmaid, laundrymaid – or artisan or tradesman's families, looking for a maid-of-all-work. There is much discussion among historians about the contribution of the widespread employment of young peasant or working-class girls to the spread of middle-class aspirations and notions of domesticity.[70] It is indeed plausible to see such employment as one means of channelling views about domesticity and family relationships: though to be receptive to such views, a family would require a small surplus income, with a stable, assured wage coming in. The question is an important one, and will be discussed in the next chapter. Yet the dominance of domestic service among female occupations may also be seen as indicating the lack of alternative occupations. In England in 1851, 40 per cent of the female labour force was employed in domestic service, in France in 1856 22 per cent (the difference is largely accounted for by the higher proportion of Frenchwomen engaged in agriculture). However, the number of women employed as domestic servants varied greatly with local economies. In a wealthy, urban environment, with no textile industry, the majority of young women would be likely to enter domestic service: as in York, where in 1851 they made up almost 60 per cent of the female labour force, according to the census. One analysis of the census pointed to the fact that where in Leeds only 1 in 14 women over 20 were in domestic service, and in Birmingham, 1 in 11, in Bath that figure was 1 in 4, and in London 1 in 6.[71] Service could mean more personal mobility for women, a way of becoming accustomed to life in an urban environment, away from one's family. Yet it also meant life in a disciplined, controlled environment, with long hours of labour, and a wage often to be sent back to one's family. It meant work in the often isolated conditions of the individual household. Though there is the isolated example of the Edinburgh Maidservants' Union Society which in 1825 issued a broadside threatening to strike against unfair conditions, most associations among servants were the result of philanthropic initiatives by middle-class employers. Census figures moreover must distort the real extent of domestic labour among women: for married women throughout the nineteenth century, part-time, casual and irregular domestic work – laundrywork, charring, ironing, sewing – were the staple resource, with some street selling and trading, and of the scope of this we have very little indication. Henry Mayhew, however, recorded its fundamental importance for the poor of mid-nineteenth-century London, when he wrote, for example, of the dock labourer's wife who 'has 3s a week for washing, charring and mangling', and of many more, whose work depended on their own skills but also on the location and seasonality of their husband's job.[72]

The poor position of such workers in the labour market is emphasised by the groups from which domestic servants were largely drawn in the United States. The majority of free black working women were likely to do some kind of domestic work. An 1859 survey of Philadelphia suggested that over 80 per cent of black working women were domestic servants. No black women worked in the

*by little formal organisation
else out work women's work important
to family*

182   THE ORIGINS OF MODERN FEMINISM

cotton mills of Philadelphia or New England though there were several thousand slave women in factories in the South. No black women participated in the new unions.[73] Immigrant women also similarly found domestic service the most accessible occupation. In 1845 the *New York Daily Tribune* estimated that of 10,000–12,000 young women in domestic service in the city, 7000–8000 were Irish and about 2000 German. Horace Greeley commented in the same newspaper in 1846: 'when Yankee girls, nine-tenths prefer to encounter the stunning din, the imperfect ventilation, monotonous labor, and excessive hours of a cotton factory in preference to doing housework, be sure the latter is not yet what it should be'.[74] The choice, for those who had it, was not an unusual one.

The economic situation for working women was therefore by the 1850s one of considerable confusion. For the majority, especially married women workers, work was poorly paid, unskilled, irregular – but essential to their own and their families' wellbeing. Such qualities might make their continuing employment on those terms all too enticing – for the entrepreneurs in the 'sweated trades' of the great cities of the western world. But technological changes were also slowly, but inevitably, overtaking the advantages which domestic industry had to offer, and for many in the old-established trades the prospects of paid employment at home were steadily decreasing. Women working in factories, mostly younger unmarried women, though slowly learning the language of association, were not yet by the 1850s ready to take the steps which the Lowell mill girls had dared to do. The links between feminism and the growth of organisation among working-class women are difficult to trace and await much further research, as will have been apparent. But on the evidence available to us, it would seem that in the early nineteenth century the conditions of women's work, like those of the great majority of unskilled male workers, did not encourage formal organisation, though the hardships of early industrial capitalism brought women, like men, to protest at the worst times against their political and economic impotence. The differing interests of men and women workers could create a defensive reaction among women, who were aware of the conflict yet needed to defend their livelihood; but women's movements were likely to be at their strongest when there was co-operation between men and women.

1. A British satire on the Parisian women's march to Versailles in October 1789 (Note 1).

2. The conservative Edmund Burke, scourged by radicals, women as well as men, including, from left to right, Helen Maria Williams, Mrs Barbauld, the female figure of Justice and Liberty (wearing the cap of liberty) and Catherine Macaulay (Note 2).

3. Millet, *The Angelus* (1855–57).

4. The monthly meeting of the women Quakers of Houndsditch, 1843.

5. 'The Scotch Cottage of Glenburnie', an illustration to the novel by Elizabeth Hamilton, showing the reaction of visitors to the domestic conditions of this Scottish household (Note 3).

6. Daumier, *The Washerwomen of the Quai d'Anjou* (1850/2).

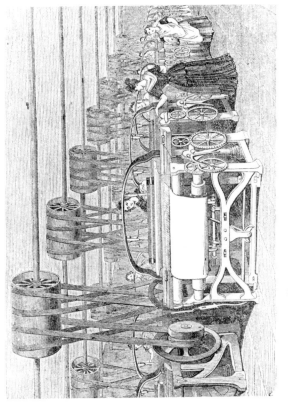

7. Women powerloom weavers in 1844.

8. Delacroix, *Liberty Guiding the People* (1830).

9. Attack on the workhouse at Stockport, 1842.

10. A coarse satire on the Female Reform Societies of 1819 (Note 4).

11. Peterloo, showing a woman carrying the banner of the Manchester Female Reform Society on the platform with Henry Hunt, and women attacked by the yeomanry (Note 5).

12. 'Bravo, Bravo, that's even finer than Jeanne Deroin's last speech', from
Daumier's series, *The Women Socialists* (1849).

NEW DEMANDS AND NEW JOBS

However, links between feminism and occupational changes can also be traced in the ways in which middle-class women came to understand and, to some extent, to identify with, the problems of working women. From the 1790s onwards, Mary Wollstonecraft and others like her had lamented the loss of traditional female areas of work to male expertise or capital, or professional skill: millinery, bookbinding, brewing, hairdressing.[75] A key example, one raising unique issues, was the job of the midwife, whose position at the higher levels of society was threatened with the growth of professional medical education from the early eighteenth century. With the professionalisation of medicine came the continuing, eventually successful efforts of doctors to regulate and supervise midwives, whose skills might (or might not) be considerable, but who received no formal training. *The Lancet* wrote, in 1841, that:

> With regard to the advocacy of midwives, the women of England are, happily for their sons, wholly deficient both in the moral and physical organisation necessary for performing the duties of that most responsible office.[76]

Jean Donnison has most effectively described the complexity of the conflicts of the nineteenth century, as obstetrics became a respectable, even exclusive, branch of medicine, and as midwives themselves called for a Female College for proper training to be given. The question was not to be resolved in this period, though Florence Nightingale attempted briefly to set up a school for midwives in 1861, which failed because of an outbreak of puerperal fever. The majority of women in the country were still probably only attended, if at all, by a midwife in childbirth.

There was not merely regret for past 'traditional' occupations, but also, clearly, demand for new kinds of employment. In the earlier part of the period, that demand might be seen in terms of small-scale crafts and trades. Priscilla Wakefield's list of 1798 included, among jobs that could be done by both sexes, watchmaking, retail stationery, pastry and confectionery making, toymaking, the management of public houses, pharmacy and farming.[77] But by the 1840s and 1850s the extent of the demand for work from both working and middle-class women and the existence of a glut of female labour, were clearly understood – the evidence lay in the conditions of work of governesses and needlewomen. Women were constrained both by industrial changes and by cultural limitations in the work that they might undertake. By 1859 Harriet Martineau could write of the 'jealousy of men' for the 'industrial independence' of women. Her article, 'Female Industry', in the *Edinburgh Review* was remarkable for its direct, historical and realistic discussion of the problems of women's employment. She drew upon the work of feminist Barbara Leigh Smith, *Women and Work* (1857) and the important study by John Duguid Milne, *The Industrial and Social Position of Women in the Middle and Lower Ranks* (1857), and her argument was for the ending of that 'artificial depreciation' of women's work, caused by the assumption that women were primarily dependent on fathers and husbands for financial support. Half a million 'surplus' women, the single and the widowed, would not be supported; already, more than two million women, out of six million over 20, worked for their living. Martineau's case ultimately rested on fair, unfettered competition for women's labour in the market-place. Though the case was well put, certain ambiguities still remained.[78]

For the essentially liberal feminists of Britain in the 1850s, the answer to the expanding demand for work lay both in a better education for women and in new kinds of occupations. Such arguments were not new: Anna Jameson, Harriet Taylor Mill and others had pointed the way.[79] Leigh Smith suggested shopwork, book-keeping, medicine, clerical work, telegraphy, art and design, as appropriate jobs. The columns of the *English Woman's Journal* were to add, enthusiastically, more and more occupations to that list: wood engraving, watchmaking, hairdressing, architecture, piano-tuning, 'sanitary teaching', and even attendants in the British Museum Reading Room! The list, which was more seriously to stress the importance of nursing and all kinds of charitable work, lay significantly almost entirely within the expanding service sectors of the economy.[80] Such feminists could not, and did not, escape all contemporary assumptions about the nature of women and the domestic orientation of women who married: the latter question could not be actively challenged. Their case still tended to rest on the occupations thought *appropriate* to women. Their concerns can be seen in the work of the new National Association for Promoting the Social Sciences, and in the pages of the *English Woman's Journal*. The NAPSS, which tended to reflect a fashionable philanthropy, had by 1857 set up a committee on the employment of women. In 1859 the Earl of Shaftesbury, when opening the annual conference of the society, offered a classic definition of the work to be deemed suitable:

> the instant that the work becomes minute, individual and personal; the instant that it leaves the open field and touches the home; the instant that it requires tact, sentiment and delicacy; from that instant it passes into the hands of women.

At the same meeting, Fanny Hertz distinguished between the 'natural' barriers to women's work and those created by prejudice – which she hoped, in this 'higher phase of social excellence' would be overcome.[81] That cultural problem of the distinction between the 'natural' and the artificial was to remain a critical one for the feminists of 1860. And though they were aware of them, they chose not to avail themselves of the very much bolder arguments by John Duguid Milne, whose work put a strong case for the participation of middle-class women not only in such service-oriented occupations, but in productive industry itself, first in minor salaried offices, then in the highest positions. Such an entry into industry would not only mean a greater sharing of interests with middle-class men, but it would also improve the situation of working-class women, offering them a model for their aspirations and encouraging their own self-improvement and mobility. But such an uncompromising statement of the middle-class ethic, applied to the situation of women, was uncongenial: in its radicalism it remains worthy of comparison with the much better known study by John Stuart Mill, *The Subjection of Women.*[82]

Through the inspiration of Jessie Boucherett, and active and enthusiastic supporter of Leigh Smith, and initially under the patronage of the NAPSS, the Society for Promoting the Employment of Women was founded in 1859. That society, run by the 'ladies of Langham Place' where both the Society and the *Journal* had their offices, together with a few local branches, launched a series of pilot projects to train women for fields in which they were not currently employed. A printing press, the Victoria Press, was established by women trained as compositors, and ran successfully. Maria Rye (who was also to advocate and put into practice the defeatist remedy of emigration for single women) set up a law stationer's office staffed by women. Jessie Boucherett organised classes in clerical and commercial subjects. Wherever possible, they advocated the entry of women into the medical profession, into which Elizabeth Blackwell had shown the way. They saw their work as merely exemplifying what might be done: 'the rest remains to be accomplished by the real impetus of the movement: namely its necessity, its justice, and its expediency'.[83] The *English Woman's Journal* compared the prejudices against women's employment to the irrationality of religious taboos:

> custom and prejudice are at work to exclude us from earning a living: here we contend, and will not cease to contend, is a great evil. There are innumerable employments for which women are fitted: there are but few from which they are not excluded.[84]

The theory was brave but the practice, of necessity, limited. The demand was still as yet very small for women's employment in the service sector of the economy. But throughout the second half of the nineteenth century, and indeed until the present day, it was steadily to grow, offering new kinds of employment to both working-class and middle-class women. These feminists of the mid-nineteenth century, though identifying most closely with the single, educated women, were well aware that the oversupply of women's labour affected all classes, equally subject to wage differentials based upon sex. Their case was for the expansion of available labour and for the lowering of barriers to women's employment: their problem, though it could not have been identified, that both their own instincts and the demands of the market were directed towards a new kind of womanly work – work for which women especially were fitted, work which offered a new way of extending the sexual division of labour into the capitalist economy. The expansion of teaching by women, the foundation in 1860 of the Nightingale School for Nurses, the new department stores employing young women assistants, all were signs of the future, in which young women would find employment in new, but equally 'natural', jobs.[85]

In the aftermath of 1848 in France, feminist activities were necessarily limited. Jeanne Deroin and Desirée Gay, in exile, had no immediate successors. Observers of women's employment such as Jules Simon, whose important work *L'Ouvrière* was published in 1861, saw women's future as being primarily, and desirably, in the home. Individual feminists continued to attempt to meet such strongly held male views, in socialist, republican and liberal circles alike. There were exceptions. Elisa Lemonnier founded the Society for the Professional Education of Women and the first of her vocational schools in 1862, to meet girls' need for technical training for commerce or industry. Julie-Victoire Daubié, in 1861 the first woman to earn the *baccalauréat*, published, five years later, her work *La femme pauvre au XIXe siècle*, a valuable contribution to the study of women's work which clearly identified the demand for employment among women of all classes, and the need for opening up new areas of employment, especially in public employment – railways, the post office, administration – and in paid and unpaid philanthropic work.[86] In the United States there was relatively little writing or organisation around the theme of women's employment, though there was to be so after the Civil War. The demand for a married woman's right to her own earnings, and for a much wider range of occupations to be open to women, still clearly figured in the debates of the women's rights conventions. In Rochester in 1848, Sarah Owen spoke of the condition of needlewomen, and of the monopoly of most occupations by men, praising the initiative of Elizabeth Blackwell in opening up the field of medicine.[87] Caroline Healey Dall, an active member of this American movement and editor of the feminist newspaper, *Una*, and organiser of several Boston conventions, in 1860 published the text of three lectures given in Boston on '*Women's Right to Labour*': or, Low Wages and Hard Work. In this she was clearly influenced by English feminists, by Anna Jameson to whom she dedicated her work, and by the information from the *English Woman's Journal*. Like that *Journal* she claimed free access to employment, unfettered by 'the laws and customs that cripple women', to the extent of driving women from the overstocked market for needlewomen on to the street as prostitutes. But it was not merely new kinds of occupations that were needed, but ability and self-confidence among women to take up new jobs, and an end to prejudice against such employment:

> When men respect women as human beings, consequently as labourers, they will pay them as good wages as men; and then uncommon skill or power to work will be set free from the old forcing-pump and siphon, and we shall see what women can do.[88]

The conditions of early industrial capitalism did not favour association among women at the workplace, except in exceptional circumstances. They had little industrial strength. Yet they might, and did, protest on their own behalf and for their families, at their

work, changing ... were important feminist thinking

treatment by employers. Michelle Perrot has emphasised how women working together might use informal, but powerful weapons – ridicule, songs, gossip – and how, in urban life as well as in the countryside they were able to draw upon a rich tradition of collective action, direct, spontaneous and based on the life of the neighbour-hood, the *quartier*.[89] Such direct action, reflecting the relationship between household, workplace and community, was still very much a feature of French life in the first half of the nineteenth century, and was carried into new urban worlds, even as the relationship between domestic and paid labour was being redefined. Perhaps, in Britain, that retreat from collective action among working-class women noted by Dorothy Thompson did mark a greater dislocation between public and private worlds – or between workplace and community – in a society increasingly more urbanised than that of France. In the United States, it is not clear that such a basis for collective action among working-class women or those in rural communities did exist in the same way: if so it was probably in long-established craft communities like Lynn, Massachusetts. Yet these themes have to be explored not only from the perspective of the workplace – the modern perspective – but also from that domestic framework which shaped the lives and thinking of the great majority of women.

Only among the important minority of women who worked in the new factories might the conditions of industrial militancy exist, and those conditions and the rewards, even then, were rarely sufficient in this period. But the demand for work, and the circumstances of women's work, were nevertheless continuing and important factors in the generation of feminist thinking. For those allied in the 1830s and 1840s to different kinds of co-operation, especially in France and England, socialism on a small scale could offer the opportunity to reorganise women's work, perhaps even to recognise their particular needs. But such movements were doomed, as their strength, especially among artisans, decayed. In Britain, liberal feminists identified the barriers to wider employment that imposed low wages upon women, in the artificial construction of 'women's work'. Yet, caught between principle and realism, they had little choice but to offer a different version of 'women's work', one which was far broader, but which also, in the last resort, derived from a particular view of women. The principles of political economy, of free and unfettered competition, co-existed uneasily with that domestic framework which still shaped so much feminist thinking.

6. Domestic Questions

THE domestic focus of women's lives, to be narrowly limited to home and family, was justified and given ideological unity in the nineteenth century by a range of arguments, resting on women's nature, on God's ordinances, on the evidence of past and present societies, which have already been outlined. Common reactions to women's employment outside the home in the early nineteenth century – the descriptions, for example, of Dr Gaskell of Manchester life, of Louis Villermé of the French working classes, of Jules Simon on women's work – draw not only upon humanitarian feeling but upon these arguments. Yet the changing realities of domestic life – the availability of piped water, the quality of housing, the existence of a maid-of-all-work – can tell us as much about private life as the assumptions of observers. The changing balance between paid and unpaid labour within the home, the possibility of migrating to a new urban environment and its material conditions, technological changes and the creation of a home-based consumer demand: more detailed study of these areas may well suggest how far women did in fact retreat within the domestic sphere in this period. But these issues, especially those relating to the conditions of domestic life, remain much neglected questions.

What is relevant here is the extent to which the conditions of domestic life brought women together, in shared identifiable concerns, in work, in protest. Twentieth-century assumptions about the 'separation' of domestic life from the public sphere may well blind us to a different pattern of separation in the nineteenth century, one which depended on long-established popular beliefs, and patterns of work and behaviour. The most distinguished recent study of rural life in nineteenth-century France has stressed that in the peasant household, while labour was not entirely segregated, the focus of women's work lay within the house, yet 'it is the exterior extension of their domestic tasks which takes women out of their houses', and brought together the women of the village, to work and socialise together. Similarly, Perrot stressed the militancy and collective participation of urban women, used to working together, in forms of urban protest most related to the subsistence of the household.[1] Some examples of such protests by women within their community, taking part, often a leading part, in its defence, have already been noted: protests against the erosion of the communal rights of villagers in France, against enclosure in Britain, and against large-scale evictions in the Highlands of Scotland. Women's participation in bread riots is still very much in evidence in mid-nineteenth-century France. The importance of local customs in dictating the shape of household life can be seen too, in a number of ways: in the different patterns of household relationships in Provençal and northern France, for instance, or in the extent of 'free unions' among urban men and women, rather than the use of legal marriage ceremonies. Such customary patterns might be imported also, as immigrants from Ireland did to the United States. Their survival depended on both material and cultural factors. The question of the effectiveness of a specific and heightened ideology of domesticity was also that of the penetration of a dominant culture: there were many different barriers, for the mid-western farmers of the United States, the peasants of the Massif Central or the Scottish Highlands, the urban masses of Lille and Manchester, the Irish immigrants to London, Liverpool, New York, Boston. Language, illiteracy and the depths of poverty could all be impenetrable obstacles.

Domesticity could both limit and broaden horizons. Feminists of the early nineteenth century attacked the sacrifice of selfhood which was required; they identified the legal and economic framework of marriage as deeply oppressive remnants of a past feudal world. Yet on the whole they did not attack the view that women's maternal responsibilities, where they existed, should be primary. Many, like John Stuart Mill, shared the view that women would probably choose to remain within a domestic environment, but that they should have the freedom to choose such a life, and the possibility of independence outside it.[2] For working women such a choice did not exist: for them the prospect of domesticity could represent a higher standard of living, a chance of a better life for all members of the family, an end to an economy of casual makeshifts and irregular work, to be made possible only by the higher and more secure wages of men. Still, such identification with their families' interest could, in the circumstances of urban migration and poverty, lead them to participate in the protest movements of the early industrial age not less than in the countryside.[3]

DOMESTIC MYTHS AND DOMESTIC REALITIES

There is much to suggest that the sexual division of labour for the great majority of rural and urban women, and the elevated concept of 'domesticity', which had such meaning for the upper and middle classes, failed to coincide at all for much of this period. The central responsibilities of married women remained the fundamental domestic ones: caring for children, fetching water, cooking, washing and cleaning for the household. But such tasks, far from being private, individual ones, undertaken within the home as a refuge from the outside world, were impossible within the strictly limited resources of most working peoples' homes, and were as likely to be dependent on communal resources, and undertaken with other women. The fetching of water was one of the most fundamental of daily tasks for both urban and rural women throughout this period: it remains largely unacknowledged work by historians, though it was essential to the life of the household. Water might be fetched in the countryside from springs or from a village well, often at some distance from the household. Rainwater was used, but obviously provided an insufficient supply. In towns or cities there was normally some means of public supply, with rainwater butts, private and public wells, and public taps, where there were unreasonable supplies of piped water, all being used, as well as rivers. Though their supplies were nearer their homes, urban women might well face long waits for supplies of poor, often infected, water. One engineer of the Southwark water company in London commented in 1844 that he had seen 'as many as from 20 to 50 persons with pails waiting round one or two standpipes'. In Gateshead, with 38,000 inhabitants, most of those in search of water were said to have to wait between one and three hours in 1845. By 1845 the Second Report of the Commissioners for Inquiring into the State of Large Towns and Populous Districts had judged the problem an overwhelming one, with only 6 out of 51 major towns having a good water supply – even that did not imply the provision of piped water to the homes of the poor.[4] The situation gradually changed after the 1840s and 1850s. Between 1846 and 1876 Manchester managed to supply around 80 per cent of its houses with some kind of internal water supply. Most local authorities lagged a long way behind that. In France the situation was little different. In Lille, for instance, the inhabitants had to rely on public wells, often dry, often infected by the many canals in the town, throughout this period. And the majority of rural dwellings in Britain and in France were to lack internal water supplies even by the beginning of the twentieth century.[5]

This question has been stressed because it is fundamental to the whole issue of domestic labour for the household in this period. By modern standards the majority of rural and urban households used very little water – one estimate is between 3 and 5 gallons a day. Much housework must therefore have taken place outside the house, and what could be done within the house was extremely limited. As Davidson has suggested: 'the spread of piped water was very significant in changing the locus of several household activities and encouraging women to stay at home'.[6] The implications of this for women's history have still to be explored. In the country, for instance, it might be easier to prepare food for cooking beside a well or a stream. Laundry, especially, could be done much more easily and practically by the nearest public well or washing place than at home. In the remoter rural areas, this might still be done by 'beetling' or trampling linen in rivers or stream. Elsewhere women might together manage the laborious business of preparing lye, by passing water through clean ashes or, as recorded by Dr David Boswell Reid, in his evidence to the Health of Towns Commission in England, they might collect urine in a common barrel from streets or groups of houses, sufficiently ammoniacal to serve as a washing agent.[7] Soap remained expensive, though it might be used in conjunction with other materials. The heating of the copper, often just the largest receptacle shared by a number of households, was both expensive and time-consuming, and demanded the co-operation of women together: often it would be done outside. Wash-houses, when built, in Britain were likely to provide communal rather than individual facilities. Wash-day could be an important social occasion, and a means of asserting women's solidarity, as recounted by one Breton folklorist:

> The washing is rinsed, twisted and beaten at the wash-house where the tongues are quite as active as the washerwomen's beetles; it is the seat of feminine justice, with little mercy for the

menfolk. Soaped from head to foot, soaped again, and rinsed down, they go through some bad times.[8]

Perrot has described how in French urban life in this period, the *lavoirs* or wash-houses remained the central meeting place for women, not only a place of work, but of gossip, quarrels and mutual support: 'the sites of practical feminism'.[9] They could, as they did for professional laundresses, provide the foundation for more formal associations of workers, the Parisian co-operative of washerwomen in 1848. The demolition of the old Parisian washing boats, and the coming of the new, more regulated *lavoirs* in the first years of Napoleon III, with their emphasis on the values of cleanliness, order and individual domesticity, marked a significant shift.

Other domestic activities too were likely to involve some collective labour. Cooking for the majority in this period still meant the heating of the pot over the fire that served as the major source of heat, to cook the simplest of stews, potatoes or puddings. When hot meals were cooked they were largely simple, monotonous dishes, depending on the supplies of food. Though by the end of this period the cast-iron oven was becoming more common in most homes above the poorest, still urban and rural labourers' wives alike were more likely to depend on the communal bread oven or the baker's shop for their bread. The gathering of wood for the fire, though an activity for all the family, would be one in which women and children would play a major part, until, in Britain, coal became more plentiful in the period after the 1840s.[10] Other kinds of work might also be done together. Gatherings could take place over knitting or sewing or lacemaking, gatherings known as the *covize* in the Auvergne, the *covégis* in Velay, the *veillée d'été* in the South. American women shared in the pleasures of the 'quilting bee', which was a more occasional event, but equally a source of mutual support. In the rural mid-West of the United States, and elsewhere too, the isolation of farms and homesteads and the relative newness of these communities gave women far fewer opportunities to join together.[11]

Such labours, the work of women together, may begin to suggest how far the domestic realities of life for working women were from notions of household management among well-intentioned, middle-class observers. That distance is equally clear when one looks at the formal framework of marriage. The economic factors likely to determine women's age at marriage have already been briefly touched on. It is also relevant to see how far the changing legal framework of marriage, which was increasingly subject to closer restrictions by the state, affected the majority. The state in this period had a considerable interest in the regulation of marriage, whether through the Napoleonic Civil Code, Lord Hardwicke's Marriage Act of 1753 or, in the United States, in the interest of state legislatures in the subject after the American Revolution. Nevertheless, such regulation was not in this period particularly effective. Among the working classes of the cities many observers noted the existence of free unions, unsanctified by Church or state. Louis Villermé, in his survey of French cities, noted large numbers of free unions; he found at Rheims in 1836, for instance: 'a large number of [textile workers] live in concubinage . . . many remain attached to one partner for life'.[12] Duveau noted, in France, that such free unions were found every-where except in the South. In Paris, some workers, especially apparently those in the metal trades, might commit themselves to free unions rather than marriage as a question of principle. The concern of both Church and government at this situation led to the establish-ment of the St-François Régis society in 1826 for the purpose of encouraging the legitimisation of such unions. Their work in Lille did mark a considerable increase in the marriage rate: there in the 1850s the society was influential in effecting between 300 and 700 marriages a year.[13] In Britain the situation was not dissimilar. Henry Mayhew, writing of London, found at one of his meetings of needlewomen many women who could not afford to marry their partners:

> I am advanced in the family way at present. I am living with a man now, but not in the married state. It's not in his power to marry me, his work won't allow it; and he's not able to support me in the manner he wishes and keep himself. . . . I think he would marry me if he had the marriage fees, willingly.[14]

A marriage licence could cost 5–12s. Some refused marriage for anti-clerical or anti-Anglican feelings, others in different areas of the country simply followed a local custom. Among the weavers of Norwich, for example, the woman in a free union was treated as a lawful wife. The London City Mission noted with horror the extent of such co-habitation, with one report in 1848 coming from an area of Westminster where only 200 out of 700 couples had been found to be married.[15] The extent to which the new form of civil marriage introduced in Britain in 1837 was used, especially by very different social groups, can be used as an indicator of the diversity of community attitudes on this: in rural Wales among Nonconformists, in industrial Wales and the North East, in new boom towns, and on the Borders where irregular patterns of marriage, on the Scottish model, were common, the form of civil marriage was used from its beginning.[16] Historians need to examine the differing practices of communities, rather than the bare legal framework. A further, well-known example of this is the custom of 'the sale of wives', essentially a popular form of divorce, probably at its height between 1785 and 1845.[17]

Early nineteenth-century rural and urban communities were thus likely to have their own standards of sexual behaviour; standards which were much more tolerant and flexible towards sexuality than the evangelical puritanism increasingly dominant among the upper levels of society. Observers' comments on the sexual morality of the poor, especially in the industrial towns, should be seen as an indication of the gulf that existed between the attitudes of different classes. Evidence to the Mines Commission in 1842 on women's work in the mines suggests, for instance, a greater interest in women's sexual conduct than in the effect of such work on their health. Mr John Thorneley gave evidence:

> The system of having females to work in coal pits . . . I consider to be the most demoralizing practice. The youths of both sexes work often in a half-naked state, and their persons are excited before they arrive at puberty. Sexual intercourse decidedly frequently occurs in consequence . . . women brought up in this way lay aside all modesty and scarcely know what it is by name.[18]

The same accusations were thrown at women working in the mills, Dr Gaskell alleging that:

> The chastity of marriage is but little known or exercised among them: husband and wife sin equally, and a habitual indifference to sexual rights is generated which adds one other item to the destruction of domestic habits.[19]

Yet the evidence of working people themselves in front of successive commissions, and some clearer sighted comments bore out the view that there was no greater degree of sexual promiscuity among women working in the mines or the cotton factories: in practice such women were probably less likely to become prostitutes than the more vulnerable women in the sweated trades, or domestic servants.[20] The assumption of middle-class observers was that the mixing of the sexes, in the place of work outside the home, would inevitably lead to sexual relations; yet in practice young women, in the factories as in rural communities, were separated from men largely by the sexual division of labour, their own courtship and sexual relations governed by the standards of family and community.

In France, the same readiness to focus on the sexual lives of women workers is apparent. Louis Villermé wrote of the domestic incompetence and the promiscuity of working women, of the mixing of male and female workers in Lille factories:

> Are you then ignorant of the licentious discourses which this mixture provokes, of the lessons of bad morals which result . . . and of the driving passions which you encourage as soon as their voice begins to make itself heard. . . . You will never be allowed to escape the reproach of having allowed girls to be lost whose morals you could have saved by wise and honest precautions.[21]

Simon, too, writing from a republican standpoint, believing that 'a woman, once become a worker, is no longer a woman', denounced the spread of concubinage, and wrote that: 'there is nothing that the imagination could add to the ravages of prostitution and incest in our great industrial towns'.[22] There are close parallels, as one might expect, between the comments of French and English writers, of Gaskell and Villermé, on the industrial towns. Whether they address themselves to the domestic incompetence or the sexual manners of the working classes, it is clear that it was not merely the horrific material conditions of such towns, but also the potential moral dangers within them which were so alarming. Their view of the latent sexuality of women, when unrestrained by domestic order, was focused upon the woman working outside the home.

In the United States, rapidly becoming a pluralistic, polyglot society, the effect of the ideal of 'true womanhood' on a range of different family forms is only now beginning to be evaluated. To middle-class Americans, including both abolitionists and pro-slavery writers, belief in unrestrained black sexuality was one example, though the most clear-cut, of that 'simple truth', stated by the *New York Daily Tribune*, 'that enslaved, degraded, hopeless, races or classes are always lewd'.[23] The inevitable comparison, frequently made, was between black people and the urban northern poor, most notably the Irish immigrants. Sexual restraint, within the bounds of ordered domestic family life, was an essential part of American civilisation; those who might threaten such a way of life were to be identified. Such beliefs apart, the experiences of free and slave black people, and of Irish immigrants, were of course entirely separated, influenced by their own past cultures. Herbert Gutman has charted the cultural process which dictated the Afro-American way of family life, through the mingling of the two cultures, through 'the everyday choices made by slave men and women', in the choice of husbands or wives, in the naming of children, in the maintenance of the network of kinship: the maintenance of such domestic, kinship and community patterns – in the face of the conditions of slavery – being a means of assertion, of resistance to denial of their humanity.[24] Immigrant populations in the early nineteenth century have not been studied with this depth: but studies of such populations in the later nineteenth century have suggested that for Irish, Italian and Jewish families, cultural legacies from pre-industrial Europe were of great importance, though they were to be modified by the structure of employment available in the cities. But in almost all cases, married women attempted to confine their labour to the home, or to casual part-time work.[25]

One specific example of a clash between popular assumptions and those of legislators may be given. In Britain, rising illegitimacy rates, and the expense of the Poor Law, had both caused increasing concern, and the legislation of 1834 which attempted to reshape poor relief in Britain contained new 'bastardy clauses'. Where the older Poor Law had required the putative father to contribute towards the support of the illegitimate child, the new one placed the burden of support and, by implication, of guilt, entirely on the woman. Such an imposition cut across local communities' assumptions of the joint responsibility of man and woman, and meant that one of its most important sanctions, financial payment, which often led to the admission of responsibility and subsequent marriage, was lost. There were many protests, and a significant increase in illegitimacy in certain counties: the provision was eventually repealed, though previous provisions never entirely recovered. The intention was that women, as the politician Lord Althorp indicated, would learn 'always to bear in mind their individual responsibility and be either the wives of their lovers, or nothing at all'.[26]

As awareness of class differences sharpened, so too did the awareness of different patterns of domestic life. Responses structured by class have made it extraordinarily difficult for historians to recover any sense of the reality, the quality of life at home, for the working classes of the nineteenth century. One distinguished attempt to do so is that by David Vincent, who has relied on working-class autobiographies, a source necessarily biased towards male experience. Even so, the impression received is one of affectionate relations, but relations at all points structured by the overwhelmingly harsh necessities of earning a living. Whether waiting to marry until a modest degree of security existed, scraping a living with a mother's casual earnings helping, or making the decision to take young children from school to send them to work, the home was never a refuge from the outside world, but, in Vincent's words, 'a cockpit, the arena in which the consequences of exploitation and inequality were experienced and battled with'.[27] These, by definition, atypical working-class men who left autobiographies did not regard their wives as 'equal partners in the search for reason and truth', though some hoped for a real improvement in the future in the education of women.[28] The same ambiguity was to be found among many Owenites.[29] The dominant view, of the legislators and of the middle classes, indicated that women and children were not to be regarded as free agents in the market place for labour, and that their future was to lie in the home and at school (even though that view might be overridden by immediate labour requirements). That view was too, towards the end of this period, to be very clearly expressed among working men: both as a means of securing a better family future and to restore the centrality of male earnings to the family economy. That concern at the reversal of roles in the family, already mentioned above, voiced by so many observers, brought reassertion of the new framework of women's domestic orientation, in an increasingly urbanised and industrialised world. As the Chartist R. J. Richardson wrote, recalling addressing a group of female calico printers: 'your places are in your homes: your labours are your domestic duties: your interests in the welfare of your families, and not in slaving thus for the accumulation of the wealth of others, whose slaves you seem willing to be'.[30] The same view can of course be found elsewhere. Among the artisans of Lyons, there was considerable hostility to married women working outside the home, though they had certainly shared to the full labours within it. Louis Vasbenter, a Lyonnais worker, expressed this:

> Woman's life is the life of the home, of the domestic, the interior. Not that I pretend that she must serve as a slave her master, not that she be entirely submissive to the wants of men . . . [but] her ideas will hardly ever differ from those of her tutor.[31]

The complexities of shifting family roles in early industrial society remain very difficult to understand. The married woman's management of domestic responsibilities meant that it was she who controlled the family budget. Sometimes, where members of the family still worked at home, this might mean negotiating over piece rates. In other situations, the wife might be given the whole of the husband's wages, to distribute as necessary, as the sociologist Le Play observed in the Parisian carpenter's family. Or the husband might make the wife an allowance from his wages, keeping the rest. Much depended on local and occupational custom.[32]

One promising line of investigation into the structure of family relationships has been based on legal records. Nancy Tomes's study of working-class violence between husbands and wives in London between 1840 and 1875 offers a fascinating discussion of assumptions about sexual roles, and the complex relationship between community standards, changing economic roles, and the diffusion of middle-class beliefs about the passivity and vulnerability of women. In the families which she describes, male dominance, together with the right to punish a wife physically – to an extent regulated by community standards – was accepted; but the level of recorded violence did decline during this period. Perhaps the higher level of the earlier period was due to the greater insecurity of sexual roles in a period of considerable economic change. Perhaps the diffusion of middle-class values, seen in the increasingly deterrent sentences given by magistrates to offenders, and in the desire for 'respectability' among some working-class families, was equally important. Perhaps, too, community standards and controls were beginning to have less effect.[33]

Such speculations suggest how far the experience of working-class women in the home in the course of industrialisation remains to be charted. Male dominance remains a continuing theme: so does co-operation between husband and wife in the maintenance of the household economy, though in a different guise. Opportunities for paid labour for married women were decreasing, except for the limited kinds of work that could be done at home. The slow spread of elementary education meant that more time would be spent in caring for children. The home was less likely to be the focus for training children in an occupation, though they might continue to help the family economy. Awareness of middle-class values, whether through domestic service, through much popular literature, or through its adoption by working-class leaders, must have reinforced such shifts. But the timetable for such changes was to vary greatly, with the pace of industrial and urban growth, and the strength of dominant cultures.

WOMEN AND COMMUNITY PROTEST

However, such experiences need to be recovered if we are to explain that withdrawal from public life by working-class women which Dorothy Thompson has suggested took place in Britain, and Michelle Perrot, in a slightly later period, in France.[34] Comparison with the United States is difficult, since for so much of the American working class, the first initiation into an urban industrial society coincided with immigration into an alien culture. Language and cultural barriers could mean that newly arrived immigrant women, while playing a central role in the family's struggle for survival, were less likely to participate in any militant collective action. But study of the nature of that transition from collective and community action to more formal political and workers' organisation may perhaps tell us something about the likelihood of organisation among working-class women themselves in this period.

Certainly, in the early nineteenth century, women did participate, and often played a leading part in collective protests, especially on issues of major concern to the subsistence of their families. In particular, the participation of women in bread riots throughout the eighteenth century, and earlier, has been observed, and clearly continued well into the nineteenth century. In 1795 at Haverfordwest in Wales, an old-fashioned JP dealing with rioting in a mining community, recorded 'the women were putting the men on, and were perfect furies. I had some strokes from some of them on my back'.[35] In England, large-scale food riots in East Anglia in 1816 were characterised by female leadership and participation. Helen Dyer, arrested for her part in the Brandon riot, where a crowd of 1500 had paraded with flags and pikes, had carried the paper containing the crowd's demands to be put to the magistrate. It was widely suggested that women in such crowds encouraged the men to more violent action. It is not, however, clear whether such riots were primarily a women's form of action, or rather, as is more likely, that their prominence in these was unusual compared to other forms of action, and attracted more newspaper reports. When they did play a major part, then women tended to focus on very specific targets, targets which were probably most familiar to them, such as shops and market-stalls. They might also attack millers and mill dealers. In 1812, a Manchester mill was visited by a crowd of rioters, and six women were subsequently prosecuted for removing 8 or 10lbs of flour, apparently the amount which it was judged the average apron held. Women quite clearly shared and understood the assumptions of the moral economy that dictated the crowd's actions, especially in the setting of prices. In crowds, women would hiss and abuse their opponents, throw stones, overturn stalls, carry away sacks of flour, and even on occasion confront troops. They might also offer a symbolic representation of their protest, whether simply exhibiting adulterated bread around the town or, as in Nottingham, putting a loaf dashed with red ochre with black crepe around it on a pole to parade around town. Perhaps, to some extent, women's participation was due to an apparently greater reluctance of magistrates to proceed against them, but to set against this there are many examples of harsh retribution. Hannah Smith, for example, was hanged in Manchester in 1812 for highway robbery, or rather for taking potatoes, butter and milk from carts coming into town, to resell to the crowd at lower prices. Such forms of action were on the decline, though potatoes were seized in the old way from a cart at Whitehaven in 1838 and resold to the public. And in the Scottish Highlands, they apparently survived well into the 1840s, perhaps later.[36]

The history of such movements in France is similar, though not systematically charted. There too women kept a close eye on markets and on prices, and in times of dearth on carts and the movements of grain. In the hardships of 1817, for instance, a number of women were sentenced to prison, transportation, even death, for their share in such riots. In 1816–17, 1828, 1831, 1839–40, especially in western France, the pattern still very clearly survived. In the widespread disturbances in the scarcity before the Revolution of 1848, many women in the north and west of France took part in action.[37] There were, too, scattered later examples, but better communications, especially the railways, and agricultural improvements meant that the age of the food riot had basically disappeared by the second half of the nineteenth century.

Involvement in such community action was not limited to the bread riot alone but could be extended to other issues of major concern in domestic life. Kenneth Logue has demonstrated the participation of women in riots against the militia and against lay patronage in the Church in Scotland in the late eighteenth century.[38] They were prominent, as already suggested, in riots against enclosure. In Wales at the beginning of the nineteenth century this was particularly marked. In 1809 women were arrested at St Clears for pulling down fences, and again in 1812, two Caernarvonshire women, Margaret Rowland and Anne Humphrey, were sentenced to six months imprisonment for helping to pelt magistrates and constables with clods of earth. In 1820 a crowd of Cardiganshire women dug a pit for the interment of every surveyor who invaded their rights.[39] A late example of enclosure protest in England is to be found in the women involved in the protests against the enclosure of Otmoor in 1830.[40] In the Scottish Highlands, where women continued to protest sporadically against the price of potatoes and grain, they also stood in the front line of defence against their homes, in the face of sheriff's officers and constables, whose task it was to clear the peasants from the land. At Greenyards in Ross-shire in 1833, 300 crofters, two-thirds of them women, armed with sticks and stones, greeted the police forces, and 15 to 20 women were seriously injured.[41] In the same way, in France, women were also involved in occasional attempts to reassert rights once communally owned, to forest lands, as in Tourrette lès-Vence in the Var in 1828, where the forest guard impounded illegally cut vine-props and tried to sell them:

> At this point a crowd of people – both men and women, young and old – gathered in the public square where the said vine-props were displayed. They declared furiously and with great anger that these vine-props belonged to the commune, that they should not be sold but ought to be burned on the spot, and produced many other arguments of a kind to rouse the entire population, most of whom had assembled in the square. Many people even began to take the vine-props away.[42]

These movements were most typical of the remoter areas of the countryside, but such crowd responses can be found in the town as well as the country.

For example, in 1811–12, a series of food riots in northern England, in which women like Hannah Smith were prominent, were accompanied by machine-breaking, in which women were equally prominent. A number of women were arrested and sentenced, and two transported for their destruction of the new looms.[43] But their participation in the crowd action should be seen very much as the reflection of popular hostility to the new machinery rather than the direct threat to their own employment: powerlooms, after all, offered jobs particularly to women, even if they threatened old-established patterns of family work. Perrot suggests that from being initiators of protest, women came to be rather its auxiliaries. In France too food riots were mixed with protests against *machines anglaises*. In 1831 in St-Etienne, women with aprons full of stones threw them at the National Guard, as the crowd outside the arms manufacturer attempted to destroy a new machine.[44] Those crowd movements discussed in the previous chapter should perhaps be seen as much in this context as in the more modern context of shifting patterns of employment. Collective protest might be directed against innovations which hit at men's or women's work or indeed at whatever most affected the subsistence of the family. But women's participation was most noted and most obvious in matters which were still primarily their concern: in others, increasingly, they played a lesser part.[45]

In England, it has been suggested that:

the turning point for women's social protest . . . was the campaign against the New Poor Law of 1834, for this movement was the bridge between the older form of direct action, involving violence, and newer forms of political organization, and the use of political techniques.[46]

Such a claim is a difficult one, since there is clear evidence that working-class women did associate together in political movements before the 1830s: but the agitation against the new Poor Law is certainly an important example of the extension of the family's struggle for survival in an urban context, directed against institutions and policies. The campaign was centred, though not exclusively, in the industrial North, and by 1838 both direct and forceful action and organised political campaigning were being undertaken by women against the New Poor Law. In Elland, Leeds, in February 1838, a party of women, unable to disrupt a meeting of Assistant Commissioners, took revenge by rolling the local Guardians in the snow. Women were prominent in riots in Dewsbury in the same year. Mary Grassby of Elland, one of the leaders of the campaign, suggested that women had more need to oppose the Poor Law than men, because they had more to fear from it in the break-up of their families, to which their feelings were more susceptible. Women here had a crusade which was an acceptable one: defence of their homes and families, defined as their particular concern. That mixture of traditional methods and new directions can be seen in the action of a crowd of over 100 women in 1838 in Combe St Nicholas, Dorset, who stole a cartload of bread for distribution among paupers, in protest against the withdrawal of outdoor relief to the able-bodied. A range of female anti-Poor Law societies were founded in early 1838 in Yorkshire, Lancashire and Cheshire, the first probably that in Elland. Women rapidly came to organise and chair their own meetings, with female speakers addressing the audience, as when the women of Carlisle promised Fergus O'Connor that they would: 'follow our husbands, our fathers, our sons and our brothers to the battlefield, to cheer and comfort them in the hour of danger, bind up their wounds, and instigate them to fresh deeds of valour.'[47] A Carlisle banner is said to have shown a Poor Law Guardian tearing a child from his mother, and on the reverse side separating husband and wife. Women invoked the Scriptures, sang hymns and took part in chapel meetings to defend their conduct. In 1843, a group of women accompanied a crowd attacking Carmarthen workhouse, many of them carrying brooms with which, they said, they would sweep away its foundations. The campaign, which involved far more women's societies than any previous one, embodied both class protest and an assertion of the particular domestic concerns of women. This suggests that women were perhaps shifting their ground from the older patterns of collective action to protest in a different setting. But such protest contained within it a narrowing of the possibilities of action, a recognition of the limits set by domestic life. In the Chartist movement in Britain, and in the French crowds in 1848 and 1851, women did play a part which will be explored later: the question must remain, how far that part was an auxiliary one, reflecting a declining participation in what was becoming political, rather than community, action.

That domestic labour had collective aspects, and continued to do so throughout the second half of the nineteenth century, has been stressed. But domestic life was becoming more entirely women's territory, as the slow separation of home and work continued. In the French countryside, women's association together was related to their work, and to their Church. As Segalen suggests, perhaps the 'feminisation' of religious practice was accompanied by a clearer focusing of male sociability outside home and Church.[48] Agulhon has traced the 'great surge in popular sociability' in the rural Mediterranean department of the Var from the beginning of the nineteenth century, with the growth of *chambrées* and *cercles*, informal male societies modelled by peasants and artisans on similar bourgeois societies. Universally, such societies excluded women. In the Var, and in cities like Marseilles and Toulouse, such societies, and the cafés and cabarets, the male institutions of sociability, were playing a vital role in disseminating political information, sometimes clandestinely, and in building political loyalties. It is likely that, even if less marked in northern France, this was not entirely a Mediterranean phenomenon.[49] Thompson suggests that the pub similarly had become too important a focus for political action in Britain by the 1840s, and that women were increasingly excluded from it.[50] The issue was not a new one. Women had always been excluded from certain aspects of public life – most guilds and all guild offices, *compagnonnages*. Masonic lodges and local government, to name but a few – but as working-men's politics slowly became more formalised, and the politics of the crowd less important, so women's participation in public affairs declined. The conditions of domestic labour, even in urban communities, might mean that women's presence still informally dominated the streets. Yet where the centre of production was shifting from the household, and as the centres of male sociability also came to lie outside home and family, then the 'separation of spheres' was likely to have some reality for the working-class woman. For the great majority, the ideals of 'domesticity' were still very distant. For a few better-off groups within the working class, in skilled, secure jobs, those complex notions of domestic relationships derived from middle-class experience might begin to have some meaning.

MIDDLE-CLASS DOMESTICITY AND ITS BOUNDARIES

The quality of that experience for the wives and daughters of the middle classes in Britain, France and the United States still needs much further study. For them also, the separation of spheres was not merely a prescriptive ideal but a material reality. Yet relatively little has been written about the economic role of the middle-class Victorian housewife. The proliferation of all kinds of advice manuals, addressed to daughters, wives, mothers, has left historians at times confused as to the extent to which such advice was ever taken, ever practicable. Those domestic themes which define the setting of so much nineteenth-century literature can be a better guide. The greatest novelists could evoke a world through its domestic detail, as did George Eliot:

> There were particular ways of doing everything in that family; particular ways of bleaching the linen, of making the cowslip wine, curing the hams, and keeping the bottled gooseberries; so that no daughter of that house could be indifferent to the privilege of having been born a Dodson, rather than a Gibson or a Watson . . . in short there was in this family a peculiar tradition as to what was the right thing in household management and social demeanour.[51]

Lesser novelists, like Elizabeth Hamilton in *The Cottagers of Glenburnie* (1808) (Plate 5) or Mrs Gaskell in *Mary Barton* (1848), could use such detail for didactic purposes, pointing to the lack of domestic competence of Highland peasants or northern factory workers. But most revealingly, some historians have used neither prescriptive nor imaginative work, but have attempted to reconstruct, through correspondence and diaries, the particular worlds of middle-class women, as Nancy Cott has done for the early nineteenth-century New England woman, and Bonnie Smith for the well-to-do bourgeoises of the department of the Nord, in northern France. Leonore Davidoff has looked, in microcosm, at the Taylor family of Ongar, and Mary Ryan at the development of a domestic ideology among the women of Utica, New York State. What is perhaps surprising are the common themes of that ideology, which can only be summarised here.

The moral qualities with which the domestic sphere was invested were described in Chapter 3. But beyond this, the business of household management itself acquired an emotional charge for which there is abundant evidence in diaries and in correspondence. Sexual and work roles were to be fused. What was new was not the question of 'love' or 'romance' but the weight of cultural and psychological expectations placed upon the life of the family, and especially on the woman at the centre of that family. The household was no longer a place for productive activity, but the setting for the internal life of the family, its physical qualities – cleanliness, order, comfort – reflecting the achievement of the woman at its heart. Domestic management was not a job but a vocation, and the task of motherhood in particular had become the most demanding of vocations. For the middle-class women of New England and Utica, New York, the transition from involvement in production to mainly domestic responsibilities did involve a commitment to, an internalising of, the values and sacrifices required of them. In the department of the Nord, in France, Smith has pointed to the declining involvement of the wives of manufacturers in their husbands' businesses from the mid-nineteenth century, and their search for fulfilment in 'the rhetoric of reproduction', the internal life of the home. For Britain there are no such comparable studies, though Patricia Branca has described the demanding tasks of the suburban wife and mother, and her adoption of 'a modern set of values' in the course of the second half of the nineteenth century.[52] Davidoff, in her portrait of the Taylor family of Ongar in the early nineteenth century, has suggested a not dissimilar development to that in New England: the two Taylor sisters, strictly evangelical, identifying with the 'natural' and God-given division of the spheres of the sexes, yet at the same time feeling some degree of ambivalence about the possibility of wider activity.[53] There is therefore evidence that some early and mid-nineteenth-century women did see their future as the creators of the quality of family life, as the nurturers and socialisers of children and, sustained by religious faith, aiding in the moral regeneration of social life. Such a view could give a woman both solidarity and confidence. Cott records the reaction of an 18-year-old, in her diary, on first reading Hannah More's *Strictures on the Modern System of Female Education*:

> What an important sphere a woman fills! how thoroughly she ought to be qualified for it – but I think hers the more honourable employment than a man's – for all men feel so grand and boast so much – and make such a pother [sic] about their being lords of the world below – if their mothers had not taken such good care of them

when they were babies, and instilled good principles into them as they grew up, what think you would have become of the mighty animals – oh every man of sense must bow before woman. She bears the sway not man as he presumptuously supposes.[54]

Sexual purity, maternal responsibilities and administration of the household were all part of the domestic world of middle-class women.

The roots of the ideal of sexual purity in women pre-date the Victorian age by many years. The double standard of morality for men and women has a long history, and its relationship to patterns of inheritance and property relations as a means of securing legitimate succession to property, still remain to be charted.[55] Still, there is no doubt that the outward tone of public life did change in the first half of the nineteenth century, and that not only chastity but the denial of sexual passion was an element in the assertion of woman's moral superiority. The development of this has already partly been traced in Chapters 1–3. The strength of the evangelical movement in Britain and in the United States completed that shift, already apparent in the eighteenth century, away from earlier views of women as having sexual appetites equal to, if not greater than, men's. The evangelical case rested both on woman's natural modesty, passivity and delicacy, and on her superior ability to control and to renounce her passions. As Cott has suggested, such a theme could have attractions for many women who, like Mary Wollstonecraft, preferred to emphasise women's power to control and subdue than to accept the determinism of nature. Women were elevated by this 'passionlessness', through their own conquest of passion, their greater moral and spiritual strength. Angelina Grimké, abolitionist and feminist, wrote of the possibility of being married to a man, who, like the great majority, felt 'that women were made to gratify their animal appetites, *expressly* to minister to their pleasure – and Christian men too. My soul abhors such a base letting down of the high dignity of my nature as a woman.'[56] A number of historians have suggested that such a justification for denying passion provided a way in which women might refuse sexual relations within marriage and, perhaps, control the number of births.[57] Whether that was indeed so must remain open. Yet there is much evidence of the widespread acceptance of such standards of female purity. In Utica, New York, 'sexual matters had been relegated beyond the pale of private conversation by mid-century'.[58] Those criticisms of the sexuality of the lower orders, in Britain, France and the United States quoted above, are the converse to a world which for the most part equated denial of female sexuality with a higher level of refinement and civilisation.

Such views are often regarded as typical of Protestant countries. Yet it was in France that the double standard of morality was perhaps most rigidly entrenched, both within the marriage codes and in the official toleration of prostitution.[59] It might perhaps be surmised that its strength in France was due at least in part to the pattern of middle-class marriage, which remained very much a question of parental alliances, a linking of property as much as of individuals. Certainly the qualities of purity and innocence for young girls, the importance of virginity before marriage, were overwhelmingly emphasised, by writers on maternal education, in the doctrines of the Church, and in the teaching of the convents. There was of course no single conception of women's sexuality. One important development in western society was the emergence of more clearly defined medical views of women's sexuality, adding to the authority of the social science of the Enlightenment that of the natural sciences.[60] Their views might vary greatly. At mid-century, for example, one can contrast the notorious statement of Dr William Acton, in his *Functions and Disorders of the Reproductive Organs* (1857) that 'the majority of women (happily for society) are not very much troubled with sexual feeling of any kind' with the work of Dr Auguste Debay. Debay's *Hygiène et physiologie du marriage* (1849), which went through 172 editions in 40 years, portrayed sexual pleasure as entirely normal, and indeed a necessity, for women as well as men.[61] In the United States, the rise of the study of gynaecology and obstetrics went along with a tendency, among some medical writers, to see female sexuality and the reproductive system as the key to a wide range of disorders both physical and mental – thus stressing how far woman's biological functions determined her life. But this theme still remained to be explored by the medical profession throughout the second half of the nineteenth century.[62] Still, such stress on the need for purity among women, in all three societies, must surely have influenced the quality of intimate family life – with the consequences of which we still live – while offering, to some women, the chance of self-assertion.

An outstanding feature of nineteenth-century domestic life is the increasing responsibility which mothers were asked to bear for the upbringing and socialisation of their children. The implications of 'maternal education' in the early nineteenth century have already been described. It should be stressed that, if not in the precise way described by aristocratic French writers such as Mme Necker de Saussure, much was required of mothers in the training of young children and daughters. Mary Ryan recorded how in Utica magazines appealing especially to mothers took over from the evangelical periodicals, as the strength of the revivalist impulse declined. There the *Mother's Magazine* and *Mother's Monthly Journal*, in the 1830s, described the gentle means of discipline which the mother might employ, no longer harsh punishments which recalled Calvinist will-breaking. The mother was to use the quieter tactics of emotional withdrawal, of emphasising her own care and sacrifices. Such a method obviously required constant and unceasing care and vigil-ance, into which the mother's energies should be put, to inculcate desirable values: honesty, industry, frugality, self-control. Ryan suggests how such practice of late eighteenth- and early nineteenth-century educational theory directed towards the training of the will in children might be seen as developing the values pre-eminent among the Utica middle classes. In the longer term, the mother's task was to direct the family strategy towards the training for future careers of the sons of the family, through emotional, domestic and financial support, made possible, if necessary, by the earnings of daughters.[63] That pattern is perhaps not so different from the one to be found in Britain.

Branca has told us much about that weight of concern which overwhelmed middle-class mothers in mid-nineteenth-century Eng-land. Examples, among many, include Dr Bull's *Hints to Mothers* (London 1833) which rapidly went through 14 editions, and the appearance of the *British Mother's Magazine*, which published from 1845 to 1863. The high infant mortality rate, which showed no signs of declining, placed a very heavy responsibility indeed on mothers. One advertisement of the period, in *The Mother's Friend*, begins: 'Do not let your children die. Fenning's *Every Mother's Book* contains everything a mother ought to know about her child's Feeding, Teething, Weaning . . . .' Similarly, too, changes in attitudes to childrearing pointed to the responsibility of mothers in shaping the whole future careers of their children, through the quality of their care in early infancy. It was this, 'the most sacred duty which devolves upon the sex', which would shape 'the character of the whole of society'. The question of discipline, reflected in the correspondence of mothers with magazines, was a controversial one, though by mid-century the advocates of gentle, enlightened training were prevailing, in the prescriptive literature at least.[64] These high expectations, combined with a high death rate, could make the life of the woman committed to motherhood extraordinarily hard. Mrs Gaskell, married in 1832, lost her first child, and that loss was recalled by her in a sonnet 'On Visiting the Grave of my Stillborn Little Girl', in 1836, after the birth of a second daughter. She became absorbed in the detailed progress of that daughter, Marianne, starting a diary to record it when Marianne was just six months old, and which lasted for three years. In it she noted every detail of the child's ways: but the diary also became a strict self-examination of the mother which allowed no indulgence.[65]

The extent to which new ideas of childrearing, following the advice of early nineteenth-century writers on maternal education, were having their effect in France is not so easy to judge. Church authorities, including Bishop Dupanloup, continued to stress the values of authority. But Paul Janet, writing of the bourgeois family in 1861, praised 'the intimacy, confidence and liberty that reigns today in families' and, a little later, a work by Gustave Droz, *Monsieur, Madame, et bébé* (Paris, 1866), an immediate bestseller, wrote of the value of affectionate family relations, between husbands and wives, parents and children. The middle-class French mother was certainly in the course of the nineteenth century increasingly less likely to employ a wet-nurse, more likely to direct her attention to the upbringing of her children. Yet the degree of control retained by middle-class parents over their children in France throughout the nineteenth century (and into the twentieth century) suggests perhaps that, relatively, girls were subjected to a more authoritarian regime than in Britain or the United States. Perhaps, among the smaller and less mobile French middle classes, the assumption that children were likely to continue very much in the paths already established by their family may have had something to do with a generally more conservative outlook. But the question must remain still very much an open one.[66]

The economic role of women in the nineteenth-century middle-class household is often forgotten. It was to the housewife, as the administrator of the household, that the advertisements, the new magazines and the household manuals were addressed; it was the housewife who played a leading role in spending the family's surplus income. In this period, the middle classes were undoubtedly growing in number and manuals, proliferating in all three countries, were addressed to all income levels. J. Walsh's *Manual of Domestic Economy* (1853) was specifically written for those with incomes of from £100 to £1000 a year. The impact of such manuals and magazines can only be supposed. Their insistence on the appropriate standard of living at different income levels must surely have encouraged aspirations of higher status, at every level. What is changing in this period is the adjustment of the household to the new consumer economy. To a much greater degree than before, the middle-class household was becoming a major consumer of the products of the industrial revolution. For example, a variety of closed cast-iron ranges and stoves were available in the United States from the 1840s. After mid-century bath tubs were beginning to require a separate room, especially when piped water became more easily available. Cooking utensils, kitchen gadgets of all kinds, were advertised in manuals and in magazines. New pottery, furnishings, carpets, curtains: all were increasingly available, and could be bought on a new structure of credit if necessary: hire purchase.[67] There were perhaps important differences in the orientation of different kinds of households to such products. In France the bestselling book on domestic economy, *La maison rustique des dames* (1844–5) by Cora-Elisabeth Millet-Robinet, was apparently intended for country housewives but proved increasingly popular among city women. The task of the manager of the rural household was still in many ways a productive one: she had both to attend to the affairs of the household and to supplement her husband on the farm, overseeing the servant girls, managing the farmyard and so on. The emphasis on British manuals is directed very much more explicitly to the urban woman, who can rely on shops and markets for produce and purchases of all kinds. In the United States there was of course immense variation between the rural household of the mid-west and the city woman, whose role was not unlike that of her British contemporary.[68]

But in spite of such variations, clearly the household, increasingly defined as women's space, had taken on new meaning in the course of the nineteenth century. The domestic interior and its qualities were to display above all the achievement of the mistress of the home, the emotional strength, the creativity, which went into it. Ornaments, dress, even cooking, were all a part of this female world, a world which had its own symbolism, explored by Smith and by Davidoff.[69] Cleanliness was not only hygienic, but also virtuous. Domesticity in the nineteenth century was never merely a question of a heightened division of labour, but also a powerful duty which drew upon both the labour and the emotions of women. Its dynamism gave them a powerful role in the purchase and the creation of demand for the consumer goods which were a product of the new industrial world.

The particular boundaries of such domesticity are difficult to judge. Cott, in describing the women of New England in the first quarter of the nineteenth century, suggested that the separation of spheres offered a vocation for women which cut across class differences and met the democratic requirements of American society.[70] Yet very different emphases are of course possible. In societies where sharper class distinctions already existed, to be refined in the process of industrialisation, then the implications of domesticity were not at all above class. Notions of gentility, of being a 'lady' were already common currency by the end of the eighteenth century in Britain, especially among satirists, who accused farmers' wives or grocers' wives of aspiring to gentility in their displays of conspicuous leisure.[71] Such accusations, indicating that withdrawal from productive labour already noted, should be taken seriously only in so far as they indicate the degree to which such purely domestic, but not productive, concerns had already become identified with class. Clearly, a certain amount of surplus income was essential to the creation of the domestic interior. Works by Ryan and by Branca have suggested that domesticity, as an aspiration if not a reality, was central to the concerns not merely of the upper middle classes or the professions in the nineteenth century, but equally to merchants and manufacturers, and also to shopkeepers, tradesmen and to those increasingly entering the different kinds of white-collar employment, dependent not on capital but on educational qualifications.[72] Catherine Hall has put the most fundamental question, in her preliminary study of the Birmingham middle classes between 1780 and 1850. How far was the separation of spheres, the elaborate definition of the different worlds of men and women 'one of the fundamental organising characteristics of middle class society in late eighteenth and early nineteenth-century England?'[73] She suggests that it was not merely the material separation of the home from the place of work, but also the political and cultural redefinition of public and private worlds which distinguished the middle classes from the rest in English industrial society. Whether the lines of distinction were quite so sharp, at least by 1850, is an issue which must wait much further research. There is evidence to suggest – some of which has been cited in the course of this work – that materially and culturally, a kind of separation of worlds was similarly emerging between men and women in the nineteenth-century working class. Its quality – perhaps less private, more influenced by community and neighbourhood concerns – still remains to be traced.

Here it is worth noting that the ideal of the 'lady', relevant in practice only to those women of the upper and middle classes who could afford to employ substantial numbers of domestic servants but by aspiration to many more, could, and did, cut across that common domestic vocation which women theoretically shared. Anne Summers has charted the complex relations between 'ladies' and nurses in the nursing party sent out to the Crimea. Ladies and domestic servants, in fact, by definition, shared a common bond of dependence, on husbands and employers; but in the unusually close circumstances of the nursing party in the Crimea, the ladies found the most important differences between themselves and the rest not economic, but their own greater cultivation and refinement. Middle-class women could and frequently did internalise that view of the working classes which, as has been seen, was an important theme of nineteenth-century social comment: yet it could also be overcome. Perhaps, as Summers suggests, that sense of superiority felt by 'ladies', however repugnant to modern instincts, could also be 'a first stage towards assuming responsibility for other, disadvantaged, women'.[74]

There were many complexities at the heart of the domestic ideal. Its emotional force, and that definition of women's nature which lay at its centre, carried with it the potential for a role beyond private and domestic life. Increasing stress on the separation of spheres, on definitions of womanhood, could lead women to reach out to other women, to explore the possibilities of 'sisterhood' on the common ground of domesticity. They could be missionaries, not only in God's name, but in carrying their own message of morality, their own qualities of compassion and caring, into a wider world. Women found that their identification with the nurturing and caring qualities of womanhood could be a basis for female friendship, for the common concerns of their own sex. Common education, in the academies of New England, for example, or common religious experiences, could strengthen such attachments, It has been suggested, both by Cott and by Ryan, that with the decline of hierarchical relationships in the new American republic, what took their place were the associations of peers. Women came to value relationships among their own sex. If gender prescribed their future, then they could best escape their inferiority by exploring their own special qualities, in imbuing them with particularity and moral superiority. The recognition and the consciousness of womanhood were an essential prerequisite to any attempt to challenge it. Historians have been able to recover in a few instances the kind of supportive networks which such women built, based not on patterns of work but on their reproductive and caring roles. Carroll Smith-Rosenberg's study of female friendships, often lasting a lifetime, points to the way in which such relationships among women might foster and build a sense of their own worth and self-esteem in a world in which they might have little public status. And the passion and intimacy of such friendships, their emotional centrality in women's lives, is an important contrast to the 'passion-lessness' expected in heterosexual relations. Such friendships might also develop to become sensual, even sexual.[75]

But such networks could become more formal. Ryan argues that in Utica, the association, with its religious roots, but its focus, for women, on the maternal role, could have played a vital part in easing that transition from religious revivalism to the privacy of strictly domestic life. Maternal Associations were in fact short-lived, and found little support in Britain. Yet it is also clear that such associations, whether with a specifically religious purpose or not, limited to women of fairly similar social class, could fulfil a need. And between 1800 and 1860 such associations, with political and philan-thropic aims, did multiply. Their intentions were to be, as will be shown, directed towards the extension of women's particular qual-ities and concerns into the outside world, and, wherever possible, towards their own sex. The pursuit of the qualities of domesticity could lead women into association with others, and perhaps further, into the male public sphere, into organisation, campaigning, speak-ing and the recognition of the disabilities of their sex. For middle-class feminists, that route was a common one.

CHALLENGES TO DOMESTICITY: INDIVIDUAL AND COLLECTIVE

Yet there were also those who directly confronted the dominant view of domestic life. One way of doing this was to make direct attacks on the constraints placed upon sexuality, and in particular the denial of female sexuality. But sexual radicalism was to prove unable to counter the combined effects of religious strength and the domestic ideal, and the association between such radicalism and feminist ideas was a dangerous one for feminists, as Mary Wollstonecraft and William Godwin had found. Defiance of convention in sexual matters was not to be lightly undertaken, and perhaps it is not surprising that the most notable example of such defiance in the early nineteenth century is that of Percy Bysshe Shelley, a man himself close to the Wollstonecraft tradition, and a poet whose way of life and declared hostility to Christianity had put him beyond the bounds of respectability. Some of his greatest epic poetry denounced the narrowness and timidity of convention and celebrated on a heroic scale the power and strength of women as free and equal to men. Many of his political works were to be frequently reprinted in the interest of the working-class movement, but much of his most radical material on sexual matters was not printed till well after his death.[76]

Other individual writers were to celebrate the power of passion in women. Mme de Stael, the liberal opponent of Napoleon I, was to advocate faithfulness to one's passions, in *De l'influence des Passions sur le bonheur des Individus et des Nations* (1796). In *Delphine* (1802) and in *Corinne* (1807), the passionate heroine, the anti-clericalism, the justification of divorce all earned the author a notorious popularity.[77] George Sand, too, especially in her early novels of the 1830s, assaulted the conventions of marriage with determination. In the preface to her first novel, *Indiana* (1832), she wrote:

> Indiana . . . is a type; she is woman, the feeble being whose mission it is to represent *passions* repressed, or, if you prefer, suppressed by *the law*; she is desire at odds with necessity; she is love dashing her head blindly against all the obstacles of civilisation.[78]

Later, in 1842, even after the controversy caused by the book, she reprinted it again, denouncing the laws that governed women in wedlock as 'unjust and barbarous'. Yet the ending of that novel recalls the Tahitian idylls of Diderot: passions could be fulfilled, after an unhappy history, only in a cottage, hidden away far from civilisation, in the West Indies. Sand's feminism was individualistic: she was not prepared to make a political stand or to co-operate with the feminists of 1848 in France.[79] Yet in Britain, where she was equally notorious, she won much praise from such diverse sources as the radical *People's Journal* of William and Mary Howitt, in which Mazzini praised her for declaring 'the secret of her sex, its inward life', and G. H. Lewes, who in the *Westminster Review* saw her work as exemplifying what women writers, at their best, could achieve.[80] The work of a much lesser known English novelist, Geraldine Jewsbury, was strongly influenced by Sand. Her first novel, *Zoe* (1845), described the passion of Zoe, a married woman, for her two suitors, Everhard and Mirabeau; in *The Half-Sisters* (1848), indebted, so reviewers said, both to de Stael and to Sand, she describes the dedication of the professional actress. In both novels there is much discussion of the role of women, and in both the call of duty finally triumphs. The comparison between Mirabeau, the would-be lover of Zoe, and Charlotte Brontë's Mr Rochester aroused contemporary critical comment: 'a wild declaration of the 'Rights of Woman' in a new aspect'.[81]

The challenge to monogamy was not limited to individual heroines portrayed in such exceptional works, but was to come also from those who advocated co-operative living and the abandonment of domestic privacy and its values. The example had already been set, as suggested in Chapter 3, by such sects as those of Luckie Buchan and the Shakers, sexually unorthodox in different ways. Their successors were to be found in the early nineteenth-century secular sects: Owenites, Saint-Simonians, Fourierists, Icarians, Perfectionists. Attitudes towards sexuality, domestic arrangements and the status of women within these groups varied greatly, but they all advocated some kind of radical transformation of social life, including family life. The contribution of such movements to the range of feminist ideas and practice in the 1830s and 1840s was vital: yet the force of the inspiration was brief, leaving few direct heirs.

One of the earliest expressions of such views was William Thompson's *Appeal of One-Half the Human Race, Women, against the Pretensions of the Other Half, Men . . .* (1825). An Irish landowner and Owenite economist, Thompson's denunciation of marriage – 'Home . . . the eternal prison-house of the wife' – is one of the most radical so far encountered.[82] His friendship with Anna Wheeler, a woman of great originality, a rebel from an Irish gentry family, who had met both Saint-Simon and Charles Fourier, the two leading 'utopian socialists' in France, greatly influenced him. He dedicated the work to her, declaring that though he could not *feel* like her 'the inequalities of sexual laws', from her he had understood 'those bolder and more comprehensive views which perhaps can only be elicited by concentration of the mind on one darling though terrific theme'.[83] They argued, against the utilitarian James Mill, that the interests of women could not simply be identified with those of their husbands, and opposed a collective ideal to this version of individualism. The entry of women into their political rights was to be made possible by 'Mutual Co-operation in large numbers'. The values of equality were insufficient because of women's disadvantages: 'permanent inferiority of strength and occasional loss of time in gestation and rearing infants'.[84] Only a society based on co-operation and collective possession of property in which children were equally educated and provided for by the whole group could make equality possible. Their views on women's sexuality were radically and frankly stated, in a specific denunciation of the double standard of morality imposed upon women, and of the despotism exercised by men within marriage, over wives and daughters. The 'isolated breeding establishments, called married life' allowed men to maintain women in a condition of slavery, justified by all legal, political and social codes. Such a situation profoundly degraded women themselves and the political implications were clear – no identity of interest between husband and wife existed. The *Appeal* was an important feminist statement, and its idealism expressed the tone of the Owenite view of marriage in this 'old immoral world'. Wheeler and Thompson were to take that case further and to state a full programme for the emancipation of women, in their published work and in, for instance, Wheeler's translation of Saint-Simonian feminist periodicals, and in her own public lectures from 1829.[85]

Owen's *Lectures on the Marriage of the Priesthood in the Old Immoral World* were published in 1835. To Owen the artificiality of the marriage contract, at odds with natural desires and impulses, was responsible for very many of the evils which affected both men and women: prostitution, for example. Bound by convention as they were, it was impossible for most women to act as rational beings while the marriage system remained, and it was not possible to bring up children in a rational way. The plan was to remove men and women from single families into large-scale communities, where domestic labour and the care of children would be communally performed. Marriage procedures too would be regulated by the community. His *Lectures* became notorious, crowding Owenite meetings, forcing

Owenites to admit the abolition of marriage was not an immediate prospect.[86] Yet there is also much evidence that across the country Owenite lecturers, men and women, met with much support, especially from women, for their denunciation of current legal arrangements, notably the absence of divorce. Such a response perhaps reflected the more tolerant and flexible attitude to sex and marriage among working people described above. A number of well-known Owenite figures, men and women, themselves entered into free unions or lived together before marriage. Yet the concerns of women for the enforcement of male obligations, and the prospect of free unions without male responsibilities in the unreformed world led Owen and many others to modify their views, to suggest that the abolition of marriage could only take place at the same time as a complete reform in property relations. Two of the leading women lecturers of the movement, Margaret Chappellsmith and Emma Martin, were to stress this revision, evidently more acceptable to large audiences of women. Frances Morrison, in *The Influence of the Present Marriage System* . . . (1838), insisted that strict enforcement of marriage laws was necessary 'to insure that fidelity which the vehemence of temporary passion could never guarantee'.[87] In the future, for such women, soundly based monogamous partnerships would be encouraged, not the language of free love; it is important that for them, the language of passion was rejected for that of reason and sympathy: as Taylor has put it:

> The equation of sex with compulsive processes was a male mode of thought: women on the other hand, firmly asserted the ruling place of reason in all properly ordered human relations.[88]

The seven Owenite communities established between 1821 and 1825, with high aspirations towards collective living, similarly foundered on the radicalism of the leap to be made. The women joining them were mostly working-class and married. The communities made real attempts to restructure patterns of work, yet given their difficulties in surviving at all their scope was limited. Communal housework among women certainly seems to have been introduced, at, for instance, the Spa Fields community in Islington and others, and women did participate in varying degrees in agricultural and manufacturing work. But collective housework was itself very time-consuming, and there seems to have been no question of women's primary responsibility for housework. The amount of work required of women, its collective conditions and male dominance in decision-making: all contributed to evident resentment among female members of these communities. Though the declared aim was to put new marriage relations into practice, most members came already married. Only in one community, Manea Fen, did the leader proclaim his intention to put sexual freedom into practice: by so doing he clearly contributed to the collapse of the community, though there was support for his aims from some of the women members.[89]

These divergencies, between co-operative ideals and women's reactions in practice, can also be traced within the Saint-Simonian movement. In the theory of the disciples of Saint-Simon, the rehabilitation of the material world, which was necessary for the synthesis of matter and spirit, was not merely a philosophical issue, but one which required the rehabilitation of the flesh, of sexual passion. While they gave great publicity to the question of the emancipation of women, the association between feminism and the free fulfilment of the passions was again to be dangerously close. Leaders of the movement were mainly male – Olinde Rodrigues, Prosper Enfantin, Henri Bazard – but an important and interesting group of women were also associated with it. They were influenced not only by Henri de Saint-Simon, but by his contemporary Charles Fourier who had similarly argued, in his *Théorie des quatre mouvements* . . . (1808), that the liberation of men and, equally, the emancipation of women, must depend on the liberation of the passions. His critique of civilisation and his insistence on radical social changes were to continue to influence French socialists throughout the 1830s and 1840s.[90]

Such work, as Sullerot suggests, provided a stimulus rather than a direct inspiration for French feminists who between 1832 and 1834 directly challenged existing conventions of marriage. The group who founded the *Tribune des Femmes*, which appeared from 1832 to 1833 under several different titles (*La Femme Libre, La Femme Nouvelle, La Femme Affranchie, La Femme de l'Avenir*), have been described as having 'for the first time a real awareness of belonging to a female community, and they transcended, by their militant feminism, that proud individualism of the newly independent'.[91]

The paper was in some ways more feminist than Saint-Simonian. The founders, Desirée Gay, the author of the *Adresse aux femmes privilegiées* (1832), and Marie-Reine Guindorff, had both taken part in

Saint-Simonian organisation of tailors' and dressmakers' associations but by 1833 had moved towards Fourierism. Two other likely contributors were Suzanne Voilquin, embroideress and midwife, who had gone with her husband to Egypt on the Saint-Simonian quest for the Woman Messiah, but was later divorced, and Jeanne Deroin, the self-educated teacher. Others also wrote for the paper, including correspondents from the provinces, who have not yet been identified. What distinguished their work was their consciousness both of class and of the links which bound women together. In their first number, they appealed to middle-class women (given in Anna Wheeler's translation): 'Let us not form two camps – that of the women of the people, and that of the women of the privileged class. Let our *common interest* unite us to obtain this *great* end.'[92] That appeal did not prevent them from criticising the *Journal des Femmes* of Fanny Richomme for its triviality. They identified a further division among women, that between the respectable and those who lived outside convention. They appealed to the respectable to see how far their lives simply reflected man-made laws and customs, of which both virtuous women and prostitutes were equally the victims. Their solutions were of two kinds: firstly, the material provisions, of education and equal employment, and secondly, more radically, the reform of marriage, the acceptance of divorce, and even the acceptance of sexual freedom for women.

Among this group, the case for sexual freedom was put most strongly by Claire Demar, whose work *Ma loi d'avenir* was published in 1834, after Demar's death by suicide. She had left the decision to publish to her friend, Suzanne Voilquin, who in her introduction pointed to the miseries faced by a woman who attempted to live out, in practice, the task of regenerating the moral world in the old corrupt society. Demar had been shocked by the moderation of the *Tribune des Femmes* on this issue, advocating rather a liberty without rules or limits: only in the love of the sexes could spirit and flesh come together. The facts of inconstancy, of shifting affections, could only be bravely recognised. Her work was cast in Saint-Simonian language and she drew also upon *The Children of God* . . . (English translation, London, 1833) by James Lawrence, whose *Empire of the Nairs* has already been mentioned earlier and who was now associated with the Saint-Simonians. Like Lawrence, Demar rejected the concept of certain paternity, but unlike him looked not for a matrilineal society but for a communal upbringing for children by those with the training

and capacity for it. In her work the echoes of the romanticism of
Diderot, of Lawrence, even Shelley, were strong, but Suzanne
Voilquin was more in tune with the other authors of the *Tribune* when
she suggested that moral and sexual liberty must depend first on the
achievement of economic independence by women.[93] When the
Tribune des Femmes collapsed, women Saint-Simonians, mostly
middle-class, continued to contribute to other journals on aspects of
women's situation. Pauline Roland, for instance, wrote of the
necessity of an onslaught on the professions by women, as did Louise
Magnaud on the need for education, in the *Journal des Femmes* or the
short-lived *Conseiller des Femmes* published in Lyons by the ex-St-
Simonian Eugénie Niboyet.[94] The sexual radicalism attributed to the
group, like Owen's ideas on marriage in England, led to an
association being formed in the public mind between feminism and
free love which was, for the most part, quite unfounded. Within such
movements, the ambiguities felt by educated working women might
be expressed. They were tempted to identify the harshness of their
situation – bound to men they did not love, entirely vulnerable to
desertion – with the conditions of marriage. Yet at the same time, for
their immediate survival and that of their children, they needed the
enforcement of what legal sanctions to maintenance existed. Perhaps
also they hoped for some material improvement in the future, for
some glimpse of the domestic relations enjoyed by that class
immediately above their own.

American examples of such challenges to convention were more
diverse and more experimental. New Harmony, established by
Robert Owen in Indiana, failed for much the same reasons as his
communities in England. Frances Wright, a woman from an
orthodox Scottish background, already unconventional in the
breadth of her travelling experience and for her friendship with the
French liberal, Lafayette, was both inspired by the practice of Robert
Owen and determined to take that practice even further. She had
been greatly shocked on her first visit to America in 1818 by the
institution of slavery, and on her later return, in 1824, attracted by the
applicability of the Owenite co-operative village to the southern
plantation. From 1826 she planned the establishment of Nashoba, in
Tennessee, to be sustained by the manual labour of slaves, but in
which free members of black, white and mixed race would be
admitted equally to membership. In her 'Explanatory Notes respecting the Nature and Object of the Institution at Nashoba . . .' she

proclaimed her commitment not only to 'the amalgamation of the races' but also to abolishing 'the tyranny usurped by the matrimonial law':

> The marriage law existing without the pale of the institution [Nashoba] is of no force within that pale. No woman can forfeit her individual rights or independent existence, and no man exert over her any rights or power whatsoever beyond what he may exercise over her free and voluntary affection.[95]

Her attempts were rapidly defeated in the face of practical and financial obstacles, and the notoriety which her community attracted. A more influential and long-lasting community preaching sexual nonconformity was that founded first at Putney, Vermont, and then at Oneida by John Humphrey Noyes. Noyes, who emerged in that halfway sector between millenarian Christian sects and utopian socialism, himself bred in fundamentalist American sects, came to be a Perfectionist, a believer in the possibility of achieving Christ's kingdom on earth. Noyes' ideal community was based upon a system of 'complex marriage', built on the ideal of sexual liberation, to be made possible by a method of controlling births, male continence or 'coitus reservatus': it was also regarded as a means of breeding better children. His work was influential among birth control campaigners, yet though he recognised the need for women to have sexual relationships without bearing children, the regulations which governed Oneida, and its patterns of sexuality, were still primarily male-dominated and controlled. However, not many experimental communities were as successful or as long lasting as that of Oneida.[96]

In general, the communities born of utopian socialism reflected one response to the harsh conditions of early industrial life, appealing to the displaced, to artisans and the lower middle classes, as well as to those with experience in the new factories. Such communities attempted to escape the harshness of the new market economy by the values of a collective way of life, a collectivism which did not separate domestic and productive spheres and therefore could still challenge domestic as well as industrial conventions. Yet by the 1840s the ambiguities of such a challenge, in the face of the increasing strength of new modes of production, were overwhelming. But the potential for effective criticism of the notion of 'woman's sphere' was certainly present in such movements, as seen in the energetic campaigns, and in the unprecedented public lecturing, of such figures as Anna Wheeler, Frances Morrison, Margaret Chappellsmith, Suzanne Voliquin and Desirée Gay, and Frances Wright. Such women were, however, rapidly made aware of the punishment that established society could and did mete out to such heretics and the aftermath of such radicalism was to be a retreat from confrontation on these issues.

In 1848 Karl Marx touched on these themes in the *Communist Manifesto* when he denounced 'the bourgeois claptrap about the family and education . . . the hallowed co-relation of parent and child'. His view sprang from an historical analysis of family changes, illustrating how the dominant bourgeois view, from the eighteenth century onwards, reflected property relationships and exclusivity, and was linked to the formation of capital. But the 'actual' family bound by affection and duty was in the process of dissolution, increasingly so among the proletariat, where nevertheless some examples of 'family affection, based on extremely real relations, can be found': perhaps those studies of family life which Engels, for example, cited in his *Condition of the Working Class in England in 1844* (1845). For Marx, 'the relation of man to woman is the most natural relation of human being to human being' and therefore from this relationship, from the condition of women, the level of emancipation of humankind might be judged. That view remained a romantic one, in which the nearness of women to nature remains the touchstone. Marx, like most other contemporary socialists, could not take that theme further or conceive of the political practice of women as relevant to the changing of their situation.[97]

Clearly a further question arising must be how far women were able to assert a right to limit their own families, to control their fertility. There is of course a massive literature on this subject: the problem here lies in distinguishing between family responses to changing circumstances – legal, social or economic – which may or may not reflect the influence of women within marriage, and assertion of women's right and need to restrict childbearing in their own interests. Even in a period of rising fertility demographic historians have been able to trace declining birthrates among the Leicestershire framework knitters in the second quarter of the nineteenth century, the French peasantry throughout the nineteenth century, and in the United States in, for example, late eighteenth-century Rhode Island and Pennsylvania.[98] The problems of establishing the responsibility for such decisions are so great that they will not be attempted here, though it has been suggested that the declining middle-class birth rates of mid-nineteenth-century Britain and America may indicate an assertion of female power, a degree of 'domestic feminism'.[99] It is difficult to know how such a suggestion, though it fits increasing stress on women's family roles, could be substantiated.

Discussion of the possibility of birth control and available methods did, however, surface in the early nineteenth century, for a variety of motives. The most common was the conservative, neo-Malthusian argument: the need to limit population to fit available resources. Women popularisers of political economy, such as Mrs Jane Marcet and Harriet Martineau, wrote didactically for a working-class audience on the need for moral restraint and the postponement of marriage.[100] Unsurprisingly, that case was not welcomed by the leaders of working-class movements or by most early socialists who, in looking to the future state of motherhood, in the 'New Moral World' saw no case for the individual woman to control the size of her family. It was virtually impossible for women to advocate birth control openly in the first half of the nineteenth century. A few exceptional male campaigners did so. Following the tracts which Francis Place, the London radical, had distributed on this subject in London and the Midlands, Richard Carlile, the radical bookseller, in 1826 published *Every Woman's Book; or What is Love?* . . ., describing three methods of contraception, one of which, the use of the vaginal sponge, was for a woman's use. Carlile shared his views, especially his anti-clericalism, with Elizabeth Sharples, with whom he lived, in defiance of convention, from 1831 to 1843. Two other works first printed in the United States, Robert Dale Owen's *Moral Physiology* (New York, 1830; London, 1832) and Charles Knowlton's *Fruits of Philosophy or, the Private Companion of Young Married People* (New York, 1832; London, 1834) advocated similar methods, though Knowlton doubted the efficacy of the sponge.[101] William Thompson, in the *Appeal of One Half the Human Race* . . ., had praised the possibility of the control of fertility, and John Stuart Mill, in his *Principles of Political Economy* (1848), perhaps spelt out most clearly of all the consequences, for women, of family limitation, that relief from '(along with all the physical suffering and at least a full share of the privations) the whole of the intolerable domestic drudgery resulting from the excess'.[102] Perhaps, through some of these writers, the influence of Elizabeth Sharples, Frances Wright, Anna Wheeler and Harriet Taylor Mill was heard. Perhaps also, there is more to be learned of the extent to which women lecturers, such as Emma Martin, did 'diffuse a knowledge of the human organisation', as advertised in the *Reasoner* in 1848.[103] The first direct evidence of support by substantial numbers of women for such writings came from 1856, when Dr George Drysdale, whose major work on contraception, *Physical, Sexual and Natural Religion* was published in 1855, received in the correspondence columns of his journal *Political Economist and Social Science* a number of letters from women supporting the cause, claiming to be diffusing such knowledge themselves.[104] There is much still to be learned on the relationship between feminist activities and sympathies and activism in the cause of birth control, but the case for improving the health and the wellbeing of married women through limiting births was increasingly being heard.

Yet for most women the question remained one over which they might exercise certain old-established and unreliable, even dangerous, means of control. Abortion became a crime in England for the first time in 1803, though disapproval had increasingly been expressed by the medical profession throughout the eighteenth century. Herbal preparations and quack remedies – 'Female Pills' – continued to be widely advertised, and very probably used, in the next century. Observers in both Britain and France pointed to the increasing rate of abortion, especially among working women in the cities. As one French doctor wrote: 'it is especially in the city that this scourge carries out its greatest ravages; there, and in certain gatherings, the ending of pregnancies by abortifacients is noted almost daily; friends do not even hide it from each other; it is a thing understood, excused, accepted.'[105] Such patterns were noted by English observers, especially in the textile districts, from the 1830s onwards. Perhaps the experience of working together offered women new sources of knowledge and support, in their own methods of family limitation. Middle-class women, too, might seek to use it, as they did in Britain and in the United States, where by the 1860s the medical profession were commenting on the very different attitudes of their women patients, mainly well-to-do, to themselves.[106] Certainly, even in rural France, abortion as well as infanticide was well known. The imperial prosecutor at Agen in France referred to infanticide as an aid to birth control, or a means of redeeming failures in birth control, suggesting that the number of infanticides by married women was increasing because of their determination to limit the number of their children.[107] There is thus much scattered evidence, of a kind which historians are only beginning to recover, that married women did feel the need to limit their families.

There was another, more direct and public way of assaulting the established framework of marriage: a way which could only be carried out effectively by members of the middle or upper classes though, as has been indicated, it was not without meaning for poorer women. This implied the recognition of the oppressive nature of the legal bonds of marriage and campaigns directed against them. Strangely, domesticity could itself fuel such campaigns. When Caroline Norton called in 1837 for the law in England to recognise the bonds existing between mothers and children, in allowing her access to, if not custody of, her own three young sons, she touched on an area where those who administered the law had already expressed some disquiet at the distance between the practice of the common law and the requirements of motherhood.[108] In the United States, in some states, legal practice was already more favourable to women than in Britain, and the issue of law reform had already been raised in the course of the American Revolution.[109] In both countries, some couples, such as Robert Dale Owen and Mary Jane Robinson, or Harriet Taylor and John Stuart Mill, or Lucy Stone and Henry Blackwell, preferred to write their own marriage contracts, even though they also underwent the legal marriage ceremony. Stone and Blackwell were to declare jointly in 1855 that:

> we deem it a duty to declare that this act on our part implies no sanction of, nor promise of voluntary obedience to such of the present laws of marriage as refuse to recognise the wife as an independent rational being, while they confer upon the husband an injurious and unnatural superiority.[110]

In 1836 Mrs Ernestine Rose presented the first petition for a Married Woman's Property Act to the state legislature of New York. Between 1839 and 1850 most states passed some legislation permitting married women to own property, but they still might not have legal rights to their own earnings or to custody of their children. And when in 1848 a group of women, dominated by the abolitionists Elizabeth Cady Stanton and Lucretia Mott, organised the Seneca Falls Convention for women's rights, their Declaration of Sentiments and Resolutions included lengthy denunciation of woman's legal situation, second only to her lack of citizenship in the catalogue of 'repeated injuries and usurpations on the part of man towards women': the civil death of married women, the absence of any right to their earnings, their irresponsibility if in their husband's presence, his right to control and chastise, and the laws of divorce.[111] The convention was to be followed, in the mid-1850s, by a series of petitions and campaigns which were to mobilise feminist opinion, at the same time as in Britain the petition of the married women's property committee was to draw together campaigners on this issue.

One of those who took up the cause of reform was Barbara Leigh Smith, daughter of a wealthy Unitarian and radical MP, who had given his daughter an excellent education. In 1854 she published the *Brief Summary in Plain Language of the Most Important Laws concerning Women*, whose forcefulness and effectiveness attracted the attention of legal reformers, already convinced of the inefficiency of existing laws. The committee formed by Leigh Smith to promote reform of the property laws was to draw together for the first time in England, in an organised way, a group of self-consciously feminist women.[112] It included besides Leigh Smith, Bessie Rayner Parkes, Anna Jameson, Elizabeth Reid, the founder of Bedford College, and Eliza Fox, daughter of W. J. Fox. The secretary was Mary Howitt who, with her husband, William, had come from a rather humble Quaker background and made a considerable success of a career in popular journalism. The feminist campaign coincided with an increasing willingness among lawyers to contemplate a reform which would regulate the institution of marriage, be applicable to all classes of society, and unite the different provisions of the common law and of the courts of equity. Two powerful articles in the *Westminster Review*, in 1856 and 1857, by Caroline Frances Cornwallis, were strongly to reinforce the case made by Leigh Smith.[113] Petitions with more than 26,000 signatures were collected and sent to the House of Commons, including some distinguished names, featured at the head of the petition: Elizabeth Barrett Browning, Elizabeth Gaskell, Harriet Martineau, Geraldine Jewsbury, Anna Blackwell and Marian Evans (George Eliot). The petition was based on the necessity for protecting the earnings of married women of all classes of the population, and was supported by the Law Amendment Society. Yet although a bill passed the second reading in the Commons by 120 to 65, the question was overtaken by the passing in August 1857 of the Divorce Act, which made divorce legal, though it embodied different moral standards in sexual conduct for men and women, and protected, to some extent, the economic situation of the divorced, separated or deserted woman. The campaign lost its momentum, yet the effect of its organising power was considerable, the more so in that it coincided with a growing current of legal reform, and with that support, the committee could realistically hope for some success. The importance of the reform of the law of marriage as an initial basis for organisation among middle-class women should certainly be stressed.

In France, no such basis existed. In 1837, Mme de Mauchamps of the *Gazette des Femmes* had petitioned against the articles of the Civil Code which prescribed a wife's obligation to obey and to reside with her husband, as contrary to the French Constitutional Charter of 1830. In 1836 she had petitioned for the institution of divorce, as did Flora Tristan in 1838. In 1848, feminists were to return to that issue, though when the question of divorce was raised in the National Assembly by a sympathiser it received little support: this was to be characteristic of all attempts to reform the legal basis of marriage in this period.[114] The problem was not merely one of legislation. The attempt by the Napoleonic Code to impose one system, the community of marital property, as uniform throughout France, was strongly resisted in some areas, especially the South, and in practice, people married with a wide variety of legal options, as far as the distribution of property between husband and wife was concerned. What was distinctive, however, was the maintenance of the dowry system, which gave the husband the use of his wife's income but not of the capital, embodied in law. Historians have pointed to the great regional diversity of marital practice, and equally to the ways in which families used the system gradually to adapt it to their own social and economic needs. The continued use of the marriage contract, stipulating under what legal regime the marriage would take place, must have helped to stress the material basis of marriage, for families as for individuals, and arranged marriages, for the bourgeois family, remained the accepted pattern.[115] There was to be no support forthcoming for reform of the legal structures of marriage. Not until 1884, when republicanism had a secure basis for anti-clerical policies in the Third Republic, did divorce return to France – and even then for political reasons rather than from any sympathy with feminist pleas.

There was of course one more way to challenge the married state, and that was from outside: to assert the possibility and indeed the desirability of remaining single. A number of feminist writers of the

1840s and 1850s made a case for the desirability of singleness, denouncing the ridicule poured upon 'old maids' and young women's expectations of marriage at all costs.[116] Feminists themselves were frequently identified with the single, the ugly, the sex-starved. In the cartoons of Daumier, in the columns of *Punch*, the satire abounded (Plate 12, and back cover). But when, in addition to this, the inevitable accompaniment of singleness seemed to be poverty, the case in its favour remained difficult to make. The first priority, for single women, was to secure the possibility of independence.

There was one acceptable way in which, even if in domestic isolation, educated middle-class women, married or not, might explore the tensions of domesticity. It lay, of course, in that one source of employment open to such women: the creation of imaginative fiction, journalism and the writing of popular literature. The impact of women on the literary scene in the first half of the nineteenth century, in all three societies, was considerable. By the 1840s critics, especially in Britain and the United States, had come to recognise the 'domestic novel' as a specific genre, the work mainly of women. The celebration of domestic virtues, the growth of children's personalities, the abandonment of the purely romantic for the realistic depiction of domestic detail: these were features of the work of the best minor novelists, such as Elizabeth Gaskell or Harriet Martineau. Journalists such as Mary Howitt in *Howitt's Journal* or Sarah Hale in *Godey's Lady's Book*, might, in different ways, celebrate women's domestic power. In the United States, from Catherine Sedgwick's early novels of the 1820s to those of the Warner sisters in the 1850s, novels by women were to develop themes of domesticity which illustrated the expansion of domestic virtues into moral and religious reformation of that world outside the home.[117] Male critics, employing a double standard of criticism, were all too likely to see this as a reflection of 'the natural limitations of feminine power'.[118] Yet in such a work as *Jane Eyre* (1847), the emergence of an adult woman with strong but controlled passions from the confining yet demanding conventions of Victorian womanhood was charted, powerfully and imaginatively. But Jane Eyre's rebellion and self-assertion were nevertheless constrained at the last by the limits which she herself placed upon them.

7. Politics, Philanthropy and the Public Sphere

Confusion has seized us, and all things go wrong,
The women have leaped from 'their spheres,'
And instead of fixed stars, shoot as comets along,
And are setting the world by the ears! . . .

They've taken a notion to speak for themselves,
And are wielding the tongue and the pen;.
They've mounted the rostrum; the termagant elves,
And – oh horrid! are talking to men!

Maria Weston Chapman 'The Times that
Try Men's Souls' (1837)[1]

NINETEENTH-century women did cross the boundary that separated private and public life, for a variety of reasons. Exploration of these reasons should help us to establish how far such ventures came to be undertaken on behalf of women themselves, even though they may have originated in women's identification with their community, their class and their church. Women clearly supported the political ambitions of their men and their communities in this period, though they may have seen their own role as auxiliary to those who might properly take part in public life. They might be drawn by their religious principles to go to meetings, join associations and even speak in public, as they were in the abolitionist campaign. Both working-class and middle-class women might support the issues most immediately relevant to their class, where they identified with it. All these sources of political action could provide a vocabulary, a language, which was not relevant to the world of men alone: the language of slavery and natural rights, of citizenship and representation, of individualism that was both religious, in emphasising the responsibility of the individual soul, and economic, in stressing the laws of the market-place. Such language could provide a very powerful set of images which women could adapt to their own struggle for political recognition. But, most of all, women did feel drawn by the argument that the qualities which they were expected to exercise in domestic life should be carried into the outside world, infused into public life. It was an argument which was by no means incompatible with the case for citizenship. But this understanding of the possibility of expanding and redefining the sphere of women's action is perhaps the most important element in the making of nineteenth-century feminism, and is found in all three societies, though in different degrees. It was not found in one class alone, though middle-class women very clearly dominated feminist action by the 1850s. It carried the potential for a focusing on specifically female issues, in which the concerns of women might aspire to cut across the barriers of class.

CROWDS, RADICALISM AND REVOLUTION

It has already been seen that when it was a question of demanding bread at a fair price, or attacking new machinery which might threaten a family's income, women were ready to take part. Whether they were likely to be so prominent in crowds that gathered at moments of political tension is less clear. Eugène Delacroix is said to have based his famous allegorical painting *Liberty Guiding the People* (1830) (Plate 8) on the courage of a young working woman, Marie Deschamps, at the barricades in the July Revolution in France.[2] The liberal observer Alexis de Tocqueville noted that women took as much part in the June insurrection in Paris as men, preparing their ammunition, carrying 'the preoccupations of a housewife into battle' – by which he meant that they hoped for better things for their families.[3] Yet only 'a tiny group' of women were arrested after that demonstration, and there were very few reports of women's participation in the newspapers, however they figured in artistic impressions. Perhaps, given the military nature of the action, they were less likely to take part.[4] But they might still have an important part to play in the rituals of crowd action, not just a symbolic role for artists of the new Republic. William Reddy, for example, has traced the changing pattern of crowd action at Rouen, where in August 1830, a month after the fall of the conservative Charles X in the July Revolution, an *état d'agitation* spread throughout the town, as crowds shut down mills and about 600 gathered outside the town-hall, demanding that the *tambour* or drum should lead the *cortège* or procession around the town in a mock-military march. Such crowds were not unusual, similarly occurring, for example, in Armentières and in Roubaix in 1830. And the crowds, according to Reddy, were 'almost certainly made up of as many women as men'.[5] Such crowds might well not distinguish too closely between 'economic' and 'political' reasons for action, and direct their hostility, once roused, against mills or public offices indiscriminately. Women might play an important symbolic role in such collective actions. In Lyons, in March 1848, after the news of the February Revolution in Paris, a crowd of working women first took to the streets, to demonstrate in favour of increased wages and reduced working hours, and to intimidate those who would not join them. Within the same month, a crowd of some 400 women, set to march in brigades to the sound of the *tambour* to the prison, where the prisoners were freed, were joined by male workers and by soldiers.[6] In the small town of La Garde Freinet, in the department of the Var, the authorities noted with disapproval in October 1849 a procession *en farandole* down the streets, led by women and followed by youths chanting political cries.[7] They might be involved too in organising a local *charivari* or carnival, with a clearly seditious political message.[8] The question is whether women were regarded as playing a purely symbolic role – at the head of the procession, bearing a flag – or whether their active political support was invoked. Much contemporary comment still referred to the role of the women of the people as 'veritable viragos, furies, shrews, enraged female devils', compared to the calm, graceful female figure, the proper allegorical representation of the republic, which was so much more acceptable to conservative republicans and to many on the left.[9] Women clearly did still have some public role to play in demonstrations, in *charivari*, in crowd action, but only, perhaps exceptionally, in military confrontations.

In the insurrection of 1851 in France, against the *coup d'état* of Louis Napoleon Bonaparte, women gave active encouragement to their men, but mostly remained behind, as the marching columns of peasants and artisans went off from villages and small towns. When the men of La Garde Freinet marched to overthrow the local prefect, their women urged them to bring back *La Bonne*, the authentic republic, and stayed behind as a garrison. In that department over 3000 men and only 16 women were to be arrested. They were mostly young married women, there with their artisan husbands. One at least, Mme Césarine Ferrier, was encouraged to march at the head of her procession, carrying a red flag and wearing the cap of liberty, so that other women would come to join. Four other women also accused of bearing flags came from the same village, where, 'when they announced that the people were sovereign, all we women and girls of the hamlet got together to dance the *farandole*'.[10] Some women, exceptionally, did take more violent action. Men, women and children followed 200 armed men in an onslaught on the gendarmerie of Clamécy in the department of the Yonne, and took brutal vengeance on those within.[11] The rising of 1851 was in many ways unusual, in that peasants and artisans took up arms against a well-armed and well-equipped state. However, it was not a spontaneous rising but one based on a network of secret societies. The democratic socialist message, spreading out from Paris, as the republic turned increasingly to the right, continuously attempted from 1849 to 1851 to build an organisation. And for the most part, that was an organisation based on the institutions of male sociability – the *chambrées*, the cafés, the trade associations – which excluded women. There were exceptions. Agulhon's study of the Var has shown how in areas where male leaders, perhaps sympathetic to aspects of Saint-Simonianism, recognised the importance of women's support – and also where there was well-paid work for women – evidence of strong political commitment and activism among women is present for some communes. In La Garde Freinet, for instance, they formed their own *société de prévoyance* or mutual insurance society, in 1848, and took a strongly anti-clerical view.[12] But we have too little evidence to know how exceptional this was.

The *coup d'état* crushed political activity after December 1851. But the example of that brief period of political association and action was to be a most significant one for the French working class, although the experience of the republic had offered little to women. Universal manhood suffrage had been achieved, in however limited a way: women would find no allies on the question of the franchise, no model as in Britain and the United States. The line was clearly drawn between the sexes. The majority of republican leaders had been contemptuous of political pretensions or even political interest shown by women, seeing little need to win their support. With the exception of a small minority, prepared to take feminist claims more seriously, the view, from the left as well as from the right, was most likely to be that of the socialist Pierre-Joseph Proudhon:

Women's role is not to be found in public life, the life of action and agitation, but truly in the internal life, that of sentiment and of the tranquillity of the domestic hearth. Socialism has not come only to restore work, but also to revive the household.[13]

The republic brought new forms of political association to France, but they were forms which tended to exclude women, as the tradition of crowd and community action became less important, though this would happen slowly in France.[14] The repressive political regime of the Second Empire brought few changes in the possibilities of political action for women, officially or unofficially. Those who claimed political interest, apart from a privileged few, had to confront directly a strongly entrenched code of male authority: that confrontation can be seen, at times, between 1848 and 1860.

In Britain too women had taken part in bread riots, enclosure protests and Luddism, and in the years immediately following the Napoleonic Wars they began to be drawn into more organised political action for the reform of the parliamentary system, as they had not been in the 1790s. In June 1819 the Blackburn Female Reform Society was founded, its aim 'to assist the male populations of this country to obtain their rights and liberties' and its members 'to use their utmost endeavours to instil into the minds of their children a deep and rooted hatred to their tyrannical rulers'.[15] Other such societies, in Manchester, Stockport, Nottingham and a number of other, mainly northern towns, followed. Female Reform Societies met weekly, made speeches, passed resolutions and showed their support for leaders such as Henry Hunt and William Cobbett. The situation was recognised as novel for all concerned. When the Stockport Female Reform Society met on 19 July, women members felt inhibited at the presence of men, and the president, a Mrs Hallworth, asked the gentlemen to withdraw:

with a view that in our debates (for it is something new for women to turn political orators) we should for want of knowledge make any blunders we should be laughed at, to prevent which we should prefer being by ourselves ... the male brethren immediately obliged.[16]

Cartoonists and satirists recognised the novelty too, and were not slow to portray these women as promiscuous and lustful harridans (Plate 10).[17] Though they were often received patronisingly, and clearly saw themselves as supporting 'husband, father or brother', the degree of organisation – and it was separate organisation – which they achieved was greater than any seen among French working women in this period. They too though could play a ceremonial part, as at Peterloo, when women in white dresses, with flags, banners and caps of liberty, were placed at the head of formations and on the main stage, with Mary Fildes, President of the Female Reform Society of Manchester, dressed in white in Hunt's own carriage (Plate 11). In the clash at Peterloo, when the yeomanry charged an unarmed political meeting, over a hundred women were wounded, and two were killed. After Peterloo, several women were charged with political libel or sedition as a result of their attempts to expose the affair. And in 1820–1 women in a number of major cities tried to demonstrate through addresses and the collection of money and petitions their sympathy, as women, for the apparently wronged Queen Caroline.[18]

One continuing concern of working-class radicals in the 1820s and 1830s was for a free press.[19] Richard Carlile, whom we have already met as an active supporter of birth control, did this as a part of his wider campaign through the press for radical free thought. On his imprisonment in 1820, his wife Jane attempted to carry on his newspaper, *The Republican*, but was herself rapidly tried and imprisoned for seditious libel. A volunteer, Susannah Wright, a Nottingham lace-maker, came to take charge, and herself faced imprisonment. Throughout the 1820s the paper depended on women for its distribution, and it kept up an enthusiastic correspondence with female republican societies where they still managed to exist. In the paper Susannah Wright made strong demands for improved education for women. The struggle was to continue into the early 1830s. In July 1832 a female group known as the Friends of the Oppressed was founded 'to aid and assist the wives and families of those who suffer in the people's cause'. One of their central aims was also 'to support . . . a really free and untaxed press'. In October 1832 a group of about 100 women assembled to welcome May Willis, an 'intrepid old lady' who had spent fourteen days in the House of Correction for selling the *Poor Man's Guardian*. One woman was to take that cause very much further. Elizabeth Sharples, a well-brought-up young woman from Bolton, a disciple of Carlile's from a distance, offered her help to him when he was again imprisoned in 1831. She not only took over the paper, like

Susannah Wright, but also gave public lectures at the Rotunda, the lecture hall in Southwark which had become a platform both for Carlile's freethinking rationalism and for the National Union of the Working Classes, founded in 1831 to express working mens' views on the reform crisis. Sharples spoke as a radical and as a rationalist:

> I propose to speak . . . of superstition and of reason, of tyranny and of liberty, of morals and of politics. Of politics! politics from a woman! some will exclaim. YES, I will set before my sex the example of asserting an equality for them with their present lords and masters and strive to teach all, yes ALL that the undue submission which constitutes slavery is honourable to none; while the mutual submission which leads to mutual good is to all alike dignified and honourable.[20]

Public opinion was shocked by the 'lady of the Rotunda'. She opposed the hierarchies both of Church and state, attacking the panacea of co-operation as one which did not meet the real strength of the ruling power, the Church and the army. She had in fact more in common with Thomas Paine than with the working-class radicals of the 1830s, and she took approval of Paine's work as a test for professedly radical candidates at a general election. She pointed to the tyranny of Church and of state as barring improvement in women's condition and appealed to her 'sisters' to seek equality with her. She was to put her beliefs fully into practice, lecturing and editing her paper the *Isis*, living with Richard Carlile and bearing him three children, and in 1849 adopting the 16-year-old Charles Bradlaugh.

The debate about the reform of parliament was to generate new interest in politics for the two years after the introduction of the first Reform Bill by the Whig government of 1830. A few female societies were newly formed, like the Female Radical Reform Society of Manchester, a branch of the National Union of the Working Classes, and others elsewhere in Lancashire. Other Political Unions, like that of Birmingham, were prepared to accept women as members. Women also took some part, though we do not know how great, in the riots of October 1831, certainly in Bristol and probably in Nottingham. In Merthyr Tydfil, women were a part of the massive rising of that community in May and June of 1831.[21] In London, the Friends of the Oppressed supported wives and families of the imprisoned, and M.A.B. of Bristol called upon women to employ the technique of exclusive dealing, that is, dealing only with politically sympathetic shopkeepers: 'The spending of money (especially in domestic concerns) is the province of women, in it we can act without the risk of being thought politicians'.[22]

For some years before the emergence of the Chartist movement, women had been aware of and ready to play some part in political associations directed towards the reform of the British Parliament. The manufacturing districts of the North had seen the most active organisations, but artisan politics in London, too, had drawn upon women's support. Whether via freethinking radicalism or from a background of evangelical respectability, like the women radicals of Elland, Leeds, some working women were in this period clearly being introduced to formal political organisation. The extent to which women participated in the struggle against the New Poor Law has already been discussed. Clearly that campaign had both a domestic and a political focus, and can be seen in the context too of a range of political movements of the 1830s. Between 1815 and 1850 women in Britain came to use the form of the political association quite extensively, and this is nowhere more apparent than in the development of the Chartist movement. Historians, particularly David Jones and Caroline Martin, have recently pointed out just how extensive working women's involvement in Chartism was: not limited geographically, as were earlier examples, but drawing in women from all over the country into a national movement.[23] It is clear that the vast majority of women in the movement participated in order to further the explicit aims of the Charter: a parliamentary voice for their husbands, fathers and brothers. Though the Charter mentioned political rights for women themselves only in a first draft, a number of leading Chartists still remained sympathetic to the principle: John Frost, William Lovett, Ernest Jones. Perhaps such aspirations simply seemed too distant from the problems of everyday life for the rank and file. The language of female Chartists is very clearly that of women who did bear the brunt of domestic life, and were even in some respects coming to share some of the assumptions of a more exalted view of domesticity. They were assumptions which might underlie the words of both male and female Chartists: Thomas Wheeler, for instance, appealing to the women of Britain:

> Women of Britain, you have ever been foremost in every good, in every noble cause: we entreat your assistance: this is pre-eminently

your cause; you have to bear the greater burden, the greater share
of our misery and distress; you have to endure the insult and
contumely of a class of avaricious and unfeeling shopkeepers, who
prey upon your indigence and want, you have to bear the thousand
varieties of domestic vexations, which to the impatient spirit of man
would be worse than the actual distress; you are then even more
interested than ourselves in procuring a fair day's wages for a fair
day's work; lend us then your powerful assistance; animate us in
the glorious struggle; cheer us by your approbation, enliven us by
your presence, and we cannot, we will not, fail in your success.[24]

Women members too assumed that they had a particular contribution to make to Chartism which arose from their own concerns: it
might be that of educating future Chartists, for they 'hold in their
hands the character and consequently the destiny of a nation. What
they are themselves, so are their children.'[25] It may be too that some
women found their way to Chartism through nonconformity: the
hymns sung at meetings, the banners covered with scriptural texts,
the meeting place sometimes in chapel or Chartist Church – all these
would have brought together Chartism and the language of the
evangelical movement.[26] The interest of women Chartists in temperance associations was widely assumed too, and lecturers often spoke
on the cause as one close to women's hearts. Another tactic which
they assumed to be peculiarly their own was that of exclusive dealing.
A number of Female Chartist Associations pledged themselves to
purchase only from 'those who are willing to be co-workers with us in
the great work of national redemption' like the Carlisle Female
Reform Association in December 1838.[27] Some writers came even
closer to the language of domesticity, in denouncing women's work
outside the home, as did S.S. writing of 'Female Slavery in England'
in 1848 in *The Labourer*: 'Withdraw women from their homes: break up
the family compact . . . make women day-labourers with men and
thus efface the peculiar modesty and delicacy of the female character. . . .'[28] The view echoes the better known and already quoted work
of R. J. Richardson, *The Rights of Women*, who stressed as he wrote it
(in jail) that his hopes for women's future were for 'good laws, happy
homes, cheerful hearths, loving husbands and prattling children'.[29]
Yet, at the same time, he believed that women had 'a natural right, a
civil right and a political right' not merely to a voice in political affairs
but to a vote. Though by no means all the leaders would have gone as

far as that, his work does illustrate a view which seems to have been prevalent: that women were qualified to take an interest and, at the very least, a supportive role, in the political campaigns of their class. To some extent, that view might depend on the extremity of the situation, the degree of distress which working people were feeling. The Birmingham Female Political Union wrote to the East London Female Radical Association, addressing 'Dear Sisters in Bondage', urging them not to confine their interests to the home, for:

> when that home becomes impoverished and desolate – when she sees the pallid countenances and tattered garments of her children – when she feels that the wages of husbands are inadequate to the support of his family, then it is woman's privilege to leave her home and join with her husband, father, or brother, to seek redress for their grievances.[30]

It is the extent of women's involvement which is very evident. From 1839 onwards large numbers of women, across the country, were forming Female Political Unions, Patriotic Societies, Chartist Associations and so on. About a third were in the old radical centres of Yorkshire, Lancashire and Cheshire, but the most active ones included societies of London, Birmingham, Bath and Nottingham. Birmingham and Nottingham societies recorded over 1000 recruits in 1838. Perhaps half the societies were formed in 1838–9, another quarter in 1842, and the rest later.[31] Sometimes they were the result of the initiative of male leaders, like that of Thomas Clutton Salt at Birmingham, sometimes of the coming together of women in the same street or workplace. An estimated average attendance at the usual weekly meetings would be between 25 and 75. Female societies would meet separately, have their own subscription and committee, hear guest speakers and discuss activities: the raising of petitions, the passing of resolutions, the fund-raising. Although the scale of such activities certainly reduced after 1842, it was by no means completely in decline. Individual women continued to be active, and some of the largest and most vigorous female associations were founded from 1847 to 1850. In public their activities were in the main supportive. They joined large meetings and demonstrations, often very much to the front of processions, ceremonially dressed, with white and green banners. Societies might begin by getting up a petition and house visiting for signatures, often of women only, like that from Merthyr

Tydfil for John Frost's release. They raised funds for all kinds of purposes: the National Rent, the Land Company, the Chartist Convention – but Martin's evidence suggests that they felt particular enthusiasm for supporting the families of imprisoned Chartist leaders.[32]

While women's societies may be seen as auxiliary to the main movement, and while the dominance of their domestic concerns should not be missed, still the radical nature of such involvement, seen in comparative perspective, should not be underestimated. No such widespread female organisation existed to support the French republican cause, neither did leading figures in the French working-class movement actively support such female participation. Clearly to some extent the support of Chartist leaders was a deliberate political tactic, in that some feared women's conservatism and commitment to religious values, and there were attempts to play explicitly, among women, on the heroic personal qualities of Chartist leaders such as Fergus O'Connor and Henry Vincent. Nevertheless, the level of organisation achieved required a level of political interest and experience which is far greater than that found in France at the same date. Some women did declare their readiness to take part in any struggle for their rights, however violent. But more significant is perhaps the literacy and articulacy of some Chartist women and the number of female lecturers, rapidly gaining experience in public speaking. In the early 1840s female lecturers were common within the Chartist movement, following the Owenite lecturers, at a time when that right had hardly been won by middle-class women. Prominent women among the Chartists included Susannah Inge and Mary Ann Walker of the City of London Female Chartist Association, both accustomed and confident speakers. So too was Elizabeth Neeson of Tower Hamlets Female Chartists Association, who with her husband consistently encouraged women's participation in the movement. Many lesser known women also addressed their local associations and others, on a variety of public affairs.[33] Their written contributions, too, were impressive, like those of 'Sophia' or of Helen Macfarlane, a writer and poet in Chartist periodicals, or even the letters of Elizabeth Hanson, the leader of the Elland radicals. It is among these women that some more direct assertions of women's own political potential were beginning to be heard. Susannah Inge, in her 'Address to the Women of England', wrote in 1842 that:

the period has . . . arrived when woman . . . has taken her stand in
the arena of politics . . . and has embarked with her light boat upon
the ocean of agitation to assist in steering the shattered bark of
liberty to a smooth and shattered haven.[34]

And 'Sophia' wrote to the *English Chartist Circular* that women had
indeed a far greater effort to make than men, since:

> Not only have we to assist *them* in the regeneration of our beloved
> country but to contend against those old prejudices which have so
> long militated against our improvement.[35]

Such arguments came most clearly from leading figures such as these,
though 'a working-woman of Glasgow' did write, as a 'Real
Democrat' to the *Northern Star* in 1838, that 'it is the right of every
woman to have a vote in the legislation of her country and doubly
more so now that we have got a woman at the head of our
government'.[36] G. J. Holyoake and Julian Harney, among Chartist
leaders, both pointed to the lack of demand among working women
themselves for the inclusion of female suffrage in the Chartist
programme.[37] But it should not be assumed, because this demand
was not made, that the domestic focus of women's lives entirely
excluded all political interest: the case could be, and was, made by
them for supporting and acting with male Chartists, on the grounds of
the most immediate political priority. If most women did not
themselves claim the suffrage, at least the issue had surfaced in the
context of the claim for universal manhood suffrage, among male and
female leaders of the movement.

What happened to that radicalism, in the course of the 1850s and
following decades, remains problematic. A few women Chartists, of
Sheffield, were to make the case for female suffrage, though not a
lasting one, and we need to know a good deal more about the later
careers of women active within Chartism. Clearly there were many
shades of opinion among female as among male Chartists, and the
growth of temperance and religious activity, of self-education movements and co-operative societies, may have had more appeal for
women. In the revival of the franchise question in the mid-1860s,
women played little part in organisations such as the Reform League.
Was this due to a wider diffusion of the values of domesticity, to a
more effective separation of the worlds of home and work? It is

difficult to see, both from the history of Chartism and from that of middle-class feminism, why this necessarily would destroy women's political interests, expressed on behalf of their families. Perhaps we should look rather, in Britain as in France, at the economic and social shifts strengthening the institutions of male, rather than community-based, sociability and association in the working class: the new trade unions for highly skilled labour, the growing economic importance of areas of new heavy industry with an entirely male workforce (transport, metallurgy, chemicals).[38] Chartism, on the other hand, had drawn much of its energies from artisan and textile communities, especially those of Yorkshire and Lancashire. Diana Gittins, in her study of twentieth-century regional variations in women's family lives, has pointed to the importance of women's employment, before as well as after marriage, especially in relatively large units of production with other women, in determining degrees of equality in family relationships, and in extending women's interests beyond the domestic circle.[39] Perhaps, for the second half of the nineteenth century, we need to look harder at local variations. David Jones has sensed, in Leeds and in Keighley, in the early 1850s: 'the excitement of building an alternative culture, with the family at its heart, and self-education and political rights as its message'.[40] And Jill Liddington and Jill Norris have established for the end of the nineteenth century the relationship between Lancashire women's work and their political commitment.[41] Clearly no simple split between domestic and public life will offer the key to women's participation in political action: community loyalties, male and female patterns of work and association, and domestic relationships must all be taken into account.

POLITICAL ISSUES: CLASS, SLAVERY AND RACE

The political involvement of middle-class women in Britain was in these years more limited. After 1832 their husbands were enfranchised: though there were important indications of the beginnings of activity by political parties, we do not know whether women were to any extent drawn into this, except as observers. Outstanding women, those of the aristocracy, had for many years both in Britain and in France presided over salons and provided some kind of focus for political groupings. Such a role was played in Britain, for instance, in the first decades of the nineteenth century, for the Whigs by Lady Holland, at Holland House. Other women of a slightly less elevated social standing, close to political affairs through the political or journalistic talents of their families, could also aspire to political influence. Harriet Grote, for example, played a not insignificant role in the Philosophic Radical group, which aimed to build a third party in the House of Commons, both through her influence on her husband, George Grote, and as a determined hostess.[42] For women who were literary lionesses themselves there were no barriers to active, if indirect, participation in political activity. Harriet Martineau found her opinions on the tactics of the Anti-Corn Law League sought by its leaders, and felt free to advise Cobden on his relationship with the Prime Minister, Sir Robert Peel, and to intervene on Cobden's behalf with Peel in the 1840s.[43] The intervention of such exceptional women was not new in political affairs; yet they were also to be in a position, at a later stage, to guide and to inform the first political steps of feminists who turned to parliamentary affairs.

On a broader stage, however, there are few indications of an active role comparable to that of Chartist women in the affairs that dominated conventional political life in Britain: with the one exception of the campaign to repeal the Corn Laws in Britain. From the beginning of 1841, in Manchester in particular, middle-class women, especially those previously prominent in philanthropic and anti-slavery work, gave themselves most energetically to the fund-raising and petitioning activities of the Anti-Corn Law League, dedicated to repeal those laws which protected English agriculture, it was believed, to the detriment of the consumer, and therefore of the manufacturer. By 1841, Manchester women had organised an 'Anti-Corn Law' tea party, and a bazaar, which, as J. Croker wrote, 'did not even pretend to be for any *charitable* object but entirely for the purposes of *political agitation*'.[44] By December of that year, the *Anti-Corn Law Circular* recorded that they had raised more than 50,000 signatures to a memorial against the laws, and that they were actively being followed by women in other Lancashire towns.[45] It was the middle-class women of the League who raised to a new degree of effectiveness a long-established fund-raising technique: the bazaar. Those in Manchester in 1842 and in Covent Garden in 1845 were clearly most successful and spectacular affairs, the latter especially, lasting 17 days and raising £25,000. Women had suggested the fair of

1845 and the Ladies Committee of the Manchester Anti-Corn Law League Bazaar played a significant role in its organisation: it had 360 members from all parts of the country, each acting as a link with her own community. In Manchester itself, a Mrs Woolley, who had been active in organising the fair of 1842, suggested division into districts, with women canvassing throughout their district for contributions. These were major organisational efforts: the techniques could be applicable both to political and to charitable exercises.[46] It is interesting that where Croker, quoted above, saw these actions as improperly political, another observer, the French economist Frédéric Bastiat, believed that women's efforts sprang from a charitable view of the role of the League: 'she [woman] has comprehended that the effort of the League is a course of justice and reparation towards the suffering classes; she has comprehended that almsgiving is not the only form of charity'.[47] The truth surely lies between the two – that philanthropic experience (and, to a certain extent, motives) could contribute significantly to the gradual extension of public activity among middle-class women, who would also have surely shared the common middle-class perception of the Corn Laws as symbolising the continuing strength of aristocratic and landed power in British society. But leaders of the League also appealed to well-to-do women to create, from their own property, votes from 40s freeholds which could be used in the interests of the League, even though such women could not themselves vote.[48] Such appeals must surely by their very nature have led women to reflect on the possibility of female suffrage? Perhaps it is no coincidence that such an issue, which symbolised the aspirations of an increasingly self-conscious class, but also had a vital social dimension, was more likely to draw women into the political sphere than the parliamentary battles of Whigs and Tories. But unlike similar fundamental conflicts in France, this clash was also contained within the politics of a pressure group: neither 1832 nor 1846 approached the level of revolutionary conflict.

There were, however, other kinds of action, which though not directed towards the orthodox political institutions of society, might still, for women, take on an important political dimension; which would lead them to associate together, speak in public and practise political skills. Certain kinds of association could emerge, as has already been seen, from religious commitment. The most notable examples of this, which united women's religious, domestic and moral concerns, were the movements against slavery and the slave trade in Great Britain and the United States. In Great Britain the campaign against the slave trade emerged at the end of the 1780s, reached a series of peaks in the 1790s, and was eventually successful in 1806. The issue revived in the form of a movement for the emancipation of slaves in the British West Indies in the 1820s and early 1830s and, once that was achieved in 1833, surfaced again in 1838 in the campaign to end the period of apprenticeship stipulated in 1883. There was a further revival, following and in sympathy with American abolitionism, before the American Civil War. It was a movement whose timing and impulse coincided with the evangelical revival, though its boundaries stretched some way beyond evangelicalism, and which similarly was to cut across class.[49] Much work still remains to be done on the contribution of women to the cause of abolition in Britain, but it is clear that from the 1780s it was never insignificant. Even in 1788, 11 per cent of the contributors to Granville Sharp's Society for the Abolition of Slavery established the previous year were female; by 1830 there were numerous ladies' anti-slavery auxiliary societies, encouraged most actively by male leaders. Women clearly attended meetings and public lectures in large numbers throughout the 1820s, and once there might be persuaded to form their own societies.[50] Local ladies' associations undertook a very considerable amount of fund-raising, gathered signatures for petitions, distributed tracts, and might, as did the local society of Sheffield, direct their energies 'chiefly among the poor of this town'. The Sheffield society had 80 members in 1825. Women were asked to exercise their talents within these acceptable ways:

> We would remind every lady in the United Kingdom that she has her own sphere of influence, in which she may usefully exert herself in this sacred cause; and the effect of that influence (even if it were quietly and unobtrusively confined to the family circle, or to the immediate neighbourhood) in awakening sympathy, in diffusing information, in imbuing the rising race with an abhorrence of slavery and in giving a right direction to the voices of those on whom, under Providence, hang the destinies of the wretched slaves. . . .[51]

Not only members of the middle classes but also working-class nonconformists joined the movement against slavery, though they might also compare black slavery to white wage slavery, and the separation of families under slavery with that forced upon white workers by the New Poor Law. A number of Chartist leaders were, however, convinced abolitionists.[52] In 1842, the attempt by the Quaker Joseph Sturge to launch the Complete Suffrage Union uniting Chartist and middle-class demands briefly brought Chartism and abolitionists closer together. It attracted the support of radicals, who were also sympathetic to women's rights and organisation: W. A. Ashurst, the Owenite, William and Mary Howitt, popular writers and editors of the *People's Journal*, W. J. Fox, editor of the *Monthly Repository*, and Elizabeth Pease, daughter of the great Quaker industrialist family of Darlington who declared herself a Chartist. A number of British women – Elizabeth Pease, Marion Reid, Matilda Ashurst, Mary Howitt and Anne Knight – had been present at the World Anti-Slavery Convention held in London in 1840, when the position of women in the movement was raised.[53] Continuing visits by American abolitionists to England won over more support for the American cause, especially among Chartists, and also acquainted British women in the anti-slavery movement with the links between the two causes.

Seymour Drescher has contrasted the strength of the anti-slavery movement in Britain, as a broad social movement, using the weapons of mass association and propaganda, with that of France, small, élitist, working from within.[54] The absence of a powerful evangelical network underlying the campaign in France, where there was a hierarchical state Church preoccupied at least initially with its own survival, explains much of the difference. French Protestants, individually, like Mme de Stael, and institutionally, through the 'Société de la morale chrétienne', founded in 1821, a socially distinguished, liberal reforming group in which Protestants were strongly represented, played a significant part in such anti-slavery action as there was. Signs of growing abolitionist interest in 1848 were rapidly silenced with the granting of colonial emancipation and the crushing of the revolution. Only in the aftermath of the American Civil War did French working-class opinion begin to support the ex-slaves' cause, and women begin to appear in such organisations as the Freedmans' Aid campaign in 1865.[55] The parallels with the slow growth of feminist activity in France are surely important, for the anti-slavery campaign was a highly significant one for the emergence of women in public life in both Britain and the United States. Its links with other movements, both religious and political, its organising dynamics and above all, of course, the imagery of oppression which it offered, made it an extraordinarily powerful example of the possibilities of organisation.

In the United States the abolitionist movement gathered real strength at a later date than the British campaign, from the 1830s to the 1850s, and it united evangelical religious opinion and political radicalism in the challenge not only to slavery, but to the entrenched political and economic system of the southern states. In so doing, it allowed women to continue to organise and to associate together which, as we have seen, they had begun to do as a consequence of the religious movements of the early nineteenth century. Those for whom the issue was one of survival, the black slave women, were able mostly to protest only in the simplest possible forms of resistance. Some were able to flee; others might, exceptionally, join communities of escaped slaves, or take part with their men in slave revolts. But the vast majority had no option but to continue working, resisting where possible by trying to acquire a little education, by trying to maintain family relations and to protect their children.[56] A few were able to do much more, especially free black women in the North. Perhaps the first American woman, black or white, to lecture in public was Maria Stewart, free-born in New England, who both in her writings and in her speeches appealed to black women to use their own talents and to educate their people: 'never will the chains of slavery and ignorance burst, till we become united as one, and cultivate among ourselves the pure principles of piety, morality and virtue'.[57] In September 1832, in a speech to a mixed audience in Boston, she pointed to the condition not only of enslaved but of free blacks, doomed even in enlightened Boston to be domestic servants only. She called too for coloured people to take their rightful part in the new Anti-Slavery Society. She did not continue her public speaking long, partly because of the hostility it raised, but in her farewell address in 1833 she defended her right to speak as a woman with reference to the Bible and to European history:

Did St Paul but know of our wrongs and deprivations, I presume he would make no objections to our pleading in public for our rights. Again; holy women ministered unto Christ and the apostles; and women of refinement in all ages, more or less, had had a voice in moral, religious and political subjects'.[58]

However, the movement and the contribution of free black women to it were to continue. Sarah Mapps Douglass, for instance, of a free black Philadelphia family, taught school for black children and was a Quaker, a member of the Philadelphia Female Anti-Slavery society almost from its inception, and corresponding secretary in 1838, attending a number of abolitionist conventions. Her friendship with the Grimké sisters led to their questioning of the racial prejudice existing in the Society of Friends.[59] Yet the argument which Maria Stewart had put was one quite fundamental to the origins of feminist action, and the abolitionist movement from the 1830s to the 1840s saw the emergence of a recognisable feminist theory and practice.

Some intimations of the issue had already appeared in the writings of Elizabeth Chandler, a young Quaker woman of Philadelphia, who in 1826 at the age of 19, sent contributions to an anti-slavery journal, *The Genius of Universal Emancipation*. Three years later she was placed in charge of the 'Ladies Repository' section, and after 1831 contributed also to William Lloyd Garrison's *The Liberator*. In her first column, 'An Appeal to the Ladies of the United States', she wrote:

> By all the holy charities of life is *woman* called upon to lend her sympathy and aid . . . . Will Christian sisters and wives and mothers stand coldly inert, while those of their own sex are daily exposed, not only to the threats and reviling, but to the very *lash* of a stern unfeeling taskmaster.[60]

She died young, in 1834, after founding the first anti-slavery society in Michigan in 1832.

The same arguments were clearly to be put by Garrison's paper *The Liberator* which launched from Boston in 1831 upon a policy of immediate and unconditional emancipation. As in England he and his associates took care to appeal to the 'Women of New England'. In 1832, responding to this call, the wealthy Maria Weston Chapman founded the Boston Female Anti-Slavery Society, an auxiliary to Garrison's male New England Anti-Slavery Society.[61] This, like other female societies, at first concentrated on fund-raising then on petitioning campaigns. Maria Chapman herself, however, gave very substantial assistance to Garrison, acting in effect as general manager of the national American Anti-Slavery Society which was founded in 1833. Lydia Maria Child, author of *The Mother's Book* and influential in Boston literary circles, backed the movement fully with her *Appeal on Behalf of That Class of Americans Called Africans* (1833) which, in line with Stewart, condemned not only slavery but also racial prejudice in the North. Initially, women were accorded no place at the official conventions. At the first one, Lucretia Mott, a leading Philadelphia Quaker, helped to draft the Declaration of Sentiments and Purposes yet was neither officially recognised as a member nor expected to sign the Declaration. Rapidly, however, an all-female national group was organised. Mott, as a Quaker used to public speaking, was a dynamic and influential leader. The movement and the number of female societies grew very fast.

In 1837 the first national organisation, the Anti-Slavery Convention of American Women, met with around 100 delegates: this convention came to focus most clearly on what women could achieve. Two women who actively participated were Sarah and Angelina Grimké from South Carolina, whose careers were to exemplify the links between the abolitionist and the feminist causes.[62] Originally from a slave-owning, well-to-do family, they had come to the liberal atmosphere of Quaker Philadelphia but found their efforts, even there, were limited. They noted the segregation that existed at Quaker meetings and began to shift their views away from Quaker orthodoxy, while increasingly studying the political message of *The Liberator*. Angelina Grimké was invited by the secretary of the American Anti-Slavery Society to speak privately to women on the subject. Instead, initially, she wrote her *Appeal to the Christian Women of the Southern States* (1836), appealing to the Bible, to the Declaration of Independence, but ultimately to the slave's natural right to be free. Southern women should take the responsibility, should free, or at the very least educate, their slaves, and move towards abolition by every possible peaceful means, especially by petitioning. The work was widely distributed, and the two sisters, defying the strictures of orthodox Quakers, took up pressing invitations to train as agents for the American Anti-Slavery Society. As soon as they had completed the training, they began to speak publicly, first in parlours and then, because of the numbers, in local churches, often to over 300 women. Throughout January and February 1837 their lectures continued, as the two sisters took active steps to ensure that black women also would attend the all-female Convention. When it met, uniting 71 delegates, run efficiently by women, the Grimkés stressed not just the evil of slavery, but that of racial prejudice as well: 'They [female slaves] are our countrywomen – *they are our sisters*; and to us women, they have a right to look for sympathy with their sorrows, and effort and prayer for their rescue'.[63] They believed that women should have a particular understanding for the nature of this oppression, for they too had been accused of 'mental inferiority' and denied education.

In their tour of 1837 through New England, the sisters focused all the prejudices of American society about the appearance of women as public speakers. They spoke for instance at Lynn, in June 1837, in the open air, to a mixed audience of over 1000, and as Angelina commented: 'It is wonderful how the way has been opened for us to address mixed audiences, for most sects here are greatly opposed to public speaking for women, but curiosity and real interest in the antislavery cause . . . induce the attendance at our meetings.'[64] Most of the older New England churches had supported a gradual commitment to emancipation and received travelling abolitionist agents with hostility. The Grimkés were to be attacked both as abolitionists and as women. Angelina Grimké herself took the step of criticising Catherine Beecher, that pioneer of women's influence in the home, who took a conservative view of female abolitionist tactics. In her *Letters to Catherine Beecher* (1837) Angelina Grimké defended such tactics, attacked all forms of racial prejudice and defended woman's rights as a citizen, including the right to petition, and

> to have a voice in all the laws and regulations by which she is to be governed, whether in Church or State, and the present arrangements of society, on these points, are a violation of human rights, a rank usurpation of power, a violent seizure and confiscation of what is sacredly and inalienably hers.[65]

Conservative churchmen retaliated, and in a Pastoral Letter, one to be read in all the Congregational Churches of Massachusetts, denounced the sisters and exhorted women to remember 'the appropriate duties and influence of woman' which might be reflected in 'the unostentatious prayers and efforts of women in advancing the cause of religion at home and abroad', but clearly not in the character of itinerant lecturers and teachers.[66] Sarah Grimké's reply was a clearly feminist statement, *Letters on the Equality of the Sexes* (1837) first published as a series of articles in the *Spectator* and reprinted in the *Liberator*. Grimké based her argument on the Scriptures, and defended the moral equality of men and women. The moral duties which women, like men, should undertake would be better carried out by better educated women. She challenged that 'sphere marked out for us by man', a sphere which left women carrying out the subordinate work in religious and benevolent activities, for if women were allowed to be ministers, they would clearly interfere with existing patterns of ecclesiastical male authority. It was an attack not only on religious authority, but on the contemporary legal and economic situation of women.[67]

The Grimké sisters were led by their participation in the anti-slavery cause to challenge most forcibly not only the racial prejudices of American society and the practice of slavery, but also the clerical authorities of that society. Their radicalism in speaking to large mixed audiences could of course be paralleled in Britain in the 1830s and 1840s: yet it was a very major step. Public speaking, the right to petition, to organise, to act as a paid and travelling agent – all these were new ways of assertion for women. The Grimké sisters, though continuing their steady commitment, withdrew from the limelight after 1838, but by that stage, women's participation had expanded very greatly. A survey of the spurt of petitions growing out of the first Female Anti-Slavery Convention suggests that in the petitions sent to Congress in 1837–8, over 40,000 women's signatures were obtained, outnumbering men by more than two to one.[68] The distribution clearly followed that of the all-female societies set up in the wake of the Grimké's tour. An organised network had been established very rapidly. From petitioning, it was not a long step to canvassing the opinions of politicians, even campaigning for them. But the dominance of women, and the threat to clerical authority, helped to bring about a significant split in the movement by 1840, when the women asserting the feminist case remained with Garrison, though others seceded with the clerically-dominated group. The conflict came to a head in the World Anti-Slavery Convention held at London in the same year, when American women delegates, including Lucretia Mott and others, demanded to be accepted as full members, a demand still quite contrary to English practice. Both English and American representatives defended the women's rights, but were outvoted by a great majority. The consequence was that Lucretia Mott, and the young wife of a delegate who had defended women's membership, Elizabeth Cady Stanton, agreed that they would on their return 'hold a woman's rights convention', since the men to whom they had just listened were so much in need of further education.[69] Such a meeting did not in fact take place for another eight years, since Stanton remained absorbed in domestic life and Mott in anti-slavery campaigns. Women continued their anti-slavery work, whether as journalists, like Lydia Maria Child, or as lecturers, still often rebuked and reviled, like Abby Kelley, who took over as a travelling agent where the Grimké sisters had left off. The appeal of the movement and the connections between feminism and abolition-ism were growing, as were the links of women involved with the issues of legal reform, of temperance and of health reform.

But there could of course be conflicts of interest between the two movements, though these were not so easily apparent before the Civil War as afterwards. Frederick Douglass, the great black pioneer of the abolitionist movement, played a leading role at the first Woman's Rights Convention in 1848 in Seneca Falls; and on his initiative the National Convention of Coloured Freedmen also passed a resolution on the equality of women. The famous ex-slave, Sojourner Truth, who had won her freedom when New York abolished slavery in 1827, had managed to retrieve her son, illegally sold away, and support herself by domestic work in New York City, before she became a travelling abolitionist, and spoke at the women's rights convention in Akron Ohio in 1851, to meet male ridicule of women's aspirations: 'I have ploughed and planted and gathered into barns, and no man could head me! And ain't I a woman'.[70] Such contributions did not, however, imply an absence of racial prejudice among white women – seen in the reluctance of many to allow Sojourner Truth to speak at all. Another leading black woman, Sarah Remond, from Salem, Massachusetts, had belonged to local anti-slavery societies from an early age, and was in 1856, at the age of 30, appointed an agent of the American Anti-Slavery Society, appearing at the Woman's Rights Convention in New York City in 1858. In 1859 she travelled to England to press her cause, and lectured forcefully on the harshness of slavery, on the separation of families, and on 'the female slave, the most deplorably and helplessly wretched of sufferers'. In the same year, she also enrolled as a student at Bedford College, boarding with the founder Elizabeth Reid. Her career was to attract the notice of the *English Woman's Journal*, which was entirely sympathetic to the abolitionist cause.[71] In these years, the language of natural rights, the sense of religious mission, and that of women's particular fitness for the task at home, meant that feminists and abolitionists continued to fight on both fronts together, though often with very different emphases.

MORAL REFORM AND PHILANTHROPY

Linked to this campaign in the United States, and to a wide range of philanthropic concerns in Britain, were the secularly oriented social and moral issues which came most to concern middle-class women, and into which much of their organising ability went, especially as the intensity of the religious revivalism of the earlier period receded. Women organised to achieve the reform of society, both through individual moral reform and through awareness of the broader social issues that affected societies divided by class. In the process they might come to challenge male authority, both in terms of men's differential standards of sexual morality, and more directly in relation to the power which men exercised inappropriately over women. Two examples of campaigns for the moral reform of individuals were those against temperance and against vice, both actively under way by the 1850s in Britain and in the United States. The earliest temperance associations in Britain, from 1830, were built on a shared Anglo-American foundation of evangelicalism and humanitarianism, and on the campaigning experience of anti-slavery. But the campaign had a complex history: at first it drew together only abstainers from spirits, and then, in the early 1830s, the mainly working-class teetotal societies gathered strength.[72] By 1853, with the founding of the United Kingdom Alliance, a strong case was made by radical reformers of all classes for legislative intervention. The part which women played within this history is by no means clear, and still awaits further discussion. Yet it is relevant that both in the early working-class movement, and at a later date, the case for temperance appeared to have an immediate relevance for women, even, as Brian Harrison suggests, being 'a modest form of feminism: the belief that resources should be diverted from purely male pleasures to expenditure which could benefit the whole family'.[73] It drew from those progressive, radical sections of middle-class opinion which were likely also to support anti-slavery, peace movements and the repeal of the Corn Laws, and among whom evangelical and Quaker opinion was strongly represented.

It has already been suggested that Chartist leaders believed temperance to be an issue of particular interest to women, and a number of Female Chartist Abstinence Unions were established. Women, when organising Chartist social activities, might, as did a group in Halifax in October 1840, offer a Chartist Temperance Tea Party.[74] In January 1841 the East London Female Total Abstinence Chartist Association published a long address on the necessity for abstention from drink and tobacco:

> Come then, sisters and countrywomen ... let us form Total Abstinence Chartist Associations without delay, in every town and village throughout the United Kingdom; nor cease agitating until our exertions are crowned with success.[75]

Mary Smith of Leeds, writing in April 1842, similarly proposed a National Female Anti-Tobacco and Temperance Association.[76] As Harrison suggests, teetotalism and Chartism had much in common, appealing to those Chartists who believed in the possibilities of individual self-improvement and self-education. For women, though, surely the temperance movement had a deeper dimension: it was about the use and control of family resources and leisure time, an assertion of domestic priorities.

In its early years, temperance won strong support from Primitive Methodists, from Bible Christians and from other seceding Methodists. But increasingly it was linked with more orthodox denominations, until by 1859, with the adherence of Anglican evangelicals, it became very much more of a religious than a radical movement. One phenomenon which accompanied this was a stress on rearing sober children. In 1847, a Mrs Anne Carlile, the widow of a Presbyterian minister, whose activities included prison-visiting, temperance work and the rescue of prostitutes, while visiting Sunday Schools in Leeds first applied the term 'Band of Hope' to children committed to temperance. By September 1847 a ladies' committee of the Leeds Temperance Society was appointed to visit local schools, and the new Band of Hope was founded with, by 1849, some 4000 children under 16 having taken the pledge. From its Leeds origins it rapidly became a national movement. A study by Shiman suggests that in spite of its foundation by Mrs Carlile, women did not act as agents in the national movement except as unpaid assistants – but one might perhaps expect women's influence through Sunday School teaching to be strong.[77] It seems more likely that active middle-class women temperance reformers would by the 1850s be committed to the religious and respectable National Temperance League, rather than to the United Kingdom Alliance, committed to legislative change through complete prohibition. Several women in particular played a part in the Anglican revival of interest in temperance in the late 1850s. Clara Lucas Balfour, an extraordinarily prolific moral writer, Bible Christian and temperance lecturer, published in 1849 her *Woman and the Temperance Reformation*, which viewed women as 'the most influential moral teachers of society' with a particular responsibility to promote virtue, and a mission to reform husbands, children, even vulnerable women themselves. In 1853 the Birmingham Ladies Temperance Association, in which the Quaker Mrs Sturge was prominent, was founded as a response to a ladies' conference held in London in the same year. The Birmingham Association called 'attention to the destruction of domestic happiness in this country which may be traced to intemperance', and gave its energies to the local distribution of tracts.[78] Middle-class women were drawn through parish visiting or through charitable work into such societies. This was especially the case with one pioneer reformer, Mrs Julia Wightman of Shrewsbury, a vicar's wife, whose *Haste to the Rescue* (1859) was extremely influential in converting members of the Church of England to the cause. Influenced by the 'gospel temperance' of the American temperance preacher J. B. Gough, she founded a total abstinence society at Shrewsbury, after pleas from the wives of two drunken parishioners. She rapidly won working men to sign the pledge, and linked her work to prayer and Bible meetings, and to social activities centring on a Working Man's Hall.[79] Her work was followed by many, and by the Church of England Total Abstinence Society founded in 1862, though it was not until 1876 that the separate British Women's Temperance Association was set up. Again, we know very little about the participation of women in different elements of the temperance movement, though there are clear indications of an overlap between sympathisers with teetotalism and feminists of the 1860s and 1870s: though, of course, there was no complete alignment, and some temperance reformers such as the politician John Bright were quite hostile to women's rights.[80] The *English Woman's Journal* reviewed with sympathy the efforts of Clara Lucas Balfour, Julia Wightman and Mary Bayly, whose *Ragged Homes and How to Mend Them* (1860) seemed to exemplify the results of such labours.[81]

In the United States, the energies of feminists were to be put not so much to the cause of reform among the working classes as to legislative change, and for a short time after 1848 the causes of temperance and women's rights ran together. Early temperance societies did permit women an auxiliary role from the late 1820s, and a new energy entered the movement after 1840 with the foundation of the Washington Society, independent of churches and attempting reform on a much wider scale. It rapidly developed a women's auxiliary in the Martha Washington Society, to be followed in the 1840s and 1850s by the Sons, and then the Daughters, of Temperance. Women participated actively in the 1840s in campaigns for local options. Some women apparently 'took power into their own hands, visiting saloons, breaking windows, glasses, bottles, and emptying demijohns and barrels into the street'.[82] Temperance by the 1840s was a matter not just for individual and social reformation but for political change, cutting across political loyalties. After Seneca Falls, with their abolitionist experience, women claimed a share in this political campaign.[83] When forbidden to speak in the convention of the New York Sons of Temperance in January 1852 or to send delegates to the World Convention in 1853, women formed their own Woman's State Temperance Society for New York in 1852. Elizabeth Cady Stanton's address to that society showed how fundamental she felt the links between temperance and women's rights were. It was, she said, 'a woman's rights society' – women claimed the right to speak, to be present at councils, to be agents of the society. They had also to care for the legal disabilities of the drunkard's family: only reform of the marriage laws, and ultimately the suffrage, could remedy their situation. Similarly, the reformer Amelia Bloomer linked the causes of feminism, abolitionism and temperance in her newspaper founded in Seneca Falls in 1849, the *Lily*. Stanton herself published a series of articles in the paper. The *Lily* argued that female suffrage was essential to control the liquor laws and to legislate for other reforms, including the right of women to escape from drunken husbands. It was a case which rested on a belief in the necessity of social and political reforms which would allow women to exercise their proper influence, to regenerate society. Some regarded Bloomer as too cautious in her reforming aims; yet she was prepared to champion women typesetters against the male printers on her paper, and to be identified with that 'short dress' which became so easy a target for ridicule, though she defended it in radical terms: 'in dress, as in all things else, we have been and are slaves, while man in dress and all things else is free'.[84]

There was also a strand running through the temperance movement which extended individual reform and self-help to personal health. Tobacco was frequently seen as as much of an evil as alcohol: coffee and tea might also be banned. Women were to show a particular interest as a movement for improvement in personal health, based on greater knowledge of physiology and on self-help, grew. Homeopathy, the 'botanical medicine' of Samuel and John Thomson, as spread by Samuel Hahnemann in the United States from the 1820s, and the teaching of Silvester Graham on diet reform, all had considerable appeal for women. 'Ladies Physiological Reform Societies' were founded in the United States, on the explicit model of charitable and anti-slavery societies. Women such as Paulina Wright Davis and Mary Gove Nichols began to lecture on hygiene and on dress reform. Harriot Hunt, who helped to set up the Ladies Physiological Society in Charlestown, Boston, explained:

> If women could be induced to meet together for the purpose of obtaining a knowledge of physical laws, it would enable them to dispense in great measure with physicians, put them on their own responsibilities, and be a blessing to themselves and their children.[85]

Harriot Hunt and her sister set up in medical practice without training, gave lectures on physiology in working-class districts and through what they learnt of working-class women's ignorance and deprivation came to identify with the women's rights movement. By the end of the 1840s the reforming crusade among women health reformers had reached the point where a case could be made for the education of women physicians, especially since several women already practised, though they were unqualified. Elizabeth Blackwell, who graduated from Geneva College, New York, in 1849, was to point to the necessity of 'the application of scientific knowledge to women's necessities in actual life', and to the phenomenon of medical lectures and societies amongst women. Though unsatisfactory, they were evidence of how such themes bore on women's interests, and their immediate inclination to diffuse that knowledge: 'As teachers, then, to diffuse among women the physiological and sanitary knowledge which they need, we find the first work for women physicians'.[86] But the hostility of orthodox medical schools in the United States to the idea of educating women led to the formation of women's medical colleges: Boston Female Medical College and the Female Medical College of Philadelphia in 1850. A few small reforming colleges, unorthodox and sectarian to the mainstream medical profession, such as Central Medical College of Syracuse, New York, were to initiate co-educational medical education. Both forms of medical school were slowly to develop, though in the 1850s, only three women, including Elizabeth Blackwell, were to gain admission to regular medical colleges and to graduate. But the impetus clearly arose from the need to spread medical knowledge among women more generally, given their particular need of it, as well as to provide professional employment for women. In Britain, middle-class feminists of the *English Woman's Journal* similarly showed interest in health reform, in hygiene and in the improvement of physical education among women. Emma Martin, the secularist lecturer, trained as a midwife and began to agitate against the male domination of health care and for women's right to be trained in obstetrics and gynaecology. She was herself to offer lectures in gynaecology and courses in midwifery.[87] It is probable that much still remains to be learned of the movement for health reform in Britain in the first half of the nineteenth century.

Temperance and health reform were thus both causes to which women reformers were drawn: though by no means all temperance reformers were feminists. A further example of reforming zeal may be seen in the attempts to confront that social evil which most contravened the standards of domesticity. From the 1830s city missions pioneered the reclamation of the 'fallen' and in taking part, as an extension of Christian missionary work, women were led both to question the double standard of morality which permitted such a social evil, and the restraints on respectable women which sought to prevent them understanding and reforming it. In New York, in the early 1830s, as a part of the missionary work undertaken in the aftermath of Finney's revival, women involved in Sunday Schools and Bible classes came to visit prisons and hospitals, and to be drawn into the problems of the inmates.[88] A group of women established the New York Magdalen Society, and opened a House of Refuge: when they were greeted with public hostility, they were forced to retreat. But gathering strength, they returned, and in May 1834 founded the

New York Female Moral Reform Society which, aiming in the long term at a morally pure world, in the short term hoped for the reclamation of individual prostitutes. Through their journal, the *Advocate of Moral Reform*, and through paid agents, they built a network of 445 auxiliary societies, mainly in the New England countryside. Male missionaries led the visiting, but in their company middle-class women too might go the city's brothels. A new House of Refuge was founded, though it was never very successful. Their work began increasingly to take a preventive turn, such as setting up an employment agency for poor but 'honest' women, and extending their home visiting. The moral reform movement, as seen in New York, gave such middle-class women the means of organisation, extended their moral influence, allowed them to express hostility to male behaviour, and also, in warning against it, to propose means of monitoring and limiting it. Their paper contains many militant statements, as when, for example, in 1837 it was suggested that ladies should retire from the field, they replied:

> We regard ourselves as acting on the behalf and in the name of a large portion of our sex to whom we have virtually pledged ourselves, and as occupying ground which none but women could so appropriately or so efficiently fill.[89]

New York work aroused much notice in Britain in both the orthodox and the radical press. David Nasmith, a peripatetic evangelical Scottish Presbyterian missionary in New York at the foundation of the City Mission there, brought the concept to London in 1835.[90] Together with a group of evangelical clergy, he founded the London City Mission, with its Tract Society, Reading Room, Adult School and London Female Mission. It was the conduct of the latter, and its closeness to mission work, which led his backers, shortly afterwards, to withdraw. Nasmith defended himself but eventually withdrew from London activity. There is no indication that women played much part in the London mission, unlike that of New York, though they had contributed for many years to charitable organisations with some relevance to this work. In Britain, it was only in the 1850s that women made out the case for their active intervention to aid the fallen.[91] The penitentiaries and the houses of refuge for women in the early nineteenth century were harsh places, requiring strict discipline. Anglican sisterhoods opened new houses, which were similarly harsh, in the early 1850s, but in the same decade more serious attempts were made to meet the problem by leading evangelicals, including the Rev. Baptist Noel from the London City Mission. The Rescue Society (1853), the London Female Preventive and Reformatory Institute (1857) and the Homes of Hope (1860) were all established in these years. And in 1858, as a subcommittee, the Female Mission of the Fallen was set up, as a 'woman's mission to woman'. Women were to play a continuing role in both the management of institutions and in rescue work. Male workers were at a disadvantage in that their intentions were likely to be misunderstood, and female reformers did take a particular interest in prostitution, as the most destructive of all the evils of family life. Emma Sheppard, in *An Outstretched Hand to the Fallen* (1860) wrote that 'a woman's hand in its gentle tenderness can alone reach those whom *men* have taught to distrust them'.[92] Faced with contemporary views about respectable women even coming into contact with the fallen, let alone going on to the streets and into brothels, some women accepted such limitations – but the boldest did not. That same Mrs Julia Wightman of Shrewsbury who was prominent in the temperance movement equally recorded how she had been able to save young women from the penitentiary, in *Annals of the Rescued* (1861). It is difficult to estimate the effect of such work on the middle-class women who took part and on those 'rescued'. Middle-class women were brought immediately into contact with quite different and hostile world, and with women of a class previously perhaps unknown to them. Some prostitutes were genuinely reclaimed and helped.[93] For others, 'rescue' could mean merely entry into a disciplinary refuge where little real understanding of their problems was shown and the numbers returning to the streets were high.[94] Prostitution was seen in Britain before the imposition of the Contagious Diseases Act as a moral issue, not one for legislation: rescue work by 1860 had begun to develop the theme of women's mission in the cause of purity and of their sisters.

In the United States, the work of the Female Moral Reform Society in New York continued, and was paralleled elsewhere by the many local moral reform societies which corresponded with it. By 1848, after a hard fight, it had succeeded in getting the Act to punish Seduction as a Crime on to the statute book of New York State. Renamed the American Female Guardian Society, it continued its work, though gradually the emphasis shifted from the moral reform of the individual to a greater understanding of the environment of the prostitute and of the need to work on all fronts to prevent prostitution, in the home and family, by offering alternative and better paid employment, and by extending 'women's mission' most clearly into those institutions where destitute women were likely to be found: hospitals, asylums, prisons. By the 1850s the *Advocate* had become a clearly feminist paper, one which celebrated and consciously sought to extend into the public sphere the work of women. In 1852 an article on 'What Rights have Women?' reviewed the evidence of the Bible, and came to the conclusion that '*the rights and privileges of the sexes are equal – are the same.*[95] Moral reform was indeed one distinctive way in which women moved from association in the name of religion to association which might, though inspired by religious belief, be turned to secular purposes and social reform. In France, that route does not seem to be present in the same way at this period. Prostitution was tolerated and regulated by the French state. Individual French feminists had denounced it, as did the *Femme Libre* and the *Gazette des Femmes* in the 1830s, Jeanne Deroin in *La Voix de Femmes* in 1848 and Julie-Victoire Daubié in 1866.[96] Yet no organised movement was generated until the mid-1870s, and then under the inspiration of Josephine Butler's English campaign. In Britain, middle-class women were slower to organise in movements of moral reform, and at this date, less committed to legislative intervention – with its implication of a political role for women – than their American counterparts: moral reform was a less direct, less immediate route to feminist thinking and organisation. But the connection was clearly made, and the double moral standard denounced in, for example, the work of Anna Jameson,[97] and an organisational basis was to be found in the campaign led in the 1870s by Josephine Butler against the attempt to impose a limited state regulation in Britain in the Contagious Diseases Acts.[98]

Middle-class women also undertook in this period a wide range of philanthropic work, which rested primarily on their religious commitment and on their desire to spread knowledge of a better way of life, based on cleanliness, order and domesticity, in the face of the unpromising urban environment. In doing such work middle-class women both learnt organising skills and acquired an occupation for themselves: it was an occupation inseparable from a notion of superiority, of class, of education, perhaps of race; though it was also undertaken from a view that women had something unique to offer to their fellow women, in aiding them to come to terms with the conditions of urban life in an industrial society. Organised philanthropy was of course by no means new in the nineteenth century. Prochaska has illustrated how women's contributions to charities, and female charities, grew with evangelical inspiration between 1790 and 1830.[99] Only one such society existed before 1795 in Britain, though seventeen were founded and managed by ladies between 1795 and 1830. In a sample of twenty societies of which two subscription lists survive, Prochaska has traced 'a dramatic rise in the percentage of women contributors within these expanding charities'. Most strikingly, for example, among contributors to Sir Thomas Bernard's Society for bettering the Condition of the Poor, the proportion of female contributors rose from 13 to 31 per cent from 1798 to 1805. Those energies which have been traced in tractarian, missionary and educational movements were also to be applied to the purpose of social reform, though reform which mainly had a conservative aspect. Catherine Cappe's career, for instance, shows the way such work might progress, from her early interest in Sunday Schools and Female Benefit Clubs, to her work for charity schools in York, to the setting up of a Ladies' Committee in York under the inspiration of Sir Thomas Bernard's society, to her pamphlet, written in 1816, on the importance of female visitors in charitable work in general.[100]

The same developments can be traced at a similar time in the United States. Isabella Graham founded the first all-female benevolent society in 1787, the Society for the Relief of Poor Widows with Small Children. Both she and Mrs Stillman, who in 1800 set up the Boston Female Asylum, found themselves ridiculed but rapidly followed by others, as female associations began to proliferate after 1820. There was much doubt of women's capacity to manage their own affairs, and some societies were indeed assisted by 'a committee of gentlemen'. Some women were, like Isabella Graham and her daughter Joanna Bethune, both devout evangelical Presbyterians, active in many causes. Bethune played a major part in the Society for the Relief of Poor Widows, in the Orphan Asylum (1807), the Society for the Promotion of Industry among the Poor, the New York Female Union Society for the Promotion of Sabbath Schools (1816) and the Infant School Society (1827), all in New York and all expanding rapidly in the early nineteenth century. Already it was a characteristic of such societies that they aided women who found it hard to gain occupation or employment in the city. As has been noted, women tended to support charities dealing with 'pregnancies, children, servants, and the problems of aging and distressed females'.[101] Yet middle-class women's priorities, as philanthropists, were to shift in important ways in the course of the nineteenth century, while their contributions overall, both in money and labour, steadily increased. Their priorities were related not only to their sense of mission to their own sex, but also to the interaction of state and voluntary associations, especially in Britain.

Women certainly had a distinctive part in the routine charitable work undertaken by them. In the course of the century their methods of fund-raising and organisation saw much development: the organisational efforts which went into the charity bazaar, or in the mobilisation of children as contributors and collectors of funds, have been most clearly traced by F. K. Prochaska.[102] Perhaps what is most relevant here, firstly, is the extent to which charitable effort was directed towards the homes of the poor, and secondly, the claims made by women to a share in institutional authority, as their voluntary role appeared to be displaced by the intervention of the state. Visiting societies existed well before the end of the eighteenth century in Britain, though the first systematic movement for district visiting was founded by a Methodist, John Gardner, in 1785, and rapidly followed, initially by other Methodist and male-managed societies and then by early female societies. By the middle of the nineteenth century, there were hundreds of such societies, some with an evangelical inspiration, others, like the 'Ladies of Charity', supported by the Catholic Church. If a male society it normally had a ladies' subcommittee. Normally, women formed the majority of visitors, with the time and concern to act. From the beginning they were concerned both to aid the sick and needy, or the woman lying in, and also to foster the virtues that suited domestic life, either for the servant or for the poor married woman. There were many specialised charities for the servant class, including benefit clubs, in the early nineteenth century, but just as important was the almost universal tendency to put across the view that the situation of the poor could be improved by the practice of the domestic virtues. From Mrs Trimmer's *Oeconomy of Charity* onwards, the particular qualifications of women for the task were celebrated. Most of the pioneers of charitable reform in the course of the nineteenth century learnt their trade through first visiting the homes of the poor. Mary Carpenter, for example, teaching to earn her living, first understood the reality of the lives of the poor living not far away from her in Bristol when her father founded a Working and Visiting Society, on the inspiration of a Boston visitor. By the 1850s the practice had become increasingly more systematic, organised by societies and missions. It is clear that, for some at least, the difficulties of the relationship between the middle-class woman visitor, and the visited, were apparent:

> to enter a laborer's cottage to put the wife and mother there through a catechism before her own children as to what she has to live upon, how she manages, filled up with reproaches as to why she does not keep her children cleaner and her cottage more tidy, has always seemed to me both unladylike and uncharitable, and that it effects no good purpose I am also morally convinced. The poor woman is most likely thinking in her heart 'If you had as much to do as me, ma'am, I daresay you would not be any more tidy'; and it is very likely as soon as the visitor's back is turned that she may mutter,'Does she think that poor and rich are two different flesh that she talks to me so?'[103]

One woman who openly faced the barriers of class was Ellen Ranyard, a Londoner, and a visitor for many years before, in 1857, she conceived that a way of reaching the very poorest families, those untouched by Sunday Schools and respectable charities, might be to use the 'Bible-woman', a working woman paid by the Bible and Domestic Female Mission to carry the Bible right into the homes of the poorest, where she would be accepted as a 'lady' would not, welcomed as 'a motherly woman, *of their own class*'. Such women might provide the 'missing link' between rich and poor, for 'the necessity for re-establishment of intercourse between the higher and lower grades of female society in our great city was alike imperative and immediate'.[104] The first Bible-woman, Marion Bowers, had found herself giving out not only Bibles, but a fund of domestic advice, so much so that the religious and secular work of the mission needed to be administratively kept separate, though the Bible-woman remained the only agent in the home. To Ranyard, the relationship between the supervising lady and the Bible-woman was 'our kind of sisterhood', a Protestant kind, one which should be expanded. The key rule was that 'a poor woman is the best agent for carrying [the Bible] to women in those depths, and that she requires the constant aid and sympathy of a Christian sister from the *educated classes*.[105] By 1862 there were some 170 Bible-women in 76 districts of London, including 'Sarah' of Clerkenwell, 'Hannah' of Spitalfields, 'Rebecca' of Shoreditch, and many more, known by their Christian names, carrying 'the gospel of the scrubbing brush':

> The woman is appointed for the physical civilisation of communities. She is to 'guide the house' whether small or great; and this part of the education of the women of the working classes has been little cared for. The misery surrounding them is a voice from the depths saying 'Teach us how to mend it'. It is women of their own class who must answer their cry just because of these only will they learn what is wanted to be known.[106]

The middle-class feminists of the *English Woman's Journal* were in sympathy with the visiting movement, though for them it had to serve a secular rational purpose. In the work of the National Association for the Promotion of Social Science, founded in 1857, was found an organisation and a cause which could channel their efforts, no longer based on religious inspiration, but on the possibility of changing the environment of the poor, through 'sanitary reform'. The Ladies National Sanitary Association, based at the same offices as the *Journal*, planned to diffuse knowledge about 'the laws of health and the management of the household', and the care of infants and children through 'the action of *women* in every parish'. Those accustomed to district visiting, the 'clergyman's wife', the 'doctor's daughter', the 'squire's lady' and the parish nurse, as well as religious visitors, should all learn to give 'minute domestic instruction' in sanitary matters. The coming of social science, and better understanding of the 'laws of health' offered women both an occupation and a vocation:

> The amelioration of humanity under its varied phases of misfortune has now become a science, the appliances of which are studied to an extent which removes many obstacles to good works. The spirit of association involving unity of purpose and division of labour which is of late so much the character of our social institutions, while it offers the means of realisation to the loftiest enterprise, gives efficacy to the humblest efforts.[107]

A further article by Parkes discussed how best such a science might be popularised, through discriminating visiting and maternal meetings, by personal example and by the introduction of such matters into girls' schools. The habits and customs of the population could be changed, it was argued, by women alone, even though men might 'drain, cleanse, and build' to transform the urban environment.[108] Parkes makes it very clear that she is looking not for fundamental changes in the sexual division of labour but for the best possible application of that division, as seen by women as well as men:

> What we, in the moral struggle of England, and of America, have to accomplish is not so much a change in the practical duties, which from the earliest ages have been performed by our sex, but a change in the public estimate of the value of those duties, so that they may be henceforth accomplished in freedom, and under the sanction of better laws.[109]

Philanthropic activity was not, however, directed only to the homes of the poor but also to the institutions in which the deprived and destitute were to be found. And it was not in domestic visiting, but in claims to share influence and even authority in such institutions, that women met and disputed male prerogatives. In the second decade of the nineteenth century, as Prochaska notes, the number of institutions admitting women visitors increased, often after effective campaigning. York County Hospital and Lunatic Asylum were persuaded by Catherine Cappe to accept female visitors in 1813 and 1814 respectively, and the Leeds Infirmary in 1816. In these early decades women were distinguished for their contributions, in particular, to prison visiting. Sarah Martin, a dressmaker of Great Yarmouth, converted in 1810, first visited in Yarmouth Gaol to read the Bible to prisoners in 1819, and then, gradually, by her influence over the next twenty years, transformed the gaol, introducing not only the Scriptures, but cleanliness, occupations and aid in dealing with the world outside. The much better known work of Elizabeth Fry, through her own influence and that of the British Society of Ladies for promoting the Reformation of Prisoners, founded in 1821, brought 'cleanliness, godliness and needlework' to women in Newgate.[110] But they also faced the resistance of male authority, the view that reforms benefiting women prisoners – separate buildings, female officers, women visitors – represented interference on a considerable scale. The report of the Commission on Prisons set up in 1835 was unfavourable to Mrs Fry's reforms and, as the state increasingly regulated and controlled prisons through the establishment of a new national inspectorate, the role of women visitors became much less.

As a result of the introduction of the New Poor Law in Britain in 1834, women's visiting of the poor was also curbed. Outdoor relief was restricted, so that entry into the workhouse became much more common. Attempts to visit the workhouses, which began in the 1840s and 1850s, frequently revealed to the middle-class visitors a state of shocking squalor, but were seen as interference by local Boards of Guardians. After 1850 a number of women clearly managed to gain some access to workhouses. Mrs Sheppard of Frome, for example, succeeded in getting pauper children out of the workhouse and received as local boarders. She hoped to establish asylums for the aged poor. Louisa Twining, youngest daughter of a large middle-class Anglican family, had begun charitable visiting in 1847.[111] She found her original requests to enter the Strand Union Workhouse refused officially, though her visits continued unofficially, from 1853. She began to publish a number of works on the issue, including the pamphlet *Workhouses and Woman's Work* (1857). The interest which was aroused helped in the founding, in 1858, of a new Workhouse Visiting Society, under the aegis of the Social Economy Department of the National Association for the Promotion of Social Science. Twining acted as secretary to the Society, which started its own journal in 1859. One particular interest was the rescue of 'the better class of girls' for whom in 1861 a house of refuge was opened by the Society. In 1860 Twining gave evidence on pauper schools to the Royal Commission on education. Her view, and that of the Society, was that women should be introduced into all aspects of workhouse management – household, schools, nursery, infirmary – for 'how could men alone be fit judges of what went on there?':

> No Boards of Guardians, and no officials, can be expected to manage girls' schools as they ought to be, neither can *male inspectors alone inspect them.* Results would be far different if the influence of women of feeling, and education were introduced . . . and constant lady visitors, who would cultivate the affections of the children, and help to counteract the fatal effects of life in an institution and in a mass for girls.[112]

The *English Woman's Journal*, which reprinted a number of Twining's articles, protested in an article on 'Interference' that women could be seen by Boards of Guardians as interfering, when doing 'the ordained and proper work of women'.[113] Throughout the 1860s and 1870s a carefully planned onslaught on officialdom by some of the most effective social reformers of the period continued: the logical extension of their policies was the appointment of women as Guardians and as Inspectors, for which Twining called in 1861.

Besides the workhouse movement, women were active in other institutions, especially those caring for children and for girls. The work of Mary Carpenter for ragged schools is well known.[114] A Unitarian and a teacher, influenced by American abolitionism, in 1846 she began in Bristol a new school for the children of the streets, and of the more respectable poor. Unlike organisers of previous ragged schools, she concentrated on the quality of the teaching, with trained teachers. Her account in *Ragged Schools* (1849) was about education, not delinquency. After that, however, she turned her attention to the criminal child, as they were known, and systematically explored reformatory systems, in England and abroad. *Reformatory Schools* (1851) and succeeding works on the same subject made her a national authority, though her compassionate arguments for education rather than punishment were by no means accepted. In 1854 she founded the first girls' reformatory school in England, Red Lodge: although it was not a particularly successful experience, largely for want of good staff. Like Louisa Twining, Mary Carpenter played an active role in the first meetings of the National Association for the Promotion of Social Science, and her public speaking there was much admired. Such campaigns were extended to other institutions – to hospitals, for example, especially such a hospital as the new one for sick children at Great Ormond Street, run entirely by men.[115]

It could be suggested that within the National Association for the Promotion of Social Science, and in the columns of the *English Woman's Journal*, certain themes in relation to philanthropy were emerging which were to be a significant part of the feminist case of the 1850s. Women's influence – as defined by themselves – was to be felt both in working-class homes through an appeal to working-class women and in the new institutions of the state: for this to happen, middle-class women had to organise, to speak in public and to write for the press. 'Association' and 'sisterhood' were terms commonly used for such organisations. There was a relationship, too, between this need for women's influence and the desire of women of all classes for more varied occupation and employment. What was needed were not only visitors and administrators, but nurses, female prison officers, workhouse matrons, instructors in household economy and sanitary reform. Such posts would clearly require professional or practical training: this was fully realised by such women as Anna Jameson and Louisa Twining. Of course, not all women philanthropists used arguments that challenged convention. Many, perhaps most, were socially conservative and either inflexible in their view of women's role or ambivalent, as was Mary Carpenter on women's right to the suffrage. But such activity could develop organising and political skills and lead women to demand a share in male authority, and to extend the theme of the common concerns of all women. In the context of the 1850s it had radicalising potential.

In the United States, similar developments from the earlier activities of moral reform and benevolent societies were taking place. Women from the moral reform societies were becoming interested in the condition of female prisoners, including prostitutes. From 1838 Dorothea Dix strove singlehandedly to expose conditions prevailing in prisons and in asylums, reporting to state legislatures and lobbying to secure federal legislation to support asylums for the insane: this failed only through presidential veto. In New York, reformers urged a separate association to aid female convicts, and in 1844 a Female Department of the New York Prison Association was founded. In the same year Eliza Farnham, freethinker and author, was appointed the first women prison matron, at the women's division of Sing Sing, where she had marked success. Later she continued her career in prison and asylum work elsewhere, became involved in abolitionist and women's rights activity, and wrote, in *Woman and her Era* (1864), a work which celebrated women's moral superiority, and their reproductive role. Eventually a home for former women convicts was set up by the Women's Prison Association, directed by Catherine Sedgwick, a leading author of domestic novels from 1848 to 1863. Lydia Maria Child, too, spent much time in this work. In so doing they appealed to their own mission, as women, and to their fellow feeling with the deprived and outcast:

Among the most precious of woman's rights is the right to do good to her own sex. . . . Every woman in misfortune and disgrace is the proper object of care to the happier and safer part of her sex.[116]

Other associations dealing with the welfare of women – aged, sick, impoverished – grew up in all the major cities. In 1849 in New York the Home for the Friendless and House of Industry had its cornerstone laid by the Female Guardian Society, and was imitated in many other cities. There were others: the Wilson Industrial School for Girls in 1853, the Brooklyn Industrial School Association in 1854, the Nursery for the Children of Poor Women in the same year. The Women's Hospital Association in the 1850s was able to purchase a private home and rapidly expanded the medical facilities available to New York women: best known was the New York Infirmary for Women and Children, founded by Elizabeth Blackwell in 1853 'to afford poor women the opportunity of consulting physicians of their own sex'.[117] Such a hospital must be seen not only in the context of women physicians' struggle for professional status and the wider diffusion of medical knowledge, but also against the background of the explosion of benevolence towards those of their own sex. The missionary impulse of evangelical Protestants led to the founding of the Five Points House of Industry in New York's worst slum; its history suggests, like that of Ellen Ranyard's Bible-women, that missionaries were overwhelmed not by the need for Christianity, but by the sheer social problems of the new urban life and the needs of the poor. Prayer meetings, even temperance meetings, were not enough: Louis Pease, running the Five Points House with the aid of a ladies' committee, found he had to provide employment – a sewing workshop – to reclaim the poor. Increasingly disillusioned by their task, New York missionaries turned to work with children, and to understanding of the economic and environmental background of the city's problems.

Such interests were, as in Britain, by no means confined to the greatest American cities. In Utica, Mary Ryan has shown how from 1830 the Female School of Industry (a sewing circle) had established the Utica Orphan Asylum and Benevolent Association, and by the 1830s a whole network of philanthropic societies existed, including the Ladies' Society for the Relief of the Poor, which ran an industrial school. In fund-raising again they played a major part, especially in running bazaars and carnivals. In such a small city it was largely such women, sometimes through their different denominations, who provided public welfare, which might be haphazard and sometimes capricious. Ryan describes the extent to which such charity by the 1850s was administered by women of the social élite, white-collar and professional families.[118] The picture is probably not untypical of many small and middling towns.

By the 1850s, in Britain and in the United States, organised philanthropy had reached new heights. Religious fervour – which could be Catholic, Episcopalian, High Anglican, as well as strictly evangelical – could lead women into voluntary campaigning associations, which brought them together on the basis of their shared concerns. Comparison between British and American philanthropy is difficult here: clearly the two movements had much in common and learned from each other. Yet it is possible to suggest that the priority given to the abolitionist issue, by women who by their background and their religion were committed to radical and progressive beliefs, meant that that philanthropy which had its roots in the largest American cities played a rather less central part in the American feminist movement than it did in Britain. A correspondent of the *English Woman's Journal* explicitly compared 'Abolitionism' to the 'Condition of Englishwoman Question', for the power of both movements to generate awareness of the situation of women, and in Britain there is a strong case for suggesting that social issues – employment, sanitary reform, the reform of state institutions – had priority over the political issue of the vote in generating a feminist movement.[119] It was to be a movement which, given the rapidity of urban and industrial growth, and the state of the franchise, incorporated a strong awareness of class differences.

So far, voluntary and philanthropic associations have been considered purely in Anglo-American terms, to the exclusion of French charity and philanthropy. Yet French work in this field was greatly admired, by English reformers at least, who frequently wrote with admiration of the work done among the Parisian working class, for instance, by Soeur Rosalie of the Sisters of Charity, whose crèche, infant school, industrial school and institution for the aged seemed the model of possible action by women, though too socially conservative in outlook. The practicality and the training for such work of the Catholic religious orders was frequently referred to.[120] Yet it does not seem, before 1860, that a background of charitable work played much part in developing French feminist activity. One acute observer of the

situation of women in France, Julie-Victoire Daubié, in *La femme
pauvre au dix-neuvième siècle*, wrote with bitterness that the work of
public assistance was given over 'to the encroachment of the cloister
and the usurpation of men' and that women in secular lay associations were at a considerable disadvantage to religious orders which
were trained, secure and with financial resources. She suggested
that in the care of foundlings, the running of hospitals, the care of
former convicts, the establishment of friendly societies, there was
much that women – of all classes – should be doing, yet the weight of
official organisation was stifling the zeal and inventiveness of private
initiatives. She was fully aware of the extent of work in Britain and in
America, contrasting, for instance, early British attempts to introduce aid and a continuing moral purpose into the lives of domestic
servants to the French situation where male employers were inhibited
by no moral or sexual constraints and there was a great need for
'the moralising of domestic life'. For her, only the part which women
of the poorer classes might play, thus gaining employment, could
redeem the situation: 'To woman belongs the great mission of
regenerating charity: it is she who will reconcile the suffering class
and the idle class'.[121]

It is worth considering how accurate her view was, and whether it
helps to explain the real differences between French and Anglo-
American feminism. Clearly the first half of the nineteenth century
did see a massive expansion of charitable activities by religious orders
and lay societies in France as elsewhere. Under the Restoration the
'Congrégation', the famous and influential lay society founded in
1801, first at Paris but followed by many other towns and cities, with
its organisations for men, women and the young, generated a number
of charitable societies and programmes. In 1833, the young layman
Frédéric Ozanam founded the Society of Saint-Vincent de Paul,
which was to create lay pastoral societies of men and women, mainly
though not entirely from the social élite, who pioneered visiting
among the poor. The work of Soeur Rosalie in Paris helped to inspire
that of Armand de Melun, who in the 'Société d'Economie charitable'
pioneered awareness of social issues among Catholics. Nevertheless,
although there was an important current of liberal Catholicism, even
of Catholic socialism, under the July monarchy, the organisation of
charitable work was still more characteristically associated with those
who took a conservative, often legitimist view of the social order, like
Armand de Melun himself. That connection was strengthened under

the Second Empire.[122] One important group was the 'Société de la morale chrétienne', a 'liberal replica' of the 'Congrégation', already mentioned for its interest in the slave trade, but which equally took an interest in all kinds of humanitarian activity. It had a small but very distinguished membership, in which Protestants were strongly represented, with numbers rising from 116 in 1822 to 337 in 1830. In 1828, a *Comité des dames* was set up. Eugénie Niboyet, the feminist from Lyons, served from 1829 on different committees of the society, including those on charity and on prisons. She helped to found a school for the children of prisoners in St-Lazare prison and praised the work of a number of distinguished women on these committees, both Catholic and Protestant.[123]

It is difficult to sense the range of charitable activity by women, since there were few distinguished women pioneers, with some exceptions. Mme de Pastoret founded the *salles d'asiles* or kindergartens, though with a stronger charitable than educational purpose, in Paris in 1800, and the movement steadily expanded until in 1837, when the *salles d'asiles* were officially recognised, there were just over a hundred in France. Much was to be due to the internationally admired work of Marie Pape-Carpentier, who with some Protestant support founded an *école normale* in Paris in 1847, and was particularly interested in the educational methods adopted. By mid-century, middle-class French women across the country were aiding the *salles d'asiles*.[124]

Yet perhaps if one looks at two approaches to philanthropic provision in Lille in this period, by Pierre Pierrard, on working-class life, and by Bonnie Smith, on the philanthropic activities of middle-class women, some sense of the interaction between state, religious and voluntary lay charity begins to emerge. There was evidently a most important relationship between the official *bureau de bienfaisance* of the town, aided by the *bureau de charité* in every parish, and directly after 1855 by the work of the sisters of Saint Vincent, one of whom, Soeur Sophie, was indeed regarded as the Soeur Rosalie of Lille. The major hospice in Lille was run, by agreement with the town, by the nuns of the Congrégation des Filles de l'Enfant Jesus. A refuge and a penitentiary for young women were both run from 1831 by the Soeurs du Bon Pasteur, and another order ran one for the aged. The Soeurs de Notre-Dame de la Treille, founded in 1845, kept up a number of female charities in their house: to Christian mothers, servants, working women, and so on. Much was also done by the laymen of the societies of Saint-Joseph and Saint-Vincent de Paul. After around 1840, well-to-do laywomen took their place alongside these societies, as *dames de charités*, though the initiative clearly lay with the male leadership. Smith stresses that from mid-century bourgeois women were involved in founding *salles d'asiles* and crèches, in setting up sewing workshops for young women and running Sunday recreational meetings for them. They were particularly committed to maternal societies, offering help to those lying-in, and domestic advice. In all these activities, they, like Anglo-American middle-class women, were concerned primarily with the problems of their own sex and with domestic life.

In this context – admittedly resting on a single example – there would seem to be some truth in Daubié's analysis. The direction and implementation of charitable activity in Lille lay mainly with local administrators and with the religious orders. Female religious orders did, indeed, under the control of the administration, control and regulate those public institutions to which English women, for instance, were so keen to gain access. And in the context of regulation by state and by Church, both committed, certainly by the 1850s, to the maintenance of conservative social values in the aftermath of the revolution of 1848 – a commitment which the French middle classes, broadly, shared – there was little scope for the extension of charity into a more radical and innovatory critique of social institutions. Charitable work by middle-class women, directed to similar, though not such extensive, aims as elsewhere, seems in France to have a more conservative bias than the voluntaristic associations of Britain and America, which extended to challenge the double standard of morality, and to demand that women's influence be felt in public institutions, even in legislation.

8. The Feminist Case

By the middle decades of the nineteenth century, the cause of feminism, the explicit assertion of the individual autonomy of women, against their husbands, against the state and against prevailing stereotypes, had clearly emerged. It can be seen in the arguments of individual writers, following Mary Wollstonecraft and William Thompson, outlining the case for equality from varying political perspectives. It can be seen too in the lives of lesser known women, associating together, writing, agitating, signing petitions, sitting on committees. Such women addressed themselves to the issues that have been discussed here: to legal reform, to the question of women's education, to employment, to the part that they could play in public life – and in so doing they came to demand the right to citizenship. The demand for the vote was not a single demand, growing out of the envy of propertied women for their husbands' rights, but one which grew from decades of action. By 1860 the ground was clearly laid, and in Britain and the United States a small but recognisable feminist movement was established. In France the defeat of 1848 was a disastrous one, and the regime of the Second Empire uncongenial to any kind of political association. But more fundamental reasons may explain the long delay before the emergence of feminist association in France, and its weakness when it did. The arguments put in the mid-nineteenth century were indeed arguments for the political equality of women and men: but they sprang too from a sense that women, given the freedom to define their own sphere of life, would still not see it as identical to that of men, though it would overlap in very many areas. But that sphere was one which entitled them to an equal share in political rights, to citizenship. They undoubtedly inherited, like the Chartists, the revolutionaries of 1848 and the abolitionist leaders, the language of republicanism. But they contributed to the themes of democracy, freedom and individual citizenship a specifically domestic focus, one which assumed the common interests of women on the basis of their domestic responsibilities and their moral qualities. The barriers of class remained, and the majority of active feminists at this time were from middle-class backgrounds, often dissenting in religion and radical in politics. Yet the number of women from the lower middle class and some from working-class backgrounds who took part in feminist activity might suggest that under the right circumstances the cause did appeal to women of different classes. Those circumstances surely included the same factors which determined political association among working-class *men*: a degree of political consciousness, in a revolutionary or reforming movement, or employment sufficiently secure or well paid to allow permanent association around their interests as workers. Such circumstances were found, but rarely, among working-class women in this period: in the French Revolution of 1848, and among the Lowell mill girls. Domestic life for working-class women remained more a struggle for survival than a route to formal association among their own sex. For the slightly better off, the achievement of a degree of domestic stability must have seemed too vulnerable, too dependent upon male earnings, for them to endanger it in this period.

THREE WRITERS

The individual writers considered here will be Flora Tristan, Margaret Fuller and John Stuart Mill. Each made a very consider-able contribution to feminist thinking, yet as individuals rather than as part of a movement, though all were prepared to, and did, advocate their ideas in the practice of their lives as well as in their writings. None can be categorised simply as 'liberal' or 'individualist' or 'socialist': their arguments are more complex, aware of that different, domestic focus to women's lives which made male categories of political debate inadequate. Flora Tristan's feminism sprang from a quite unorthodox career, which illustrated for her the realities of a married woman's situation in early nineteenth-century France, and gave her increasing awareness of the miseries of working-class life in France. Herself illegitimate, her marriage to André Chazal, her employer in lithographic colouring, was an unhappy one. Leaving him, she travelled to Peru to claim a share in her father's inheritance, but failing to do so she returned to France and, in 1837, petitioned the Chamber of Deputies for the re-establishment of divorce. In these years she first became acquainted with Saint-Simonian and Fourier-ist ideas. In 1839 she visited England on which she wrote a commentary revealing her interest in the position of women there – as in her discussion of the extent of London prostitution, and the sterility of English middle-class marriages – and also her identification with the work of Robert Owen and the Chartist political movement.[1] In 1842, after returning to France, she published in the second edition of her *Promenades dans Londres* an appeal to French workers to organise so as to avoid the English example, and in 1843 she offered, in *L'Union Ouvrière* (The Workers' Union) her own vision of the future.

In this, she visualised the transformation of the working class, made possible through the transformation of working-class women. It was both a Christian and a socialist view. She believed in the development of harmonious social relations which would allow human nature itself to develop its potential: emotional, moral and active. Such harmony could only be achieved through the association and unity of all members of the working class. Her God was a Saint-Simonian God, embodying the highest qualities of men and women, of love and intelligence: a Being whose spirit should pervade all humanity. Christ offered a personal example of that loving humanity to which a female messiah might also aspire: 'as a woman who feels faith and force, why shouldn't I go, just like the apostles, from town to town announcing the good tidings and preaching fraternity and unity in humanity to the workers'.[2] The message was one of the means of unity among workers, the ending of small associations, the coming of the universal union which would give workers the social strength and consolidation to enforce their power, winning representation, education, employment and the ability to confront the triumphant middle class which had dominated French society since 1789. Perhaps the longest section of the work is that entitled 'Why I Mention Women', and it is here that Tristan elaborates her view of woman as a true 'pariah', 'cast out of the Church, out of the law, out of society', deemed inferior by all authorities. The transformation of the working class could come about only through the transformation of working-class women themselves, brought up, according to Tristan, ignorant and brutal-ised, through no fault of their own. Tristan called for *'absolute equality'*, for women to have their 'natural and inalienable rights' because 'woman is everything in the life of a worker':

it would be most important, from the point of view of intellectually, morally, and materially improving the working class, that the women receive from childhood a solid and rational education, apt to develop all their potential so that they can become skilled in their trades, good mothers capable of raising and guiding their children and to be for them . . . free and natural schoolteachers, and also so that they can serve as moralising agents for the men whom they influence from birth to death.[3]

If regarded as an equal, her husband's 'associate, friend and companion', she will intelligently create a loving domestic environment which will be the means of attracting her husband from the tavern, for 'with half of what a drunkard spends in the tavern, a worker's whole family living together could go for meals in the country in summer'.[4] Though the 'rights of man' had been proclaimed, it remained for the men of 1843 to complete the emancipation of 'the last slaves of society', guaranteeing to women full equality within the Workers' Union. Yet it must also be said that in elaborating her plan for the implementation of the Workers' Union, Tristan permitted to women a share in public affairs, but a lesser one. Local committees of seven were to include 5 men and 2 women, and the central committee for all France 40 men and 10 women. The central committee was to issue an appeal to the king of France, to the Catholic Church, the French nobility, to employers and to women 'of all stations, ages, opinions, and countries' to contribute towards the establishment of Workers' Union palaces, in which men, women and children would all work and be educated, and in which the sick, elderly and disabled would be cared for. Tristan was interested in progressive ideas on education, in vocational training and in the organisation of labour in the palaces, though she enters into little detail in these matters. Here then was a utopian scheme, one which rested on women as 'the moral agents for the men of the masses'. Tristan seems to have envisaged a degree of co-operation between the different classes of French society, as well as appealing to wealthy women. She asked that such women give not to charity, but to the creation of jobs, the instruction of workers about their rights and duties being 'a sacred and sublime mission worthy of the truly charitable and religious woman'.[5]

It is a form of socialism which still has at its heart that heightened ideal of womanhood, derived from Saint-Simon and Fourier, but sharing much with evangelical and pietistic views. Tristan toured France after the publication of her work, and it is clear that in some towns her visit did have an important radicalising effect on the organisation of workers, as Agulhon has confirmed in Toulon.[6] She met with success also in Lyons and in Marseilles, though she found considerable hostility to her chapter upon women from journals popular among male artisans, *La Ruche Populaire*, *L'Atelier* and *L'Echo de la Fabrique*. Louis Vasbenter, already quoted above, and S. Hugont, both Lyonnais artisans, wrote to Tristan to protest and to defend the domestic 'inner life' of woman.[7] Yet she did attract women in her meetings, both mixed and separate ones. In Lyons, for example, she brought 120 women in the working-class Croix Rousse to a meeting on 27 May 1844, and on 8 June felt pleased at the interest and responsiveness of 20 women silk-reelers with whom she spent the afternoon.[8] But although she met and became friendly with Eléonore Blanc, a laundress from Lyons who became her first biographer, her comments on the level of education and intelligence among working women are sometimes harsh, and she could, as she did in her journal just before she died in 1844, express feelings of disillusion and isolation in an environment alien to her.[9] Ultimately, she was caught between her view of the necessity of transforming working women's lives and the priorities of the male artisan movement to which she appealed.

The American feminist, Margaret Fuller, much better educated than Tristan, but equally unconventional in her life, also died young.[10] Born in 1810, she was the daughter of a prominent Massachusetts lawyer, who gave his daughter a masculine education in the classics of a very high standard. In the late 1820s her breadth of knowledge and conversational skills were to gain her admission to the intellectual society of Cambridge, Massachusetts. In the 1830s, as her religious ideas shifted from more orthodox views towards an almost pantheistic belief in the spirit of Creation, she built an acquaintance with Ralph Waldo Emerson, philosopher and essayist of Concord, Massachusetts, met Harriet Martineau, and in 1836 was hired by Bronson Alcott, the father of Louisa Alcott, to teach languages in his progressive school in Boston. There she taught, became friendly with Elizabeth Peabody, and continued her study of German literature, in 1839 publishing a translation of Eckermann's *Conversations with Goethe*. By then she was at the heart of an intellectual movement known as

Transcendentalism, which drew together Fuller, Peabody, Emerson, the minister Theodore Parker, Alcott, and a number of other distinguished men. She held a series of Conversations from 1839 to 1844 in Boston on a wide range of topics – mythology, art, education, and, of course, women's rights – in which women like Lydia Maria Child and the Peabody sisters were participants. In 1840 she joined with Emerson in producing the *Dial*, a quarterly Transcendentalist journal, which she edited jointly and for which she produced many contributions. Her best known work on women's rights, *Woman in the Nineteenth Century* (1845), was an expanded version of an essay first published in *The Dial* in July 1843, 'The Great Lawsuit. Man *versus* Men, Woman *versus* Women.' In 1844, she went to New York to work for the *New York Daily Tribune*, and among other themes wrote a series of articles on the charitable and public institutions of the city, including the home for former women convicts set up by the Women's Prison Association.[11] In 1846 she set off for Italy as the *Tribune*'s foreign correspondent, and became involved in the cause of Italian freedom, together with the man she met and married in Italy, the Marchese d'Ossoli. When the Roman Republic was proclaimed in February 1849, she worked in an emergency hospital in Rome, doing all she could to aid the revolution. On the fall of the republic she fled to Florence, but on her return to America was drowned, in 1850, at the age of 40.

In some ways Margaret Fuller's work derives from a rather different intellectual tradition from any of those described in this book. Her interest in German literature brought her to the study of the philosopher Immanuel Kant, and the German Idealists who wrote after Kant. Transcendentalism derived from such writings, and rested on the theme of a cosmic purpose, pervading the universe, of which individual human beings were but one small part. It is a vague, loosely defined, highly abstract philosophy, which allowed those who shared it to discuss the aspirations of the human spirit towards ideal truths, without the constraints of any carefully defined doctrines. What Margaret Fuller contributed to this theme was the view that both men and women should be free to attain an understanding of their destiny in the divine purpose: their complementary destiny:

By Man I mean both men and women; these are the two halves of one thought, I lay no especial stress on the welfare of either. I believe that the development of the one cannot be effected without that of the other. My highest wish is that this truth should be distinctly and rationally apprehended, and the conditions of life and freedom recognised as the same for the daughters and the sons of time; twin exponents of a divine thought.[12]

She protested at the lack of freedom permitted by those too concerned with 'little treatises' marking the precise boundaries of 'woman's sphere and woman's mission', and defended those taking part in public affairs, whether writing or lecturing. Every freedom should be enjoyed by women as by men, and women, like negroes, should not be held in bondage: the better to fulfill the divine purpose: 'What woman needs is not as a woman to act or rule, but as a nature to grow, as an intellect to discern, as a soul to live freely and unimpeded, to unfold such powers as were given her when we left our common home'.[13] Yet, Fuller suggests, woman even in current society did enjoy power in all classes above the poorest, albeit a power which normally involved the indulgence of 'her ignorance and childish vanity'. The corrupt state of marriage was harmful to both parties. Yet when equality entered into the partnership, then a progressive improvement could be traced, from the practical egalitarian partnership of the 'good provider' and the 'capital housekeeper', to those couples who in intellectual and religious terms were able to share 'a common faith and a common purpose', and aspirations towards a true freedom.[14] Mary Wollstonecraft and William Godwin, Catherine and Goodwyn Barmby, Mary and William Howitt, all presented true examples of an intellectual partnership, though the highest grade was that of truly united religious partnership. In such partnerships, Fuller does not suggest that the precise division of labour is of importance – it is the freedom to choose and to speak that is essential. Nature offered a variety of interests and employments, and that variety had to be accepted. But she protested against the view that women should be better educated in order that they might be 'better companions and mothers *for men*'. While motherhood was indeed a most demanding occupation, Fuller denied that the intellect should be developed exclusively with reference to any single relationship: rather, by its very existence, God signalled his desire for its perfection in women and in men. But women of capacity and genius were still likely to be enslaved by emotion and the senses: the world expected a degree of self-regulation and harmony not yet achieved. Fuller discusses an 'electrical . . . magnetic element' in woman, the quality of awareness and intuition of the world around her. Women of genius, torn by such powers, by their intellectual strength, and by the world's expectations, could be wounded and destroyed, especially in close relationships with men, if they were not given the space to develop their powers.

It is clear that though Fuller did not accept mean-spirited, authoritarian descriptions of 'woman's sphere' she did believe in the complementary natures of men and women. For her there were two aspects of woman's nature: Muse and Minerva. Of the former, she wrote:

> The especial genius of Woman I believe to be electrical in movement, intuitive in function, spiritual in tendency. She excels not so easily in classification, recreation, as in an instinctive seizure of causes, and a simple breathing out of what she receives, that has the singleness of life, rather than the selecting and energising of art.[15]

For Fuller, male and female natures still represented 'the two sides of the great radical dualism', even though 'there is no wholly masculine man, no purely feminine woman'.[16] Men and women might share each other's qualities, without exclusiveness. Only in the current context, as the debate grew more acute, did she give preference for Minerva, given the need for women to exert their intellectual powers, in asserting their independence and abandoning their reliance upon men's judgement. There were indeed, she believed, contemporary signs that women's situation was changing. The works of the German mystic Swedenborg, of Fourier and of Goethe are praised for their understanding of women's need for fulfilment. So too are other women writers, and two comments on works already discussed here are worth considering.

Fuller found Anna Jameson a 'sentimentalist' though with redeeming qualities. But on one matter she was most fully in accord with her, in her discussion of the question of prostitution and the hypocrisy of legislators and men of the world. Fuller contrasted the situation of women of fashion, whose exploitation of their advantages to seek male approval brought admiration, jealousy and flattery, with that of women she met in prison, prostitutes who attributed their fall to just the same motives: love of dress, love of flattery, love of excitement. In the 'world of souls' the prostitutes were the less guilty. But only the publicity which women like Anna Jameson and Lydia Maria Child gave to the condition of prostitutes was bringing people to question whether perhaps men should not be required to observe the same standards of virtue as those expected of women.[17] Men too, suggested Fuller, should be expected to discipline their passions. Fuller commented also on the work by Mme Necker de Saussure, discussed above, which she thought had both positive and negative qualities.[18] It was harmful in its acceptance of the inferiority of women to men, and of the dissimulation of women, concealing their real feelings within marriage. Yet in writing of women's lyrical inspiration, and in its fine feeling for women's situation, the book had something to recommend it. Thus Margaret Fuller drew from the work of earlier generations what she found acceptable, but she, accepting the complementarity of masculine and femine in human nature, nevertheless stresses the autonomy of each individual woman in the realisation of the divine purpose. Whatever occupations that took them to – even to being a sea-captain – they should follow. Whatever pastimes little girls chose – even playing with a carpenter's tools – they should follow. Many would doubtless give themselves to motherhood: but all would not be constrained to do so. So 'the perfection of each being in its kind – apple as apple, Woman as Woman' would be achieved.[19] Individual autonomy was to be seen within the context of participation in that greater whole Man (meaning humanity), and the sharing of each woman in that greater Womanhood.

The best known individual feminist writer of this period is probably John Stuart Mill, whose work can only be considered briefly here. Though the *Subjection of Women* was not published until 1869, the first and essential draft was made in 1860–1, after the death of Mill's wife, Harriet Taylor Mill, in 1858. Behind this classic work lay a diverse intellectual and personal inheritance. Mill himself, the son of the utilitarian, James Mill, had grown up in an atmosphere of Benthamite radicalism. Though his father's patron, Jeremy Bentham, had offered theoretical support for women's suffrage, but not as an immediate possibility, James Mill had clearly suggested that a woman's interest should be regarded in public affairs as identical with her husband's, thus inspiring William Thompson's *Appeal of One-Half the Human Race, Women.* . . . John Mill, experiencing a mental crisis as he struggled with the utilitarian legacy, was open to more radical influences, from Francis Place and Richard Carlile, for instance, who led him to distribute tracts on birth control at an early age.[20] In an early article in the *Westminster Review*, in 1824, he attacked the application of differential moral standards to men and women.[21] In 1830 he met the woman who was to shape the rest of his life, then Harriet Taylor, at the home of W. J. Fox, the Unitarian editor of the *Monthly Repository*, at the centre of an interesting group of radical and freethinking men and women. Among this group, unorthodox views about the position of women had for some time been circulating, and as early as 1831–2 Harriet Taylor and John Mill both wrote essays, which were never published, on the existing state of marriage and the desirability of divorce.[22] The influence of Taylor upon Mill is a controversial issue. He attributed to her the highest intellectual qualities, which subsequent historians have doubted. At the same time, there would seem to be a good case for Taylor's influencing him in a radical direction on the question of women's situation. Her essay on 'The Enfranchisement of Women', written in 1851, was, as will be seen, considerably more radical in some ways than Mill's *Subjection of Women*. Mill was also increasingly interested in Saint-Simonian ideas. In 1830 he visited Paris, and was attracted by the historical outlook of the group there, though repelled by its religious messianism. In 1832 he contributed an article to one of the last issues of *Le Globe*. This interest was to have some lasting effect in, for example, his discussion of co-operative and socialist associations in the *Principles of Political Economy* (1848).[23]

The influences of Harriet Taylor and her friends, and of Saint-Simonian ideas, were probably of some importance in leading Mill towards an unusually sympathetic treatment of women's situation.[24] He approached the issue from two angles: first, in considering the consequences of the position of women for society as a whole (the utilitarian perspective); and, secondly, in estimating the effects on women's individuality, on their potential for growth (the liberal view). Historically, he regarded male dominance as an inheritance from a past in which the law of the strongest regulated human affairs. This survival remained 'an almost solitary exception' to the disappearance of primitive conditions. Yet modern society, with this exception, was built on a very different principle, that of individual freedom of choice and opportunity. If this principle was justified, then women too, as individuals, should similarly enjoy the freedom to develop and compete, and no longer suffer from disabilities which were 'the single relic of an old world of thought and practice'.[25] As he met objections to such equality, Mill suggested that there was no evidence at all that the nature of women should disqualify them from sharing in all aspects of life: for women's nature as known in his own society was 'an eminently artificial thing'. Women had been brought up from their early years to believe in submission, in yielding, in living for others, in being attractive to men. Changes were recent, seen for instance in the emergence of women of letters, themselves also 'artificial products'. The lack of opportunities for achievement, in literature, the arts and other fields, meant that it was impossible to estimate the potential of women. He entirely rejected the case for women's biological inferiority, as put by August Comte.[26] Freedom of choice of a different way of life should be left to women themselves. Compulsion and direction were surely irrelevant, in any case, for those who saw a domestic life as natural to women. Only if it was thought that the vocation of wife and mother was both necessary to society and repugnant to women, could the argument for compulsion be logically put.

Mill argued that to achieve the equality which he believed necessary, the legal treatment of women in marriage in Britain should be reformed, allowing a married woman control over her person, her property and her children. While many happy marriages did survive in spite of such conditions, an institution should not be judged by its best examples. In all classes the possession of power could bring about its corruption and the exercise of despotism within the family: he denounced in particular the brutality and violence exercised against women in the lowest classes of society. In a voluntary association between partners, there was no necessity for one to rule, as in a business partnership. A division of powers was possible, and the weight of influence would depend eventually on age, character and intelligence, and, Mill suggests, also 'a more potential voice' from whoever brought the means of support into the family. So, in most cases, given the current state of society, the man was likely to have the greater say – but there was no need for legislation on the issue.[27]

While attacking legal restraints on married women, Mill also believed that such women should have the '*power* of earning'. If marriage were an equal contract, and all honourable employments were open to women, *then* she might freely choose to marry, and, normally, to bring up a family and manage a household or to follow an occupation. Here Mill suggests that 'the common arrangement, by which the man earns the income and the wife superintends the domestic expenditure, seems to me in general the most suitable division of labour between the two persons'.[28] Therefore in general he did not think it best that a wife should contribute financially to the support of the family. There are two points which Mill does not make here, surprisingly, given the state of the contemporary debate. Firstly, it was clear to many reasonably unprejudiced observers that for the majority of married working-class women some contribution to the family finances was essential. Secondly, the prevailing problem for women's employment in nineteenth-century England remained a glut of female labour, concentrated in a very few occupations: needlework, governessing, domestic service. Only in the *Principles of Political Economy* does he refer, fairly briefly, to 'the opening of industrial occupations freely to both sexes', and criticise the 'disproportionate preponderance' of the 'exclusive function' of motherhood in women's lives.[29] Nowhere in the *Subjection of Women* does Mill consider the realities of women's employment, confining himself to 'functions of a public nature'. He did not, like, for instance, John Duguid Milne, consider the benefits of the entry of middle-class women into industrial and managerial occupations, or the need to extend the range of working-class occupations open to women. Nor does he, like the feminists of the *English Woman's Journal*, discuss the importance of the expansion of women's occupations in what we would call the 'service sector' of the economy. It is perhaps surprising that, as an economist, he did not look harder at the situation of women in the economy, leaving others to deploy the arguments of the *Principles of Political Economy* in this context.[30]

Mill argued that women should be admitted on an equal basis to all public functions and occupations. First, there was no shadow of a reason for not permitting women to enjoy the suffrage, given the arguments so far outlined. Secondly, women should be free to compete for public office, to enter professions with high public responsibilities. If they succeeded in doing so, they were evidently well qualified. Even if only a few did so, there could be no case for exclusion. Again, the evidence of the past offered no guide at all as to women's potential, since they had been carefully trained to avoid such occupations, though where, by the accident of birth, women had ruled, a high proportion had shown great talents. Of the differences between men and women as they existed at that time, women's talent for practice as compared to speculation could be invaluable, as could women's quickness of understanding and judgement. Their so-called 'greater nervous susceptibility' was in large measure a product of excess, unchannelled energy. If women's minds were, as they seemed at present, more mobile, less capable of absorption in a single issue, then that too had its positive values.

Therefore Mill argued the case for an equality in marriage to be achieved by lifting the profoundly unjust disabilities which distorted the proper relations between men and women. He did so partly that the individual woman might achieve her potential. She would learn a proper degree of assertion:

> I believe that equality of rights would abate the exaggerated self-abnegation which is the present artificial ideal of feminine character, and that a good woman would not be more self-sacrificing than the best man: but, on the other hand, men would be much more unselfish and self-sacrificing than at present, because they would no longer be taught to worship their own will as such a grand thing that it is actually the law for another rational being.[31]

She would begin to enjoy the freedom and the choice to govern her own conduct, and to share as a citizen in the duties of the community. That citizenship which Mill marks out for her is in some ways still a 'republican' notion:

> Whatever has been said or written, from the time of Herodotus to the present, of the ennobling influence of free government – the nerve and spring which it gives to all the faculties, the larger and higher objects which it presents to the intellects and feelings, the more unselfish public spirit, and calmer and broader views of duty that it engenders, and the generally loftier platform on which it elevates the individual as a moral, spiritual and social being – is every particle as true of women as of men.[32]

Women also would aspire to that self-culture, that moral cultivation which Mill saw as characteristic of the liberal individual.

Mill's view of women must be related also to the benefits which he believed that the equality of women would have on society taken as a whole, especially the moral benefits. A sense of justice would pervade the relations between men and women, rather than that awareness of superiority and selfishness bred into every boy from an early age.[33] That awareness had 'a perverting influence of such magnitude' that it was difficult to imagine, undercutting all the influences of education and civilisation. And also the 'intellectual power of the species' would be greatly improved by allowing women free use of their talents. Consequently, the immense accession of new concerns and responsibilities for women would broaden their own moral horizons and transform, for the better, their influence upon society. For Mill was critical of the effect of women's influence on public virtue in his own society. The moral principles impressed upon them were frequently negative, having little to do with the broader issues of morality. Women rarely supported disinterestedness in public life, actions which brought little or no benefit to the immediate family. Similarly, he condemned the ways in which their influence was felt, through religious proselytism – which merely embittered religious animosities – and charity:

> the education given to women – an education of the sentiments rather than of the understanding – and the habit inculcated by their whole life, of looking to immediate effects on persons, and not to remote effects on classes of persons – make them both unable to see, and unwilling to admit, the ultimate evil tendency of any form of charity of philanthropy which commends itself to their sympathetic feelings.

For Mill it was just this kind of shortsighted benevolence which would sap 'the self-respect, self-help and self-control' on which 'individual prosperity and social virtue' were both based. With horizons enlarged and enlightened, women would be able to take a broader view, help to shape a more informed public opinion. That 'mediocrity of respectability' which women, especially of the middling classes, were frequently responsible for, as 'the auxiliary of common public opinion', operating always on the side of trivial considerations, restraining the aspirations, perhaps the nobler ones, of a husband, would be reduced.[34] Mill's writing on women should also be related to that fear of the tyranny of mediocre public opinion, stifling individuality, expressed in On Liberty (1859). The quality of married life, too, no longer so predictably a relationship between beings of very different abilities and interests, would be greatly enhanced. The progress of civilisation had turned men towards domestic life:

> The association of men with women in daily life is much closer

and more complete than it ever was before. Men's life is more domestic. Formerly their pleasures and chosen occupations were among men, and in men's company; their wives had but a fragment of their lives.[35]

But men had been disillusioned while women remained so much inferior to themselves. Mill's ultimate aim is clear:

> The moral regeneration of mankind will only really commence when the most fundamental of the social relations is placed under the rule of equal justice, and when human beings learn to cultivate their strongest sympathy with an equal in rights and cultivation.[36]

Mill thus offers an alternative version of the domestic relationship, based on equality and justice between men and women, with women free to compete for all professions and all public offices, though with most married women choosing to remain at home. Through public involvement, through the unity of private and public life, women too might achieve that moral fulfilment, that cultivation, which for Mill is the purpose of human life, and at last become full citizens. Mill has been criticised for his acceptance of the sexual division of labour within the home: it should be remembered that he shared this acceptance where married women with young children were concerned with the majority of feminist writers of the period. The argument for *citizenship*, still, for Mill, viewed in almost classical terms, was prior to any direct challenge to the sexual division of labour. His case is left to rest on the moral and intellectual capacities of women, primarily middle-class women. It is a curiously abstract piece of work, which offers no reflections on the relationship between the sexual division of labour within the home and outside in the labour market. He asserts that women should have the right to choose employment or domestic life, without confronting its reality, the narrow range of employments open to women of any age, or the limitations placed upon women by their domestic orientation. All this could be found in other contemporary work. Mill extended the case for citizenship to women, but ignored the relationship between economic and political strength. His language remained that of political theory, not of the reality which faced feminists in practice. Still, it was a fundamental challenge to notions of women's 'nature' and an uncompromising statement of belief in women's capacities:

though the radicalism of the arguments may be exaggerated by Mill's reputation.

FEMINIST PRACTICE:
DEFEAT AND DIFFICULTIES IN FRANCE

To turn to the world of practical feminist agitation is to recognise the force of the resistance to such demands. That is particularly so with respect to the development of French feminism. It has been seen that throughout the 1830s and 1840s Saint-Simonian and middle-class feminists continued to put arguments for the improvement of women's education, for higher wages and for legal reform, especially divorce. Léon Abensour suggested that the concerns of middle-class women, affronted at the radicalism of Saint-Simonian views, were above all for equality in marriage, then for the possibility of careers being open to them, with less interest in the achievement of political rights, or the improvement of the situation of working-class women: perhaps such preoccupations were typical of the narrow, rather static bourgeoisie of Louis Philippe's reign.[37] Yet the revolution of 1848 was to see a brief explosion of feminist activity, in which middle- and working-class women acted together, extending their concerns for employment and education to the fundamental demand for political and civil equality. Women active in the revolution came from very different backgrounds: Eugénie Niboyet, a middle-class woman from Lyons, from a Protestant liberal background, with experience in philanthropy, Saint-Simonianism and journalism, Desirée Gay, the dressmaker, Suzanne Voilquin, the midwife, the teachers – Jeanne Deroin, Pauline Roland, Elisa Lemonnier – together with some wealthier women, past contributors to the *Journal des Femmes*, and women of letters.[38]

The first sign of such activity came in the petition from a group of women, mainly middle-class, led by Antonine Andrée de Saint-Gilles, to the Provisional Government, on 16 March, for political and social rights for women. The sovereign people of the new republic should exemplify that marriage of complementary qualities to be found in the union of man and woman.[39] On 20 March 1848 that petition was reprinted in the first number of *La Voix des Femmes*, a publication initiated by Niboyet, which lasted until 18 June, publishing 46 issues. Niboyet probably received some financial help from the ex-Saint-Simonian banker, Olinde Rodrigues. *La Voix des Femmes*, like all the feminist papers published in the revolution, was printed by a woman printer, the widow Lacombe. From the beginning the journal identified the parallel aims of workers and of women. As Niboyet stressed in the first issue, 'with the slavery of work should end the slavery of women'.[40] On 27 March Jeanne Deroin published in *La Voix des Femmes* an appeal to the people to recognise women as citizens, so that they might play their part in that great work of social regeneration which was to begin.[41] Those who wrote for the journal were united in their commitment to the ideals of the revolution, and in a common interest in socialist ideas; ideas of the kind taught in the past by Saint-Simon and Fourier, and in 1848 by such socialists as Etienne Cabet, Pierre Leroux and Victor Considérant, to whom they looked for aid. They were united also in a kind of sentimental Christianity. The demands of the journal, for women, are clear. Contributors stressed again the need for improved education, for *lycées*, for teachers. They asked for the same education as that received by boys, though given separately, or at a different time. Some mentioned divorce, though it was clearly regarded as a more dangerous topic. They hoped to relieve the condition of prostitutes, though they saw this as coming about only through the achievement of a more socially just society. And they demanded political and civil rights: legal personality, the right to vote, equal wages to men for similar work, the right of association, of petitioning, the right to have the paternity of illegitimate children recognised by law. All kinds of petty discrimination were brought to light: why, it was asked, had boys' schools received ten days holiday to celebrate the coming of the republic, where girls had not had that pleasure?[42]

Not only did their journal draw these women together, but they began to play a part in the rapid growth of political clubs taking place in Paris after the revolution. They hoped for much from Etienne Cabet, the most popular French socialist, with a considerable following and reputed to be sympathetic to the women's cause. On 19 March, his club, crowded with women, debated the question 'Should women have the same political and social rights as men?' and almost every hand went up. But Cabet was himself unwilling to give unequivocal support, even though he had shown much concern about the oppression of women.[43] At the Club Lyonnais, a working woman spoke from the platform, demanding that women should no longer be regarded as slaves, that they should be admitted to the National

Assembly, receive sufficient wages for subsistence, and that the shame of seduction and illegitimacy should rest rather with the seducer than with the abandoned girl. At the 'Club de l'Emancipation des Peuples' one of the contributors to the *Voix des Femmes* spoke to a male audience to demand a proper education for women. And, from its first appearance, the *Voix des Femmes* had its own society, at first open only to women, which met at the office of the journal. Reports of the meetings are given in the paper, mostly discussions about the founding of new associations of working women. The group, popularly referred to as the Club des Femmes, attracted very great hostility: caricatures of viragos, of ugly women wearing the cap of liberty, began to invade the rest of the press. When Niboyet announced a meeting of the group, later opened to men, to discuss the question of divorce, she found that it was broken up by determined vandals, and then shut down by the police.[44]

Still, the newspaper had been able to put across its viewpoint, though it was frequently attacked. Deroin, for instance, from March onwards replied to a series of attacks from the newspaper *La Liberté*, which displayed a 'letter from an unemancipated woman . . .' and called for women to be vowed to 'obedience, silence, trusting love and humble devotion'.[45] The paper's views remained fairly consistent, increasingly leaning towards the socialist viewpoint. Writers shared a veneration for the ideal dignity of work. 'Marie Pauline' published one article, 'Woman must work', in which work was seen, for women, as the means of freedom.[46] The paper wrote of examples of collective organisation, both in current forms of socialism and in the past. Its outlook was internationalist, pacifist, sympathetic to the cause of anti-slavery. Anne Knight, the English Quaker, was a contributor to the *Voix des Femmes*.

But the pursuit of political and civil rights was to be very hard. On 22 March a group, forming a committee for the rights of women, went to the *Hôtel de Ville* to state the case, but was fobbed off. Pauline Roland had already, in the small town of Boussac, attempted without success to claim the vote in the local municipal election. But the elections for a new constituent assembly, to draw up a new constitution for France, were imminent. The feminists of the *Voix des Femmes* considered two lines of attack. They drew up a list of recommended male candidates, at first including all republicans and socialists, but narrowing it later to those sympathetic to their own cause. But the idea of electing at least one woman was attractive, and the name of George Sand was suggested, as a woman whose achievements and opinions would be respected. But Sand rudely rejected the invitation, in an open letter addressed not to the *Voix des Femmes* but to the major republican paper *La Réforme*, in which she totally disassociated herself from the club, the opinions and the women of the *Voix des Femmes*. Her letter was followed by a host of insults and ridicule, which attributed all possible sexual failings to these women.[47] Journals announced demonstrations in favour of divorce which had never taken place, and the club was broken up in the wake of this affair. Niboyet took up the defence, in the most moderate of tones:

> We do not aspire to be good male citizens [*citoyens*], we aspire simply to be good women citizens [*citoyennes*], and if we demand our rights it is as women and not as men. . . . It is in the name of the holy obligations of the family, in the name of the tender labours of the Mother, that we come to say to you: Yes, we like you have the right to serve our country in proportion to our abilities.[48]

As a last resort the paper published a petition to the Provisional Government, asking for the right to vote, given the state which civilisation had reached, given republican values and the clear fitness of women for the task.

With the June insurrection came changes. *La Voix des Femmes* was crushed by new press laws and was briefly replaced by *La Politique des Femmes*, directed by Desirée Gay, 'published by a society of working women in the interests of women', but it only lasted for two issues, to be followed by Jeanne Deroin's *L'Opinion des Femmes*, which appeared once in August 1848, and then regularly from January to August 1849, four times a month. In this paper, and in her *Cours de droit social pour les femmes* (n.d. 1848?) Deroin preached an uncompromising yet evangelistic feminism, one which rested not merely on egalitarianism, or on the organisation of labour, but on an inspired, exalted belief in the distinctive, unique part which women might play in the new social order. In the *Cours de droit social*, she suggested that now social science might develop the three divine principles, Liberty, Equality, Fraternity, and that the moment was come to inaugurate the reign of God on earth. Woman, called to play her part by the Christian Redeemer, was gradually comprehending her social destiny: 'Man is able to establish order only by despotism; woman is able to organise only through the power of maternal love; the two united will be able to reconcile order and liberty.'[49] In her journal, in a series of articles on 'The mission of woman in the present and in the future' and in her debate with the socialist Pierre-Joseph Proudhon, she maintained that position. But at the same time she also carried on the fight for political rights, and stood for election to the legislative assembly in the May elections in 1849. She carried her programme to the clubs and spoke within them to defend her view that democratic socialist politics could not come about without the emancipation of women, and she appealed to the electoral committee of the democratic socialists, the strongest group on the left, if not to support her, at least not to oppose her actively on the grounds of her sex. But Proudhon's paper Le Peuple denounced her candidature; she replied and her reply was widely printed. She wrote that she believed woman was the equal of man, yet different, and for that reason she should take part in the work of social reform, since only she could supply what man lacked to complete the work.[50] Her candidature was officially refused, and though she tried to put her case at a number of political meetings, at most of them she was refused the right to speak. Rapidly she turned to her project for a union of associations, drawing together both women and workers, which she initiated and developed. For this, in May 1850, she together with the others involved, including eight other women, was arrested. Her trial gave her a dramatic opportunity to defend her political and social views.

The revolution of 1848 represented a substantial defeat for the feminists, both in the lack of sympathy shown them by potential allies on the left and in the increasing conservatism of the majority in the National Assembly. Few male supporters had been prepared to propose legislative change in the Assembly. The proposal of Crémieux, a member of the Provisional Government, for a new divorce law was allowed to fall in May 1848. Victor Considérant, the one exception, a disciple of Fourier, on 13 June proposed that women should have political rights. Aware of the unpopularity of the demand, he nevertheless felt that at least one voice should be raised in its favour but it was not even discussed. And in the aftermath of the June insurrection, on 25 July, the government specifically decreed that women were not to be members of, or take any part in, political clubs. With the election of Louis Napoleon Bonaparte as president of the Second French Republic, politics moved steadily to the right and after the coup d'état of December 1851, and the coming of the Second

Empire, there was little scope for political activity of any kind except that favourable to the empire and the established order.

Many of these feminists had no immediate alternative but exile. Voilquin joined a Fourierist commune in Louisiana. Gay went first to Switzerland and then to Belgium. Niboyet, who had more sympathies with Bonapartism, returned to Lyons, continuing life as an increasingly conservative writer and journalist. Deroin went to England and continued writing, first publishing *L'Almanach des Femmes*, the first issue from Paris, the second and third in England: many of her old associates, especially Pauline Roland, contributed. This too contained the message of her 'Evangile social', a projected new work. But Deroin, absorbed in the struggle for survival with her family in England, never returned to France. She died in England in 1894, with William Morris and English socialists at her funeral.[51] Yet clearly feminism in France did not disappear, though under the conditions of the early years of the Second Empire the cause could be taken up only by individuals, and no organised movement was to appear before 1866, with the founding of the 'Société de la Revendication du Droit des Femmes' and, in 1871, the 'Association pour le Droit des Femmes' by the militantly republican and anti-clerical Maria Deraismes and Léon Richer. Between 1852 and 1881 women were formally prohibited by law from political commentary and newspaper directorships.

It is clear that the character of French feminism was different from that of Britain or the United States.[52] Much of the force of the movement of the 1830s and 1840s sprang from its strong associations with utopian socialism; that inheritance was by no means over by the 1860s, as survivors such as Jenny d'Héricourt, a disciple of Cabet and friend of Deroin, continued to fight the literary battles, and others – Victorine Brochon, Nathalie Lemel and Marguerite Tinayre – established small-scale co-operatives among Parisian workers.[53] Yet within the French socialist movement, which was to revive and reorganise after 1864, as well as among republican politicians, very strong hostility to the rights of women was expressed. The most notorious anti-feminist was P. J. Proudhon, already seen as an opponent of Jeanne Deroin in 1848. But his views, the doctrine of the *femme au foyer*, were largely shared by the republican historian Jules Michelet, expressed in *L'Amour* (1858) and *La Femme* (1860), and by the positivist Auguste Comte. Proudhon's tirade against women, in his *De la Justice dans la révolution et dans l'église* (1858) was drawn from his own controversy with Jenny d'Héricourt in the columns of the

Révue philosophique, beginning with her own article, in December 1856, 'M. Proudhon et la question des femmes'[54] Proudhon believed, without compromise, in the inferiority of women, their value in relation to men even being mathematically expressed (as 8 to 27!). Physically, intellectually and even morally, they were lesser beings, and only in fulfilling that lesser role within the institution of marriage, under the authority of a husband, would they take their proper rule in a society ruled by the principles of justice.[55] Proudhon's work aroused many replies, including those from Hermance Lesguillon, *Les femmes dans cent ans* (1859), and Adèle Esquiros, *L'Amour* (1860). More substantial were the replies of Juliette Lamber, later, as Mme Adam, a leading republican, and of Jenny d'Héricourt. Their differences indicate something of the spectrum of feminist opinion. Lamber's *Idées anti-proudhoniennes* (1858) denounced Proudhon's reduction of woman to a *femelle*, a female animal, his reliance on the natural superiority of man. Historical progress had brought civilisation to a point where society could begin to realise the ideal, harmony between masculine and feminine elements.[56] Women should exercise their qualities not only in the family but in society at large, in education, medicine, philanthropy and administration: and many tasks and occupations would overlap between men and women. Women needed an occupation, not only for single women, but for those older women, too, whose families had grown up: 'Work alone has emancipated men, work alone can emancipate women'.[57] Equality in marriage, and before the law, allowing woman an 'autonomous personality', could co-exist in a society in which women, and men, would be free to determine their own sphere.[58] It is a work which rests on a view of the different functions which men and women performed in society, but which permitted a freedom of choice, of self-determination of those functions. Later French feminists judged her short work to be 'the most explosive and the most effective' reply to Proudhon.[59]

Yet d'Héricourt's *La Femme affranchie* was in many ways more substantial. She reviewed not only Proudhon, whose ideas she had already assaulted, but a complete range of opinion in France, from the Saint-Simonian and Fourierist socialists and their successors, to liberal republicans such as Emile de Girardin and Jules Michelet, and the positivist Auguste Comte. D'Héricourt was iconoclastic. She was disrespectful to the republican revolution: 'Woman is like the people: she wants no more of your revolutions, which destroy us and profit only a few ambitious windbags'.[60] She also disliked the metaphysical nonsense, the androgynous constructions, of a Saint-Simon or a Pierre Leroux, though she acknowledged the importance of their work for the feminist cause. The time was over for sentimental conceptions of 'woman's mission' and ripe for practical action along American lines. She rejected the ways in which de Girardin and Michelet excluded women from the public world. Her critique of Proudhon suggested that it was as yet impossible to generalise reliably about the nature and potential of women. Given equal education and opportunities, the two sexes could indeed be fitted to the same functions in society, except in what concerned reproduction alone.[61] Women should have equal civil rights, though d'Héricourt was torn as to whether, given the current state of political education, they should have the vote; finally she suggested a common qualifying examination for all women and men over 25.[62] She called for middle-class women to exercise their responsibilities, to claim their rights and to give their children a rational education. Practically, she suggested a new 'Comité des femmes du progrès', an *institution polytechnique* for training women, and a new journal: all to achieve the kind of liberty and equality which would enable women to find their own place in society.[63] Perhaps, as P. K. Bidelman suggests, the poorer reception given to d'Héricourt's book was due to her challenge to the progressive forces in French politics, her warning that women might challenge republican doctrine.[64]

The ultimate future of French feminism was to be that of a moderate and bourgeois movement, connected with the republican cause, following 'a cause of prudence and moderation which might better be described as timidity', sharply divided from the small groups of feminists within the French socialist movement. James McMillan has pointed to the difficulties of understanding the weakness of the French feminist movement, suggesting that we need 'a thorough investigation of the deeply entrenched forces of anti-feminism'.[65] Certainly the republican tradition of 1789, in France, unlike that of the United States, retained an unyielding hostility to women's participation in the public life of the republic. In the 1760s the ideas of Rousseau had appeared to offer something positive to women in all three societies considered here; by the 1860s his themes had in France become hardened into a reactionary and inflexible *masculinisme*, as Bidelman calls it. Some key differences in French society have been noted here. Most obviously, there is the absence of that background of widespread, active and innovatory association among middle-class women, around religious and philanthropic purposes, found from around 1800 in both Britain and America. Though such associations also existed in France, they were of later date and less important, given the growth in strength of the religious orders, and the degree of control exercised by the Church and by a centralised state bureaucracy of a kind which did not exist in the other two societies. There was no easy route to humanitarian and political activity, such as the anti-slavery or anti-Corn Law movements in Britain. It is perhaps not surprising that women of the Protestant minority – such as Eugénie Niboyet and Hortense Wild – were prominent in feminist action both at mid-century and in a later period. The religious model of voluntary action and organisation is an important element in understanding the roots of feminist organisation.

This should be related to the difference in the composition of the French bourgeoisie and the Anglo-American middle classes. Generalisations here are almost impossible, given the regional and sectional variations. Daumard portrayed, under the July monarchy, a Parisian bourgeoisie which in the upper ranks saw little mobility, and which still looked to landed property and to public employment as a source of status, rather than to industrial growth. The differential patterns of economic growth in France and, say, Britain, in the nineteenth century had their effects on the size and the outlook of the French middle classes. Among the textile manufacturers of the North, for example, the interests of the family and of industry might be identified and expanded through the continuing control of marriage alliances and the dowry system. Economic historians continue to discuss the degree to which the French bourgeoisie did develop an entrepreneurial rather than a dynastic outlook in the second half of the nineteenth century. The question must surely be of great relevance to the situation of middle-class women, and must await further discussion. Certainly the upper ranks of the French bourgeoisie did not offer recruits to feminist activity in this period as did, for example, the leading circles of Manchester. And the contrast between the women from industrialists' families in Lille, as Smith has portrayed them, absorbed in a life of children, charity and household, increasingly distant from public life, and those of Manchester, whom we have seen in campaigns against slavery and the Corn Laws, and who were by the mid-1860s to be drawn into the suffrage issue, is a striking one. Surely one explanation must lie not only in the socially and politically conservative outlook of this class in France, but more fundamentally, in a family structure which did not permit the expansion and enlargement of the domestic world.[66]

That slower rate of economic change also, of course, affected the size of the French urban working classes, still a minority of the population at mid-century, and the extent of large-scale industry. There were no working-class women's organisations in France comparable to those which campaigned against the Poor Law or supported the Chartists in Britain. The political climate from 1815 to the Second Empire permitted for the most part only brief periods of revolutionary action and continuing undercover organisation centred on male institutions. Neither offered women the opportunity to organise in support, or to develop political ideas, except in a spontaneous and informal way. After 1848, the achievement of universal male suffrage, however ineffective in practice, offered no common cause, no opportunity to reopen the suffrage question. Women entered large-scale production only slowly in France, and found few opportunities there in this period for association together. A further question must surely be one which cannot yet be answered: did the segregated worlds of the French peasant family, varying in degree between the North and Mediterranean regions, survive into the world of the French urban working classes, to which they were still so closely bound?

THE UNITED STATES: FEMINISM AND THE CURRENT OF REFORM

In the United States the progress of feminist practice from 1848 was rapid, drawing on that wide range of activities which have been traced in the previous chapter, but increasingly focusing on the suffrage issue. In 1848, the Seneca Falls Convention employed the language of the Declaration of Independence in their own 'Declaration of Sentiments', proclaiming the self-evident truth: 'that all men and women are created equal', and denouncing 'a history of repeated injuries and usurpations on the part of man towards woman'. The Declaration covers women's right to suffrage, the oppression of women in marriage and the absence of divorce, the masculine monopoly of employment and education, women's subordination in religious matters, and the application of dual moral standards. Moreover, men had usurped the right which belonged to God alone to define that 'sphere of action' within which women should move, and had attempted by the destruction of women's confidence and self-respect to secure their acquiescence in 'a dependent and abject life'. It is a comprehensive catalogue, one which marks out the range of concerns traced here. The resolutions which followed included also the affirmation of women's right to speak and preach in public. The only resolution which was not passed unanimously was that put by Elizabeth Cady Stanton and Frederick Douglass: 'it is the duty of the women of this country to secure to themselves their sacred right to the elective franchise'.[67] The Convention was seriously divided on this issue, and the resolution was passed only by a narrow majority.

Elizabeth Cady Stanton was to emerge as one of the dominant personalities of the American movement of the 1850s. The daughter of a New York lawyer and a product of Emma Willard's seminary at Troy, she experienced Finney's revivals, and played, with her husband, an active part in the anti-slavery movement, speaking in the 1840s before the New York legislature. In 1847 she moved to Seneca Falls, in western New York State, where, although she found many congenial friends, she also realised the practical difficulties facing women in a small community:

> The general discontent I felt with woman's portion as wife, mother, housekeeper, physician, and spiritual guide, the chaotic conditions into which everything fell without her constant supervision, and the wearied anxious look of the majority of women impressed me with a strong feeling that some active measures should be taken to remedy the wrongs of society in general and women in particular.[68]

It was this feeling which led her, on a visit to Lucretia Mott and other Quaker families, to propose the notion of a convention, following that conversation remembered from the London Anti-Slavery Convention in 1840. On the question of the suffrage, however, Mott had opposed Stanton's resolution, probably because she shared the view of W. H. Garrison, who while supporting women's suffrage thought that no one committed against slavery, man or woman, should vote in the present immoral state of the government.[69] For whatever reason the split took place, it did not recur in subsequent conventions throughout the 1850s, though the question of priorities was to split the movement seriously after the Civil War. The demand for the suffrage came to be seen as 'the one cardinal demand' on which all others depended, and equally as the one which, most symbolising women's step into public life, was to be most fiercely opposed. Successive conventions reaffirmed the demand. Two weeks after Seneca Falls, in Rochester, New York, a woman presided over a further Convention against the doubts of Mott and Stanton, who believed it 'a most hazardous experiment' for a woman with no knowledge or experience of guiding public meetings.[70] A series of conventions were held in the early 1850s, the first two national conventions at Worcester, Massachusetts in 1850 and 1851, and the third in Syracuse in 1852. The abolitionist movement continued to be closely linked to the cause, as did that of temperance. Male abolitionists were frequently convinced supporters, and might play an active part within the movement. Female anti-slavery agents were powerful missionaries for the feminist cause as well.

From the junction of abolitionism and broader movements to expand woman's sphere had sprung a potentially powerful feminist movement. Its leaders, Cady Stanton and Mott, were joined by two other women who would continue to play a leading role for many years. Lucy Stone, the daughter of a Massachusetts farmer, had had the benefit of an education at Oberlin College, which she paid for after teaching for nine years. Originally of a Congregationalist background, she rejected such orthodoxy and became a Unitarian. By 1847 she had become a lecturer in the dual cause of anti-slavery and women's rights. In 1855 she married Henry Blackwell, brother of Elizabeth and Emily Blackwell, in a simple ceremony which embodied their own protest at the current state of marriage. Susan B. Anthony, also born in Massachusetts of a Quaker home, had a father who was an active supporter of temperance, anti-slavery and even women's rights. Susan taught early and attended a seminary. By the 1830s the family was deeply involved in the abolitionist movement. Initially, in 1848, she was not attracted by the Seneca Falls Convention, but when she was refused recognition at a series of temperance conventions in 1852 and 1853 she was converted to the cause. She gave up teaching in the early 1850s and became a full-time anti-slavery, temperance and women's rights worker, in 1856 becoming chief agent of the American Anti-Slavery Society in New York. She remained unmarried. These leaders were supported by activists who, like them, were constantly travelling, visiting small towns, cultivating women who were most likely to be sympathetic, sowing ideas which may well have taken years to find fulfilment.

But the movement, which leant so heavily on abolitionism, still lacked an organisation of its own. The successful annual conventions were not planned by any state or national bodies, but by constantly changing committees. There was considerable reliance on abolitionist funds, lecturers and newspapers. There were a few feminist journals. In 1852 Anna Spencer started the *Pioneer and Woman's Advocate*, in Providence, Rhode Island, its motto 'Liberty, Truth, Temperance, Equality'. Paulina Wright Davis founded the *Una*, committed to women's enfranchisement, in 1853. Wright Davis, from western New York, who experienced Calvinist conversion very young, married Francis Wright, a fervent abolitionist from Utica, and there became active in anti-slavery, moral reform and temperance societies. In 1836 she took her first step on behalf of women's rights by circulating petitions in favour of the married women's property bill in New York. On her husband's death in 1840 she moved from Utica to be drawn into the wider national currents of reform. She spent some years lecturing, especially in the cause of health reform. She presided over the two conventions held at Worcester in 1850 and 1851. The *Una* was published first in Providence, then in Boston, where Caroline Dall acted as assistant editor, and was an important means of publicising feminist ideas and reports of conventions. Much of the paper was devoted to Wright Davis's own commitment to the reform of the structure of marriage: 'the starting point of all the reforms which the world needs'. The progression of Amelia Bloomer's paper, the *Lily*, from the cause of temperance to that of women's rights has already been mentioned. In 1855 Anna McDowell began to publish in Philadelphia the *Woman's Advocate*, owned, printed and written by women. And in 1853, one of the few European-born women to take part, Mathilde Anneke, a political refugee, published her *Deutsche Frauenzeitung* for the German community in Milwaukee, without much success.[71]

One study of American feminist-abolitionist women in this period, by Hersh, has examined in depth the background of 51 women prominent in the movement, suggesting something of the complex interplay of influences underlying nineteenth-century feminism. The great majority of these were organisers and propagandists for the movement. Of the 51, 33 could claim New England ancestry. The great majority came from comfortable middle-class or upper middle-class homes, only four growing up in relative poverty; and they retained both a sense of class and of pride in New England values, which could border on nativism. Their commitment to end racial prejudice has been contrasted with a rather less enlightened view of Irish immigrants, which also had some roots in religious prejudice. They had grown up in families with a radical outlook, often with strong-minded mothers. Fifteen of the group had come from Quaker homes, accustomed to seeing Quaker women ministers. The most outstanding characteristic uniting them was the high degree of education which they had achieved, in a variety of ways, for the period: at the same time a number had experienced immediate personal frustrations as women, from a lack of occupation, or low salaries. Most critical was the way in which belief for the need for reform in society had grown from religious commitment, much of which might remain with them. They had rejected orthodox, especially Calvinist, Protestantism. It is clear that Quakerism and Unitarianism drew a number brought up in evangelical faith; others found a commitment to social reform replacing any formal religious commitment, yet tended to retain a sense of a special mission, an absorption with duty and with the struggle against evil in the world. The failure of the established churches to take a stand against slavery, and their conservatism on women's rights, offered them little. But many of the group were attracted to a liberal, freethinking and speculative kind of religion, to a God who had both male and female qualities, as the Boston Unitarian Theodore Parker had preached. Quakerism had a strong appeal, yet, as the Grimkés found, male Quaker leaders could still attempt to regulate women's sphere of action.[72]

So far, the identification of the American movement with the argument from individual natural rights, rooted in the Enlightenment, and with the American Revolution, has been stressed. And this inheritance was undoubtedly of fundamental importance to the movement, providing it with a familiar and appealing rhetoric. Most directly, that analogy can be seen in feminist protests against taxation without representation, widely urged by speeches of Lucy Stone in the 1840s and 1850s. Dr Harriot Hunt submitted a protest with her taxes every year. In 1858 Lucy Stone refused to pay taxes at all and allowed her goods to be sold at auction (though they were bought by a friend).[73] Women had to resist the 'aristocracy of sex'. The language of slavery, which came both from the revolutionary movement and from abolitionism, provided perhaps the most powerful of all images: the parallel between woman and slave. The bondage and confinement of women were stressed: as Lucy Stone wrote, 'marriage is to woman a state of slavery'. Yet in spite of such condemnation of the current conditions of marriage, most American feminists accepted the idea of a difference in the economic and social roles of men and women, and found congenial that sense of women's special mission which still owed something to the evangelical spirit. Such a belief was an essential part of women's contribution to the anti-slavery and temperance movements, and could entail belief in woman's moral superiority. But such differences should in no way limit participation in a broader public life to which both men and women should equally contribute, as citizens. There were of course differences within the movement, as in this exchange, for example, at the Syracuse National Convention in 1852:

> Clarina Howard Nichols ... Woman must seek influence, independence, representation, that she may have power to aid in the elevation of the human race. When men kindly set aside woman from the National Councils, they say the moral field belongs to her; and the strongest reason why woman should seek a more elevated position is because her moral susceptibilities are greater than those of men.
> Mrs Mott thought differently from Mrs Nichols; she did not believe that woman's moral feelings were more elevated than man's; but that with the same opportunities for development, with the same restrictions and penalties, there would probably be about an equal manifestation of virtue.[74]

Nichols' view was probably the predominant one, though some feminists, such as Susan B. Anthony, did raise the issue of the effect of educational and environmental differences on women's nature.[75]

Movements of moral reform, which implied the moral superiority of women, were, as has been emphasised, one important route to feminist activity, but not all those who supported such movements were likely to take up the cause of women's rights. Catherine Beecher has been seen as a pioneer of education for women, committed to raising the status of domestic labour, yet as an opponent of the Grimké sisters. The difference surely lies in the aspiration towards female autonomy, towards self-definition of one's 'sphere'. Yet there could be recognisable contradictions. A fierce debate took place in the New York Convention of May 1860, as Cady Stanton and others called for the acceptance of a divorce law, to allow women to escape from the degrading conditions of an unhappy marriage:

> Do wise Christian legislators need any arguments to convince them that the sacredness of the family relation should be protected at all hazards? The family, that great conservator of national virtue and strength, how can you hope to build it up in the midst of violence, debauchery and excess.[76]

It was a controversial debate, with the resolution opposed by Antoinette Brown Blackwell, one of the strongest defenders of the view that women and men were 'two halves of a great whole', on grounds of principle. It was opposed by Wendell Phillips on tactical grounds: it was too dangerous an issue to confront, and it would involve a battle with the influential Horace Greeley of the *New York Daily Tribune*, a strong opponent of divorce. It is interesting that this should be the most divisive issue, before the cessation of feminist activity with the coming of the American Civil War, for it did most clearly confront the rights of the individual woman with that more exalted notion of woman's destiny within marriage.

Clearly only the sketchiest account of the character of the American suffrage movement can be given here. Based in the northern and middle states, deriving much of its strength from its unity with other reforming currents of opinion at mid-century – temperance, peace, above all abolitionism – activists shared for the most part a common background in their education, their religious dissent and their relative prosperity. There were few echoes of the movement from the Southern states. Black women activists such as Frances Harper and Charlotte Forten Grimké tended to give their full energies to the anti-slavery campaign, although, like Sarah Remond, they did not forget the connection between the two.[77] Alice Rossi has stressed the 'status deprivation' of the first generation of American feminists, drawn from rural, literate, small-town America, threatened by the growth of the major urban conurbations, and by the new pattern of immigration.[78] It is certainly likely that these women shared the concerns of their class, and the rural background of American feminism perhaps helps to explain its reliance on revolutionary ideology and its relative (compared to British feminists) lack of interest in questions of employment and 'sanitary reform', and its preoccupation rather with 'moral reform'. There were of course exceptions to this, such as the work of Caroline Dall on women's employment, herself influenced by the British example. Ideas on women's suffrage did of course spread to the West. Keith Melder points out how this spread followed the lines of 'Yankee' settlement, from central Massachusetts and central New York state, to northern Ohio, northern Indiana, southern Michigan, central and northern Illinois, to Wisconsin, Iowa and Kansas. Some women, such as Mary Livermore and Clarina Howard Nichols, went to Kansas with the anti-slavery migration from New England in the 1850s. Nichols saw herself as a missionary in the cause of women's rights also, and felt, on speaking in Missouri: 'that I had not only won a respectful consideration for woman's cause and its advocacy, but improved my opportunity to vindicate New England training, in face of Southern prejudices'.[79] In subsequent years, feminism, because of its origins, could be interpreted as a means of extending, of asserting the power of a particular 'American' way of life: yet it was to continue to develop after the Civil War in diverse ways, as a growing movement.

GREAT BRITAIN: FEMINIST POLITICS AND THE POLITICS OF CLASS

In Britain, the decade from 1850 to 1860 saw significant develop-ments in the organisation of women, with the coming of the first avowedly feminist paper, the *English Woman's Journal*, the formation of a number of related societies and increasing public focus on issues affecting women. There were a number of different, though some-times overlapping, centres of activity. Radical attitudes inherited from the Owenite movement were still very much alive. William Thompson and Anna Wheeler had in 1825 advocated the admission of women to full political rights. The contributions of Catherine Barmby to Owen's *New Moral World* were considered earlier. In the early 1840s she published her 'Demand for the Emancipation of Woman, politically and socially' as a tract. She called for political emancipation to come first through the addition of female suffrage to the People's Charter, ecclesiastical emancipation through the entry of women into the priesthood, and the institution of 'woman societies' wherever possible, and domestic emancipation for women on the basis of their own independent labour. And she believed that a 'Woman's Magazine' should be published to spread these ideas. She wrote as a communist, as one who believed still in the complementarity of the sexes and the qualities they represented:

> Woman and man are two in variety and one in equality. Their physical frames are as various as are the stems of the poplar and of the oak, but yet should the sun of equal rights be alike shining upon them. In woman, sentiment; in man, intellect, variously prevail; but society should equally provide, through its institutions, that the sentiment of the woman should be strengthened by intellect, and the intellect of the man refined by sentiment; in fine, society should be so organised that without identifying the sexes, it should give to them equal educational opportunities and equal general advantages in every sphere.[80]

In a later article on 'Woman's Industrial Independence' in 1848, she argued that 'the greatest want of woman is industrial independence' which was 'as necessary for woman as for man', but possibly only attainable through association.[81] Both Catherine and Goodwyn Barmby were contributors to the *People's Journal* of Mary and William Howitt. In 1847 George Holyoake, Chartist and secularist leader, wrote to encourage the establishment of just such a magazine as Catherine Barmby suggested, in the rationalist *Free Press*, and claimed to have approached some prominent women with the idea: Harriet Martineau, Barbara Leigh Smith, Bessie Rayner Parkes. The suggestion of course took ten years to bear fruit.[82]

Among the Chartists themselves, few were actively prepared to commit themselves to women's suffrage, as has been seen. Yet one initiative had some effect. The Quaker, anti-slavery campaigner and Chartist sympathiser, Anne Knight, was informed by a leading Sheffield socialist in 1851 that seven Chartist women were actively interested in taking independent action on the suffrage issue; on 20 June 1851 Knight wrote to a Mrs Rooke of Sheffield asking for all patriotic women to aid in the revision of the Charter, 'the first article of which is in error, calling that universal which is only half of it'. A month later the Sheffield Female Reform Association had its first meeting, with an ambitious programme of establishing sister bodies throughout the country. Its Address to the Women of England called quite clearly for women to enjoy 'all the political, social and moral rights of man'. The association submitted a petition to the House of Lords, for the inclusion of adult women within the suffrage.[83] In 1852, the *Northern Star* also reported another group of which Anne Knight was a member, the Women's Elevation League, based in Camden Town, whose object was the 'Social, Moral, Professional, Pecuniary, Political Elevation of Women'.[84] Unfortunately, we know nothing more of the development of these societies.

The most direct inheritors of Owenite radicalism were those women who continued a public career, lecturing and agitating within the secularist movement. The most direct successor to Emma Martin was Harriet Law, born in 1831, from the London lower middle classes and originally a strict Baptist, who first met preachers of freethought in East London, and came to doubt her faith: most notably, St Paul's injunction to women. She met and married another freethinker in 1855, and in 1859 she began a career as a lecturer: she was to be hailed as the best woman lecturer since Emma Martin. Along with freethought she continuously supported the cause of women's rights, maintaining the cause through the 1860s and 1870s in secularist and republican circles. It may well be that, as Barbara Taylor has pointed out, in her audiences and in the clubs that survived the decline of Chartism, there remained much more interest in women's rights than has yet been traced.[85]

The cause of women's suffrage was not of course new. Individuals had raised the issue in the 1830s and 1840s. The debate about the franchise in 1832 quite clearly had the effect of stimulating a few women to think about the question. Margaret Mylne recalled: 'as soon as ever I understood the benefits expected from a £10 franchise, I began to wish that female householders should have it too, thinking it only fair play they should.'[86] Just after the Reform Act, W. J. Fox, editor of the *Monthly Repository*, published his article on 'A Political and Social Anomaly', in which he condemned the reception given to the petition of Mary Smith of Stanmore for the inclusion of unmarried females with property qualifications in the franchise: for the first time, the franchise was specifically made a male preserve.[87] It was undoubtedly in these terms, referring to the propertied and the non-dependent, that much early discussion in Britain was carried on. Mary Leman Grimstone, writing on 'Quaker Women' in the *Monthly Repository*, foresaw a time when women would speak in Parliament. Margaret Mylne, in 1841, in the *Westminster Review* put forward the argument which was to dominate many later debates – that women should be enfranchised on the same terms as men. That meant that only women who were £10 householders in the towns, who by definition, given the existing state of the property laws, had to be single or widowed, would qualify. This measure of equality might, she thought, calm any agitation. She herself accepted the identification of the interests of married women with their husbands, though she accepted that changing social conditions might create particular anomalies.[88] That was not the view of Anne Knight, who in 1847 published a leaflet which called for the introduction of women's qualities into the political life of the nation:

If woman be the complement of man, we may surely venture the intimation, that all our social transactions will be incomplete, or otherwise imperfect, until they have been guided alike by the wisdom of each sex. The wise, virtuous, gentle mothers of a State or nation might contribute as much to the good order, the peace, the thrift of the body politic, as they severally do to the well-being of their families, which for the most part, all know, is more than their fathers do.[89]

Both Marion Reid and Anne Richelieu Lamb, in sharp and stimulating works published in 1843 and 1844, denounced 'sentimental effusions' about 'woman's mission', though neither doubted the domestic focus of women's lives. Reid took the argument further, in considering women's claim to equal civil rights, in an extended and thoughtful discussion which in effect preceded many of the points made by Mill. Women's domestic duties were to be compared rather to men's professions, in no way disqualifying them for civil rights. The exercise of such rights would ennoble and elevate women themselves, and allow their interests to be properly represented. Woman's duty was 'to the higher end of her being, the development of her whole nature, moral and rational': the more she fulfilled this, the better she would perform her other, less vital tasks. Such rights would allow women to make their own choice, and would hardly detract from their commitment to domestic life. Many objections were trivial: the indecorum and tumult of elections, for example. She defended the exposure of women to 'some painful but salutary shocks to her delicacy', which might perhaps keep them better informed of the facts of life. Reid denied that representation would mean the loss of that intangible moral influence of which so many writers made so much. For her, that moral influence could be better expressed through political rights, and no conflict was foreseen by her between influence and representation.[90]

Harriet Taylor Mill's 'The Enfranchisement of Women' was prompted by the news of the conventions held in the United States in 1850. Again, unsurprisingly, many of her arguments later reappeared in the *Subjection of Women*. She too rejected any kind of 'sentimental priesthood' for women, by implication denying the popular view of the complementarity of the sexes. For her, equality meant equality of access to all occupations, an equality of competition, as well as equality of political and civil rights. Only individuals, given complete liberty of choice, could determine what constituted their 'sphere'. No conflict necessarily existed between politics and maternity, unless women were to be barred from all other careers except motherhood. In employment, 'so long as competition is the general law of human life, it is tyranny to shut out one half of the competitors': women's earnings were likely to win her greater respect, even if the earnings of men were to some degree lowered by them.[91] There could be no real substance to the view that politics would have a hardening effect upon women. That 'improvement in the moral sentiments of mankind' which had made home so much the focus of men and women's lives had produced the possibility of real companionship, yet a degree of selfishness on the side both of men and of women, exploiting dominance on the one hand, weakness on the other, was harmful to the emancipation of humanity, in its broadest sense. And women, under the influence of those to whom they were subordinate, cherished their habits of submission. Taylor Mill had no qualms: reason and principle, not sentimentality, were what was required in the cause of equality, and she welcomed as its first sign the petition from Sheffield. Her case was a strongly individualistic, certainly optimistic one, and in spite of one major difference – over the employment of married women – there are very close parallels with Mill's essay.

In 1855, Agnes Davis Pochin, married to a leading Salford industrialist, published a short pamphlet, *The Right of Women to Exercise the Elective Franchise*, in which she put forward a liberal case, arguing that the 'restrictive civil policy applied to women' was not one which could be justified by any public advantage. Such restrictions were harmful to the individual development of women's

faculties; unlike men excluded from the franchise they could never
hope to enjoy that right. And by this women's interests and horizons
were artificially narrowed and their education limited. The entry of
women into public life would not detract from their domestic lives,
but give them greater social importance:

> one of the best means of securing domestic and maternal efficiency
> is to give to women sound views of the sciences of government and
> political economy; and as means and incitement to this end, I
> would advocate such an extension of the franchise and such an
> opportunity of acquiring political distinction as would not be
> inconsistent with the social discharge of their social duties.[92]

Objections were to be countered: the possibility of domestic dissen-
sion, the argument from military strength, the dangers of tumult at
elections, the present ignorance of women – none had foundation.
And,

> As it is the Divine Will that the two sexes *together* shall constitute
> humanity, so I believe it to be the Divine intention that the
> influence and exertions of the two sexes *combined* shall be necessary
> to the complete success of any human institution, or any branch of
> such institution.[93]

Yet the claim was a modest one: enfranchisement on the same terms
as men, which would in fact have enfranchised only wealthy single
women and widows, with a right for women to have some accommodation in the House of Commons, if not yet female Members of
Parliament. She does not discuss these limitations, which surely
affected her argument; it is clearly an argument directed to women of
the middle classes, whose frustrations at their limited lives, she
suggests, are all too evident. When, in 1868, Henry Davis Pochin
presided over the first meeting of the National Society for Women's
Suffrage, it was to be Agnes Davis Pochin who introduced the second
resolution, following Lydia Becker.[94] Interest in reform of the
franchise was reviving in Britain in the late 1850s, and when in 1858
the Northern Reform society proclaimed itself as campaigning for
universal suffrage and invited women's subscriptions, a number of
women showed interest, only to be disappointed. Commenting on

this, Matilda Ashurst Biggs, daughter of the Owenite lawyer, W. Ashurst, wrote to the *Newcastle Guardian* in February 1859:

> I have never given my rights to be merged in those of any other person, and I feel it an injustice that I, who am equally taxed with men, should be denied a voice in making the laws which affect and dispose of my property, and made to support a State wherein I am not recognised as a citizen.[95]

Debate, and agitation, for the extension of the franchise were to continue. It would be interesting to know how far such agitation did encourage many women to reflect on the possibilities of a wider suffrage, before 1866.

The question of women's suffrage was thus a live one in Britain in the late 1850s, but was not to be the initial basis for organisation. As the *English Woman's Journal* had suggested, the 'Condition of English-woman Question' was to provide the spur in Britain which Abolition-ism had done in the United States: and it was the *Journal* which provided a forum and a basis for organisation. The women who wrote in it were gradually putting together a coherent case for the expansion of women's political power, though they were not at first concerned with the suffrage question. The *Journal* asserted that women should have the independence and the powers of mind to define their 'sphere' for themselves, and that both men and women would benefit from its extension into public life. It put a case for the particular mission of women to other women to be recognised in the granting of authority, employment and training. It suggested that the practice of collective organisation should be regarded as being as important as unfettered competition, in the employment and well-being of women. It suggested that women's self-assertiveness, political skills and powers of organisation should be fostered. It rested, of course, with its associated societies, on the background of those middle-class women involved: on their awareness of class, but also on their wish to deal with the common concerns of all women.

A detailed study of women active in feminist concerns in the 1850s and 1860s would be extremely valuable. Only an impressionistic view can be given here. The cause which first brought together a group of active campaigners was, as has already been seen, that of reform of the married women's property law. Lee Holcombe has suggested that the appearance of a new committee to work for that reform in 1855 signalled 'the beginnings of an organised feminist movement'.[96] Led by Barbara Leigh Smith, Mary Howitt and Bessie Rayner Parkes, the committee, as has been seen, won the support of a number of distinguished women. Some who joined in that campaign were subsequently to come together in 1858 to found the *English Woman's Journal* and the societies associated with it.[97] The women who were closely involved as activists were mostly unmarried. Like Barbara Leigh Smith, several were daughters of the dissenting middle classes. Leigh Smith's father and grandfather were both noted radical MPs, her father active in the Corn Law campaign, unorthodox on his views both on marriage and on the education of women. Bessie Rayner Parkes was the daughter of the Philosophic Radical MP Joseph Parkes. Anna Mary Howitt, who contributed to the *Journal*, was the daughter of Mary Howitt, author and journalist. Two women, Isa Craig, daughter of an Edinburgh tradesman, and Adelaide Proctor, daughter of the poet 'Barry Cornwell', had ambitions for literary careers, especially in poetry. Matilda Mary Hays as an actress was a close friend of Charlotte Cushman and while living in Rome had translated some of the novels of George Sand. Several came from large, not too well-off professional families. Emily Davies and Jessie Boucherett were the daughters of provincial clergymen. Davies had attempted to build a network of societies in Newcastle before coming to London to begin a lifetime's labour for women's higher education. Maria Rye was the oldest of nine children of a London solicitor. Emily Faithfull was similarly the daughter of a Surrey clergyman. Elizabeth Garrett, the future doctor, and friend of Emily Davies, whose family contributed so much to the early women's movement, was the daughter of the prosperous Essex corn merchant, Newson Garrett. Some had taken advantage of the new colleges for women, Leigh Smith at Bedford, Proctor at Queen's College, but more had simply acquired a better than average education through their family, probably via fathers and brothers. Religious dissent is a very common theme in their backgrounds. Parkes and Leigh Smith were both from Unitarian backgrounds, like, of course, Harriet Taylor Mill, Harriet Martineau and Mary Carpenter. The Howitt family was plagued by religious doubt, alternating between Quakerism, Unitarianism and Catholicism. The involvement of Christian Socialism in the cause of women's education had helped to develop Emily Davies' interest. Those at the heart of these new developments were young women,

aged between 25 and 35, some from well-to-do but radical backgrounds, others from professional homes which could offer them little
future occupation.

If one looks at a broader picture, at those women associated with a
wider range of campaigns from the 1850s to the 1870s – at the suffrage
campaign, at the movement to achieve higher education for women,
at the campaign for the repeal of the Contagious Diseases Acts – a not
dissimilar pattern emerges, though one which was to incorporate the
energies of far more married women. An evangelical interest in
anti-slavery and philanthropy was similarly to inspire Anne Clough,
a Liverpool merchant's daughter and the first Principal of Newnham,
and Josephine Butler, who led the campaign against the Contagious
Diseases Acts and the operation of the double moral standard in the
1870s. Walkowitz, in her study of the leadership of this campaign, the
Ladies National Association, stressed the importance of abolitionism
and temperance in the shaping of feminist commitment and the
extent to which involvement in the repeal campaign was accompanied by continuing work for medical reform and for social purity.
And, both in the leadership and at a local level, the strong
representation of Quakers and Unitarians has been stressed.[98] That
representation is evident too in the list of leading supporters of the
women's suffrage campaign. It could also overlap with the notable
presence of some leading industrialists' families: the Quaker Brights
of Manchester, the Quaker Peases of Darlington, the Wedgwoods of
Etruria. The Quaker Eliza Sturge, daughter of teetotaller and radical
Joseph Sturge, was there too. There were of course other routes:
individually distinguished women such as Harriet Martineau, Harriet Grote and the astronomer Mary Somerville were there. Ernest
Jones, the ex-Chartist, still remained as a supporter of women's
suffrage. Three out of the four daughters of the radical, Owenite
London lawyer, W. A. Ashurst, were associated with the movement,
Caroline as the wife of James Stansfeld, leader with Butler of the
LNA, Emilie, similarly, as a leading figure in that movement, and
Matilda as an early suffrage supporter. The majority of feminists
within such campaigns were therefore linked to liberal and radical
middle-class families, likely to be unorthodox in their religious
beliefs.[99] But women from the lower middle classes, such as the
daughter of the London engraver, Frances Mary Buss, educated at
Queen's College, and the badly-off daughters of clergymen and
professional families, might also provide the personal energies and

commitment in their own careers especially in expanding the fields of education and employment.[100]

In looking at the programme of the *English Woman's Journal*, the relationship between the different elements of its campaigns has been stressed. To deal with the practical problems of women – the shortage of occupations, low wages and the restrictions of prejudice – what was needed was both better education and a broadening of the occupations open to women. To deal with the conditions in which so many working men and women lived, what was needed was the employment of the surplus powers and energies of middle-class women, and the paid employment in suitable tasks of the not-so-affluent women of all classes. Only the association of women together could unite these ends. The work which most clearly reflected the aspirations of those who wrote in the *Journal* was in fact not that of either of the Mills, but of Anna Jameson, the veteran author of the 1830s onwards, whose name is frequently invoked in its pages. Two of her lectures, *Sisters of Charity* and the *Communion of Labour*, together with her 'Letter to Lord John Russell . . .' offer some indication of the outlook, in general, of the magazine. She argued that what educated Englishwomen now looked for was some share in the government of all those public institutions in which women and children were brought together – through the 'communion of labour':

> that the *maternal* as well as the *paternal* element should be made available, on the principle which I believe is now generally acknowledged, that the more you can carry out the family law, the 'communion of labour' into all social institutions, the more harmonious and the more perfect they will be.[101]

For the qualities of men and women were indeed distinct, but to be regarded as equal in value and to be jointly employed. What Jameson is tracing, is, precisely, the means of expanding 'woman's sphere,' like Julie-Victoire Daubié in France, Eliza Farnham in the United States, and many others. Jameson condemned that 'silent social antagonism' between men and women rooted in a degrading dismissal of women's powers and, equally, that dual moral standard set in a 'tide of profligacy', with dissolute moral habits on the one side, ignorance on the other.[102] The application of a single moral standard, for men and women, was best brought about through the 'communion of labour', the infusion of female responsibility into public institutions affecting women and of male responsibility into the duties of the home. One part of the answer was the desperate need for trained and equipped women, as nurses, midwives, physicians, 'sanitary reformers', district visitors, and so on, in refuges, reformatories, hospitals, training and industrial schools, and all those developing institutions which are characteristic of urban, industrial societies. One model, which offered an important framework of the discussion, was that of the sisterhood: both Catholic and Protestant sisterhoods offered organised training in practical charitable work.

That theme, of 'sisterhoods', is a recurring one, both in the *Journal* and in the work of other writers such as Louisa Twining. Bessie Rayner Parkes used it to introduce her articles on 'What can educated women do', and 'A year's experience in woman's work'; the Blackwell sisters referred to the lack of such sisterhoods in 'Medicine as a profession for women' in May 1860. A. R. L. (Anne Richelieu Lamb?) noted the lack of training and organisation among English women, compared to sisterhoods abroad:

> our women have already innumerable forces to war against, in the varied forms of poverty, ignorance, disease and crime. To mitigate these evils is, assuredly, work for woman, as well as the work by which she is to obtain a livelihood; and we think no better means can in the first instance be tried than the plan of carrying out by association on a wider scale, what is now being done partially.[103]

The work of Jameson, and of other women such as Nightingale, Twining and Carpenter brought together the themes, traced here, of education and training, of the need for employment, of the expanding sphere of women's lives from their domestic centre. The question of 'sisterhood' was in fact one of contemporary Anglican concern: what were the dangers, and the possibilities, of Protestant religious orders? Michael Hill has stressed that the growth of religious sisterhoods in the mid-nineteenth century in England should be viewed not only in theological terms, but also for the 'transitional' functions which they performed, before the state and the minor professions absorbed the work of women. Hill has labelled sisterhoods in the Church of England as 'the first signs of incipient feminism among women of the middle class'. This is perhaps to exaggerate their real importance, but not, surely, the significance of the language of association.[104]

A further theme of such writing is the difficulty of reconciling the laws of political economy with the task of improving women's situation. Matilda Hays wrote that 'where political economy has failed, the economy of nature [i.e. the 'communion of labour'] may succeed', and of the possibility of 'women *versus* political economy'. Parkes, writing on John Stuart Mill, considered the effects of competition and overcrowding on women's work and the relationship between such unmoderated competition and the domestic position of married women. Individual efforts could do little to help: women needed both to understand and to meet the challenge of the market-place:

> the more completely society is infused with those ideas which modify the action of purely scientific laws, the easier it will be for women to work without being crushed by its machinery. We will now draw attention to a parallel observation; namely that the more human creatures cast behind them the savage theory that might makes right, which may be termed the political economy of wild beasts, the more possible become the independent labours of the gentler sex.[105]

In their different ways, Parkes suggested, both Mill and Elizabeth Blackwell had urged the necessity of co-operation among women. Parkes pointed to Utopian socialism in France, to the Rochdale co-operative society, to industrial associations and female friendly societies, all suggesting the same theme. One modern historian, Judith Walkowitz, has reminded us that 'a significant discrepancy existed between the rhetoric of female solidarity, and the actions of most female moral reformers'.[106] And it is true that the rhetoric and aspirations of such pioneers can tell us little about the practical reception of well-meaning projects, of the limitations of those who might attempt to put such schemes into practice. Nevertheless, the language of such feminists does suggest that sympathy towards a degree of collective practice, which Evelyne Sullerot has noted, with respect to French feminists in 1848, as being a recurring theme: it was to be found even among these women of the English middle classes.[107]

Only in the early 1860s did this group come to formulate its demand for suffrage.[108] In July 1864 an article on 'The Enfranchisement of Women' put the arguments of Harriet Taylor Mill before the readers of the *English Woman's Journal*, as a case which seemed too clear-cut to dispute. In the main, her views were summarised, though with some additions; the view, for instance, that the admission of women to the representation could ultimately have some effect in influencing those classes of the great cities, likely to be brought within reach of the franchise:

> Women of the higher and middle classes are brought into more immediate contact than men with those whom we may call the lower-middle class, and such influence as they exercise is even now often good in its effects; but how immeasurably would it be increased and improved by their own greater cultivation.[109]

Women did indeed themselves desire the franchise, though that was often denied – because of the fear of appearing unfeminine.

> Let all honorable paths to distinction be open to both sexes, and the event will prove whether women really desire and have within them the capacity for that intellectual and moral development, which hitherto has only been attained by individuals, and in the face of difficulties which only genius or an almost superhuman perseverance could have overcome.[110]

In the Kensington Ladies' Discussion Society, founded in 1865, Barbara Leigh Smith (Bodichon) at the second meeting led a discussion on the suffrage question: the near unanimity among her audience led her to form among her associates, including Boucherett, Garrett and Davies, a Women's Suffrage Committee. A petition launched to the Commons gained some 1500 signatures and the Committee, with Emily Davies as its first secretary and the Unitarian Clementia Taylor as its treasurer, stayed in existence, drawing up further petitions, corresponding with new similar groups in Manchester and Edinburgh. In 1868 it was to join with these and other groups in the National Society for Women's Suffrage, the society which, though undergoing some transformations, was to steer the demand for women's suffrage for the rest of the nineteenth century. The route to that demand had followed a rather different course from that taken in the United States. In Britain, the existing state of the franchise and of the law affecting married women meant that the demand for suffrage on the same terms as men had a very different resonance: in spite of the similarities in language and ideas between the British and

American movements, the realities of class difference were an intrinsic and conscious part of the movement of the 1850s and 1860s.

In 1851, Jeanne Deroin and Pauline Roland wrote from the St-Lazare prison, in similar terms to the second national convention held in the United States, in Worcester, Massachusetts, and in Britain, to the Sheffield Female Reform Association. They greeted their 'sisters', of America and of Great Britain, united with them 'in the vindication of the right of woman to civil and political equality', which, they believed, could be achieved only through 'the power of association based on solidarity', the union of associations of both men and women.[111] The feminists who have been discussed in this book were few in number, isolated within their societies, and without any kind of mass organisation by the 1860s. But it is quite clear from any study of their writings, that they were informed by a close awareness and understanding of international developments. After the World Anti-Slavery Convention in London in 1840, British and American anti-slavery and feminist activists remained in correspondence. The development of American feminist ideas provided an important source of inspiration to Harriet Taylor Mill, to Jenny d'Héricourt, to Julie-Victoire Daubié. The inspiration of the work done on women's employment by the writers of the *English Woman's Journal* in London strongly influenced the writing of Caroline Dall on women's employment in America. The Blackwell sisters exemplify that link in their own persons. Jenny d'Héricourt's career was to lead her to Chicago, and in 1869, attending the convention of the Equal Rights Association in New York, she proposed a 'Universal League for Woman's Rights and Peace', to be achieved by Emancipation Societies in every country.[112] Her speech was overshadowed by the conflict between priorities in the American movement: black suffrage or women's suffrage? Yet this, and many other examples which could be given, do suggest that though the origins and character of feminist movements need to be viewed within the context of their own societies, they had, by the mid-nineteenth century, acquired an independent ideological force, which transcended national boundaries.

Moderate shaped by close + politics

Conclusion

By 1860 the common language within which, in all three societies, the question of women's political rights was discussed, was still the language of republicanism and citizenship: yet that question arose not only from the application of republican rhetoric to the situation of women but from the exploration of those definitions of women's unique qualities and family roles that have been traced here. The moralising and regenerating power of those qualities, of domestic life strengthened, first in the household, and then, by extension, into the worlds of employment, of philanthropy, of politics, have been traced here. In the context of time and of place, such views as expressed, for instance, by Marion Reid, by Elizabeth Cady Stanton and by Jeanne Deroin might indeed by radical.[1] Yet the emergence of such arguments, and of feminist movements, should not obscure the fact that the numbers involved were very small and that such women were indeed isolated and frequently ridiculed, treated with often brutal hostility and even imprisoned. Their aspirations, for the recognition of political and civil equality, for the possibility of choice, to participate in public life, to take up employment, or to run a household, and for the opening up of new areas of employment in the caring and servicing occupations may indeed seem modest to twentieth-century feminists and historians: but any understanding of the development of the occupational segregation of the late twentieth century will suggest how long such hopes have waited for fulfilment.

Certain common themes have arisen in this discussion of the origins of feminist debate and action in three western societies: though conclusions must of course of their nature be speculative. It is clear that the character of each movement owed much to the pattern of class and political conflict in each society. In France the size and social conservatism of the French bourgeoisie, as well as, in general, their political acquiescence in this period, meant that feminism had a relatively limited appeal: to individually distinguished and able women, to Protestants and those with a liberal freethinking background, to lower middle-class and working-class women of strong character fighting for subsistence in a harsh urban environment. In the United States, on the other hand, the high educational levels and the relative security of white native-born women of rural New England and the middle states allowed them to apply the language of revolutionary republicanism to the situation of women. They remained relatively untouched by the problems of working women in the cities, though strongly engaged by issues of individual moral reform, and most of all by the issue of slavery, that issue which touched not only individual consciences but the major political theme of the period, the future relationship between two very different societies, the North and the South of the United States. In Britain, in a society increasingly shaped by consciousness of class, the feminist movement too was moulded by its dependence on that great army of domestic servants, by a sense of superiority which carried with it a belief in the possibility that sex might transcend class. At the same time there was also an unease about unfettered liberalism and, among some, a sense of collective values. Part of the difference between the British and the American women's movements must surely be explained in the difference between rural and urban perspectives. And a contrast with the French movement is apparent in the clear appeal of feminism in Britain to women from leading industrialists' families, from precisely that progressive, dissenting, reforming sector of middle-class opinion which had so great an impact on British political life in the second half of the nineteenth century.

It has been suggested here that religious factors were of vital importance in explaining the development of association among women, and the growth of that moralising force – whether religious or secular – which is so strong a feature of women's action by the mid-nineteenth century. Evangelical religion provided a model for association, and a powerful imagery which embodied and gave strength to the particular qualities of womanhood – as, materially, domestic life did indeed increasingly separate itself from the world of work. Association, for religious and philanthropic purposes, was to give middle-class women most important practical skills: speaking in public, chairing committees, writing reports, keeping accounts. Yet it is interesting that leading feminists of the 1840s and 1850s had characteristically rejected, though they had often intimately experienced, the force of orthodox evangelical teaching, and had shifted towards the rationalism of Unitarianism, towards Quakerism or to secularism. That shift has been observed for the United States: a similar case could be made for British feminists.[2] Indeed, the dominant feminist case by the mid-nineteenth century carried with it the possibilities of rigidity, of the inflexible maintenance of a position of both moral and class superiority, seen in the narrowness and prejudice, based upon both race and class, of sections of the British and American suffragist movements by the end of the century. In France, the absence of such a moralising force, tied to a voluntarist pattern of association, is important: for although missionary and philanthropic impulses were an important part of the Catholic revival of the first half of the nineteenth century, the established and hierarchical Catholic Church, with its growing religious orders, offered relatively less encouragement to spontaneous association among laywomen.

Though the middle-class character of the movement appears dominant by the 1850s, it has been suggested here that working-class women could and did associate together and identify their common interests. Yet at the same time the conditions of such association were hard to meet: how far were working-class women able formally to build on that separate domestic world which middle-class women were expanding, or on their interests as workers? As has been suggested, women's employment was limited, often isolated, and unlikely to provide a living wage, with a few exceptions in artisan trades and textile factories. And the conditions of domestic life were still such as to make survival, which depended on the male wage, the first priority. Nevertheless, the strength of female Chartism suggests that those family bonds could be translated into political association, although association which was not in the 1840s to give the expansion of women's public role priority. There remain questions to be asked about the nature of that shift from crowd and community action, on a spontaneous basis, in which women were likely to take part, especially if the issue touched the family income directly, to the emergence of formal, segregated patterns of association, in work and politics, among working-class men. Utopian socialism for a brief period offered the prospect of a better world, based on the transformation of both work and domestic life, drawing upon an older view of economic partnership in the household and family, and a newer one, of the moral strength of women: hence its importance in the history both of early socialism and of early feminism.

The question remaining is how far feminist action should be related to the possibility of identifying the separate world of women: as a preliminary to challenging that separation? Association among women was more likely in the first half of the nineteenth century to take place on the basis of the expansion of domestic worlds than of women seeing themselves as individual workers, outside the framework of home and family. The tensions that have been suggested here are tensions between the desire for individual autonomy for women, and the sense of collectivity to which women coming together were drawn. The demand for female autonomy, the necessity for association: both were the hallmarks of feminist theory and practice in these years.

Abbreviations

EWJ	*English Woman's Journal*
HWS	Elizabeth Cady Stanton, Susan B. Anthony and Matilda Joslyn Gage (eds), *History of Woman Suffrage* (vols I–IV, Rochester, 1881–1902), reprinted New York, 1969
MR	*Monthly Repository*
NAW	Edward T. James, Janet W. James and Paul S. Boyer (eds), *Notable American Women: a Biographical Dictionary*, 3 vols, Cambridge, Massachusetts, 1971
NMW	*New Moral World*
PP	*Parliamentary Papers*

Notes and References

INTRODUCTION

1. The *Supplement* to the *Oxford English Dictionary* gives as the first usage of the word: '*Daily News*, 12 October 1894 "What our Paris correspondent describes as a 'Feminist' group is being formed in the French Chamber of Deputies" '; for the French use of the word, see *Trésor de la langue française*, vol. 8, Paris, 1980.

2. See Gerda Lerner's contribution to Ellen DuBois, Mari Jo Buhle, Temma Kaplan, Gerda Lerner and Carroll Smith-Rosenberg, 'Politics and culture in women's history: a symposium', *Feminist Studies*, 6 (Spring 1980), 26–63; see also, among many items, G. Lerner, *The Majority Finds its Past. Placing Women in History* (New York, 1979); B. A. Carroll (ed.), *Liberating Women's History* (Urbana, Illinois, 1976), especially the essays in Part I; Juliet Mitchell, 'Women and equality' in A. Oakley and Juliet Mitchell, (eds), *The Rights and Wrongs of Women* (London, 1976). For other references, see the Bibliography.

3. The best starting point on this issue remains M. Anderson, *Approaches to the History of the Western Family 1500–1914* (London, 1980); see also M. W. Flinn, *The European Demographic System, 1500–1820* (Brighton, 1981); J. L. Flandrin, *Families in Former Times Kinship, Household and Sexuality* (Cambridge, 1979); Louise Tilly and Joan Scott, *Women, Work and Family* (New York, 1978).

4. On the legal situation of women see Lee Holcombe, *Wives and Property. Reform of the Married Women's Property Law in Nineteenth Century England* (Oxford, 1983), Chs 2–3; R. B. Morris, 'Women's rights in early American law', in *Studies in the History of American Law* (1958; reprinted New York, 1974); L. Abensour, *La femme et le féminisme avant la révolution* (Paris, 1923), Ch. 1.

5. See Lawrence Stone, *The Family, Sex and Marriage in England, 1500–1800* (London, 1977); E. Shorter, *The Making of the Modern Family* (New York, 1975).

For other comparative studies of feminism in this period, see the Bibliography.

1. THE ENLIGHTENMENT AND THE NATURE OF WOMEN

1. See, for brief and rather favourable discussions in English, D. Williams, 'The politics of feminism in the French Enlightenment', in *The Varied Pattern. Studies in the Eighteenth Century* (Toronto, 1971); Abby R. Kleinbaum, 'Women in an age of light', in R. Bridenthal and C. Koonz (eds), *Becoming Visible: Women in European history* (Boston, 1977). For more thorough examinations of the subject, see L. Abensour, *La femme et le féminisme avant la Révolution* (Paris, 1923); P. Hoffmann, *La femme dans la pensée des lumières* (Paris, 1977). Useful collections of essays include Eva Jacobs, W. H. Barber, Jean H. Bloch, F. W. Leakey and Eileen Le Breton (eds), *Woman and Society in Eighteenth-century France. Essays in honour of John Stephenson Spink* (London, 1979); Paul Fritz and Richard

Martin, *Woman in the Eighteenth Century and Other Essays* (Toronto, 1976); *Transactions of the Fifth International Congress on the Enlightenment*, Vol. IV, Section 18, 'The portrayal and condition of women in eighteenth century literature', in *Studies on Voltaire and the Eighteenth Century*, 193, (1980).

2. See G. Schochet, *Patriarchalism in Political Thought. The Authoritarian Family and Political Speculation and Attitudes, especially in seventeenth century England* (Oxford, 1975), Chs IV, V, VII and VIII.

3. John Locke, *Two Treatises of Government*, P. Laslett (ed.) (Mentor edn, 1965). Book II, Ch. VI, 'Of Paternal Power'; Schochet, *Patriarchalism*, Chs XIII and XIV.

4. Samuel von Pufendorf, *The Whole Duty of Man according to the law of nature*, fifth edn translated by Andrew Tooke (London, 1735), p. 4.

5. Ibid., p. 196.

6. Locke, *Two Treatises*, p. 353.

7. W. Wollaston, *The Religion of Nature Delineated* (London, 1724), p. 159.

8. F. Hutcheson, *A System of Moral Philosophy*, 2 vols (London, 1755), II, pp. 152ff.

9. Samuel von Pufendorf, *Le droit de la nature et des gens . . .*, trans. Jean Barbeyrac, second edn, 2 vols (Amsterdam, 1712). Vol. II, p. 169 n. 3. Quoted in James F. Traer, *Marriage and the Family in Eighteenth-century France* (Ithaca, 1980), p. 50 n. 4.

10. Voltaire, *Dictionnaire Philosophique*, *Oeuvres complètes*, . . . 54 vols (Paris, 1877–85), Arts. 'Adultère', Vol. XVII, pp. 65–73; 'Divorce', Vol. XVIII, pp. 409–11.

11. D. Hume, *A Treatise of Human Nature*, E. C. Mossner (ed.) (Harmondsworth, 1969), p. 629.

12. Ibid., p. 621.

13. Ibid., p. 418.

14. Montesquieu, *The Persian Letters*, ed. and trans. J. R. Loy (New York, 1961), p. 27.

15. See R. O'Reilly, 'Montesquieu: anti-feminist', *Studies on Voltaire and the Eighteenth Century*, 102 (1973), 143–56; Sheila Mason, 'The riddle of Roxane', in Jacobs *et al.* (eds), *Woman and Society in Eighteenth-century France*.

16. Voltaire, *Dictionnaire Philosophique*, *Oeuvres*, XIX, 'Femme' pp. 95–104, 'Homme', pp. 373–85.

17. Rousseau 'Letter to M. D'Alembert on the Theatre', in Allan Bloom (ed.), *Politics and the Arts* (New York, 1977), p. 87. For Rousseau's views on the position of women and their influence, see S. M. Okin, *Women in Western Political Thought* (Princeton, 1979): Judith Shklar, *Men and Citizens: a study of Rousseau's social theory* (London, 1969); Victor G. Wexler, 'Made for Man's Delight': Rousseau as anti-feminist', *American Historical Review*, 81 (1976), 226–91; Jean H. Bloch, 'Women and the Reform of the Nation', and P. D. Jimack, 'The paradox of Sophie and Julie: contemporary response to Rousseau's ideal wife and ideal mother', both in Jacobs *et al.* (eds) *Woman and Society in Eighteenth-century France*; Ruth Graham, 'Rousseau's Sexism Revolutionised', in Fritz and Morton (eds), *Woman in the Eighteenth Century*; Jean Bethke Elshtain, *Public Man, Private Woman. Women in Social and Political Thought* (Oxford, 1981), Ch. 4; Zillah Eisenstein, *The Radical Future of Liberal Feminism* (New York, 1981), pp. 55–88.

18. Rousseau, *Emile ou de l'éducation*, Book V, and *Emile et Sophie ou les solitaires*. *Oeuvres complètes*, 4 vols (Paris, 1969), Vol. IV.

19. Jean H. Bloch, 'Women and the Reform of the Nation', in Jacobs *et al.* (eds), *Woman and Society in Eighteenth-century France*, *passim*.

20. Mme Brulart de Genlis, *Adelaide and Theodore; or Letters on Education containing all the principles relevant to three different plans of education; to that of princes, and to those of young persons of both sexes*, trans. from the French, 3 vols (London, 1783), Vol. III, p. 46.

21. Catherine Macaulay, *Letters on Education, with observations on religious and metaphysical subjects* (London, 1790) p. ii.

22. Ibid., Letters XXI–XXIV, pp. 198–223 are relevant.

23. Diderot, 'Sur les femmes', and 'Supplément au voyage de Bougainville', *Oeuvres completès*, 20 vols (Paris, 1875–7), vol II. For Diderot's views on women, see R. Niklaus, 'Diderot and women' and Eva Jacobs, 'Diderot and the education of girls', in Jacobs *et al.* (eds), *Woman and Society in eighteenth-century France*; A. M. Wilson, ' "Treated like Imbecile Children" (Diderot): the Enlightenment and the status of women', in Fritz and Morton (eds), *Woman in the Eighteenth Century*; Adriana Sfagaro, 'La répresentation de la femme chez Diderot', *Studies on Voltaire and the Eighteenth Century*, 193 (1980), 1893–9.

24. Jacobs, 'Diderot and the education of girls'.

25. D'Holbach, *Système Social, ou principes naturels de la morale et de la politique avec un examen de l'influence du gouvernement sur les moeurs*, 3 vols (London 1873; reprinted New York, 1969), Vol. ii, Chs IX–XII: *Ethocratie ou le gouvernement fondé sur la morale* (Amsterdam, 1776; reprinted Paris, 1966), pp. 104–6, 197ff.

26. D'Holbach, *Ethocratie*, p. 105.

27. D'Helvétius, *A Treatise on Man . . .*, trans. W. Hooper, 2 vols (London, 1777), II pp. 266–8. His ideas are discussed in D. M. Smith, *Helvétius. A study in persecution* (Oxford, 1965), Chs 14 and 15; Elizabeth J. Gardner, 'The Philosophes and women: sensationalism and sentiment', in Jacobs *et al.* (eds), *Woman and Society in Eighteenth-century France*.

28. See the excellent discussion of these themes in Marilyn Butler, *Jane Austen and the War of Ideas* (Oxford, 1975), Ch. I

29. Montesquieu, *The Spirit of the Laws*, trans. Thomas Nugent, ed. Franz Neumann (Hafner edn, New York, 1949), p. 103.

30. Ibid., p. 252.

31. Ibid., p. 257.

32. Adam Smith, *Lectures on Jurisprudence*, eds R. L. Meek, D. D. Raphael, P. G. Stein, (Oxford, 1978), pp. 14–16; for Smith's discussions of marriage and the condition of women, see pp. 141–72, 439–48. For a general discussion of this theme, see S. Pembroke, 'The early human family: some views, 1770–1870', in R. R. Bolgar (ed.), *Classical Influences on Western Thought, A.D. 1650–1870. . . .* (Cambridge, 1979); R. Meek, *Social Science and the Ignoble Savage* (Cambridge, 1976), pp. 166–70.

33. Adam Ferguson, *Essay on the History of Civil Society, 1767*, ed. D. Forbes (Edinburgh, 1966), pp. 125–6.

34. W. Robertson, *History of America, The Works of William Robertson D.D.*, 12 vols (London, 1817), Vol. IV, p. 103.

35. John Millar, *The Origin of the Distinction of Ranks* (Edinburgh, 1779), reprinted in W. C. Lehmann, *John Millar of Glasgow, 1735–1801. His Life and Thought and his Contribution to Sociological Analysis* (Cambridge, 1960), p. 176.

36. Ibid., p. 183.

37. Ibid., p. 184.

38. Ibid., pp. 199–203.

39. Ibid., p. 203.

40. Ibid., p. 214.

41. Ibid., p. 219.

42. Ibid., p. 225; this discussion, which has here been traced in the work of Scottish political economists and historians, may be related to the recent and important comments of Elisabeth Fox-Genovese and Eugene D. Genovese, *Fruits of Merchant Capital. Slavery and Bourgeois Property in the Rise and Expansion of Capitalism* (Oxford, 1983), Ch. 11, 'The ideological basis of domestic economy. The representation of women and the family in the age of expansion'.

43. Antoine Léonard Thomas, *Essai sur la caractère, les moeurs, et l'ésprit des femmes dans les différens siècles* (Paris, 1772), p. 206.

44. W. Russell, *Essays on the Character, Manners and Genius of Women in different ages*, enlarged from the French of Mr Thomas, 2 vols (London, 1773; A. Thomas, *An Essay on the Character, the Manners, and the Understanding of Women in different ages*, trans. from the French of Mons. Thomas, by Mrs Kindersley, with two original essays (London, 1781).

45. W. Alexander, *The History of Women, from the earliest antiquity to the present time; giving some account of almost every interesting particular concerning that sex, among all nations, ancient and modern*, third edn, 2 vols (London, 1782), Vol. I, p. 115.

46. Ibid., Vol. I, pp. 136ff.

47. Ibid., vol. I, Chs 18–19.

48. J. Bennett (a clergyman of the Church of England), *Strictures on Female Education, chiefly as it relates to the culture of the heart, in Four Essays* (London, 1787), pp. 95–6.

49. Ibid., p. 144.

2. FEMINISM AND REPUBLICANISM: 'REPUBLICAN MOTHERHOOD'

1. M. Wollstonecraft, *Vindication of the Rights of Woman* (1791; Harmondsworth, 1982), ed. M. Kramnick, p. 254; 'Constantia' (Judith Sargent Murray), *The Gleaner*, 3 vols (Boston, 1798), Etta Palm d'Aelders, *Appel aux françoises sur la régéneration des moeurs et necessité de l'influence des femmes dans un gouvernement libre* (Paris, 1791).

2. In the discussion that follows I have drawn heavily on two excellent recent works: Mary Beth Norton, *Liberty's Daughters. The Revolutionary Experience of American Women, 1750–1800* (Boston–Toronto, 1980); Linda Kerber, *Women of the Republic. Intellect and Ideology in Revolutionary America* (Chapel Hill, 1980).

3. Norton, *Liberty's Daughters*, pp. 161–3.

4. Norton, *Liberty's Daughters*, pp. 164–7.

5. Quoted in Kerber, *Women of the Republic*, p. 84.

6. Norton, *Liberty's Daughters*, pp. 177–88

7. Kerber, *Women of the Republic*, Ch. 4, *passim*.

8. Quoted in Kerber, *Women of the Republic*, p. 127.

9. Kerber, *Women of the Republic*, Ch. 6; Thomas R. Meehan, 'Not made out of levity': evolution of divorce in early Pennsylvania', *Pennsylvania Magazine of History and Biography*, XCII (1968), 441–64.

10. Norton, *Liberty's Daughters*, pp. 191–3.

11. Murray, *The Gleaner*, III, p. 191.

12. Ibid., III, p. 217.

13. Ibid., I, pp. 209ff.

14. Ibid., III, pp. 223–4; above, p. 219.

15. Benjamin Rush, 'Of the mode of education proper in a republic', in *Essays, Literary, Moral and Philosophical* (Philadelphia, 1791), p. 19.

16. Rush, 'Thoughts upon female education, accommodated to the present state of society, manners and government, in the United States of America', in *Essays*, pp. 75–92.

17. Charles Brockden Brown, *Alcuin: a dialogue*, ed. Lee R. Edwards (New York: 1970), pp. 29–30.

18. Norton, *Liberty's Daughters*, pp. 232–4.

19. Nancy F. Cott, 'Eighteenth-century family and life revealed in Massachusetts divorce records', *Journal of Social History*, 10 (Autumn 1976), No 1, 20–4, 43; 'Divorce and the changing status of women in eighteenth-century Massachusetts', *William and Mary Quarterly*, 3rd ser., XXXIII (1976), 592–4, 605–6.

For alternative views of the changes in family roles in this period, see Ruth H. Bloch, 'American feminine ideals in transition: the rise of the moral mother, 1785–1815', *Feminist Studies*, IV (1978), 101–26; Joan Hoff Wilson, 'The illusion of change: women and the American Revolution', in Alfred Young (ed.), *The American Revolution: Explorations in the History of American Radicalism* (DeKalb, Illinois, 1976); D. Blake Smith, *Inside the Great House, Planter Family Life in Eighteenth Century Chesapeake Society* (Ithaca and London, 1980).

20. Norton, *Liberty's Daughters*, p. 295.

21. Norton, *Liberty's Daughters*, p. 256ff.; Kerber, *Women of the Republic*, p. 189ff.

22. Barbara Brookes, 'The feminism of Condorcet and Sophie de Grouchy', *Studies on Voltaire and the eighteenth century*, 189 (1980), 297–361, especially 316–19.

23. Condorcet, *Essai sur la constitution et des fonctions des assemblées provinciales* (1788), *Oeuvres de Condorcet*, (published by A. O'Connor and M. F. Arago, 12 vols (Paris, 1847), vol. 8.

24. *Lettres d'un bourgeois de New Haven à un citoyen de Virginie* (1787), *Oeuvres*, vol. 9.

25. See his 'Sur l'admission des femmes au droit de la cité, 23 juillet, 1790', *Oeuvres*, vol. 10, originally published in the *Journal de la Société de 1739*, no. 5.

26. See, in general, on this subject, Léon Abensour, *La femme et le féminisme avant la révolution française* (Paris, 1923), Ch. vi; Jane Abray, 'Feminism in the French Revolution', *American Historical Review*, 80 (1975), 43–62; Léon Devance, 'Le féminisme pendant la révolution française', *Annales historiques de la révolution française*, 49 (1977), 341–76; Paule-Marie Duhet, *Les femmes et la révolution française, 1789–1795* (Paris, 1971); Olwen Hufton, 'Women in Revolution, 1789–96', *Past and Present*, 53 (1971), 90–108; L. Lacour, *Les origines du féminisme contemporaine. Trois femmes de la Révolution: Olympe de Gouges, Théroigne de Méricourt, Rose Lacombe* (Paris, 1900); *Women in Revolutionary Paris 1789–1795*, selected documents trans. with notes and commentary by Darline Gay Levy, Harriet Branson Applewhite and Mary Durham Johnson (Chicago, 1979); Evelyne Sullerot, *Histoire de la presse féminine en France, des origines à 1848* (Paris, 1966); Baron Marc de Villiers, *Histoire des clubs des femmes et des légions d'Amazones, 1793–1848–1871* (Paris, 1910).

27. See, on the *cahiers* and petitions of 1788 and 1789, Abensour, *La femme et le féminisme*, p. 431ff; Abray, 'Feminism in the French Revolution', pp. 46–7; Duhet, *Les femmes et la revolution*, pp. 29–41; Levy, Applewhite and Johnson, *Women in Revolutionary Paris*, pp. 13–33.

28. Abensour, *La femme et le féminisme*, pp. 432–43; the *cahier* of the flower sellers is reprinted in Levy, Applewhite and Johnson, *Women in Revolutionary Paris*, pp. 22–6.

29. Abensour, *La femme et le féminisme*, pp. 432ff.

30. Abray, 'Feminism in the French Revolution', p. 47.

31. Sullerot, *Histoire de la presse féminine*, pp. 44, 47–8; Duhet, *Les femmes et la révolution*, pp. 32–41.

32. Levy, Applewhite and Johnson, *Women in Revolutionary Paris*, pp. 18–21.

33. On de Gouges, see Lacour, *Les origines du féminisme contemporaine*, pp. 44ff.

34. Duhet, *Les femmes et la révolution*, pp. 39–40.

35. *Le Moniteur*, ii, 228, 25 November 1789; see Duhet, *Les femmes et la révolution*, pp. 173–6, and the full bibliography contained in Roderick C. Phillips, *Family Breakdown in Late Eighteenth Century France. Divorces in Rouen, 1792–1803* (Oxford, 1980), pp. 232–6; James F. Traer, *Marriage and the Family in Eighteenth century France* (Ithaca, 1980), pp. 105ff.

36. *Le Moniteur.*, ii, 315, 6 December 1789.

37. Quoted in Sullerot, *Histoire de la presse féminine*, p. 48.

38. Ibid., pp. 50–4.

39. Levy, Applewhite and Johnson, *Women in Revolutionary Paris*, p. 15.

40. *Le Moniteur*, ii, 262, 29 November 1789.

41. *Le Moniteur*, iii, 703, 26 March 1790; Sullerot, *Histoire de la presse féminine*, pp. 52–4.

42. *Le Moniteur*, v, 240, 28 July 1790.

43. Reprinted in Levy, Applewhite and Johnson, *Women in Revolutionary Paris*, pp. 122. from *Archives Parlementaires*, 41, 63–4, 1 April 1792.

44. *Le Moniteur*, x, 398, 17 February 1792.

45. Villiers, *Histoire des clubs des femmes*, pp. 14ff.

46. Ibid., pp. 42ff.; Duhet, *Les femmes et la révolution*, pp. 99ff.

47. D'Aelders. 'Discours sur l'injustice des lois en faveur des hommes, au dépend des femmes, lu à l'assemblée féderatives des Amis de la Vérité, le 30 decembre 1790', in *Appel aux françoises*.

48. D'Aelders, 'Lettre d'une amie de la vérité, Etta Palm née d'Aelders, Hollandoise sur les démarches des ennemis extérieurs et intérieurs de la France; suivie d'une adresse à toutes les citoyennes patriotes et d'une motion à leur proposer pour l'assemblée nationale, lue à l'assemblée fédératives des Amis de la Vérité, le 23 mars 1791', in *Appel aux françoises*.

49. D'Aelders, 'Adressé des citoyens françaises à l'assemblée nationale', in *Appel aux françoises*.

50. Levy, Applewhite and Johnson, *Women in Revolutionary Paris*, p. 63; Villiers, *Histoire des clubs des femmes*, pp. 72ff.

51. Duhet, *Les femmes et la révolution*, p. 104; Hufton, 'Women in Revolution', p. 99; the subject is treated exhaustively in Villiers, *Histoire des clubs des femmes*, pp. 88–222.

52. Olympe de Gouges, *Les Droits de la femme* (Paris n.d. [1791]), printed and trans. in Levy, Applewhite and Johnson, *Women in Revolutionary Paris*, p. 90.

53. See, on this society, M. Cerati, *Le Club des citoyennes républicaines révolutionnaires* (Paris, 1966).

54. Pierre Caron (ed.), *Paris pendant la Terreur: Rapports des agents secrets du Ministre de l'Intérieur*, 4 vols (Paris, 1910–49), ii, p. 164. Report of Latour-Lamontagne, 21 September 1793. quoted and translated in Levy, Applewhite and Johnson, *Women in Revolutionary Paris*, p. 200.

55. *Le Moniteur*, xviii, 450, 29 brumaire, 'Aux républicaines'.

56. Villiers, *Histoire des clubs des femmes*, pp. 212–16.

57. Ibid., pp. 178–9

58. Ibid., p. 121.

59. *Le Moniteur*, xiii, 1 September 1792.

60. Abray, 'Feminism in the French Revolution', pp. 58–9.

61. C. Theremin, *De la condition des femmes dans les républiques* (Paris), An vii (1799), p. 18.

62. Ibid., pp. 42ff.

63. Ibid., p. 78.

64. E. P. Thompson, *The Making of the English Working Class* (1963; Harmondsworth, 1968), p. 178, suggests that such issues were the concern primarily of a 'small intellectual coterie'; Albert Goodwin, *The Friends of Liberty: the English Democratic Movement in the Age of the French Revolution* (London, 1979), does not touch on the question.

65. The most useful works on this circle include Charles Kegan Paul, *William Godwin: his friends and contemporaries*, 2 vols (London, 1876); H. N. Brailsford, *Shelley, Godwin, and their circle* (London, 1913); G. Kelly, *The English Jacobin Novel, 1780–1805* (Oxford, 1976).

66. Of a number of biographies the most useful are Eleanor Flexner, *Mary Wollstonecraft, a biography* (New York, 1972); Claire Tomalin, *Mary Wollstonecraft* (London, 1974); Edna Nixon, *Mary Wollstonecraft: her life and times* (London, 1971); Ralph M. Wardle, *Mary Wollstonecraft. A critical biography* (Kansas, 1951); M. George, *One Woman's Situation* (Urbana, Illinois, 1970).

67. William Godwin, *Enquiry concerning Political Justice and its influence on modern morals and happiness* (1798, Penguin edn, ed. Isaac Kramnick, Harmondsworth 1976): 'it is obvious to remark that the perfection of the human character consists in approaching as nearly as possible to the perfectly voluntary state', p. 127.

68. Thomas Holcroft, *Anna St Ives* (1792), Oxford English novels, Peter Faulkner (ed.) (Oxford, 1973), p. 278.

69. Ibid., p. 264.

70. Godwin, *Political Justice*, pp. 762–7.

71. R. Bage, *Hermsprong, or man as he is not* (1796), Folio Society (London, 1900), pp. 142–6.

72. Mary Hays, *Memoirs of Emma Courtney*, 2 vols (1796; reprinted New York, 1974, ed. Gina Luria) vol. ii, p. 219.

73. See, for analysis of her work, besides the biographies quoted above, Z. Eisenstein, *The Radical Future of Liberal Feminism* (New York, 1981); M. B. Kramnick, Introduction, Mary Wollstonecraft, *Vindication of the Rights of Woman* (Harmondsworth, 1982); K. Rogers, *Feminism in Eighteenth Century England* (Brighton, 1982).

74. Wollstonecraft, *Vindication*, ed. Kramnick, pp. 100–6.

75. Ibid., p. 122.

76. Ibid., pp. 219–21.

77. Ibid., p. 103.

78. Ibid., p. 131.

79. Ibid., pp. 252–63, 315.

80. Ibid., pp. 135–9.

81. Ibid., p. 257.

82. Ibid., p. 262.

83. Ibid., pp. 225–7.

84. Mary Wollstonecraft to Mary Hays, 12 November 1792, Ralph M. Wardle (ed.), *Collected Letters of Mary Wollstonecraft* (Ithaca and London, 1979), p. 219.

85. Mary Wollstonecraft to George Dyson, c. 15 May 1797, *Collected Letters*, p. 391, and *Maria or The Wrongs of Woman*, with an introduction by Moira Ferguson (New York, 1975).

86. Mary Hays, *Letters and Essays, Moral and Miscellaneous* (London, 1793, reprinted New York, 1974), pp. 84–5.

87. Mary Hays, *Appeal to the Men of Great Britain on behalf of Women* (London, 1798; reprinted by Garland, New York, 1974), pp. 1–25.

88. Ibid., pp. 194–9.

89. J. H. Lawrence, *An Essay on the Nair system of gallantry and inheritance; showing its superiority over marriage, as insuring an indubitable genuiness ov birth, and being more favorable tu population, the rights ov women and the active disposition ov men* [sic] (London, 1800?), p. 16. Lawrence was an advocate of spelling reform.

90. (Benjamin Silliman), *Letters of Shahcoolen, a Hindu Philosopher residing in Philadelphia; to his friend El Hassan, an inhabitant of Delhi* (Boston, 1802).

91. Quoted in Kerber, *Women of the Republic*, pp. 282–3.

92. Ibid., pp. 178–9.

93. Ibid., pp. 135–6.

94. Norton, *Liberty's Daughters*, pp. 191–3.

95. *Le Moniteur*, xviii, 2 brumaire, 293–300, quoted and translated in Levy, Applewhite and Johnson, *Women in Revolutionary Paris*, pp. 213–17.

96. *Le Moniteur*, xxiv, 5 prairial, 501–7.

97. Ibid., 6 prairial, 515; 7 prairial, 519.

98. Hufton, 'Women in revolution', pp. 101–3.

99. Duhet, *Les femmes et la révolution*, pp. 171–3.

100. Richard Polwhele, *The Unsex'd Females: a poem addressed to the author of the pursuits of literature* (London, 1798), pp. 28–9 note.

101. *Anti-Jacobin Review and Magazine*, i (1798), p. 97; ix (1801), Appendix, pp. 515–20.

102. Jane West, *A Tale of the Times* (1799), ii, 275, quoted in M. Butler, *Jane Austen and the War of Ideas* (Oxford, 1975), pp. 104–5.

3. EVANGELICALISM AND THE POWER OF WOMEN

1. See B. Welter, 'The feminisation of American religion: 1800–1860', in Mary J. Hartman and Lois Banner (eds), *Clio's Consciousness raised. New perspectives on the history of women* (New York, 1974), and the controversial work by Ann Douglas, *The Feminization of American Culture* (New York, 1977). On Britain there is nothing comparable but see C. Hall, 'The early formation of Victorian domestic ideology', in S. Burman (ed.), *Fit Work for Women* (Canberra, 1979), and the discussions in B. Taylor, *Eve and the New Jerusalem. Socialism and Feminism in the Nineteenth Century* (London, 1983), Ch. v and H. McLeod, *Religion and the People of Western Europe, 1789–1870* (Oxford, 1981), pp. 28–35.

2. W. Wilberforce, *A Practical View of the prevailing religious system of professed Christians in the higher and middle classes in this country, contrasted with real Christianity*, 2nd edn (London, 1797), p. 435.

3. N. Cott, *The Bonds of Womanhood. 'Woman's Sphere' in New England, 1780–1835* (New Haven, 1977), p. 129.

4. S. Lewis, *Woman's Mission*, 2nd edn (London, 1839), pp. 128–9.

5. The text is quoted in, for example, C. Anderson, *The Genius and Design of the Domestic Constitution, with its unanswerable obligations and peculiar advantages* (Edinburgh, 1826), pp. 18, 315–17; J. A. James, *The Family Monitor, or a help to domestic happiness* (Birmingham, 1828), pp. 38ff; R. W. Bailey, *The Family Preacher; or Domestic Duties illustrated and enforced in eight discourses* (New York, 1837), pp. 38ff.

6. James, *Family Monitor*, pp. 71, 74–5.

7. Of many examples of this genre, see F. A. Cox, *Female Scripture Biography: including an essay on what Christianity has done for women*, 2 vols (London, 1817); Clara Lucas Balfour, *The Women of Scripture* (London, 1847).

8. Cox, *Female Scripture Biography*, II, p. xcvi.

9. T. Parker, *The Public Function of Woman. A sermon preached at the music hall, March 27, 1853* (London, 1853), p. 17.

10. B. Welter, 'The feminization of American religion', pp. 141–2.

11. E. Hamilton, *Letters on the elementary principles of education*, 3rd edn, 2 vols (London, 1803), I, p. 249.

12. I have used here R. Carwardine: *Transatlantic Revivalism. Popular Evangelicalism in Britain and America, 1790–1865* (Westport, Conn., 1978); Robert T. Handy, *A History of the Churches in the United States and Canada* (Oxford, 1976); Winthrop S. Hudson, *American Protestantism* (Chicago, 1961); William G. McLoughlin, *Revivalism, Awakenings and Reform. An Essay on Religion and Social Change in America, 1607–1977* (Chicago 1978); Donald C. Mathews, *Religion in the Old South* (Chicago, 1977).

13. Cott, *Bonds of Womanhood*, pp. 132ff, and 'Young women in the Second Great Awakening', *Feminist Studies*, 3 (1975), 15–29. See also: D. Matthews, 'The Second Great Awakening as an organising process', *American Quarterly*, 21 (1969), 23–43; Barbara Leslie Epstein, *The Politics of Domesticity. Women, Evangelism and Temperance in Nineteenth Century America* (Middletown, Connecticut, 1981), Ch. II.

14. H. Martineau, *Society in America*, 3 vols (London, 1837). See also Anne M. Boylan, 'Evangelical womanhood in the nineteenth century: the role of women in Sunday Schools', *Feminist Studies*, 4 (1978), 62–80.

15. Cott, *Bonds of Womanhood*, p. 148.

16. Ibid., pp. 139–59.

17. Whitney R. Cross, *The Burned Over District. The Social and Intellectual History of Enthusiastic Religion in Western New York* (Ithaca, New York, 1950), especially pp. 84ff; E. A. Dexter, *Career Women of America 1776–1840* (Boston 1950; reprinted 1972), pp. 50–64; Mary Ryan, *Cradle of the Middle Class. The family in Oneida County, New York, 1790–1865* (Cambridge, 1981), pp. 71–5.

18. Ryan, *Cradle of the Middle Class*, Ch 2, and 'A women's awakening: evangelical

religion and the families of Utica County, New York', *American Quarterly*, xxx (1978), 5, 602–23.

19. Ryan, *Cradle of the Middle Class*, pp. 89ff.

20. Carroll Smith-Rosenberg, *Religion and the Rise of the American City. The New York City Mission Movement, 1812–70* (Ithaca and London, 1971), p. 83.

21. John Mack Faragher, *Women and Men on the Overland Trail* (New Haven, 1979), p. 119.

22. Mathews, *Religion in the Old South*, p. 110 and Ch. 3 *passim*.

23. Gerda Lerner, *The Grimké Sisters from South Carolina. Pioneers for Women's Rights and Abolition* (New York, 1971 edn), pp. 66–9.

24. Mathews, *Religion in the Old South*, pp. 116–18.

25. Mrs Virginia Cary, *Letters on Female Character, addressed to a young lady, on the death of her mother*. Second edn, enlarged (Richmond, Virginia, 1830), p. 202.

26. Mathews, *Religion in the Old South*, Ch. 4.

27. Dexter, *Career Women of America*, p. 54.

28. Bert James Loewenberg and Ruth Bogin (eds), *Black Women in Nineteenth Century American Life. Their Words, Their Thoughts, Their Feelings* (Philadelphia, 1976), pp. 127–41. See also Milton C. Sernett, *Black Religion and American Evangelicalism. White Protestants, Plantation Missions, and the Flowering of Negro Christianity, 1787–1865* (New Jersey, 1975).

29. R. Berkhofer, *Salvation and the Savage. An Analysis of Protestant Missions and American Indian Response, 1787–1862* (New York, 1972), pp. 72–80.

30. Useful secondary works among many include W. R. Ward, *Religion and Society in England, 1790–1850* (London, 1972); Ian Bradley, *The Call to Seriousness. The Evangelical Impact on the Victorians* (London, 1976); F. K. Brown, *Fathers of the Victorians: the age of Wilberforce* (Cambridge, 1961); Alan D. Gilbert, *Religion and Society in Industrial England: Church, Chapel and Social Change, 1740–1914* (London, 1976).

31. See, for example, T. C. Smout, 'New evidence on popular religion and literacy in eighteenth century Scotland', *Past and Present*, 97 (1982), 116; J. Obelkevich, *Religion and Rural Society: South Lindsey, 1825–1875* (Oxford, 1976), pp. 149–50, 313.

32. Hannah More, *Strictures on Female Education*, in *The Works of Hannah More*, 18 vols (London, 1818), viii, p. 29. On More, see M. G. Jones, *Hannah More* (Cambridge, 1952), and pp. 114–21 for the reception of this work.

33. Ibid., p. 1.

34. T. Gisborne, *An Enquiry into the Duties of the Female Sex*, fifth edn (London 1801), pp. 12–13, 223, 305.

35. Sarah Trimmer, *The Oeconomy of Charity; or, an address to ladies concerning Sunday Schools; the establishment of schools of industry under female inspection; and the distribution of voluntary benefactions . . .* (Dublin, 1787), p. 19.

36. On the spread of Sunday Schools within the Church of England and other denominations see T. W. Laqueur, *Religion and Respectability. Sunday Schools and Working Class Culture, 1780–1850* (New Haven, 1976), Ch. 2; W. R. Ward, *Religion and Society in England, passim*.

37. M. A. Stodart, *Female Writers: thoughts on their proper sphere, and on their powers of usefulness* (London, 1842), p. 162; and in *Everyday Duties: in Letters addressed to a young lady* (London, 1840), pp. 17ff.

38. F. Baker, 'John Wesley and Sarah Crosby', *Proceedings of the Wesleyan Historical Society*, xxvii (1949–50), 76–82.

39. Quoted in Leslie F. Church, *More about the Early Methodist People* (London, 1949), pp. 146–7.

40. John Baxter, 'The Great Yorkshire Revival 1792–6: A Study of Mass Revival among the Methodists', *Sociological Yearbook of Religion in Britain*, 7 (1974), pp. 46–76; *Minutes of several conversations at the sixteenth annual conference, begun at Manchester. July 25 1803, between the preacher late in connection with the Rev. John Wesley, deceased* (London, 1803), pp. 33–4.

41. Wesley F. Swift, 'The women itinerant preachers of early Methodism', *Proceedings of the Wesleyan Historical Society*, xxviii (1951–2), 89–94: xxix (1935), 76–83.

42. J. Walford, *Memoirs of the Life and Labours of the late venerable Hugh Bourne . . .*, ed. W. Ancliff, 2 vols (London, 1855), i, 164–77.

43. Swift, 'Women itinerant preachers', *passim*; Joseph Ritson, *The Romance of Primitive Methodism* (London, 1909), Ch. vii.

44. Elizabeth Isichei, *Victorian Quakers* (Oxford, 1970), pp. 48, 107–110.

45. I owe this suggestion in part to the stimulating discussion of the issue in Phyllis Mack, 'Women as prophets during the English Civil War', *Feminist Studies*, 8 (1982), 19–46.

46. Laqueur, *Religion and Respectability*, p. 3.

47. Ibid., pp. 91–3.

48. C. S. Dudley, *An analysis of the system of the Bible Society throughout its various parts. Including a sketch of the origins and results of Auxiliary and Branch Societies and Bible Associations, with hints for their better regulation . . .* (London, 1821), pp. 343–51; F. K. Prochaska, *Women and Philanthropy in Nineteenth Century England* (Oxford, 1980), pp. 24–28.

49. Dudley, *Analysis*, pp. 343–513 contains a full and detailed account.

50. Prochaska, *Women and Philanthropy*, p. 28.

51. F. K. Prochaska, 'Women in English philanthropy, 1790–1830', *International Journal of Social History*, 19 (1974), 426–45.

52. Carwardine, *Transatlantic Revivalism*, pp. 71, 95; F. A. Cox, *Suggestions designed to promote the revival and extension of religion, founded on observations made during a journey in the United States of America in the spring and summer of 1835* (London, 1836), pp. 13–15; J. Campbell, DD, *Memoirs of David Nasmith: his labours and travels in Great Britain, France, the United States and Canada* (London, 1844), *passim* for the many attempts to found such associations by a travelling evangelist.

53. Prochaska, *Women and Philanthropy*, pp. 126–9.

54. See R. Deniel, *Une image de la famille et de la société sous la restauration (1815–30): étude de la presse catholique* (Paris, 1965).

55. Louis de Bonald, *Du divorce, considerée au XIXe siècle relativement à l'état domestique et à l'état publique de société* (1801), *Oeuvres complètes de M. de Bonald* published by M. l'Abbe Myne, 3 vols (Paris, 1864), vol. ii, pp. 42–55.

56. Margaret H. Darrow, 'French noblewomen and the new domesticity, 1750–1850', *Feminist Studies*, 5 (1979), p. 41.

57. Bertier de Sauvigny, *The Bourbon Restoration* (1955) trans. Lynn M. Case (Philadelphia 1966), pp. 305–24; R. Aubert, J. Beckmann, P. J. Corish and R. Lill, *The Church between Revolution and Restoration* (London, 1981) vol vii of H. Jelin and J. Dolan (eds), *History of the Church*, pp. 120ff.

58. C. Langlois, 'Les effectifs des congrégations féminines aux XIXe siècle. De l'enquête statistique à l'histoire quantitative', *Revue de l'histoire de l'église en France*, 60 (1974), 39–64.

59. Adeline Daumard, *La bourgeoisie parisienne de 1815 à 1848* (Paris, 1963), pp. 366–8.

60. Bonnie C. Smith, *Ladies of the Leisure Class. The Bourgeoises of Northern France in the Nineteenth Century* (Princeton, New Jersey, 1981), pp. 93–122.

61. Martine Segalen, *Love and Power in the Peasant Family. Rural France in the Nineteenth Century* (Oxford, 1983), pp. 148–50.

62. L. S. Strumingher, "A bas les prêtres! A bas les couvents!": The Church and the workers in nineteenth century Lyon', *Journal of Social History*, xi (1978), 546–7, quoted in McLeod, *Religion and People*, p. 31.

63. J. Michelet, *Priests, Women and Families*, 3rd edn, trans. from the French by C. Cocks (London, 1845), *passim*.

64. C. Neames, 'Priests, Women and Families', *Blackwood's Edinburgh Review*, lviii (August, 1845), 185–96.

65. Smith, *Ladies of the Leisure Class*, p. 113.

66. Segalen, *Love and Power in the Peasant Family*, p. 144.

67. D. Robert, *Les églises reformées en France (1800–30)* (Paris, 1916), pp. 443ff.

68. J. F. C. Harrison, *The Second Coming. Popular Millenarianism, 1780–1850* (London, 1979), p. 31 and *passim*. See also Clarke Gárrett, *Respectable Folly: Millenarianism and the French Revolution in France and England* (Baltimore and London, 1975); Cross, *The Burned Over District*, pp. 37–8ff; B. Taylor, 'The woman-power. Religious heresy and feminism in early English socialism', in S. Lipshitz (ed.), *Tearing the Veil. Essays on Femininity* (London, 1978), and *Eve and the New Jerusalem*, Ch. 5.

69. Harrison, *Second Coming*, p. 110.

70. Ibid., p. 96.

71. Ibid., p. 169.

72. Garrett, *Respectable Folly*, p. 90, and Chs 2–4.

73. On the Saint-Simonians, see F. E. Manuel, *The New World of Henri Saint-Simon* (Cambridge, Mass., 1956); M. Thilbert, *La féminisme dans le socialisme française* (Paris, 1929).

74. Taylor, *Eve and the New Jerusalem*, pp. 166–82. See also A. L. Morton and John Saville, 'Catherine Isabella Barmby (1817–53) and John Goodwyn Barmby (1820–81), Chartists, Feminists and Utopian Socialists', J. Bellamy and J. Saville (eds), *Dictionary of Labour Biography*, Vol. VI (London, 1982).

75. See C. G. Bolan *et al. The English Presbyterians, from Elizabethan Puritanism to Modern Unitarianism* (London, 1968), Ch. VI; Douglas, *The Feminization of American Culture*, Chs 1–4, and the criticisms of this argument in, for instance, D. S. Reynolds, 'The feminization controversy: sexual stereotypes and the paradoxes of piety in 19th century America', *New England Quarterly*, 53 (1980), 96–106.

76. Quoted in Taylor, *Eve and the New Jerusalem*, p. 153. See also, on Emma Martin, Grace Cowie and Edward Royle, 'Emma Martin (1812–51), Socialist, Freethinker, and Woman's Rights Advocate', in Bellamy and Saville (eds), *Dictionary of Labour Biography*, Vol. VI.

4. EDUCATING HEARTS AND MINDS

1. Maria Edgeworth, *Letters for Literary Ladies: to which is added, an essay on the noble science of self-justification* (London, 1795), pp. 45ff.

2. M. Butler, *Jane Austen and the War of Ideas* (Oxford, 1975), p. 131.

3. Maria Edgeworth and Richard Lovell Edgeworth, *Practical Education*, 2 vols (1798; reprinted London and New York, 1974), ed. G. Luria. See, for instance, Vol. II, p. 713: 'the female sex are from their situation, their manners, and talents, peculiarly suited to the superintendence of the early years of childhood. We have, therefore, in the first chapters of the preceding work, endeavoured to adapt our remarks principally to female readers, and we shall think ourselves happy if an anxious mother feels their practical utility'.

4. Butler, *Jane Austen and the War of Ideas*, p. 154. See also M. A. Stodart, *Female writers: thoughts on their proper sphere, and on their powers of usefulness* (London, 1842), p. 146.

5. For Elizabeth Hamilton see Mrs E. O. Benger, *Memoirs of the late Mrs Elizabeth Hamilton, with a selection from her correspondence, and other unpublished writings*, 2 vols (London, 1818). References to the philosophy of Dugald Stewart recur throughout her major work, *Letters on the elementary principles of education*, 3rd edn, 2 vols (London, 1803). See for example, Vol. I, pp. 29, 32, 299ff, Vol. II pp. 6, 69. Maria Edgeworth shared this interest in Stewart. See *Practical Education*, Vol. I, Preface, Vol. II, p. 561.

6. Hamilton, *Letters*, Vol. I, pp. 114, 144, Vol. II, p. 30.

7. Ibid., Vol. I, pp. 3–4.

8. See V. Colby, *Yesterday's Woman. Domestic Realism in the English Novel* (Princeton, New Jersey, 1974), Ch. 3.

9. Hannah More, *Strictures on Female Education*, in *The Works of Hannah More*, 18 vols (London, 1818), Vol. VIII, Ch. XIV.

10. Ibid., Vol. VII, pp. 181–3.

11. Colby, *Yesterday's Woman*, p. 178, to whom I owe these references; Eleanor L. Sewell (ed.) *The Autobiography of Elizabeth M. Sewell* (London, 1907); Charlotte Elizabeth, *Personal Recollections* (London, 1841), has the most detailed account, for 'at six years the foundation of a truly scriptural protest was laid in my character'.

12. Lawrence Stone, *The Family, Sex and Marriage in England, 1500—1800* (London, 1977), pp. 666–7; Sarah Lewis, *Woman's Mission*, 2nd edn (London, 1839), Chs 6–7.

13. Grace Aguilar, *Home Influence: a tale for mothers and daughters* 2 vols (London, 1847), p. vi; Colby, *Yesterday's Woman*, p. 186.

14. Anna Elizabeth Pendered, *Remarks on Female Education, with an application of its principles to the regulation of schools* (London, 1827), 'Introductory Remarks'.

15. Sydney Smith, 'Female Education', *Edinburgh Review*, XV (January 1810), 299–315.

16. (Richard Wright) 'Letters on Women', *The Universalist's Miscellany; or Philanthropist's Museum. Intended chiefly as an antidote against the antichristian doctrine of endless misery.* Vol. III (1799), Letter I, and Vol. IV, Letter V, pp. 109–12, especially.

17. Francis E. Mineka, *The Dissidence of Dissent. The Monthly Repository, 1806–1838* (Chapel Hill, N. Carolina, 1944), p. 158.

18. (Harriet Martineau), 'Discipulus', 'On Female Education', *MR*, XVIII (February 1823), 77–81.

19. W. B. Adams, 'On the condition of women in England', *MR*, VII (1833), 217–31; Anon., 'On female education and occupations', ibid., 489–98.

20. Mary Leman Grimstone, 'Sketches of Domestic Life. No. VII The Insipid', *MR*, second series, IX (1835), 645–53.

21. Anon., 'Infant Education', *MR*, second series, X (1836), 141–9.

22. Harriet Martineau, *Household Education* (London, 1849), pp. 240–5.

23. Margaret Mylne, 'Woman and her social position', *Westminster Review*, XXXV (January 1841), 28.

24. Grimstone, 'Female Education', *NMW*, I, No. 17 (21 February 1835).

25. 'Kate' (Catherine Watkins), 'An Appeal to Woman', *NMW*, I, No. 42 (15 August 1835). No. 43, 22 Aug. 1835.

26. 'Eliza', 'Thoughts on the condition and character of woman', *NMW*, X, No. 13 (25 September 1841). Also Anon., 'Walk of Ellen and mother in garden', *NMW*, II, No. 75 (2 April 1836); 'Kate' (Catherine Watkins), 'The Love of Knowledge', *NMW*, IV, No. 171 (3 February 1838), and 'Conversation of Jane and Eliza', *NMW*, V, No. 10 (29 December 1838).

27. 'Marianne B', 'Education of Women', *NMW*, V, No. 28 (4 May 1839); W. H. Brontoson, 'Education and Capabilities of Women', and Eliza Murray, 'Comparison of the sexes', both in *NMW*, V, No. 33 (8 June 1839); 'Anna', 'Education of Women', *NMW*, V, No. 35 (22 June 1839); 'A Lover of Truth', 'Education and capabilities of women', *NMW*, VI, No. 39 (20 July 1839).

28. J. G. Barmby, 'Journal of a social mission to France', *NMW*, VIII, No. 4 (25 July 1840).

29. 'J', 'Emancipation of Women', *NMW*, XI, No. 29 (14 January 1843).

30. 'M.A.S.', 'On the necessary cooperation of both sexes for human advancement', *NMW*, XII, No. 9 (26 August 1843), No. 10 (2 September 1843), No. 12 (16 September 1843), No. 14 (30 September 1843), No. 16 (14 October 1843). For Robert Owen's

views, see his Address to the disciples of the rational system at Derby', *NMW*, XII, No. 10 (2 September 1843), and the 'President's address', No. 12 (16 December 1843).

31. 'Syrtis', 'Female Education', *NMW*, XIII, No. 32 (1 February 1845), No. 35 (22 February 1845), and 'Social and domestic condition of woman', *NMW*, XIII, No. 43 (19 April 1845), with the reply by 'Homo', No. 47 (17 May 1845), and rejoinder by 'Syrtis', Nos 51 (14 June 1845), 56 (19 July 1845), and 59 (9 August 1845). Also see 'Stata', 'Social condition and claims of women', *NMW*, XIII, No. 36 (1 March 1845).

32. Anne L. Kuhn, *The Mother's Role in Childhood Education: New England Concepts, 1830–60* (New Haven, 1947), p. 21 and *passim*. See also Bernard Wishy, *The Child and the Republic. The Dawn of Modern American Child Nurture* (Philadelphia, 1972 edn), especially Part I.

33. N. Cott, *The Bonds of Womanhood. 'Woman's Sphere' in New England, 1780–1835* (New Haven, 1977), pp. 118.

34. Kuhn, *Mother's Role*, pp. 46ff; Thomas Woody, *A History of Women's Education in the United States*, 2 vols (1929; reprinted New York, 1974), Vol. I, p. 305.

35. Quoted Woody, *History of Women's Education*, Vol. I, pp. 307–11.

36. Almira H. Phelps, 'Remarks on the education of girls', *Godey's Lady's Book*, Vol. 18 (June 1839), p. 253, quoted in Kuhn, *Mother's Role*, p. 57.

37. Kuhn, *Mother's Role*, p. 58–60.

38. Lydia Maria Child, *The Mother's Book* (Boston, 1831), pp. 4–5.

39. Katherine Kish Sklar, *Catherine Beecher. A Study in American Domesticity* (New York, 1976 edn), pp. 75–6, 90–1.

40. Ibid., pp. 78–89.

41. Ibid., Chs. 6–10, especially pp. 80–9.

42. See, on these writers, Barbara Corrado Pope, 'Maternal education in France, 1815–48', *Proceedings of the Third Annual Meeting of the Western Society for French History*, 4–6 December 1975 (Texas, 1976), and, 'Revolution and retreat: upper class French women after 1789', in Carol R. Berkin and Clara M. Lovett (eds), *Women, War and Revolution* (New York, 1980): Margaret H. Darrow, 'French noblewomen and the new domesticity, 1750–1850', *Feminist Studies*, 5 (Spring 1979), 41–65; P. Rousselot, *Histoire de l'éducation des femmes en France*, 2 vols (Paris, 1883), Vol. II, pp. 374 ff.; H. C. Barnard, *The French Tradition in Education. Ramus to Mme Necker de Saussure* (1922); reprinted Cambridge, 1970).

On liberal political philosophy and Scottish common-sense ideas, see D. Johnson, *Guizot. Aspects of Political Philosophy, 1787–1874* (London, 1963), Chs. 2 and 3; S. E. Grave, *The Scottish Philosophy of Common Sense* (Oxford, 1960).

43. Pauline Guizot, *Lettres de famille sur l'éducation* (Paris, 1861 edn), Vol. I, pp. 341–50, Vol. II, pp. 1–12ff.

44. Mme Necker de Saussure, *Education progressive, ou étude du cours de la vie . . .*, seventh edn (Paris, n.d.), pp. 520ff. The whole of the third book, 'Etude de la vie des femmes', is relevant.

45. Saussure, *Education progressive*, p. 303.

46. Ibid., pp. 524ff.

47. Louis Aimé-Martin, *The Education of Mothers of Families; or, the civilisation of the human race by women . . .*, trans. Edwin Lee (London, 1842).

48. Louis Aimé-Martin, *Education des mères de famille ou de la civilisation du genre humain par les femmes*, fourth edn (Paris, 1843), Ch. XIV, pp. 102ff, and Ch. XXII. Interestingly, this material was omitted by the English translator.

49. I have relied here on the discussion in E. Sullerot, *Histoire de la Presse féminine en France des origines à 1848* (Paris, 1966), pp. 187–9.

50. Ibid., pp. 164–84.

51. Ibid., pp. 186–7; Saussure, *Education progressive*, p. 522.

52. M. Wollstonecraft, *Vindication of the Rights of Women* (1791; Harmondsworth, 1982), pp. 261–93.

53. Priscilla Wakefield, *Reflections on the Present Condition of the Female Sex; with suggestions for its improvement* (London, 1798), pp. 49–53.

54. Woody, *History of Women's Education*, Vol. I, Ch. VIII; Cott, *Bonds of Womanhood*, pp. 30–5; see also the entries in *NAW* for the women mentioned here.

55. Woody, *History of Women's Education*, Vol. I, pp. 341–63; Ronald W. Hogeland, 'Coeducation of the sexes at Oberlin College: a study of social ideas in mid-nineteenth century America', *Journal of Social History*, 6 (1972–3), 160–76.

56. Woody, *History of Women's Education* Vol. I, p. 372.

57. Sklar, *Catherine Beecher*, p. 174.

58. Woody, *History of Women's Education*, Vol I, p. 482; Lawrence Cremin, *American Education. The National Experience, 1783–1876* (New York, 1980), pp. 144–7; Maris A. Vinovskis and Richard M. Bernard, 'Beyond Catherine Beecher: female education in the antebellum period', *Signs*, 3 (1978), 856–69, and 'The female school teacher in antebellum Massachusetts', *Journal of Social History*, 10 (1977), 332–45.

59. See J. Kamm, *Hope Deferred. Girls' Education in English History* (London, 1965), pp. 136ff; Carol Dyhouse, *Girls Growing up in Late Victorian and Edwardian England* (London, 1981), pp. 40–50; Joyce Pedersen, 'Schoolmistresses and headmistresses: elites and education in 19th century education', *Journal of British Studies*, XV (1975), 136–62.

60. Anon., 'On Female Education and Occupations', *MR*, VII (1833), 489–91.

61. Grimstone, 'Female Education', *MR*, second series, IX (1835), 106–12; and 'Men and Women', *Tait's Edinburgh Magazine* (March 1834), Vol. I, new series, p. 101, quoted in J. Killham, *Tennyson and the Princess. Reflections of an Age* (London, 1958), p. 51.

62. Quoted in Killham, *Tennyson and the Princess*, pp. 97–8.

63. Anna Jameson, *Characteristics of Women, Moral, Political and Historical* (London, 1875; first published 1832), p. 37; *Winter Studies and Summer Rambles in Canada*, 3 vols (London, 1838), Vol. III, pp. 311–12; 'Woman's Mission' and 'Woman's Position', first published in *The Athenaeum* (1843), reprinted in *Memoirs and Essays, illustrative of art, literature and social morals* (London, 1846), pp. 213–15; 'On the relative social position of mothers and governesses', *Memoirs and Essays*, pp. 251–65.

64. R. Mudie, *The Complete Governess. A course of mental instructions for ladies; with a notice of the principal female accomplishments* (London, 1826), pp. 1–15; Pendered, *Remarks on Female Education*, v–vi.

65. Mrs Hugo Reid, *A Plea for Woman: being a vindication of the importance and extent of her natural sphere of action* (Edinburgh, 1843), p. 8; Anne Richelieu Lamb, *Can Woman Regenerate Society?* (London, 1844), p. 18, 'That woman could in some degree regenerate society is unquestionably true; but her first task must be to regenerate herself. . . .'

66. Killham, *Tennyson and the Princess*, pp. 130–3; Kamm, *Hope Deferred*, pp. 172ff; Elaine Kaye, *A History of Queen's College London, 1848–1972* (London, 1972).

67. Asher Tropp, *The School Teachers. The growth of the teaching profession in England from 1800 to the present day* (London, 1957), Ch. II; Phillip McCann and Francis A. Young, *Samuel Wilderspin and the Education of the Poor* (London, 1982), pp. 171ff.

68. Frances Widdowson, *Going up into the next class. Women and elementary teacher training, 1840–1914* (London, 1980), Sections I–II; Tropp, *School Teachers*, pp. 22–4.

69. Lady Ellis, 'The education of young ladies of small pecuniary resources for other occupations than that of teaching', Central Society of Education, *Second Publication, Papers . . .* (London, 1838: reprinted Woburn Press, 1968). pp. 193–4.

70. Harriet Martineau, 'Female Industry', *Edinburgh Review*, CIX (April 1859), 331.

71. Bessie Rayner Parkes, 'The Profession of the Teacher. Annual Reports of the Governesses' Benevolent Institution, 1843 to 1856', *EWJ*, I (March 1858), 1–13, and

'Female Education in the Middle Classes', *EWJ*, I (June 1858), 217–27. The latter article draws this quotation from John Duguid Milne, *The Industrial and Social Position of Women in the Middle and Lower Ranks* (London, 1857).

72. Anna Blackwell, 'Elizabeth Blackwell', *EWJ*, I (April 1858), 80–100; *EWJ*, III, (April 1859), 142 refers under 'Passing Events' to increasing and deeply interested audiences for Dr Blackwell's lectures to ladies in London; Elizabeth and Emily Blackwell, 'Medicine as a profession for women', *EWJ*, V (May 1860), 145–60; Jo Manton, *Elizabeth Garret Anderson* (New York, 1965).

733. Barbara Leigh Smith Bodichon, 'Middle Class Schools for Girls', *EWJ*, VI (November 1860), 168–77; Emily Davies, 'Letters addressed to a daily paper at Newcastle upon Tyne, 1860', in *Thoughts on some Questions relating to Women* (Cambridge, 1910).

74. I have relied for this account on: Francoise Mayeur, *L'Education des filles en France au XIXe siècle* (Paris, 1979). See also P. Rousselot, *Histoire de l'éducation des femmes en France*, 2 vols (Paris, 1883), Vol. II, pp. 360–444; Johnson, *Guizot*, Ch. 3; R. D. Anderson, *Education in France, 1848–70* (Oxford, 1970); Edmée Charrier, *L'évolution intellectuelle féminine. Le développement intellectuel de la femme. La femme dans les professions intellectuelles* (Paris, 1937), Ch. II, Part 3.

75. Mayeur, *L'Education des filles*, p. 60.

76. Ibid., p. 76.

77. Ibid., p. 75; Sullerot, *Histoire de la press féminine*, pp. 152–3.

78. Mayeur, *L'Education des filles*, p. 107.

79. See, for instance, James F. McMillan, *Housewife or Harlot. The Place of Women in French Society, 1870–1940* (Brighton, 1981), p. 12; Mayeur, *L'Education des filles*, pp. 48ff., 93.

80. T. W. Laqueur, 'Literacy and social mobility in the Industrial Revolution in England', *Past and Present*, 64 (August 1974), 96–107. There is of course a huge literature on the subject, and a useful elementary guide to the maze is M. Sanderson, *Education, Economic Change, and Society in England, 1780–1870* (London, 1983).

81. G. R. Porter, *The Progress of the Nation . . .*, 3 vols (London, 1843), Section V, pp. 278–81.

82. See T. W. Laqueur, *Religion and Respectability. Sunday Schools and Working Class Culture, 1780–1850*, (New Haven, 1976), Chs. 1–2.

83. Sarah Trimmer, *The Oeconomy of Charity* (cited in Ch. 3, n. 35), pp. 68–75.

84. 'Endowed Schools at Chester', in *Of the Education of the Poor; . . . a digest of the Reports of the Society for bettering the Condition of the Poor . . .* (London, 1809), pp. 230–9.

85. Phillip McCann, 'Popular education, socialization and social control: Spital-fields, 1812–24', in Phillip McCann (ed.), *Popular Education and Socialization in the Nineteenth Century* (London, 1977), p. 23.

86. Pamela Silver and Harold Silver, *The Education of the Poor. The history of a National school, 1824–1974* (London, 1974), pp. 48–9.

87. Ibid., p. 56.

88. Beryl Madoc Jones, 'Patterns of attendance and their social significance: Mitcham National School, 1830–39', in McCann (ed.), *Popular Education and Socialization*.

89. Laqueur, *Religion and Respectability*, p. 153.

90. Quoted in M. Sturt, *The Education of the People. A history of primary education in England and Wales in the nineteenth century* (London, 1967), p. 117.

91. J. M. Goldstrom, *The Social Content of Education, 1808–70. A Study of the Working Class School Reader in England and Ireland* (Shannon, 1972), p. 127n.

92. Simon Frith, 'Socialization and rational schooling: elementary education in Leeds before 1870', in McCann (ed.), *Popular Education and Socialization*, p. 73.

93. 'Female Slavery in England', *The Labourer*, 4 (1848), 253, quoted in Caroline E.

Martin, 'Female Chartism: a study in politics', MA Thesis, University of Wales (1973), p. 47.

94. East London Female Total Abstinence Chartist Association, *Northern Star*, 30 January 1841, quoted in Martin, 'Female Chartism', p. 37.

95. B. Taylor, *Eve and the New Jerusalem. Socialism and Feminism in the Nineteenth Century* (London, 1983), p. 234.

96. Fanny Hertz, 'Mechanics Institutes for Working Women, with special reference to the manufacturing districts of Yorkshire', *Transactions of the National Association for the Promotion of Social Science* (1859), pp. 347–54.

97. See the salutary discussion in Carolyn Steedman, *The Tidy House, Little Girls Writing* (London, 1982), pp. 117–31.

98. Cremin, *American Education*, Ch. 5.

99. Carl F. Kaestle and Maris A. Vinovskis, *Education and Social Change in Nineteenth Century Massachusetts* (Cambridge, 1980), pp. 25–6.

100. Thomas W. Dublin, *Women at Work. The Transformation of Work and Community in Lowell, Massachusetts, 1826–1860* (New York, 1979), pp. 178–80.

101. Cremin, *American Education*, Ch. 12. But also see Julie Roy Jeffrey, *Frontier Women. The Trans-Mississippi West 1840–1880* (New York, 1979), pp. 87–94.

102. Vinovskis and Bernard, 'Beyond Catherine Beecher', *Signs* (1978), pp. 862–3.

103. See, on this subject, Gerda Lerner, 'Black and White Women in Interaction and Confrontation', in *The Majority Finds its Past. Placing Women in History* (New York, 1979); Angela Davis, *Women, Race, and Class* (London, 1981), Chs. 1–2; Suzanne Lebsock, 'Free Black Women and the Question of Matriarchy: Petersburg, Virginia, 1784–1820', *Feminist Studies*, 8 (Summer 1982), 271–92; I. Berlin, *Slaves without Masters. The Free Negro in the Antebellum South* (New York, 1974), pp. 74–8, 173–4, 303–6.

104. Anderson, *Education in France*, p. 31.

105. James R. Lehning, *The Peasants of Marlhes. Economic Development and Family Organisation in Nineteenth Century France* (N. Carolina, 1980), pp. 154–9; E. Weber, *Peasants into Frenchmen. The Modernization of Rural France, 1870–1914* (London, 1977), p. 321.

106. P. Pierrard, *La vie ouvrière à Lille sous le Second Empire* (Paris, 1965), pp. 313–37; G. Duveau, *La vie ouvrière en France sous le Second Empire* (Paris, 1946), pp. 449ff.; Anderson, *Education in France*, p. 112.

107. Parkes, 'The Profession of the Teacher', *EWJ*, i (March 1858), 1–13; 'Why boys are cleverer than girls', *EWJ*, ii (October 1858), 116–18, and see replies, ii, 209, 280, 426.

5. WORK AND ORGANISATION

1. John Mack Faragher, *Women and Men on the Overland Trail* (New Haven, 1979), pp. 49ff; Julie Roy Jeffrey, *Frontier Women. The Trans-Mississippi West 1840–1880* (New York, 1979), pp. 59–61; see also the excellent general discussion in E. A. Hellerstein, L. P. Hume, and K. M. Offen, *Victorian Women. A documentary account of women's lives in nineteenth century England, France, and the United States* (Brighton, 1981), pp. 272–91.

2. J. L. Flandrin, *Families in Former Times. Kinship, Household and Sexuality*, trans. Richard Southern (Cambridge, 1979), p. 113, quoting Abel Hugo, *La France pittoresque*, 3 vols (Paris, 1835), Vol. i, pp. 237–8.

3. The most important discussion of this theme is in Martine Segalen, *Love and Power in the Peasant Family. Rural France in the Nineteenth Century* (Oxford, 1983), pp. 155ff.

4. K. D. M. Snell, 'Agricultural seasonal unemployment, the standard of living, and women's work in the south and east, 1690–1860', *Economic History Review*, XXXIV (1982), 405–37; M. Roberts, 'Sickles and scythes: women's work and men's work at harvest

time', *History Workshop*, 7 (1979), 3–28; C. Emsley, *British Society and the French Wars, 1793–1815* (London, 1979) pp. 74–5.

5. *PP* 1867–8 (4068) XVII, p. 76. Appendix Part I(A) to the 1st Report of the Commissioners on the Employment of Children, Young Persons and Women in Agriculture. Quoted in Jennie Kitteringham, *Country Girls in 19th Century England*, History Workshop Pamphlet No. 11 (1973).

6. See, for instance, the evidence of Jane Long and of Mrs Britton to the Commission of 1843 on the Employment of Women and Children in Agriculture, *PP* 1843 (510), XII, pp. 23, 66, 70–1.

7. E. A. Dexter, *Career Women of America 1776–1840* (Boston, 1950; reprinted 1972), p. 183; Edith Abbott, *Women in Industry. A study in American Economic History* (1909; reprinted New York, 1969), p. 12; and see the comments on prejudice against women's agricultural labour in Caroline Dall, *'Woman's Right to Labour'; or, Low Wages and Hard Work* (Boston, 1860), pp. 53–4.

8. Gay L. Gullickson, 'The sexual division of labour in cottage industry and agriculture in the Pays de Caux: Auffray, 1750–1850', *French Historical Studies*, XII (1981), 177–99.

9. Malcolm I. Thomis and Jennifer Grimmett, *Women in Protest, 1800–1850* (London, 1982), pp. 51–6; M. Agulhon, *The Republic in the Village. The people of the Var from the French Revolution to the Second Republic*, trans. Janet Lloyd (Cambridge, 1982), p. 44; see also J. P. D. Dunbabin, *Rural Discontent in Nineteenth Century Britain* (New York, 1974), pp. 25, 85, 161.

10. Quoted in Jacqueline Jones, ' "My Mother was Much of a Woman": black women, work and the family under slavery', *Feminist Studies*, 8 (1982), 241, 253. See also E. Genovese, *Roll Jordan Roll. The World the Slaves Made* (New York, 1974), pp. 494–5; Bell Hooks, *Ain't I a Woman. Black Women and Feminism* (Boston, 1981), pp. 48–9.

11. I. Berlin, *Slaves without Masters. The Free Negro in the Antebellum South* (New York, 1974), pp. 220–6.

12. Faragher, *Women and Men on the Overland Trail*, p. 179; E. Weber, *Peasants into Frenchmen. The Modernization of Rural France, 1870–1914* (London, 1977), pp. 41ff; Segalen, *Love and Power in the Peasant Family*, p. 90; Caroline Davidson, *A Woman's Work is Never Done. A History of Housework in the British Isles, 1650–1950* (London, 1982), pp. 105–6, 184, 202–3.

13. A most useful discussion of this subject is D. Bythell, *The Sweated Trades. Outwork in Nineteenth Century Britain* (London, 1978). See also, from a rather different perspective, Joan M. Jensen, 'Cloth, Butter and Boarders: Women's Household Production for the Market', *Review of Radical Political Economics*, 12 (1980) 14–24.

14. Useful reference works include A. Milward and S. B. Saul, *The Economic Development of Continental Europe, 1780–1870* (London, 1973); D. Landes, *The Unbound Prometheus* (Cambridge, 1969); S. Pollard, *Peaceful Conquest: the industrialisation of Europe, 1760–1970* (Oxford, 1981).

15. D. Bythell, *The Handloom Weavers. A Study in the English Cotton Industry during the Industrial Revolution* (Cambridge, 1969); Ivy Pinchbeck, *Women Workers and the Industrial Revolution 1750–1850* (1930, reprint 1981), Chs. VI–VIII; G. Duveau, *La vie ouvrière en France sous le second empire* (Paris, 1946), pp. 162–86: J. Simon, *L'ouvrière* (Paris, 1861), pp. 179ff; Louise A. Tilly and Joan W. Scott, *Women, Work and Family* (New York, 1978). pp. 63–88; L. S. Strumingher, 'Les canutes de Lyon (1835–48)', *Le mouvement social* (October–December 1978), 105, 59–86; Abbot, *Women in Industry, passim*; Helen L. Sumner, *History of Women in Industry in the United States* (Washington, 1910).

16. Pinchbeck, *Women Workers and the Industrial Revolution*, pp. 202–31; Bythell, *The Sweated Trades*, pp. 97–105, 119–23. Compare similar developments in the straw industry in New England in the first quarter of the nineteenth century, Abbot, *Women in Industry*, pp. 71–5.

17. J. Vidalenc, *Le peuple des campagnes* (Paris, 1970), p. 74; Gullickson, 'The sexual division of labour . . .'.

18. See E. P. Thompson and Eileen Yeo (eds), *The Unknown Mayhew. Selections from the Morning Chronicle, 1849–50* (London, 1971); Sally Alexander, 'Women's Work in Nineteenth Century London a study of the years 1830–50', in A. Oakley and J. Mitchell (eds), *The Rights and Wrongs of Women* (London, 1976); Bythell, *The Sweated Trades*, Ch. 2; Christopher H. Johnson, 'Economic Change and Artisan Discontent: the tailor's history, 1800–48', in R. Price (ed.) *Revolution and Reaction. 1848 and the Second French Republic* (London, 1975); J. P. Aguet, *Les grèves sous la monarchie de juillet (1830–47)* (Geneva, 1954) pp. 75ff; P. Foner, *Women and the American Labour Movement, from colonial times to the eve of World War I* (New York, 1979), pp. 39ff.

19. Abbot, *Women in Industry*, Ch. VIII; Bythell, *Sweated Trades*, pp. 106ff.

20. James R. Lehning, *The Peasants of Marlhes. Economic Development and Family Organisation In Nineteenth Century France* (London, 1980), pp. 28ff.

21. *PP* 1864 (3414), XXII, p. 255. Evidence given to the Royal Commission on Children's Employment, by the manager of one of the large London houses in the trade, quoted by Bythell, *The Sweated Trades*, p. 118; C. H. Clark, 'Household economy, market exchange, and the rise of capitalism in the Connecticut Valley, 1800–1860', *Journal of Social History*, 13 (1979), 169–90.

22. Pinchbeck, *Women Workers and the Industrial Revolution*, pp. 270–81; Bythell, *The Sweated Trades*, pp. 123ff; John Duguid Milne, *The Industrial and Social Position of Women in the Middle and Lower Ranks* (London, 1857), pp. 202, 212–16.

23. Sumner, *History of Women in Industry*, pp. 222–5.

24. Aguet, *Les grèves sous la monarchie de juillet*, p. 29; Simon, *L'Ouvrière*, p. 205.

25. S. Lewenhak, *Women and Trade Unions. An Outline History of Women in the British Trade Union Movement* (London, 1977), pp. 17–22.

26. C. R. Dobson, *Masters and Journeymen. A Prehistory of Industrial Relations, 1717–1800* (London, 1980), p. 25. This point is confirmed by the view taken in P. Clark, *The English Alehouse: a social history, 1200–1830* (London, 1983), pp. 235–6, 311–12, that women visited the alehouse only on certain acceptable occasions, and did not use it regularly, or take part in the expanding use of alehouses by trades corporations in the eighteenth century.

27. L. Abensour, *La femme et le féminisme avant la Révolution* (Paris, 1923), pp. 184ff, 208; W. H. Sewell, *Work and Revolution in France. The language of labour from the old regime to 1848* (New York, 1980), p. 31.

28. Aguet, *Les grèves sous la monarchie de juillet*, pp. 12–14.

29. Ibid., p. 129.

30. Ibid., pp. 174, 336, 338; C. H. Johnson, 'Patterns of proletarianisation: Parisian tailors and Lodève woollen workers', in John M. Merriman (ed.,), *Consciousness and Class Experience in Nineteenth Century Europe* (New York, 1979).

31. R. Gossez, *Les ouvriers de Paris. L'organisation, 1848–51. Bibliothèque de la révolution de 1848*, Vol. XXIV (Paris, 1967), p. 172.

32. Lewenhak, *Women and Trade Unions*, pp. 23, 29–30;

33. Thomis and Grimmett, *Women in Protest*, p. 73.

34. Pinchbeck, *Women Workers and the Industrial Revolution*, p. 208.

35. B. Taylor, *Eve and the New Jerusalem. Socialism and feminism in the Nineteenth Century* (London, 1983), pp. 90–1.

36. Ibid., p. 96.

37. Ibid., pp. 107ff.

38. Ibid., p. 108.

39. Johnson, 'Economic Change and Artisan Discontent', *Revolution and Reaction*, pp. 105ff; Gossez, *Les ouvriers de Paris*, pp. 160–66.

40. Foner, *Women and the American Labor Movement*, pp. 46–8.

41. Ibid., pp. 42–6.

42. Abbott, *Women in Industry*, p. 251.

43. Ibid., pp. 192–3.

44. Quoted in Foner, *Women and the American Labor Movement*, p. 54.

45. See, on this subject, Gossez, *Les ouvriers de Paris*, pp. 170–3; E. Thomas, *Les femmes de 1848* (Paris, 1948), pp. 51ff; E. Sullerot, 'Journaux féminins et lutte ouvrière 1848–1850', *Le presse ouvrière, 1819–50*, Etude presentée par Jacques Godechot, *Bibliothèque de la révolution de 1848*, Vol. xxiii (Paris, 1966).

46. Besides the above items, see also A. Ranvier, 'Une féministe de 1848. Jeanne Deroin', *La Révolution de 1848. Bulletin de la société d'histoire de la révolution de 1848*, iv (1907–8), pp. 317–55, v (1908–9), pp. 421–30, 480–98.

47. Foner, *Women and the American Labor Movement*, p. 89.

48. See Angela John, *By the Sweat of their Brow. Women Workers at Victorian Coal Mines* (London, 1980), Chs 1–2; Jane Humphries, 'Protective legislation, the capitalist state, and working class men: the case of the 1842 Mines Regulation Act', *Feminist Review*, 7 (1981), 1–33.

49. Duveau, *La vie ouvrière en France*, p. 285; R. Trempé, *Les mineurs de Carmaux, 1848–1914*, 2 vols (Paris, 1971), i, pp. 132–3; M. Agulhon, *Une ville ouvrière au temps du socialisme utopique. Toulon de 1815 à 1851* (Paris, 1970), pp. 66–7.

50. Tilly and Scott, *Women, Work and Family*, pp. 112–13; F. Collier, *Family Economy of the Working Classes in the Cotton Industry, 1784–1833* (Manchester, 1964); N. Smelser, *Social Change in the Industrial Revolution: an application of theory to the British cotton industry* (Chicago, 1959); Michael Anderson, 'Sociological history and the working-class family: Smelser revisited', *Social History*, i (1976), 317–34, and *Family Structure in Nineteenth Century Lancashire* (Cambridge, 1971); M. M. Edwards and R. Lloyd-Jones, 'N. J. Smelser and the cotton factory family: a reassessment', in N. B. Harte and K. G. Ponting (eds), *Textile History and Economic History* (Manchester, 1973).

51. Thomas W. Dublin, *Women at Work. The Transformation of Work and Community in Lowell, Massachusetts, 1826–1860* (New York, 1979), p. 40.

52. Tilly and Scott, *Women, Work and Family*, pp. 106–11.

53. M. Hewitt, *Wives and Mothers in Victorian Industry* (London, 1958), pp. 14–17, 62–6; Tilly and Scott, *Women, Work and Family*, pp. 123–36; other industries could offer a rather different picture, if one affecting far fewer women: see Judith McGaw's study of Berkshire, Massachusetts, paper mill workers, who included significantly more married women, 'Technological change and women's work: mechanization in the Berkshire paper industry, 1820–55', in M. M. Trescott (ed.), *Dynamos and Virgins Revisited: women and technological change in history* (Metuchen, New Jersey, 1979).

54. Dublin, *Women at Work*, Ch. 6; Foner, *Women and the American Labour Movement*, pp. 28ff.

55. Dublin, *Women at Work*, p. 91.

56. Ibid., pp. 116–17.

57. Ibid., p. 127.

58. Ibid., p. 130.

59. Foner, *Women and the American Labor Movement*, p. 72.

60. Ibid., pp. 91ff; Alan Dawley, *Class and Community. The Industrial Revolution in Lynn* (Cambridge, Massachusetts, 1976), pp. 81ff.

61. Thomis and Grimmett, *Women in Protest*, pp. 73–4.

62. Lewenhak, *Women and Trade Unions*, pp. 46–7.

63. Thomis and Grimmett, *Women in Protest*, pp. 76–7.

64. Ibid., pp. 78–9; D. Thompson, 'Women and nineteenth century radical politics: a lost dimension', in Oakley and Mitchell (eds), *Rights and Wrongs of Women*.

65. Thomis and Grimmett, *Women in Protest*, p. 80.

66. Ibid., p. 81.

67. Lewenhak, *Women and Trade Unions*, pp. 48–52; Thompson, 'Women and nineteenth century radical politics'.

68. Simon, *L'ouvrière*, pp. 328–30.

69. Ibid., pp. 52–7, 347; Strumingher, 'Les canutes de Lyon', pp. 74–6; L. Reybaud, *Etudes sur la règime de manufactures: condition des ouvrières en soie* (Paris, 1859), pp. 330–3, quoted in E. A. Hellerstein, L. P. Hume and K. M. Offen, *Victorian Women. A documentary history of women's lives in nineteenth century England, France and the United States* (1981), p. 394.

70. See Theresa M. McBride, *The Domestic Revolution. The Modernisation of Household Service in England and France, 1820–1920* (London, 1976); L. Davidoff, 'Mastered for life: servant and wife in Victorian England', *Journal of Social History*, 7 (1974), 406–28; L. Davidoff, J. L'Esperance and H. Newby, 'Landscape with Figures: Home and Community in English Society', in Oakley and Mitchell (eds), *Rights and Wrongs of Women*; P. Horn, *The Rise and Fall of the Victorian Servant* (Dublin, 1975); Theresa M. McBride, 'The "modernisation" of woman's work', *Journal of Modern History*, 49 (1977), 231–45.

71. Tilly and Scott, *Women, Work and Family*, pp. 68ff; A. Armstrong, *Stability and Change in an English Country Town. A Social Study of York, 1801—51* (Cambridge, 1974), p. 45; Duguid Milne, *Industrial and Social Position of Women*, pp. 190ff.

72. Lewenhak, *Women and Trade Unions*, p. 32; Alexander, 'Women's Work in Nineteenth Century London', p. 99. Compare M. Agulhon, *Une ville ouvrière au temps du socialisme utopique*, pp. 66–7.

73. Foner, *Women and the American Labour Movement*, pp. 99–105.

74. Sumner, *History of Women in Industry*, pp. 178–80; Lucy M. Salmon, *Domestic Service* (London, 1897), pp. 62ff; Carol Groneman, ' "She earns as a child; she pays as a man": women workers in a mid-nineteenth century New York City Community', in M. Cantor and B. Laurie (eds), *Class, Sex and the Woman Worker* (Westport, Connecticut, 1977).

75. Wollstonecraft, *Vindication of the Rights of Woman*, pp. 261–2; Mary Ann Radcliffe, *The Female Advocate, or An Attempt to recover the Rights of Women from Male Usurpation* (London, 1810).

76. *The Lancet*, 2 (November–February 1841–2), quoted in Jean Donnison, *Midwives and Medical Men. A history of inter-professional rivalries and women's rights* (London, 1977), pp. 55–6.

77. Priscilla Wakefield, *Reflections on the Present Condition of the Female Sex; with suggestions for its improvement* (London, 1798), Chs v–vii.

78. Harriet Martineau, 'Female Industry', *Edinburgh Review*, CIX (April 1859), 293–336.

79. A. Jameson, *Sisters of Charity* (1855), reprinted in *Sisters of Charity and the Communion of Labour. Two essays on the social employments of women. New edition . . .* (London, 1859), p. 15; Harriet Taylor Mill, 'Enfranchisement of women' (1851), reprinted in Alice S. Rossi (ed.), *Essays on Sex Equality* (Chicago, 1970), p. 104.

80. Barbara Leigh Smith Bodichon, *Women and Work* (London, 1857); *EWJ*, I, 165–77, 282–3; II, p. 359, IV, pp. 353–4, 367, V, 358–9, 418, 429 – and so on!

81. *Transactions of the National Association for the Promotion of Social Science* (1859), ed. G. W. Hastings (London, 1860), pp. 10, 347–54.

82. Milne, *Industrial and Social Position of Women*, Chs XI–XII.

83. 'Society for promoting the employment of women', *EWJ*, V (August 1860), 388–96.

84. 'The *Saturday Review* and the *English Woman's Journal*. The reviewer reviewed', *EWJ*, I (May 1860), 201–4.

85. See, on this subject, L. Holcombe, *Victorian Ladies at Work. Middle Class Working Women in England and Wales, 1850–1914* (Newton Abbot, 1973).

86. Patrick Kay Bidelman, *Pariahs Stand Up! The Founding of the Liberal Feminist Movement In France, 1858–1889* (Westport, Connecticut, 1982), Ch. I; J.-V. Daubié, *La femme pauvre av dix-neuvième siècle* (Paris, 1866), Chs IV–V.

87. *HWS*, I, p. 78.

88. Dall, *'Woman's Right to Labour'*, pp. xi, 7, 86.

89. M. Perrot, 'De la nourrice a l'employée . . . Travaux de femmes dans la France du XIXe siècle', *Le mouvement social* (October–December 1978), 105, 3–10; 'La femme populaire rebelle', C. Dufrancatel *et al.* (eds), *L'histoire sans qualités* (Paris, 1979).

6. DOMESTIC QUESTIONS

1. M. Perrot, 'La femme populaire rebelle', C. Dufrancatel *et al.* (eds), *L'histoire sans qualités* (Paris, 1979); Martine Segalen, *Love and Power in the Peasant Family. Rural France in the Nineteenth Century* (Oxford, 1983), p. 138.

2. John Stuart Mill, *The Subjection of Women* (1869), reprinted in Alice S. Rossi (ed.), *Essays on Sex Equality* (Chicago, 1970), p. 183.

3. See the discussion on this subject between Jane Humphries, 'The working class family, women's liberation, and class struggle: the case of nineteenth century British history', *Review of Radical Political Economics*, 9 (1977), pp. 25–41, and Gita Sen, 'The sexual division of labour and the working class family: towards a conceptual synthesis of class relations and the subordination of women', *Review of Radical Political Economics*, 12 (1980), 76–86.

4. Caroline Davidson, *A Woman's Work is Never Done. A History of Housework in the British Isles, 1650–1950* (London, 1982), p. 12; for the United States, the same theme is developed in Susan Strasser, *Never Done. A History of American Housework* (New York, 1982), Ch. 5.

5. Strasser, *Never Done*, pp. 28ff; P. Pierrard, *La vie ouvrière à Lille sous la Second Empire* (Paris, 1965), p. 54; Segalen, *Love and Power in the Peasant Family*, pp. 85–7.

6. Davidson, *A Woman's Work is Never Done*, p. 20.

7. Ibid., pp. 138ff.

8. Segalen, *Lover and Power in the Peasant Family*, pp. 138–9.

9. Perrot, 'La femme populaire rebelle', pp. 144–6.

10. Davidson, *A Woman's Work is Never Done*, Chs 3–4; Segalen, *Love and Power in the Peasant Family*, p. 139; Strasser, *Never Done*, Ch. 1; and see the review of nineteenth-century advice on baking in Elizabeth David, *English Bread and Yeast Cookery* (London, 1977), pp. 155–90.

11. Segalen, *Love and Power in the Peasant Family*, p. 140; John Mack Faragher, *Women and Men on the Overland Trail* (New Haven, 1979), pp. 126–7; Elaine Hedges, 'The 19th century diarist and her quilts', *Feminist Studies*, 8 (1982), 293–9.

12. Quoted in Louise A. Tilly and Joan W. Scott, *Women, Work and Family* (New York, 1978), p. 96.

13. Duveau, *La vie ouvrière en France sous le second empire* (Paris, 1946), pp. 425–9; Pierrard, *La vie ouvrière à Lille*, pp. 119ff; M. Frey, 'Du mariage et du concubinage dans les classes populaires à Paris (1846–1847)', *Annales ESC*, 33 (1978), 803–29.

14. E. P. Thompson and Eileen Yeo (eds), *The Unknown Mayhew. Selections from the Morning Chronicle, 1848–50* (London, 1971), p. 171.

15. B. Taylor, *Eve and the New Jerusalem. Socialism and Feminism in the Nineteenth Century* (London, 1983), pp. 192–205.

16. O. Anderson, 'The Incidence of Civil Marriage in Victorian England and Wales', *Past and Present*, 69 (1975), 50–87; and the ensuing debate between Anderson, Roderick Floud and Pat Thane, *Past and Present*, 84 (1979).

17. S. P. Menefee, *Wives for Sale. An ethnographic study of British popular divorce* (Oxford, 1981), p. 47.

18. *PP*, xvi (1842), p. 246, quoted in Humphries 'Protective legislation, the capitalist state, and working class men . . .', *Feminist Review*, 7 (1981), 25.

19. P. Gaskell, *The Manufacturing Population of England* (London, 1833), p. 147.

20. Humphries, 'Protective legislation, the capitalist state, and working class men . . .', pp. 26–7: M. Hewitt, *Wives and Mothers in Victorian Industry* (London, 1958), pp. 57ff.

21. L. Villermé, *Tableau de l'état physique et moral des ouvriers employés dans les manufactures de coton, de laine et de soie*, 2 vols (Paris, 1840), ii, pp. 51–2, quoted in W. H. Sewell, *Work and Revolution in France. The language of labour from the old regime to 1898* (New York, 1980), p. 227.

22. J. Simon, *L'ouvrière* (Paris, 1861), pp. vi, 139.

23. Herbert Gutman, *The Black Family in Slavery and Freedom, 1750–1925* (New York, 1976), p. 96.

24. Ibid., p. 356.

25. Susan K. Kleinberg, 'The systematic study of urban women', in M. Cantor and B. Laurie (eds), *Class, Sex and the Woman Worker* (Westport, Connecticut, 1977), p. 22; see also Groneman, ' "She earns as a child; she pays as a man" . . .', in the same volume, on the mid-nineteenth century Irish community in New York City.

26. Quoted in Taylor, *Eve and the New Jerusalem*, p. 201n; see generally on this, U. R. Q. Henriques, 'Bastardy and the New Poor Law', *Past and Present*, 37 (1967), 103–29.

27. D. Vincent, *Bread, Knowledge and Freedom. A study of nineteenth-century working class autobiography* (London, 1981), p. 55.

28. Ibid., p. 44.

29. Taylor, *Eve and the New Jerusalem*, pp. 221ff.

30. R. J. Richardson, *The Rights of Woman* (1840), quoted in D. Thompson, *The Early Chartists* (London, 1971), p. 122.

31. Quoted in L. Strumingher, 'The artisan family: traditions and transition in nineteenth century Lyon', *Journal of Family History*, 2 (1977), 211–22, from Louis Vasbenter to Flora Tristan, 11 June 1843, from J.-L. Puech, *La vie et l'oeuvre de Flora Tristan, 1803–1844* (Paris, 1925), p. 474.

32. Tilly and Scott, *Women, Work and Family*, p. 139.

33. N. Tomes, 'A "Torrent of Abuse"; crimes of violence between working class men and women in London, 1840–75, *Journal of Social History*, 11 (1978), 328–45.

34. D. Thompson, 'Women and nineteenth century radical politics', in A. Oakley and Juliet Mitchell (eds), *Rights and Wrongs of Women* (London, 1976), pp. 137–8; Perrot, 'La femme populaire rebelle', Dufrancatel *et al.* (eds), *L'histoire sans qualités*, pp. 150–4.

35. E. P. Thompson, 'The moral economy of the English crowd in the eighteenth century', *Past and Present*, 50 (1971), 115. The following acccount is based on this, Malcolm I. Thomis and Jennifer Grimmett, *Women in Protest, 1800–1850* (London, 1982), and J. Stevenson, *Popular Disturbances in England, 1700–1870* (London, 1979), pp. 101–2.

36. Eric Richards, *The Last Scottish Food Riots*, Past and Present Supplement, No. 6, 1982.

37. Perrot, 'La femme populaire rebelle', p. 135; L. A. Tilly, 'The food riot as a form of political conflict in France', *Journal of Interdisciplinary History*, ii (1971), 23–58; R. Price, *The Modernisation of Rural France. Communications networks and agricultural market structures in nineteenth-century France* (London, 1983), pp. 143–95 *passim*.

38. K. Logue, *Popular Disturbances in Scotland, 1780–1815* (Edinburgh, 1979), 199–203.

39. David J. V. Jones, *Before Rebecca. Popular Protest in Wales, 1793–1835* (London, 1973), pp. 47–8, 66.

40. B. Reaney, *The class struggle in nineteenth century Oxfordshire. The social and communal background to the Otmoor disturbances of 1830 to 1835*, History Workshop pamphlet No. 3 (1970), p. 36.

41. Thomis and Grimmett, *Women in Protest*, pp. 53ff.

42. M. Agulhon *The Republic in the Village. The people of the Var from the French Revolution to the Second Republic*, trans. Janet Lloyd (Cambridge, 1982), p. 44; see also, for instance, E. Weber, *Peasants into Frenchmen. The Modernization of Rural France, 1870–1914* (London, 1977), p. 248.

43. Thomis and Grimmett, *Women in Protest*, pp. 47–8.

44. Perrot, 'La femme populaire rebelle', p. 138.

45. In this I agree with most authorities, and dissent from the conclusion of Logue, *Popular Disturbances in Scotland*. p. 203, that 'If there was a woman's view of popular direct action, there is no evidence of it'.

46. Thomis and Grimmett, *Women in Protest*, p. 58.

47. Ibid., p. 62.

48. Segalen, *Love and Power in the Peasant Family*, pp. 141–50.

49. Agulhon, *Republic in the Village*, pp. 124–50; R. Aminzade, *Class, Politics and Early Industrial Capitalism. A study of mid-nineteenth century Toulouse, France* (Albany, 1981), pp. 82–9; W. H. Sewell, 'Social change and the rise of working class politics in nineteenth century Marseille', *Past and Present*, 65 (1974), 75–109.

50. Thompson, 'Women and nineteenth century radical politics', p. 136.

51. George Eliot, *The Mill on the Floss* (Bk I, Ch. 6) quoted in V. Colby, *Yesterday's Woman. Domestic Realism in the English Novel* (Princeton, New Jersey, 1974), p. 25.

52. P. Branca, *Silent Sisterhood. Middle-class women in the Victorian home* (London, 1975).

53. L. Davidoff, *'Life is duty, praise and prayer': some contributions of the new women's history* (London, 1981), Fawcett Library Papers, No. 4.

54. Unpublished diary of Mehitabel May Dawes, 12 June 1815, quoted by N. Cott, *The Bonds of Womanhood. 'Woman's Sphere' in New England, 1780–1835* (New Haven, 1977), p. 99.

55. But see K. Thomas, 'The Double Standard', *Journal of the History of Ideas*, xx (1959), 195–216.

56. Quoted in N. Cott, 'Passionlessness: an interpretation of Victorian sexual ideology, 1790–1850', *Signs*, 4 (1978), 234–5. See also Barbara Welter, 'The Cult of True Womanhood, 1820–60', *American Quarterly*, 18 (1966), 151–75.

57. For example, Linda Gordon, 'Voluntary Motherhood: the beginnings of feminist birth control in the United States', and Daniel Scott Smith, 'Family limitation, sexual control and domestic feminism in Victorian America', both in Mary J. Hartman and Lois Banner (eds), *Clio's Consciousness Raised. New perspectives on the history of women* (New York, 1974).

58. Mary Ryan, *Cradle of the Middle Class. The family in Oneida County, New York, 1790–1865* (Cambridge, 1981), p. 157.

59. James F. McMillan, *Housewife or Harlot. The Place of Women in French Society, 1870–1940* (Brighton, 1981), pp. 16–20; T. Zeldin, *France, 1848–1945*, Vol. i (Oxford, 1973), pp. 285ff; Bonnie C. Smith, *Ladies of the Leisure Class. The Bourgeoises of Northern France in the Nineteenth Century* (Princeton, New Jersey, 1981), pp. 10–11, 82–4, 111–12, 175–6.

60. Illustration of the relationship between the writings of the *philosophes*, and of the medical profession on this subject is given in Y. Knibiehler 'Les médecins et la "nature" féminine au temps du Code Civil', *Annales ESC*, 37 (1976), 824–45.

61. The quotation, and the comparison, are drawn from Erna A. Hellerstein, Lesley P. Hume and Karen M. Offen (eds), *Victorian Women. A documentary account of women's lives in nineteenth-century England, France and the United States* (Brighton, 1981), pp. 171–5.

62. Ann Douglas Wood, ' "The Fashionable Diseases": women's complaints and

their treatment in nineteenth century America', Carroll Smith-Rosenberg, 'Puberty to menopause: the cycle of femininity in nineteenth century America', and Regina Morantz, 'The lady and her physician', all in Hartman and Banner (eds), *Clio's Consciousness Raised*; J. S. Haller and R. M. Haller, *The Physician and Sexuality in Victorian America* (Urbana, Illinois, 1974).

63. Ryan, *Cradle of the Middle Class*, pp. 157–65.

64. Branca, *Silent Sisterhood*, pp. 95–112.

65. Winifred Gérin, *Elizabeth Gaskell* (Oxford, 1976), pp. 53–6.

66. Zeldin, *France, 1848–1945*, I, pp. 315–29.

67. Branca, *Silent Sisterhood*, p. 38ff; Davidson, *A Woman's Work is Never Done*, pp. 60–3; Strasser, *Never Done*, pp. 36–7.

68. Hellerstein, Hume and Offen, *Victorian Women*, pp. 292–5.

69. Smith, *Ladies of the Leisure Class*, pp. 66–92; L. Davidoff, 'The rationalization of housework' in D. Barker and S. Allen (eds), *Dependence and Exploitation in Work and Marriage* (London, 1976); see also E. O. Hellerstein, 'French women and the orderly household, 1830–1870', *Proceedings of the Third Annual Meeting of the Western Society for French History, 4–6 December 1975* (1976).

70. Cott, *Bonds of Womanhood*, pp. 98–100.

71. For examples, see Lawrence Stone, *The Family, Sex and Marriage in England, 1500–1800* (London, 1977), p. 351.

72. Ryan, *Cradle of the Middle Class*, pp. 146–55; Branca, *Silent Sisterhood*, pp. 38–45.

73. Catherine Hall, 'Gender divisions and class formation in the Birmingham middle class, 1780–1850', in R. Samuel (ed.), *People's History and Socialist Theory* (London, 1981), p. 174; and see also the important discussion of the development of domestic economy in Elisabeth Fox-Genovese and Eugene D. Genovese, *Fruits of Merchant Capital. Slavery and bourgeois property in the rise and expansion of capitalism* (Oxford, 1983), pp. 302ff.

74. A. Summers, 'Ladies and nurses in the Crimean War', *History Workshop Journal*, 16 (1983), 33–56. See also L. Davidoff, 'Mastered for life: servant and wife in Victorian England', *Journal of Social History*, 7 (1974), 406–28, and 'Class and gender in nineteenth century England: the diaries of Arthur J. Munby and Hannah Culwick', *Feminist Studies*, 5 (1979), 87–141.

75. Cott, *Bonds of Womanhood*, Ch. 5, 'Sisterhood'; Carroll Smith-Rosenberg, 'The Female World of Love and Ritual: Relations between Women in Nineteenth Century America', *Signs*, I (1975), 1–29.

76. See, for example, R. Holmes, *Shelley. The Pursuit* (London, 1974), index; N. Brown, *Sexuality and Feminism in Shelley* (Cambridge, Mass., 1979).

77. See Ellen Moers, *Literary Women* (London, 1980), pp. 173–210; J. C. Herold, *Mistress to an Age: a life of Mme de Stael* (London, 1959); Madelyn Gutwirth, 'Mme de Stael, Rousseau and the woman question', *Publications of the Modern Language Association of America*, 86, (1971), 100–10; Susan Tenenbaum, 'Montesquieu and Mme de Stael: the woman as a factor in political analysis, *Political Theory*, I (1973), 92–103.

78. George Sand, *Indiana*, trans. G. B. Ives (Chicago, 1978), Preface.

79. See, for example, E. Thomas, *Les femmes de 1848* (Paris, 1948), pp. 40ff.

80. P. Thomson, *George Sand and the Victorians. Her influence and reputation in nineteenth century England* (London, 1977), pp. 24–7.

81. Ibid., pp. 139–42; 'Modern Novelists – Great and Small', *Blackwood's*, LXXVII (1855), 557, quoted E. Showalter, *A Literature of Their Own. British Women Novelists from Brontë to Lessing* (Paperback edn, London, 1978), p. 143.

82. W. Thompson, *Appeal of One-Half the Human Race, Women, against the Pretensions of the Other Half, Men, to retain them in political, and thence in civil and domestic slavery*, (London, 1825, reprinted London, 1983), ed. R. Pankhurst, p. 79.

83. Ibid., 'Introductory Letter to Mrs Wheeler', pp. xxi–xxx; on Anna Wheeler, see

R. Pankhurst, 'Anna Wheeler: a pioneer socialist and feminist', *Political Quarterly*, xxv (1954), 132–43; S. Burke, 'Letter from a Pioneer Feminist', *Studies in Labour History*, i (1976), 19–23; Taylor, *Eve and the New Jerusalem*, pp. 59–65.

84. Thompson, *Appeal*, xxvi.

85. Ibid., pp. 104–5.

86. See Taylor, *Eve and the New Jerusalem*, pp. 183–92, 205–16, for a thorough discussion; also, for examples of such crowded meetings, *NMW* v, No. 4 (17 November 1838), No. 5 (24 November 1838), vi, No. 48 (21 September 1839), vii, No. 83 (23 May 1840), No. 84 (30 May 1840). Such reports are numerous throughout the early 1840s.

87. Quoted in Taylor, *Eve and the New Jerusalem*, p. 212; see also M. Reynolds (later Chappellsmith) 'Permanence of marriage unions under the rational system', *NMW*, v, No. 35 (22 June 1838). For examples of the softening of Owen's own views on marriage reforms see 'Address to Congress', *NMW*, v, No. 28 (4 May 1839); 'A few words on marriage', *NMW*, vii, No. 57 (23 November 1839); 'The permanency of marriage unions in the new state of society', *NMW*, vi, No. 61 (21 December 1839); 'Condition of Woman', *NMW*, vii, No. 76 (4 April 1840).

88. Taylor, *Eve and the New Jerusalem*, p. 214.

89. Ibid., pp. 247ff.

90. On these writers, see F. E. Manuel, *The New World of Henri de St-Simon* (South Bend, Indiana, 1963), and *The Prophets of Paris* (Cambridge, Mass., 1962); J. Beecher and R. Bienvenu, *The Utopian Vision of Charles Fourier. Selected Texts on Work, Love and Passionate Attraction . . .* (Boston, 1971).

91. Evelyne Sullerot, *Histoire de la presse féminine en France, des origines à 1848* (Paris, 1966), p. 146.

92. Ibid., p. 159; Anna Wheeler's translation of the full text can be found in R. K. P. Pankhurst, *The Saint Simonians, Mill and Carlyle. A Preface to Modern Thought* (London, 1957), pp. 109–11.

93. Claire Demar, *Ma Loi d'Avenir*, ouvrage posthume, publié par Suzanne (Paris, 1834).

94. On the *Conseiller des Femmes*, based on Lyons, see, besides Sullerot, *Histoire de la presse féminine*, Laura S. Strumingher, *Women and the Making of the Working Class: Lyon, 1830–1870* (St Albans, Vermont, 1979), pp. 39ff.

95. Quoted in A. J. G. Perkins and T. Wolfson, *Frances Wright, Free Enquirer. The Study of a Temperament*, (1939; reprinted Philadelphia, 1972), p. 193.

96. See Linda Gordon, *Woman's Body, Woman's Right. A Social History of Birth Control in America* (Harmondsworth, 1977), pp. 81ff; J. M. Whitworth, *God's Blueprints. A sociological study of three Utopian sects* (London, 1975), pp. 89–119; R. Muncy, *Sex and Marriage in Utopian Communities: nineteenth century America* (Bloomington, Indiana, 1973).

97. K. Marx, *On Education, Women and Children*, ed. Saul K. Padover (New York, 1975), extracts from *The Communist Manifesto* (1848), p. 67, *The German Ideology* (1845–6) pp. 61–2, and *Economic and Philosophic Manuscripts of 1844*, pp. 54–5.

98. See, for example, the discussions in D. Levine, *Family Formation in an age of Nascent Capitalism* (New York, 1977); J. L. Flandrin, *Families in Former Times, Kinship, Household and Sexuality*, trans. Richard Southern (Cambridge, 1979), pp. 212ff; C. Degler, *At Odds, Women and the Family in America from the Revolution to the Present* (Oxford, 1980), pp. 178ff.

99. D. Scott Smith, 'Family limitation, sexual control and domestic feminism in Victorian America' in Hartman and Banner (eds), *Clio's Consciousness Raised*.

100. Quoted in A. Maclaren, *Birth Control in Nineteenth Century England* (London, 1978), pp. 46–7.

101. Ibid., pp. 51–8; see also N. E. Himes, *Medical History of Contraception* (Baltimore, 1936), pp. 209–85.

102. Thompson, *Appeal*, p. 144; J. S. Mill, *Principles of Political Economy* (London,

1848), quoted by Maclaren, *Birth Control in Nineteenth Century England*, pp. 97–8.

103. Maclaren, *Birth Control in Nineteenth Century England*, p. 97.

104. Ibid., pp. 98–9.

105. Ibid., p. 31; M. Chatagnier, *De l'infanticide* (Paris, 1855), pp. 258–9, quoted in A. Maclaren, 'Abortion in France: Women and the regulation of family size, 1800–1914', *French Historical Studies*, 10 (1978), 475.

106. J. A. and Olive Banks, *Feminism and Family Planning in Victorian England* (Liverpool, 1964), pp. 64, 86–7; Maclaren, *Birth Control in Nineteenth Century England*, pp. 123–4.

For the United States, see Degler, *At odds*, pp. 227ff; R. Sauer, 'Attitudes to Abortion in America, 1800–1973', *Population Studies*, 28 (1974), 53–67; James C. Mohr, *Abortion in America: the origins and evolution of national policy, 1800–1900* (New York, 1978).

107. Weber, *Peasants into Frenchmen*, p. 183; Maclaren, *Birth Control in Nineteenth Century England*, pp. 81–8.

108. I. Pinchbeck and M. Hewitt, *Children in English Society*, Vol. II. *From the eighteenth century to the Childrens' Act, 1948* (London, 1973), pp. 362–76.

For Caroline Norton, see Alice Acland, *Caroline Norton* (London, 1948).

109. R. B. Morris, 'Women's rights in early American law', in *Studies in the History of American Law* (1958; reprinted New York, 1974), and see Ch. 2 above.

110. Quoted in E. Flexner, *A Century of Struggle. The Woman's Rights Movement in the United States* (New York, 1971), p. 64.

111. N. Basch, 'Invisible women: the legal fiction of marital unity in nineteenth century America', *Feminist Studies*, 5 (1979) 346–66; Flexner, *Century of Struggle*, pp. 64–5, 85–8.

112. This movement is discussed authoritatively in L. Holcombe, *Wives and Property. Reform of the Married Women's Property Law in Nineteenth Century England* (Oxford, 1983), especially Ch. 4, whose discussion I rely on here.

113. Caroline Frances Cornwallis, 'The Property of Married Women', *Westminster Review*, 66 (1856), 331–60; 'Capabilities and Disabilities of Women', *Westminster Review*, 67 (1857), 42–72.

114. L. Abensour, *Le féminisme sous le règne de Louis Philippe et en 1848* (Paris, 1913), pp. 36–49, 270–4, 283–4.

115. Zeldin, *France, 1848–1945*. I, pp. 287ff; Smith, *Ladies of the Leisure Class*, pp. 57–63; Robert Wheaton, 'Introduction: Recent Trends in the Historical Study of the French Family', in Wheaton (ed.), *Family and Sexuality in French History* (Philadelphia, 1980), pp. 19–20.

116. For example, Anne Richelieu Lamb, *Can Women Regenerate Society?* (London, 1844), Ch. VII 'Old maidism!'.

117. On Britain, see V. Colby, *Yesterday's Woman*, and on the United States, N. Baym, *Women's Fiction. A Guide to Novels by and about Women in America, 1820—1870* (Ithaca and London, 1978).

118. R. H. Hutton 'Novels by the Authoress of John Halifax', *North British Review*, XXIX (1858), 257, quoted in Showalter, *A Literature of Their Own*, p. 89.

7. POLITICS, PHILANTHROPY AND THE PUBLIC SPHERE

1. Quoted in full in *HWS*, I, pp. 82–3.

2. T. J. Clark, *The Absolute Bourgeois. Artists and Politics in France 1848–51* (London, 1982 edn), p. 17.

3. Alexis de Tocqueville, *Recollections*, trans. G. Lawrence, ed. J. P. Mayer and A. P. Kerr (New York, 1971), p. 170.

4. C. Tilly and L. Lees, 'The People of June, 1848', in *Revolution and Reaction. 1848 and the Second French Republic*, ed. R. Price (London, 1975), p. 207, note 47; M. Agulhon, *Marianne into Battle. Republican Imagery and Symbolism in France, 1789–1880* (Cambridge, 1981), p. 66.

5. W. Reddy, 'The textile trade and the language of the crowd at Rouen (1752–1871), *Past and Present*, 74 (1977), 62–89, especially pp. 80–6.

6. L. Strumingher, 'Les canutes de Lyon (1838–48)', *Le mouvement social*, 105 (October–December 1978), 83.

7. M. Agulhon, *The Republic in the Village. The people of the Var from the French Revolution to the Second Republic*, trans. Janet Lloyd (Cambridge, 1982), p. 349, note 52, and for another example, p. 242.

8. Ibid., pp. 256ff.

9. Quoted in Agulhon, *Marianne into Battle*, pp. 76–7. The continuing debate on the iconography of the republican and revolutionary movements is relevant and important, but too long to discuss here. See, besides *Marianne into Battle* Chs. 3–4, Clark, *The Absolute Bourgeois*, pp. 63ff; E. J. Hobsbawm, 'Man and Woman in Socialist Iconography', *History Workshop Journal*, 6 (1978), 121–38, and the replies of Hobsbawm by M. Agulhon and by Sally Alexander, Anna Davin, and Eve Hostettler in *History Workshop Journal*, 8 (1979), 167–82.

10. Agulhon, *Marianne into Battle*, pp. 286–94.

11. Ted. W. Margadant, *French Peasants in Revolt. The Insurrection of 1851* (Princeton, New Jersey, 1979), p. 265.

12. Agulhon, *Republic in the Village*, p. 202.

13. *Le Peuple*, 27 December 1848, quoted in Thomas, *Les femmes du 1848* (Paris, 1948), pp. 60–1.

14. For some examples of later crowd action, see Reddy, 'The textile trade and the language of the crowd'. C. Tilly *et al.*, *The Rebellious Century, 1830–1930* (London, 1975), argue that 'the turbulence of 1846–51 was the last in which reactive collective action played a large part. After that, the tax rebellion, the food riot, machine-breaking, and similar events virtually disappeared', p. 61.

15. Malcolm I. Thomis and Jennifer Grimmett, *Women in Protest, 1800–1850* (London, 1982), pp. 92–3.

16. Ibid., p. 96.

17. See, for instance, the cartoons of the Blackburn Female Reform Society: G. Cruikshank, 'The Belle Alliance, or the Female Reformers of Blackburn, August 12 1819'; J. L. Marks, Much wanted a reform among females!!!' (Plate 10), M. D. George, *Catalogue of Political and Personal Satires preserved in the department of prints and drawings in the British Museum, London* (1978), Vol. IX, 1811–19, pp. 916–17, 921–2. Both are full of obscene imagery and comment.

18. Thomis and Grimmett, *Women in Protest*, pp. 97–103.

19. Ibid., pp. 104ff.

20. *The Isis*, Vol. I, 11 February 1832, quoted in R. S. Neale, 'Women and class consciousness', in *Class in English History, 1680–1850* (London, 1981), p. 208; see also I. McCalman, 'Females, Feminism and Free Love', *Labour History* (1980), 1–25.

21. G. A. Williams, *The Merthyr Rising* (London, 1978), e.g. pp. 116ff, pp. 129ff.

22. Thomis and Grimmett, *Women in Protest*, p. 107.

23. On women's participation in the Chartist movement, I have used Caroline E. Martin, 'Female Chartism: a study in politics, M.A. thesis, University of Wales (1973); D. Jones, 'Women and Chartism', *History*, 68 (February, 1983), 1–21; Thomis and Grimmett, *Women in Protest*, Ch. 6; D. Thompson, 'Women in nineteenth century radical politics', in A. Oakley and Juliet Mitchell (eds), *Rights and Wrongs of Women* (London, 1976); G. Malmgreen, *Neither Bread nor Roses: Utopian Feminists and the English Working Class, 1800–50* (Brighton, 1978), pp. 31–5. I am particularly indebted to Martin's work for the references to Chartist periodicals quoted below, and for her discussion throughout.

24. 'Address from the London Delegate Council to the Male and Female Chartists of Great Britain and Ireland', *English Chartist Circular*, Vol. I, p. 133, quoted in Martin, 'Female Chartism', p. 31.

25. *English Chartist Circular*, I, p. 102 (23 June 1841), quoted in Martin, 'Female Chartism', p. 36.

26. Thomis and Grimmett, *Women in Protest*, pp. 105–6.

27. *The Operative*, 30 December 1848, quoted in Martin, 'Female Chartism', p. 83.

28. *The Labourer*, Vol. 4 (1848), p. 248, quoted in Martin, 'Female Chartism', p. 96.

29. R. J. Richardson, *The Rights of Woman* (1840), quoted in D. Thompson (ed.), *The Early Chartists* (London, 1971), p. 123.

30. Lovett papers, Vol. 2, p. 117, Birmingham Public Library, quoted in Martin, 'Female Chartism', p. 144.

31. Jones, 'Women and Chartism', *History* (1983), 9.

32. Martin, 'Female Chartism', pp. 92–3.

33. Ibid., pp. 120–1 names many other women lecturers.

34. *Northern Star*, 2 July 1842, quoted in ibid., p. 115.

35. *English Chartist Circular*, Vol. I, p. 63, quoted in Martin, 'Female Chartism', p. 63.

36. *Northern Star*, 23 June 1838, quoted in Thompson, 'Women in nineteenth century radical politics', in Oakley and Mitchell (eds), *Rights and Wrongs of Women*, p. 123.

37. Martin, 'Female Chartism', p. 110.

38. See, for some relevant reflections, G. Stedman Jones, 'Working-Class Culture and Working Class Politics in London, 1870–1900; *Journal of Social History*, VII (1974), 460–508; E. Richards, 'Women in the British economy since about 1700: an interpretation', *History*, 59 (1974), 337–57, and in the French context, Louise A. Tilly, 'Paths of proletarianization: organisation of production, sexual division of labour, and women's collective actions', *Signs* (Winter 1981), 7. 400–17.

39. D. Gittins, *Fair Sex. Family Size and Structure* (London, 1982), *passim* and summarised in her Conclusion.

40. Jones, 'Women and Chartism', *History* (1983), 19.

41. J. Liddington and J. Norris, *One Hand Tied Behind Us: the Rise of the Women's Suffrage Movement* (London, 1978).

42. W. Thomas, *The Philosophic Radicals. Nine Studies in Theory and Practice* (Oxford, 1979), pp. 414–15, quotes Cobden on Harriet Grote, 'Had she been a man, she would have been the leader of a party; he [her husband] is not calculated for it'.

43. Harriet Martineau, *Autobiography*, 2 vols (1877; reprinted London, 1983), Vol. II, pp. 259ff.

44. J. Croker, 'Anti-Corn Law agitation', *Quarterly Review*, 71 (December 1842), 244–314, quoted in P. Hollis, *Women in Public, 1850–1900: Documents of the Victorian Women's Movement* (London, 1979), p. 287.

45. A. Prentice, *History of the Anti-Corn Law League*, 2 vols (London, 1853), I, pp. 170–3.

46. F. K. Prochaska, *Women and Philanthropy in Nineteenth Century England* (London, 1980), pp. 54, 62–4.

47. Prentice, *History of the Anti-Corn Law League*, I, p. 170.

48. Richard Cobden, *Speeches . . .*, ed. J. Bright and T. E. Rogers, 2 vols (London, 1870), Vol. I, p. 257, speech delivered 15 January 1845, at the fair in Covent Garden, quoted in Hollis, *Women in Public*, p. 288. See also, for one view of the League, Mary Howitt, *Autobiography*, ed. Margaret Howitt, 2 vols (London, 1889), Vol. II, p. 36 (13 December 1845), 'We have tickets for the monster meeting at Covent Garden Theatre on Wednesday, when all the great heroes of the League will meet. It is a noble battle that they have fought. And now, thank Heaven! they are just on the eve of their great glorious, and bloodless victory.'

49. S. Drescher, 'Public opinion and the destruction of British colonial slavery', in James Walvin (ed.), *Slavery and British Society 1776–1846* (London, 1982).

50. F. K. Prochaska, 'Women in English philanthropy, 1790–1830', *International Review of Social History*, XIX (1974), p. 429; J. Walvin, 'The propaganda of anti-slavery' in Walvin (ed.), *Slavery and British Society*, p. 61.

51. *Ladies' Anti-Slavery Associations* (n.d.), Goldsmith's Library, University of London, p. 5, quoted by Walvin, *Slavery and British Society*, p. 62.

52. The question is a controversial one. See the contrasting views expressed by P. Hollis, 'Anti-slavery and British working class radicalism in the years of reform', in Christine Bolt and Seymour Drescher (eds), *Anti-slavery, Religion and Reform: essays in memory of Roger Anstey* (London, 1980) and in B. Fladeland, 'Our cause being one and the same': Abolitionists and Chartism' in Walvin (ed.), *Slavery and British Society*.

53. Fladeland, 'Our Cause . . .', pp. 85–95; *HWS*, III, 838.

54. See the two most interesting studies, by Seymour Drescher, 'Two variants of anti-slavery: religious organisation and social mobilisation in Britain and France, 1780–1870', and Serge Daget, 'A model of the French abolitionist movement and its variations', in Bolt and Drescher (eds), *Anti-slavery, Religion, and Reform*.

55. Drescher, 'Two variants of anti-slavery', pp. 56–7.

56. Angela Davis, *Women, Race and Class* (London, 1981), pp. 19–23.

57. Maria Stewart, *Religion and the Pure Principles of Morality, the Sure Foundations on Which We Must Build* (1831), quoted in B. J. Loewenberg and R. Bogin (eds), *Black Women in Nineteenth Century American Life. Their Words, Their Thoughts, Their Feelings* (Philadelphia, 1976), p. 186.

58. 'Mrs Stewart's Farewell Address to Her Friends in the City of Boston, 21 September 1833', quoted in Loewenberg and Bogin, *Black Women in Nineteenth Century American Life*, p. 198.

59. Gerda Lerner, 'Sarah Mapps Douglass', *NAW*, I, 511–13. Angelina Grimké sent to her English friend, the Quaker Elizabeth Pease, the information given her by Sarah Douglass on racial prejudice among American quakers.

60. Quoted in Blanche Glassman Hersh, *The Slavery of Sex. Feminist-Abolitionists in America* (Urbana, Illinois, 1978), p. 8; Merton L. Dillon, 'Elizabeth Chandler', *NAW*, I, 319–20.

61. Hersh, *Slavery of Sex*, Ch. I.

62. On the Grimké sisters, and their effect on the movement, see Gerda Lerner, *The Grimké Sisters from South Carolina, Pioneers for Woman's Rights and Abolition* (New York, 1971); A. Kraditor, *Means and Ends in American Abolitionism. Garrison and His Critics on Strategy and Tactics, 1834–50* (New York, 1967), pp. 39–77; Katherine Du Pré Lumpkin, *The Emancipation of Angelina Grimké* (Chapel Hill, North Carolina, 1974).

63. Lerner, *Grimké Sisters*, p. 161.

64. Ibid., p. 169.

65. *Letters to Catherine Beecher* (1836) in Alice S. Rossi (ed.), *The Feminist Papers, From Adams to de Beauvoir* (New York, 1973), p. 322.

66. 'Pastoral Letter' in Rossi (ed.), *Feminist Papers*, pp. 305–6.

67. Letter xv, *Letters on the Equality of the Sexes* (Boston, 1838).

68. See the analysis by Gerda Lerner, 'The Political Activities of Antislavery Women', in *The Majority Finds its Past. Placing Women in History* (New York, 1979).

69. *HWS*, I, pp. 50–62; Elizabeth Cady Stanton, *Eighty Years and More. Reminiscences 1815–1897* (1898; reprinted New York, 1971), p. 83 gives a very lively account of the Convention.

70. *HWS*, I, pp. 115–17. Loewenberg and Bogin, *Black Women in Nineteenth Century American Life*, pp. 234–6. See also, on this subject, Lerner, 'Black and White Women in Interaction and Confrontation', in *The Majority Finds Its Past*; Davis, *Women, Race and Class*, Chs 2–3.

71. On Sarah Remond, see Loewenberg and Bogin, *Black Women in Nineteenth Century American Life*, pp. 222–33; Dorothy B. Porter, 'Sarah Parker Remond', *NAW*, III, 136–7; 'A Coloured Lady Lecturer', *EWJ*, VII, 269–75.

72. See, on this subject, B. Harrison, *Drink and the Victorians. The Temperance Question in England, 1815–1872* (London, 1971); K. Heasman, *Evangelicals in Action* (London, 1962); R. E. Paulson, *Women's Suffrage and Prohibition. A Comparative Study of Equality and Social Control* (Glenview, Illinois, 1973).

73. Harrison, *Drink and the Victorians*, p. 175.

74. *Northern Star*, 17 October 1840, quoted in Martin, 'Female Chartism', p. 77.

75. Ibid., 19 August 1843, quoted in Martin, 'Female Chartism', p. 78.

76. *English Chartist Circular*, Vol. 2, p. 47, quoted in Martin, 'Female Chartism', p. 78.

77. Harrison, *Drink and the Victorians*, pp. 192–3; Lilian Lewis Shiman, 'The Band of Hope Movement: Respectable Recreation for Working-Class Children', *Victorian Studies*, XVII (1973), pp. 49–74.

78. Clara Lucas Balfour (ed.), *Woman's Work in the Temperance Reformation* (London, 1868), pp. 62ff.

79. Heasman, *Evangelicals in Action*, pp. 131–4; J. M. J. Fletcher, *Mrs Wightman of Shrewsbury. The story of a pioneer in temperance work* (London, 1906).

80. See the analysis of the interests of leading teetotallers in Harrison, *Drink and the Victorians*, pp. 174–5.

81. *EWJ*, VIII (January 1862), 335–46. See also 'Park and Playground versus Gin-Palace and Prison', *EWJ*, I (July 1858), 306–17.

82. *HWS*, I p. 474.

83. *HWS*, I, pp. 472–513.

84. Hersh, *Slavery of Sex*, pp. 47–9.

85. Harriot Hunt, *Glances and Glimpses* . . . (Boston, 1856), pp. 170, 177–9, quoted in Jane B. Donegan, *Women and Men Midwives. Medicine, Morality and Misogyny in Early America* (Westport, Connecticut), p. 213. This account is based on the latter work, Chs 7–8, and on R. H. Shryock, 'Sylvester Graham and the Popular Health Movement, 1830–1870', and 'Women in American Medicine', in *Medicine in America: Historical Essays* (Baltimore, 1966); Alice Felt Tyler, 'Harriot Kezia Hunt', *NAW*, II, 235–7.

86. Elizabeth and Emily Blackwell, 'Medicine as a Profession for Women', *EWJ*, V (May 1860), 149. This paper was originally given as a lecture in New York on 2 December 1859. For Elizabeth Blackwell's views, see also her *Laws of Life with Special Reference to the Physical Education of Girls* (New York, 1852), and her *Pioneer Work in Opening the Medical Profession to Women* (1895); reprinted London, 1914).

87. See 'Physical Training', *EWJ*, I (May 1858), 145–57; 'Extracts from the *Laws of Life, EWJ*, I (May 1858), 189–90: Edwin Chadwick, 'Physical Training', *EWJ*, VI (December 1860) 262–4; B. Taylor, *Eve and the New Jerusalem. Socialism and Femininism in the Nineteenth Century* (London, 1983), pp. 154–6. Relatively little has been written on this movement in Britain, but see Lorna Duffin, 'The Conspicuous Consumptive: woman as an invalid', and P. Atkinson, 'Fitness, feminism, and schooling', in Sara Delamont and Lorna Duffin (eds), *The Nineteenth Century Woman: Her Cultural and Physical World* (London, 1978).

88. See, on this subject, Carroll Smith Rosenberg, *Religion and the Rise of the American City. The New York City Mission Movement, 1812–1870* (Ithaca, 1971); Barbara Berg, *The Remembered Gate: Origins of American Feminism. The Woman and the City, 1800–1860* (New York, 1978).

89. Quoted in Smith Rosenberg, *Religion and the Rise of the American City*, p. 120.

90. See J. Campbell, DD, *Memoirs of David Nasmith: his labours and travels in Great Britain, France, the United States and Canada* (London, 1844), pp. 311ff, 330–8; Heasman, *Evangelicals in Action*, p. 35.

91. Prochaska, *Women and Philanthropy in Nineteenth Century England.*, pp. 182ff.

92. Quoted in ibid., p. 186.

93. See the comments in ibid., pp. 198ff; Fletcher, *Mrs Wightman of Shrewsbury*, pp. 106ff.

94. For a local study which reveals the high 'failure rate' of such refuges; see: F. Finnegan, *Poverty and Prostitution. A study of Victorian prostitutes in York* (Cambridge, 1979), Ch. 6.

95. Quoted in Berg, *The Remembered Gate*, p. 260.

96. L. Abensour, *Le féminisme sous le regime de Louis-Philippe et en 1848*, second edn (Paris, 1913), pp. 52–3; A. Ranvier, 'Une féministe de 1848. Jeanne Deroin', *La révolution de 1848. Bulletin de la société d'histoire de la revolution de 1848*, 4 (1907–8), p. 334; J.-V. Daubié, *Le femme pauvre au dix-neuvième siècle* (Paris, 1866), pp. 254–89.

97. A. Jameson, *Sisters of Charity and the Communion of Labour. Two essays on the social employment of women. New edition . . . with a prefatory Letter to Lord John Russell on the present condition and requirements of the women of England* (London, 1859), p. xxvii.

98. See the study by Judith Walkowitz, *Prostitution and Victorian Society. Women, class and the state* (Cambridge, 1980).

99. F. K. Prochaska, 'Women in English philanthropy, 1790–1830', *International Review of Social History*, XIX (1974), 426–45.

100. *Memoirs of the life of Mrs Catherine Cappe*, written by herself, (London, 1822); C. Cappe, *Thoughts on the desirableness and utility of ladies visiting the female wards of hospitals and lunatic asylums* (London, 1816).

101. Berg, *The Remembered Gate*, p. 165; Mary S. Benson, 'Isabella Marshall Graham', *NAW*, II, 71–2; and 'Joanna Graham Bethune', *NAW*, I, 138–40; Prochaska, *Women and Philanthropy*, p. 30. I am indebted to Prochaska's excellent work for much of the discussion that follows. Also useful is A. Summers, 'A Home from Home – woman's philanthropic work in the nineteenth century', in Sandra Burman (ed.), *Fit Work for Women* (Canberra, 1979). See also the very helpful local study, M. Simey, *Charitable Effort in Liverpool in the Nineteenth Century* (Liverpool, 1951).

102. Prochaska, *Women and Philanthropy*, Chs II–III.

103. A.L., 'On district visitors and the distribution of tracts', *EWJ*, V (July 1860), 322–4.

104. L.N.R. (Ellen Ranyard), *The True Institution of Sisterhood; or, a Message and its Messengers* (London, 1862), p. 8.

105. Ibid., *to which is appended London Bible and Domestic Female Mission. General Principles and Rules*, p. 1.

106. L.N.R. (Ellen Ranyard), *The Missing Link; or, Bible-women in the homes of the London Poor* (London, 1859), *passim* and p. 279ff.

107. B.R.P., 'Second Annual Report of the Ladies' National Association for the Diffusion of Sanitary Knowledge', *EWJ*, III (April 1859), 73–84 (August 1859), 380–7; and 'Charity as a portion of the public vocation of woman,' *EWJ*, III (May 1859) 193–8.

108. B.R.P., 'The details of woman's work in sanitary reform', *EWJ*, III (June 1859), 217–27 (July 1859) 316–24.

109. B.R.P., 'Charity as a portion of the public vocation of women', *EWJ*, III (June 1859), 198.

110. Prochaska, *Women and Philanthropy*, pp. 138–46, 163–73.

111. Ibid., pp. 175ff; Louisa Twining, *Recollections of Workhouse Visiting and Management during twenty-five years* (London, 1880).

112. Twining, *Recollections*, p. 33; 'The Workhouse Visiting Society and the duty of workhouse visitation', *EWJ*, I (August 1858), 381–92.

113. 'Interference', *EWJ*, V (July 1860), 335–40, and see also III (July 1859), 421–4 for a review of the journal of the Workhouse Visiting Society.

114. On Mary Carpenter, see Jo Manton, *Mary Carpenter and the Children of the Streets*

(London, 1976); Harriet Warm Schupf, 'Single women and social reform in mid-nineteenth century England: the case of Mary Carpenter', *Victorian Studies*, XVII (1974), 301–17.

115. 'Hospital for sick children', *EWJ*, V (April 1860), 117–20.

116. Berg, *The Remembered Gate*, p. 220; W. David Lewis, 'Eliza Farnham', *NAW*, I, 598, 560.

117. Berg, *The Remembered Gate*, p. 237; Smith-Rosenberg, *Religion and the Rise of the American City*, Chs 7–9.

118. Ryan, *Cradle of the Middle Classes*, pp. 210–18.

119. *EWJ*, IV (September 1859), p. 69.

120. 'Soeur Rosalie', *EWJ* (November 1859), 152–62 (December 1859), 227–34 (January 1860), 298–311.

121. Daubié, *La femme pauvre au dix-neuvième siècle*, pp. 100ff, 223ff.

122. There is of course a massive literature on this subject. See R. Aubert, J. Beckmann, P. J. Corish and R. Lill, *The Church between Revolution and Restoration* (London, 1981), pp. 227–30, 294–302, and *The Church in the Age of Liberalism* (London, 1981), pp. 92–7, Vols. VII and VIII of H. Jedin and J. Dolan (eds), *History of the Church*. An authoritative study is that of J. B. Duroselle, *Les débuts du catholicisme social en France jusqu'en 1870* (Paris, 1951), which emphasises how the view of social reform pioneered by de Melun in 1839–40 was to be typical of conservative social catholicism in France throughout the nineteenth century, and stressed the mission of members of the upper classes to educate and improve the working classes through their 'patronage', in parallel with the work of the religious orders, p. 186.

123. On the 'Société de la morale chrétienne', see C. Pouthas, *Guizot pendant la restauration, Préparation de l'homme d'état (1814–30)* (Paris, 1923), pp. 342–9; E. Niboyet, *Le vrai livre des femmes* (Paris, 1863), pp. 225ff.

124. See D. Deasey, *Education under Six* (London, 1978), pp. 21–5; 'Madame Marie Pape-Carpentier', *EWJ*, VIII (January 1862) 298–307.

125. P. Pierrard, *La vie ouvrière a Lille sous le Second Empire* (Paris, 1965), Ch. VI, Ch. IX, especially pp. 383–417; Bonnie C. Smith, *Ladies of the Leisure Class. The Bourgeoises of Northern France in the Nineteenth Century* (Princeton, New Jersey, 1981), Ch. 6. For a contemporary view of the proper relationship between public and private charity, by the Napoleonic prefect of the department of the Nièvre, see M. A. de Magnitot, *De l'assistance et de l'extinction de la mendicité* (Paris, 1856).

8.   THE FEMINIST CASE

1. See *The London Journal of Flora Tristan, 1842, or The Aristocracy and the Working Class of England*. A translation of *Promenades dans Londres*, by Jean Hawkes (London, 1982). On Tristan's life, see J. L. Puech, *La vie et l'oeuvre de Flora Tristan* (Paris, 1925); J. Baelen, *La vie de Flora Tristan* (Paris, 1972); D. Desanti, *Flora Tristan: la femme révoltée* (Paris, 1972); C. N. Gattey, *A Biography of Flora Tristan. Gauguin's Astonishing Grandmother* (London, 1970); M. Thibert, *Le féminisme dans le socialisme française* (Paris, 1929), pp. 279–312; S. Joan Moon, 'Feminism and Socialism: the Utopian Synthesis of Flora Tristan' in Marilyn J. Boxer and Jean H. Quataert, *Socialist Women. European Socialist Feminism in the nineteenth and early twentieth centuries* (New York, 1978).

2. Flora Tristan, *The Workers' Union* (1843), trans. with an introduction by Beverly Livingston (Urbana, Illinois, 1983), pp. 42, 119.

3. Ibid., pp. 76–83.

4. Ibid., p. 85.

5. Ibid., p. 15.

6. M. Agulhon, *Une ville ouvrière au temps du socialisme utopique. Toulon de 1815 à 1851*

(Paris, 1920), pp. 154–163, stresses the importance of Tristan's visit in bringing together a small group of leaders, and forming the organisation which was to have effect in the major strike in the Toulon arsenal in 1845.

7. Louis Vasbenter to Tristan, 11 June 1843, and S. Hugont to Tristan, 17 June 1843, in Puech, *Vie et l'oeuvre de Flora Tristan*, pp. 474, 478. See above, p. 199.

8. Flora Tristan, *La Tour de France, journal inédit, 1843–44*. Preface by M. Collinet, notes by J. L. Puech (Paris, 1973), pp. 13–15, 95, 102, 107, 216.

9. See the comments of Pascale Werner, 'Les voix irregulières. Flora Tristan and George Sand, ambivalence d'une filiation', in C. Dufrancatel *et al.* (eds), *L'Histoire sans qualités* (Paris, 1979), p. 62.

10. Studies of Margaret Fuller's life include Arthur W. Brown, *Margaret Fuller* (New York, 1964); M. Wade, *Margaret Fuller: Whetstone of Genius* (New York, 1940); P. Miller, *Margaret Fuller: American Romantic* (New York, 1963); Ann Douglas, *The Feminization of American Culture* (New York, 1977), Ch. 8; Francis E. Kearns, 'Margaret Fuller and the Abolition Movement', *Journal of the History of Ideas*, 25 (1964), 120–7.

11. See her letter to her brother, 23 November 1844, on her visit to Sing Sing prison, M. Fuller, *Woman in the Nineteenth Century, and kindred papers . . .*, ed. A. B. Fuller (Boston, 1874), p. 373; the bibliography of her work by M. Wade (ed.), *The Writings of Margaret Fuller* (New York, 1941), pp. 595–600, contains references to her articles on 'Our City Charities' and the 'Asylum for Discharged Female Convicts' in the *New York Daily Tribune* for 19 March and 19 June 1845 respectively, and a number of others.

12. Margaret Fuller, *Woman in the Nineteenth Century*, with an introduction by Bernard Rosenthal (New York, 1971), pp. 13–14.

13. Ibid., p. 38.

14. Ibid., p. 78.

15. Ibid., p. 115.

16. Ibid., p. 116.

17. Ibid., pp. 146–8.

18. Ibid., pp. 158ff.

19. Ibid., p. 177.

20. See M. Williford, 'Bentham on the Rights of Women', *Journal of the History of Ideas*, 36 (1975), 167–76; James Mill, *Essay on Government* (1821), ed. C. V. Shields (Indianapolis, 1955), pp. 73–4; M. Packe, *Life of John Stuart Mill* (London, 1954), pp. 57–8.

21. *Westminster Review*, 1 (April 1824), 526, quoted in Susan M. Okin, *Women in Western Political Thought* (Princeton, New Jersey, 1979), p. 219.

22. On the relationship between Taylor and Mill, see the excellent introduction by Alice Rossi to her *Essays on Sex Equality* (Chicago, 1972 edn). Rossi reprints here the two early essays on marriage and divorce. See also F. E. Mineka, *The Dissidence of Dissent. The Monthly Repository, 1806–1838* (Chapel Hill, N. Carolina, 1944), Chs V–VII.

23. For the influence of Saint-Simonian ideas on Mill, see R. K. P. Pankhurst, *The Saint Simonians, Mill and Carlyle. A Preface to Modern Thought* (London, 1957); I. W. Mueller, *J. S. Mill and French Thought* (Urbana, Illinois, 1956).

24. The most useful discussions of Mill's view of women are contained in Okin, *Women in Western Political Thought*, Ch. 9; Z. Eisenstein, *The Radical Future of Liberal Feminism* (New York, 1981), pp. 113–44; J. Charvet, *Feminism* (London, 1982), pp. 30–42; Jean Bethke Elshtain, *Public Man, Private Woman, Women in Social and Political Thought* (Oxford, 1981), pp. 132–46; J. Annas, 'Mill and the Subjection of Women', *Philosophy*, 52 (1977), 179–94.

25. Mill, *Subjection of Women*, in *Essays on Sex Equality*, ed. Rossi, p. 146.

26. Ibid., pp. 198ff; Okin, *Women in Western Political Thought*, pp. 220–2.

27. Mill, *Subjection of Women*, in *Essays on Sex Equality*, pp. 170–2.

28. Ibid., p. 178.

29. John Stuart Mill, *Principles of Political Economy with some of their applications to social philosophy* (1848) Books IV and V, ed. D. Winch (Harmondsworth, 1970), pp. 125–6.

30. Consider, for example, John Duguid Milne's use of the *Principles of Political Economy*, on the question of the effects of the expansion of women's employment on levels of wages and patterns of demand, *Industrial and Social Position of Women in the Middle and Lower Ranks* (London, 1857), pp. 317ff; Bessie Rayner Parkes, 'Opinions of John Stuart Mill', *EWJ*, VI, (September 1860), 1–10, and 'Apropos of Political Economy', *EWJ*, VI (October 1860), 73–80.

31. Mill, *Subjection of Women*, in *Essays on Sex Equality*, p. 172.

32. Ibid., p. 237.

33. Ibid., pp. 217ff.

34. Ibid., pp. 227–8.

35. Ibid., p. 234.

36. Ibid., p. 236.

37. L. Abensour, *Le féminisme sous le règne de Louis-Philippe et en 1848*, second edn (Paris, 1913), p. 236.

38. Sullerot, 'Journaux féminins et lutte ouvrière, 1848–51', *La presse ouvrière, 1819–50*. Etude presentée par Jacques Godechot, *Bibliothèque de la révolution de 1848*, Vol. XXIII (Paris, 1966), pp. 96–101.

39. Edith Thomas, *Les femmes de 1848* (Paris, 1948), p. 36.

40. Sullerot, 'Journaux féminins . . .', p. 93.

41. Ranvier, 'Une féministe de 1848', *La révolution de 1848. Bulletin de la société d'histoire de la révolution de 1848*, 4 (1907–8), p. 323.

42. Sullerot, 'Journaux féminins . . .', pp. 102–12.

43. Thomas, *Les femmes de 1848*, p. 44; Christopher H. Johnson, *Utopian Communism in France. Cabet and ithe Icarians, 1839–51* (Ithaca, 1974) pp. 90–3 substantiates Cabet's equivocal view of feminism. Deroin and Niboyet were not disillusioned, though Jenny d'Héricourt realised his inconsistency; Jenny d'Héricourt, *Le femme affranchie, Réponse a MM Michelet, Proudhon, E. de Girardin, A. Comte et aux autres novateurs modernes* (Paris, 1860), pp. 21ff.

44. Thomas, *Les femmes de 1848*, p. 47; Sullerot, 'Journaux féminins . . .', p. 106.

45. Ranvier, 'Une féministe de 1848' pp. 325–8.

46. Sullerot, 'Journaux féminins . . .', p. 109.

47. E. Thomas, *Pauline Roland, Socialisme et féminisme au XIXe siècle* (Paris, 1956), p. 108 and *Les femmes de 1848*, pp. 38ff.

48. Thomas, *Les femmes de 1848*, p. 43.

49. Deroin, *cours de droit social pour les femmes* (Paris, n.d. (1848?)), p. 7.

50. Ranvier, 'Une féministe de 1848', pp. 335–9; A. Zevaès 'Une candidature féministe en 1849', *La révolution de 1848*, 28 (1931–2), pp. 127–34.

51. Sullerot, 'Journaux féminins . . .', p. 120; Ranvier, 'Une féministe de 1848', *La révolution de 1848. Bulletin de la société d'histoire de la révolution de 1848*, 5 (1908–9), pp. 492–8.

52. See, on the future development of feminist activity in France, P. K. Bidelman, *Pariahs Stand Up! The Founding of the Liberal Feminist Movement in France, 1858—1889* (Westport, Connecticut, 1982); J. F. McMillan, *Housewife or Harlot. The place of women in French society, 1870–1940* (Brighton, 1981), Ch. IV; C. Sowerwine, *Sisters or Citizens? Women and socialism in France since 1876* (Cambridge, 1982).

53. E. Thomas, *The Women Incendiaries* (London, 1966), pp. 5–7.

54. An account is given of this controversy in d'Héricourt, *La femme affranchie*, pp. 126ff.

55. P.-.J. Proudhon, *De la Justice dans la Révolution et dans l'église. Nouveau principes de philosophie pratique*, 3 vols (Paris, 1858). See pp. 335–76, 430ff.

56. Juliette Lamber, *Idées anti-proudhoniennes sur l'amour, la femme et le mariage* (Paris, 1858), pp. 80ff.

57. Ibid., p. 100.

58. Ibid., p. 166.

59. Bidelman, *Pariahs Stand Up!* p. 46, quotes the early twentieth-century feminist Jane Misme on Lamber's work.

60. D'Héricourt, *La femme affranchie*, Vol. I, p. 185.

61. Ibid., Vol. II, p. 104.

62. Ibid., Vol. II, pp. 177ff.

63. Ibid., Vol. II, pp. 210–22.

64. Bidelman, *Pariahs Stand Up!* pp. 47–9.

65. McMillan, *Housewife or Harlot*, p. 85, and 'Perspectives on the History of French Women', *European Studies Review*, 13 (1983), 483–6.

66. Relevant works include T. Zeldin, *France 1848–1945* (Oxford, 1973), Vol. I, Chs 1–6, especially Ch. 5; Adeline Daumard, *La bourgeoisie parisienne de 1815 à 1848* (Paris, 1967), pp. 328–36; David S. Landes, 'French entrepreneurship and growth in the nineteenth century', *Journal of Economic History*, IX (1949), 45–61; the view expressed in the latter work is controversial and may be considered with the discussion in, for instance, T. Kemp, *Economic Forces in French History* (London, 1971), Ch. VI; Robert Wheaton, 'Recent Trends in the Historical Study of the French Family', in *Family and Sexuality in French History* (Philadelphia, 1980).

67. *HWS*, I, 67–73. On this subject I have relied upon Blanche Hersh, *The Slavery of Sex. Feminist-Abolitionists in America* (Urbana, Illinois, 1978); Ellen DuBois, *Feminism and Suffrage. The emergence of an independent women's movement in America, 1848—69* (Ithaca, New York, 1980); Eleanor Flexner, *A Century of Struggle. The Woman's Rights Movement in the United States* (New York, 1959); Keith Melder, *The Beginnings of Sisterhood. The American Woman's Rights Movement, 1800–1850* (New York, 1977); Alice S. Rossi (ed.), *The Feminist Papers. From Adams to de Beauvoir* (New York, 1973).

68. Elizabeth Cady Stanton, *Eighty Years and More. Reminiscences 1815–97* (1898; reprinted New York, 1971), p. 148.

69. See A. Kraditor, *Means and Ends in American Abolitionism. Garrison and his Critics on Strategy and Tactics, 1834–50* (New York, 1967), p. 73.

70. *HWS*, I, p. 75.

71. Ibid., I, pp. 46, 246–9, 283–9; Mary Ryan, *Cradle of the Middle Class. The family in Oneida County, New York, 1790–1865* (Cambridge, 1981), pp. 226–9; Hersh, *Slavery of Sex*, pp. 201–2; 'Mathilde Anneke', *NAW*, I, 50–1.

72. This discussion follows Hersh, *Slavery of Sex*, Ch. 4 throughout.

73. Ibid., p. 195.

74. *HWS*, I, p. 522.

75. Hersh, *Slavery of Sex*, p. 111.

76. *HWS*, I, p. 719.

77. See Bert James Loewenberg and Ruth Bogin, *Black Women in Nineteenth Century American Life. Their Words, Their Thought, Their Feelings* (Philadelphia, 1976), pp. 243–51, 283–95.

78. Rossi (ed.), *The Feminist Papers*, pp. 265–81.

79. Keith E. Melder, *The Beginnings of Sisterhood. The American Woman's Rights Movement, 1800–1850* (New York, 1977), p. 158; *HWS*, I, p. 196.

80. Catherine Barmby, 'The Demand for the Emancipation of Woman, Politically and Socially', *New Tracts for the Times*, 1 (1848), reprinted in Barbara Taylor, *Eve and the New Jerusalem. Socialism and Feminism in the Nineteenth Century* (London, 1983), pp. 386–93.

81. 'Woman's Industrial Independence', *Apostle and Chronicle of the Communist Church*, 1 (August 1848), reprinted in Morton and Saville, 'Goodwyn and Catherine Barmby', J. M. Bellamy and J. Saville (eds), *Dictionary of Labour Biography*, Vol. VI, pp. 10–18.

82. G. J. Holyoake, *Sixty Years in an Agitator's Life* (London, 1893), pp. 222–5.

83. Caroline E. Martin, 'Female Chartism: a study in politics', M.A. thesis,

University of Wales (1973), pp. 108–10; C. Rover, *Women's Suffrage and Party Politics in Britain, 1866–1914* (London, 1967), pp. 10–11.

84. *Northern Star*, 8 May 1852, quoted in Martin, 'Female Chartism', p. 129.

85. E. Royle, 'Harriet Teresa Law (1831–97): Feminist, Secularist and Radical', in Bellamy and Saville (eds), *Dictionary of Labour Biography*, Vol. v, pp. 134–6; Taylor, *Eve and the New Jerusalem*, pp. 284–5.

86. Quoted in Helen Blackburn, *Women's Suffrage. A Record of the Women's Suffrage Movement in the British Isles . . .* (1902; reprinted New York, 1971), p. 14.

87. W. J. Fox, 'A Political and Social Anomaly', *MR*, vi (1832), 637–642.

88. Mary Leman Grimstone, 'Quaker Women', *MR*, ix (1835), 30–7; Margaret Mylne, 'Woman and her Social Position', *Westminster Review*, xxxv (1841), 24–52.

89. Quoted in Blackburn, *Women's Suffrage*, p. 19.

90. Anne Richelieu Lamb, *Can Woman Regenerate Society?* (London, 1844), p. 54; Mrs Hugo Reid, *A Plea for Woman: being a vindication of the importance and extent of her natural sphere of action* (Edinburgh, 1843), Chs v–vi.

91. Harriet Taylor Mill, 'Enfranchisement of Women', *Westminster Review*, lv (July 1851), 289–312, reprinted in Rossi (ed.), *Essays on Sex Equality*, p. 105.

92. Mrs Henry Davis Pochin ('Justitia'), *The Right of Women to Exercise an Elective Franchise* (1855). Reprinted for the National Society for Women's Suffrage . . . (Manchester, 1873), p. 17.

93. Ibid., p. 27.

94. Blackburn, *Women's Suffrage*, pp. 71–2.

95. *HWS*, iii, pp. 838–9.

96. Lee Holcombe, *Wives and Property. Reform of the Married Women's Property Law in Nineteenth Century England* (Oxford, 1983), p. 58.

97. There are no adequate studies of this group. See Holcombe, *Wives and Property* Ch. 4, and *Victorian Ladies at Work. Middle Class Working Women in England and Wales, 1850–1914* (Newton Abbot, 1973), Ch. 1, besides the *Dictionary of National Biography*. There is a short article by M. Maison, 'Insignificant Objects of Desire', *The Listener*, 86 (1971), 105–7.

98. On Anne Clough, see Deborah Gorham, *The Victorian Girl and the Feminine Ideal* (London, 1982), pp. 135–41, and M. Simey, *Charitable Effort in Liverpool in the Nineteenth Century* (Liverpool, 1951), pp. 64ff; on the leadership of the Ladies National Association, see Judith Walkowitz, *Prostitution and Victorian Society. Women, class and the state* (Cambridge, 1980), Ch. 6.

99. Blackburn, *Women's Suffrage*, pp. 96–100.

100. See Gorham, *The Victorian Girl and the Feminine Ideal*, pp. 141–3.

101. Anna Jameson, *Sisters of Charity and the Communion of Labour. Two essays on the social employments of women. New edition . . . with a prefatory letter to Lord John Russell on the Present Condition and Requirements of the women of England* (London, 1859), p. xxx.

102. Ibid., p. xxvii.

103. Bessie Rayner Parkes, 'What can educated women do'?', *EWJ*, iv (January 1860), 289–98, and 'A year's experience in women's work', *EWJ*, vi (October 1860), 112–21; Elizabeth and Emily Blackwell, 'Medicine as a profession for women', *EWJ*, v (May 1860), 145–60; A.R.L. (Anne Richelieu Lamb?) 'Organisation', *EWJ*, vi (January 1861), 331–9, and see also her 'Our Ten Thousand', *EWJ*, iv (January 1860), 31.

104. M. Hill, *The Religious Order. A study of virtuoso religion and its legitimation in the nineteenth century Church of England* (London, 1973), p. 10, and see the stimulating discussions on pp. 167ff and pp. 271ff.

105. M.M.H. (Matilda Mary Hays), 'Florence Nightingale and the English Soldier', *EWJ*, i (April 1858), 76–7 and 'Female Industrial employments in the South of Ireland, *EWJ*, i (July 1858), 330–8; Bessie Rayner Parkes, 'Opinions of John Stuart

Mill, *EWJ*, vi (September 1860), 1–10, and 'Apropos of Political Economy', *EWJ*, vi (October 1860), 73–80.

106. Walkowitz, *Prostitution and Victorian Society*, p. 131.

107. Sullerot, 'Journaux féminins et lutte ouvrière', p. 107.

108. See on the early stages of the suffrage movement, Rover, *Women's Suffrage and Party Politics*, pp. 1–6; Blackburn, *Women's Suffrage*, pp. 44–100; Ray Strachey, *The Cause. A Short History of the Women's Movement in Great Britain* (1928; reprinted London, 1978), Ch. vi.

109. 'The Enfranchisement of Women', *EWJ*, xiii (July 1864), 296.

110. Ibid., p. 296.

111. The texts of the letters of June 1851 are given in *HWS*, i, pp. 234–7, and in *Northern Star*, 14 June 1851, quoted in Martin, 'Female Chartism', p. 110.

112. *HWS*, ii, pp. 94–6.

CONCLUSION

1. See the stimulating discussion of the moral qualities of nineteenth-century feminism in G. Fraisse, 'Les bavardes. Féminisme et moralisme', in C. Dufrancatel *et al.* (eds), *L'histoire sans qualités* (Paris, 1979).

2. N. Cott, *The Bonds of Womanhood. 'Woman's Sphere' in New England, 1780–1835* (New Haven, 1977), p. 204.

NOTES TO PLATES

1. (Plate 1) King, Queen and Dauphin are driven by a crowd of women to Paris from Versailles. The woman carrying a man's head on a pike is saying to the male figure in jackboots, Lafayette, 'If you are a traitor, this is how we shall treat you'. Next to Lafayette, a group of women carry a banner headed 'District des Cordeliers'. Some drag a large wagon full of sacks of corn, saying, 'God be praised that we shall not want any more! we have our baker and the butcher and the cook's boy, and they will not escape us again'. For descriptions of this and subsequent prints, I am indebted to the relevant volumes of the *Catalogue of Prints and Drawings in the British Museum. Division I. Political and Personal Satires*, Vols 1–4 by F. G. Stephens, Vols 5–11 by M. D. George, Vols 1–2 ed. G. W. Reid, 11 vols (London, 1870–1954).

2. (Plate 2) Edmund Burke is scourged by, among other male radicals, three women writers known to be sympathetic to the French Revolution. Helen Maria Williams, on the far left, who did not in fact write a reply to Burke, says, 'Though I decline shivering lances in this glorious cause I think I made him feel the full force of a Cat-o-nine tails!'. Mrs Barbauld, an active dissenting supporter of Dr Richard Price, is shown standing next to him, violently scourging Burke, and saying to Price, 'Let me alone, Doctor, for exertion in this business; the most incorrigible Urchin in my School never felt from my hands what this Assassin of Liberty shall now feel!'. Catherine Macaulay, on the far right, was the author of the *Observations on the Reflections of the Right Hon. Edmund Burke on the Revolution in France, in a Letter to the Earl of Stanhope* (London, 1790). She says, referring to her own *History of England*, 8 vols, (London, 1763–83), 'Tickle may do as he pleases with the pen, but I am determined to tickle to some tune with this instrument in my hands! The hypocrisy of Cromwell was nothing to turn a bout!'. The three women are wearing tricolour favours.

3. (Plate 5) Three well-dressed visitors to the cottage of the McClarty family survey the dirt and disorder. The lady, Mrs Mason, asks Mrs McClarty, who is sweeping the earth floor, 'Why do you not make your Daughters assit [sic] you?' She answers 'Indeed

my Daughters can clean the House, or Milk the Ky as wee'l as I can when they like but its no often that they will be Fashed'. Notice the cobwebs on the wall, the chickens pecking at the pot and plates on the floor, the cat lapping from the bowl on the dresser, and the manure heap right outside the door.

4. (Plate 10) The woman speaker holds in her hand a document marked 'Female – Resolutions for pushing things forward', and says: '(Dear Sisters) I feel great pleasure in holding this *thing* 'um-bob in my hand, as we see our Sweethearts, and Husbands, are such fumblers at the main *thing*, we must of course take the *thing*, in our own hands, – we must not leave a stone unturn'd – we must exert every *limb*, – we must pursue the *point* as far as it will go, a REFORM is very much wanted (among us) though we should not put on Armour, or carry Guns, (it is my opinion) Though we should be start [sic] naked, we could make the whole Army *Stand*! – It is our duty as Wives to assist our Husbands in every *Push* and *Turn*, by that means we shall Increase and *Multiply* in our *under* takings.' The woman on her right has a sheaf of papers marked 'Petition' under her arm, and holds out a paper inscribed 'The Whole Duty of Women'. Two girls are holding up a Cap of Liberty on a pole. An older man hits his wife, saying 'Come home and get Dinner ready you Old Baggage I'll Reform you'. A young man says to a pretty woman 'I feel for your Sex my Dear', putting his hand on her breast.

5. (Plate 11) The full title of this print is 'To Henry Hunt Esq as Chairman of the Meeting assembled on St Peter's Field, on the 16th of August, 1819, and to the Female Reformers of Manchester and the adjacent towns who were exposed to and suffered from the Wanton and Furious Attack made on them by that British Armed Force the Manchester and Cheshire Yeomanry Cavalry'. A woman holds a banner inscribed Manchester Female Reform on which a female figure tramples on Corruption. To the left, below the platform, a woman, supported by others, is pierced by the sword of one of the yeomanry.

Bibliography

The following is intended as a brief selective guide to the most useful and accessible recent works, mainly in English.

COMPARATIVE AND GENERAL STUDIES

Michael Anderson, *Approaches to the history of the Western family, 1500–1914* (London, 1980)

Clive Banks, *Faces of Feminism. A Study of Feminism as a Social Movement* (Oxford, 1981)

Patricia Branca, *Women in Europe since 1750* (London, 1978)

Renate Bridenthal and Claudia Koonz, *Becoming Visible: Women in European History* (Boston, 1977)

Zillah Eisenstein, *The Radical Future of Liberal Feminism* (New York, 1981)

Jean Bethke Elshtain, *Public Man, Private Woman. Women in Social and Political Thought* (Oxford, 1981).

R. Evans, *The Feminists, Women's Emancipation Movements in Europe, America and Australasia, 1840–1920* (London, 1977)

Erna A. Hellerstein, Lesley P. Hume and Karen M. Offen (eds), *Victorian Women. A documentary account of women's lives in nineteenth-century England, France and the United States* (Brighton, 1981)

Susan M. Okin, *Women in Western Political Thought* (Princeton, 1979)

Ross Evans Paulson, *Women's Suffrage and Prohibition: a comparative study of equality and social control* (Glenview, Illinois, 1973)

Alice S. Rossi (ed.), *The Feminist Papers. From Adams to de Beauvoir* (New York, 1973)

Louise Tilly and Joan Scott, *Women, Work and Family* (New York, 1978)

BRITAIN

Sally Alexander, 'Women's work in nineteenth century London: 1820–1850', in Juliet Mitchell and Ann Oakley (eds), *The Rights and Wrongs of Women* (London, 1976)

Françoise Basch, *Relative Creatures. Victorian Women in Society and the Novel* (New York, 1974)

Patricia Branca, *Silent Sisterhood. Middle Class Women in the Victorian Home* (London, 1975)

Duncan Bythell, *The Sweated Trades. Outwork in Nineteenth Century Britain* (London, 1978)

Leonore Davidoff, 'Mastered for life: servant and wife in Victorian England', *Journal of Social History*, 7 (1974), 406–28

——, 'The rationalization of housework', in D. Barker and S. Allen (eds), *Dependence and Exploitation in Work and Marriage* (London, 1976)

——, 'Class and gender in nineteenth-century England: the diaries of Arthur J. Munby and Hannah Culwick', *Feminist Studies*, 5 (1979), 87–141

——, 'The separation of home and work? Landladies and lodgers in nineteenth and twentieth century England', in Sandra Burman (ed.), *Fit Work for Women* (Canberra, 1979)

——, *'Life is duty, praise and prayer': some contributions of the new women's history* Fawcett Library Papers, No. 4 (London, 1981)

——, Howard Newby and Jean L'Esperance, 'Landscape with figures: home and community in English society', in Juliet Mitchell and Ann Oakley (eds), *The Rights and Wrongs of Women* (London, 1976)

Caroline Davidson, *'A Woman's Work is Never Done'. A History of Housework in the British Isles, 1650–1950* (London, 1982)

Sara Delamont and Lorna Duffin (eds), *The Nineteenth Century Woman: Her Cultural and Physical World* (London, 1978)

Deborah Gorham, *The Victorian Girl and the Feminine Ideal* (London, 1982)

Catherine Hall, 'The early formation of Victorian domestic ideology', in S. Burman (ed.), *Fit Work for Women* (Canberra, 1979)

——, 'Gender divisions and class formation in the Birmingham middle class, 1750–1850', in R. Samuel (ed.), *People's History and Socialist Theory* (London, 1981)

Margaret Hewitt, *Wives and Mothers in Victorian Industry* (London, 1958)

Lee Holcombe, *Victorian Ladies at Work. Middle Class Working Women in England and Wales, 1850–1914* (Newton Abbot, 1973)

——, *Wives and Property. Reform of the Married Women's Property Law in Nineteenth Century England* (Oxford, 1983)

Patricia Hollis, *Women in Public, 1850–1900: Documents of the Victorian Women's Movement* (London, 1979)

Pamela Horn, *The Rise and Fall of the Victorian Servant* (Dublin, 1975)

Jane Humphries, 'Protective legislation, the capitalist state and working class men: the case of the 1842 Mines Regulation Act', *Feminist Review*, 7 (1981), 1–33

Angela John, *By the Sweat of their Brow. Women Workers at Victorian Coal Mines* (London, 1980)

David Jones, 'Women and Chartism', *History*, 68 (February 1983), 1–21

Josephine Kamm, *Hope Deferred. Girls' Education in English History* (London, 1965)

John Killham, *Tennyson and 'The Princess'. Reflections of an Age* (London, 1958)

Sheila Lewenhak, *Women and Trade Unions. An Outline History of Women in the British Trade Union Movement* (London, 1977)

Theresa McBride, *The Domestic Revolution. The Modernization of Household Service in England and France, 1820–1920* (London, 1976)

Angus Maclaren, *Birth Control in Nineteenth Century England* (London, 1978)

Ivy Pinchbeck, *Women Workers and the Industrial Revolution, 1750–1850* (1930, reprinted London, 1981)

Linda Pollock, *Forgotten children. Parent-Child relations from 1500 to 1900* (Cambridge, 1983)

Francis K. Prochaska, *Women and Philanthropy in Nineteenth Century England* (Oxford, 1980)

Eric Richards, 'Women in the British economy since about 1700: an interpretation', *History*, 59 (1974), 337–57

Katharine Rogers, *Feminism in Eighteenth Century England* (Brighton, 1982)

Elaine Showalter, *A Literature of Their Own. British Women Novelists from Brontë to Lessing* (London, 1978)

Lawrence Stone, *The Family, Sex and Marriage in England, 1500–1800* (London, 1977)

Barbara Taylor, *Eve and the New Jerusalem. Socialism and Feminism in the Nineteenth Century* (London, 1983)

Malcolm I. Thomis and Jennifer Grimmett, *Women in Protest, 1800–1850* (London, 1982)

Dorothy Thompson, 'Women and nineteenth century radical politics: a lost dimension', in Juliet Mitchell and Ann Oakley (eds), *The Rights and Wrongs of Women* (London, 1976)

Nancy Tomes, ' "A Torrent of Abuse": crimes of violence between working-class men and women in London, 1840–1858', *Journal of Social History*, 11 (1978) 328–45

Martha Vicinus (ed.), *Suffer and be Still. Women in the Victorian Age* (Bloomington and London, 1972)

——, (ed.), *The Widening Sphere: Changing Roles of Victorian Women* (Bloomington and London, 1977)

David Vincent, *Bread, Knowledge, and Freedom. A study of nineteenth-century working-class autobiography* (London, 1981)

Judith Walkowitz, *Prostitution and Victorian Society. Women, class and the state* (Cambridge, 1980)

Frances Widdowson, *Going Up into the Next Class. Women and Elementary Teacher Training, 1840–1914*, Explorations in Feminism, No. 7 (London, 1980)

FRANCE

Jane Abray, 'Feminism in the French Revolution', *American Historical Review*, 80 (1975), 43–62

M. Agulhon, *Marianne into Battle. Republican Imagery and Symbolism in France, 1789–1880* (1979), translated by Janet Lloyd (Cambridge, 1981)

Patrick Kay Bidelman, *Pariahs Stand Up! The Founding of the Liberal Feminist Movement in France, 1858–1889* (Westport, Connecticut, 1982)

Margaret H. Darrow, 'French noblewomen and the new domesticity, 1750–1850', *Feminist Studies*, 5 (Spring, 1979), 41–65

Geneviève Fraisse, 'Les bavardes. Féminisme et moralisme', C. Dufrancatel *et al.* (eds), *L'Histoire sans qualités* (Paris, 1979)

P. Hoffman, *La femme dans la pensée des lumières* (Paris, 1977)

Olwen Hufton, 'Women in revolution, 1789–96', *Past and Present*, 53 (1971), 90–108

Eva Jacobs, W. H. Barber, Jean H. Bloch, F. W. Leakey and Eileen Le Breton (eds), *Women and Society in Eighteenth-century France. Essays in honour of John Stephenson Spink* (London, 1979)

Darline Gay Levy, Harriet Branson Applewhite and Mary Durham Johnson (eds), *Women in Revolutionary Paris, 1789–95* (Chicago, 1979)

Theresa McBride, *The Domestic Revolution. The Modernization of Household Service in England and France, 1820–1920* (London, 1976)

James F. McMillan, *Housewife or Harlot: the Place of Women in French Society 1870–1940* (Brighton, 1981)

Francoise Mayeur, *L'Education des filles en France au XIXe siècle* (Paris, 1979)

Michelle Perrot, 'De la nourrice à l'employée . . . Travaux de femmes dans la France du XIXe siècle', *Le mouvement social* (October–December 1978), 105, 3–10

——, 'La femme populaire rebelle', C. Dufrancatel *et al.* (eds), *L'Histoire sans qualités* (Paris, 1979)

Roderick C. Phillips, *Family Breakdown in late Eighteenth-century France. Divorces in Rouen, 1792–1803* (Oxford, 1980)

Barbara Corrado Pope, 'Maternal education in France, 1815–48', *Proceedings of the Third Annual Meeting of the Western Society for French History, 4–6 December 1975* (Texas, 1976)

——, 'Revolution and retreat: upper class French women after 1789', in Carol R. Berkin and Clara M. Lovett (eds), *Women, War and Revolution* (New York, 1980)

Martine Segalen, *Love and Power in the Peasant Family. Rural France in the Nineteenth Century* (Oxford, 1983)

Bonnie G. Smith, *Ladies of the Leisure Class. The Bourgeoises of Northern France in the Nineteenth Century* (Princeton, NJ, 1981)

Laura S. Strumingher, *Women and the Making of the Working Class: Lyon 1830–1870* (St Albans, Vermont, 1979)

Evelyne Sullerot, *Histoire de la presse féminine en France, des origines à 1848* (Paris, 1966)

——, 'Journaux féminins et lutte ouvrière 1848–50', *La presse ouvrière, 1819–50*. Etude présentée par Jacques Godechot, Bibliothèque de la révolution de 1848, Vol. XXIII (Paris, 1966)

Edith Thomas, *Les femmes de 1848* (Paris, 1848)

Robert Wheaton (ed.), *Family and Sexuality in French History* (Philadelphia, 1980)

T. Zeldin, *France 1848–1945*, 2 vols (Oxford, 1973–7) Vol. I, *Ambition, Love and Politics*.

THE UNITED STATES

Barbara Berg, *The Remembered Gate: Origins of American Feminism. The Woman and the City. 1800–1860* (New York, 1978)

Nancy F. Cott, *The Bonds of Womanhood. 'Woman's Sphere' in New England, 1780–1835* (New Haven and London, 1977)

——, 'Passionlessness: an interpretation of Victorian sexual ideology, 1790–1850', *Signs*, 4 (1978), 219–36

Angela Davis, *Women, Race and Class* (London, 1981)

Carl N. Degler, *At Odds. Women and the Family in America from the Revolution to the Present* (New York, 1980)

Ann Douglas, *The Feminization of American Culture* (New York, 1977)

Thomas W. Dublin, *Women at Work. The Transformation of Work and Community in Lowell, Massachusetts, 1826–1860* (New York, 1979)

Ellen DuBois, *Feminism and Suffrage. The Emergence of an Independent Women's Movement in America, 1848–1869* (Ithaca, 1978)

Barbara L. Epstein, *The Politics of Domesticity. Women, Evangelism and Temperance in Nineteenth Century America* (Middletown, Connecticut, 1981)

John Mack Faragher, *Women and Men on the Overland Trail* (New Haven and London, 1979)

Eleanor Flexner, *A Century of Struggle. The Woman's Rights Movement in the United States* (New York, 1959)

Philip Foner, *Women and the American Labor Movement, from colonial times to the eve of World War I* (New York, 1979)

Linda Gordon, *Woman's Body, Woman's Right. A Social History of Birth Control in America* (New York, 1976)

Herbert Gutman, *The Black Family in Slavery and Freedom, 1750–1925* (New York, 1976)

Blanche Glassman Hersh, *The Slavery of Sex. Feminist-Abolitionists in America* (Urbana, Illinois, 1978)

Bell Hooks, *Ain't I a Woman. Black Women and Feminism* (Boston, 1981)

Julie Roy Jeffrey, *Frontier Women. The Trans-Mississippi West, 1840–1880* (New York, 1979)

David Katzman, *Seven Days a Week: Women and Domestic Service in Industrialising America* (New York, 1978)

Linda Kerber, *Women of the Republic. Intellect and Ideology in Revolutionary America* (Chapel Hill, 1980)

Gerda Lerner, *The Majority Finds its Past. Placing Women in History* (New York, 1979)

Bert James Loewenberg and Ruth Bogin (eds), *Black Women in Nineteenth Century American Life. Their Words, Their Thoughts, Their Feelings* (Philadelphia, 1976)

Julie Matthaei, *An Economic History of American Women* (New York, 1982)

Keith E. Melder, *The Beginnings of Sisterhood. The American Woman's Rights Movement, 1800–1850* (New York, 1977)

Mary Beth Norton, *Liberty's Daughters. The Revolutionary Experience of American Women, 1750–1800* (Boston, Toronto, 1980)

Mary Ryan, *Womanhood in America from Colonial Times to the Present* (New York, 1975)

——, *Cradle of the Middle Class. The family in Oneida County, New York, 1790–1865* (Cambridge, 1981)

Anne Firor Scott, *The Southern Lady. From Pedestal to Politics, 1830–1930* (Chicago, 1970)

Kathryn Kish Sklar, *Catherine Beecher. A Study in American Domesticity* (New Haven and London, 1973)

Carroll Smith-Rosenberg, 'The female world of love and ritual: relations between women in nineteenth-century America', *Signs*, I (1975), 1–29

Susan Strasser, *Never Done. A History of American Housework* (New York, 1982)

Barbara Welter, 'The cult of true womanhood, 1820–1860', *American Quarterly*, 18 (1966), 151–75

——, 'The feminisation of American religion, 1800–1860', in Mary J. Hartman and Lois Banner (eds), *Clio's Consciousness Raised. New perspectives on the history of women* (New York, 1974)

FURTHER BIBLIOGRAPHICAL AIDS

Elizabeth Fox-Genovese, 'Placing women in history', *New Left Review*, 133 (1982), 5–29

Linda Frey, Marsha Frey and Joanne Schneider (eds), *Women in Western European History. A Select Chronological, Geographical, and Topical Bibliography, from Antiquity to the French Revolution* (Brighton, 1982)

Olwen Hufton and Joan W. Scott, 'Women in history: a survey', *Past and Present*, 101 (1983), 125–57

S. Barbara Kanner, 'The women of England in a century of social change, 1815–1914. A select bibliography', Part I, in M. Vicinus (ed.), *Suffer and be Still. Women in the Victorian Age* (Bloomington and London, 1972); Part II in M. Vicinus (ed.), *A Widening Sphere. Changing Roles of Victorian Women* (Bloomington and London, 1977)

——, (ed.), *The Women of England from Anglo-Saxon Times to the Present. Interpretive Bibliographical Essays* (Hamden, Connecticut, 1979)

Barbara Sicherman, E. William Monter, Joan W. Scott and Kathryn K. Sklar, *Recent United States Scholarship on the History of Women* (Washington DC, 1980)

Index

Abbott, J. S. C., 119
Abbott, Jacob, 119
Abensour, Léon, 291
Abolitionist movement:
  black women in, 248–9, 253, 306; in
    Britain, 245–8; and the Chartist
    movement, 247; and feminism,
    247, 272, 301–4, 306, 308, 313;
    315, 322; in France, 247; and the
    temperance movement, 257; in
    the United States, 248–54
Abortion, 226
Academies, female, 41–2, 126–7
Acton, William, 209
Adams, William Bridges, 115, 116
Advocate of Moral Reform, 260–1
Aelders, Etta Palm d', 33, 34, 48, 49, 50,
  68
Agricultural labour, women's, 150–4
Aguilar, Grace, 113
Agulhon, Maurice, 234, 280
Aimé-Martin, Louis, 123–4
Alcott, Bronson, 120, 280, 281
Alcott, Louisa, 120, 280
Alexander, William, 30
American Indians, women's position
  among, 24–5, 26, 30, 86, 130
American Revolution, 34–42, 67–8; *see
  also* republicanism
Anneke, Mathilde, 303
Anthony, Susan B., 302, 305
Anti-Corn Law League, 314, 353n
  women's involvement in, 244–5
Anti-slavery, *see* abolitionist movement
Ashurst (Stansfeld), Caroline, 315
Ashurst (Venturi), Emilie, 315
Ashurst, (Biggs), Matilda, 247, 313, 315
Ashurst, William, 247, 315
Association, among men, 205, 234–5,
  243, 277, 323

Association, among women:
  and the abolitionist movement,
    245–54, 299; and the Anti-Corn
    Law League, 244–5, 254, 299;
    Catherine Watkins Barmby on,
    307–8; and the Catholic Church,
    98–9; and colleges for women,
    130; and evangelicalism, 74,
    78–82, 93–6, 100–1, 262–4, 322–3;
    and female Chartism, 238–43,
    255; and feminism, 1–2, 276–7,
    298–9, 316–18, 320, 322–4; and a
    free press, 236–7; and health
    reform, 258–9; and moral reform,
    259–62; and the New Poor Law,
    203–4; and informal networks,
    214–15; and parliamentary re-
    form, 235–6; and philanthropy,
    95–6, 263–75, 316–18, 322; and
    'sanitary reform', 266–7; in sister-
    hoods, 317; and temperance,
    255–8; working-class women and,
    293–300, 323; *see also*: Bible
    Societies; clubs; crowd action;
    friendly societies; Maternal
    Associations; trade unionism
Austen, Jane, 71, 129
Austin, Sarah, 134

Bachellery, Joséphine, 138
Bage, Robert, 56, 59–60
Bagley, Sarah G., 175, 176
Balfour, Clara Lucas, 256
Band of Hope, 255
Baptists, 79–80, 83, 85, 87, 91
Barbeyrac, Jean, 12
Barmby, Catherine Watkins ('Kate'),
  105, 117, 282, 307–8
Barmby, John Goodwyn, 105, 117, 282,
  308

Bayly, Mary, 256–7
Bazaars, 244–5, 264
Beale, Dorothea, 132
Becker, Lydia, 312
Bedford College, 131–2, 228, 253, 314
Beecher, Catherine, 2, 120, 121–2, 126, 127–8, 139:
  and the abolitionist movement, 251, 305; her educational philosophy, 121–2; on the teaching profession for women, 127–8
Beecher, Lyman, 78, 79, 119, 121
Bennett, John, 30–1
Bentham, Jeremy, 284
Bethune, Joanna, 263
Bible Christians, 93, 255–6
Bible Societies, 91, 93, 94–5, 100, 265–6, 271
Bidelman, Patrick Kay, 298
Biggs, see Matilda Ashurst
Birth control, 4, 208, 223, 224–7
Black women:
  and the abolitionist movement, 248–9, 253, 306; education of, 147; and employment, 154, 181–2; and evangelicalism, 85–6; family life of, 196–7; and feminism, 248–9, 253, 306; free, 147, 154, 181–2, 248–9; and racial stereotypes, 196–7; and the sexual division of labour, 154; under slavery, 154, 197, 182, 248
Blackwell sisters, 317, 320
Blackwell, Anna, 228
Blackwell, Antoinette Brown, 306
Blackwell, Elizabeth, 135, 187, 258, 271, 302, 318
Blackwell, Henry, 227, 302
Blanc, Eleonore, 280
Bloomer, Amelia, 257–8, 303
Bodichon, see under Smith for Barbara Leigh Smith
Bonald, Louis de, 97
Boucherett, Jessie, 185, 314, 319
Bourne, Hugh, 92–3
Bowers, Marion, 265
Bradlaugh, Charles, 237
Branca, Patricia, 210, 213
Bright, John, 256
British and Foreign Schools Society, 132, 141–3
Brontë, Charlotte, 217:
  and Jane Eyre, 230

Brougham, Henry, 115
Brown, Charles Brockden, 40–1
Browning, Elizabeth Barrett, 228
Bryan, Margaret, 129
Buchan, Luckie, 101–2, 103, 217
Buckminster, Rev. Joseph, 75
Burke, Edmund, 56, Plate 2, 363n
Bushnell, Horace, 119
Buss, Frances Mary, 132, 315
Butler, Josephine, 262, 315

Cabet, Etienne, 292, 296:
  see also Icarians
Calvinism, 77–8, 91, 113, 118, 304
Campan, Mme de, 137
Cappe, Catherine, 93, 141, 263, 267
Carlile, Anne, 255
Carlile, Jane, 236
Carlile, Richard, 225, 236, 237, 284
Carnot, Hippolyte, 138
Carpenter, Mary, 265, 269, 270, 314, 317
Cary, Virginia, 84
Catholic Church:
  and association among women, 98–9, 299, 323; and childrearing, 211; and the education of girls, 135–9, 145; in France, 12, 69, 96–9; and marriage, 194; and philanthropy, 264, 272–5; and sexual purity, 209
Chandler, Elizabeth, 249
Channing, William Ellery, 106
Chapman, Maria Weston, 231, 249
Chapone, Hester, 109
Chappellsmith, Margaret, 219, 224
Charity schools, 140–1, 142, 143, 263:
  see also Sunday Schools
'Charlotte Elizabeth' (Phelan Tonna), 113
Chartists, 204, 238–43:
  and the abolitionist movement, 247; on women's education, 144; on family life, 198; and temperance, 255; Flora Tristan and, 278; see also female Chartism
Cheltenham Ladies College, 132
Child, Lydia Maria, 42, 121, 153, 249–50, 270, 281, 284
Childbearing, 109–111, 209–11:
  collective, 20, 218; and educational psychology, 110–11, 118–19, 121; New Moral World on, 117; and temperance, 255; as women's task, 27, 29, 30, 31, 34, 38–9, 62,

Childbearing – *continued*
68, 108, 109, 119–22, 209–11; *see also* family life; motherhood; sensational theory of knowledge
Christian Socialism, 131, 314
Church of England:
evangelical movement in, 75, 86–7, 88–91; sisterhoods in, 317; and temperance, 255–6
Cigar-making industry, 167
Citizenship, for women:
Condorcet on, 42–3; women's demands for, 3–4, 44, 46–9, 50, 292, 294: rejected, 53, 295; language of, 3–4, 231–2, 276–7, 321; J. S. Mill on, 288–90; and republicanism, 3–4, 42–3, 54, 63–4, 276–7; Wollstonecraft on, 63–4; *see also* republicanism; suffrage
Clerical work, 185, 188
Clinton, De Witt, 120
Clothing trades, 158–9, 166–7:
see also needlewomen
Clough, Anne, 315
Clubs, women's:
in Britain, 55; in France, 47–52, 68, 292–3, 295
Cobbett, William, 235
Cobden, Richard, 244
Common sense philosophy, 110, 121, 122, 127
Communist Church, 105
Compagnonnage, 163, 205
Comte, Auguste, 286, 296, 297
Condorcet, Marquis de, 31, 42–3, 70
Congregationalism, 77, 78, 91, 251
Conseiller des Femmes, 125, 222
Considérant, Victor, 292, 295
Contagious Diseases Acts, 315
Co-operation, 242, 318:
among consumers, 176; in utopian communities, 217–20, 222–3; and women workers, 165, 168–70, 188, 193, 296
Cornwallis, Caroline Frances, 228
Cott, Nancy, 206, 207, 208, 213, 214
Cotton industry, *see under* textiles
Cours, 136–9
Craig, Isa, 314
Crandall, Prudence, 42, 147
Crèches, 169, 272, 275
Crimean War, 214
Croker, J. W., 244–5

Crowd action, women in:
in bread riots, 51, 69, 153, 200–2, 204; and community life, 188, 190, 200–5; declining importance of, 204, 205, 235, 323, 352n; on enclosures and communal rights, 153, 202–3; in machine-breaking, 163–4, 203; and political action, 232–5, 237; and poor relief, 153, 203–5; rituals of, 201, 232–4, 236; *see also* association, among men and among women

Dall, Caroline Healey, 187, 303, 307, 320
Daubié, Julie-Victoire, 139, 187, 262, 273, 275, 316, 320
Daumard, Adeline, 97
Dauriat, Louise, 138
Davidoff, Leonore, 206, 207, 212
Davidson, Caroline, 192
Davies, Emily, 135, 314, 319
Davis, Paulina Wright, 258, 303
Debay, Auguste, 209
Delacroix, Eugène, 232, Plate 8
Demar, Claire, 221–2
Deraismes, Maria, 296
Deroin, Jeanne, 186, 221, 262, 291–6, 320, 321
Deutsche Frauenzeitung, 303
Diderot, Denis, 7, 15, 18–19, 28, 66, 216, 222
Divorce:
and American feminism, 306; in Britain, 4, 55, 195; Charles Brockden Brown, on, 41; in France, 45, 46, 48, 53, 69, 97, 221; Harriet Taylor and John Stuart Mill on, 285; in the United States, 37, 41, 67, 306; Voltaire on, 12; women's demands on, 55, 216, 219, 221, 228, 229, 277, 292, 293, 306
Dix, Dorothea, 270
'Domestic feminism', 225
Domestic manufacture, 150, 154–61, 168:
in the clothing trades, 158–60, 166–7; declining, 80–1, 92, 104; education for, 141–2; expanding, 155–6, 157, 158, 159, 160; in glovemaking, 159–60; in lacemaking, 158; in the metal trades, 160–1; John Millar on, 27–8; in textile production, 156–8; and women's trade unionism, 161–70

Domestic service, 150, 155, 180–2, 200, 287:
  black women in, 154, 181–2; education for, 141, 142, 143; and ideals of domesticity, 180, 200; and married women, 155, 173, 181; and middle-class women, 214, 316; and prostitution, 196
Domestic violence, 199, 286
Domesticity:
  challenges to, 217–20, 223; Chartist (male and female) views of, 198, 238–40, 242; extensions of, 96, 214–15, 231–2, 243, 316–17; ideals of, 28–9, 30, 32, 96, 99, 189–90, 193, 198–9, 205, 206–15, 242; material conditions of, 189, 191–3, 206, 211–13; and men's role, 289–90; John Millar on, 28–9; and philanthropy, 264–5, 275, 316; and 'women's sphere', 66, 175, 189, 205, 206–7, 212–14, 252, 282, 316; for working-class women, 190–1, 193, 205, 222; see also childrearing; household work; motherhood; sexual division of labour
Donnison, Jean, 183
Douglas, Ann, 106
Douglass, Frederick, 253, 301
Douglass, Margaret, 147
Douglass, Sarah Mapps, 149
Drescher, Seymour, 247
Droz, Gustave, 211
Drysdale, George, 226
Dublin, Thomas, 173, 174, 176
Dudley, C. S., 94
Dupanloup, Bishop, 136, 139, 211
Duveau, Georges, 194

Eastman, Mehitabel, 175
Edgeworth, Maria, 109–12, 118, 121, 122
Edinburgh Review, 184
Education, of girls:
  and the American Revolution, 39–40; for black girls, 148; Chartist view of, 144–5; curriculum compared to boys, 3, 142–3, 148–9; conflicting with employment, 142, 145, 148; elementary, 42, 44, 53, 63, 108, 123, 132, 140–9, 200; for employment, 108, 130, 134–5, 148, 184; in female academies,
  41–2, 126–7; in female seminaries, 127–8; and feminism, 3, 132, 134–5, 145, 148, 276, 314, 316; and the French Revolution, 44, 47, 48, 49, 53; Mary Hays on, 65; and higher education, 130, 131–2, 134–5, 314; of infants, 110, 116, 118, 124; Hannah More on, 89, 112–13; for motherhood, 17–18, 38–40, 42, 90, 108, 109–25, 137, 139, 144, 209, 282; in the novel, 57, 111–12; Owenite view of, 117–18, 144; Restoration works on, 100, 122–3; secondary, 41–2, 125–39; of teachers, 42, 125–39; Flora Tristan on, 278; Mary Wollstonecraft on, 61; women's demands for, 45, 47, 48, 49, 144–5, 221, 222, 292, 293, 316; see also literacy; schools; teaching profession
Eliot, George (Marian Evans), 206, 228
Ellis, Lady, 134
Emerson, Ralph Waldo, 280, 281
Employment, women's, 3, 4, 43–4, 125, 130, 150–3, 154–61, 170–4, 180–2:
  of black women, 154, 181–2; education for, 108, 130, 134–5, 138, 148, 184; feminist demands for, 3, 151, 184–7, 188, 221, 276, 277, 287, 291, 293, 300, 307, 313, 316–18; Anna Jameson on, 130, 316–18; male attitudes to, 130, 165–8, 170, 177, 178–9, 187, 198–9, 280; for married women, 155–6, 159, 161, 172, 173, 177, 179, 180, 181, 182; Harriet Taylor Mill on, 311; John Stuart Mill on, 286, 287, 290; Charles Theremin in, 54; wages of, 163, 164, 167, 168, 173; Mary Wollstonecraft on, 63; see also domestic manufacture; domestic service; factory production; teaching; trade unionism; and under individual industries
Enfantin, Prosper, 105
Engels, Friedrich, 173, 224
English Woman's Journal, 2, 134, 307:
  and the abolitionist movement, 253; and association among women, 316–18; on education, 134–5, 145, 148–9; on employment, 184–6, 187, 287, 316–18, 320; and philan-

English Woman's Journal – continued
    thropy, 269–70, 272; and political
    rights, 313; and 'sanitory reform',
    266–7, 272; and suffrage, 313,
    318–19; and temperance, 256
Enlightenment, 2, 7–8, 38, 109:
    and feminism, 2, 7–8, 304; and
    women's role in the family, 8–12,
    15–18, 21–8, 29–30, 38; and
    women's history, 21–32; and
    women's nature, 12–21, 22, 28–9,
    30–2; *and see under* individual
    writers
Episcopalianism, 83, 272
Esquiros, Adèle, 297
Evangelicalism, 3, 73, 74–96:
    and the abolitionist movement, 246–8;
    and association among women,
    74, 78–82, 93–6, 100–1, 262–4;
    322; in black churches, 85–6; in
    Britain, 87–96; doctrines of, 76–7;
    and the education of women, 108,
    109, 112–14, 118–19, 140, 142;
    and family life, 76, 79, 84, 85, 86,
    89, 113, 207–8; and feminism, 304,
    322–3; and philanthropy, 89,
    262–4, 271–2; and revivalism,
    77–83, 85–6, 87, 92–3, 100; and
    sexual purity, 208–9; and slavery,
    83–5, 246; and temperance, 254;
    in the United States, 77–86; *see
    also* Bible Societies; missions;
    Sunday Schools; *and* individual
    denominations.
Examinations, 131, 133, 134–5, 137–9
Exclusive dealing, 238, 239

Factory production, 151, 155–9, 161,
    170–80:
    married women in, 172–3, 179, 180,
    243; and sexual morality, 196;
    single women in, 172–3, 179, 182,
    243; and women's trade unionism,
    173–4, 175–9; *see also* textile indus-
    tries
Faithfull, Emily, 314
Family, women in the, 4–5:
    among American Indians, 24–5, 26,
    86; contractual view of, 8–12;
    economy of, 4–5, 150, 168, 198–9;
    evangelical view of, 76, 79, 84, 85,
    89, 113, 207–8; expectations of, 5,
41, 190, 198–200, 206–8, 209–11;
history of, 21–8; Marx on, 224;
among the middle classes, 206–13,
299–300; John Millar on, 25–8;
Montesquieu on, 21–3; patriarchal view of, 8–9; among
peasantry, 98, 300; Rousseau on,
6–17; royalist view of, 97; in
slavery, 196–7; Adam Smith on,
23–4; and temperance, 254–5; violence and, 199, 286; among working classes, 98, 190, 198–200,
203–4, 323; *see also* childrearing;
domesticity; marriage; motherhood
Farnham, Eliza, 270, 316
Female Chartism, 238–43:
    and domesticity, 238–40; on education,
    144–5; and feminism, 242–3, 323;
    and nonconformity, 239; and
    temperance, 239, 255
Female Reform Societies, 235–7, Plates
    10, 11, 364n
'Feminisation' of religion, 73–7, 88, 97,
    98, 100–1, 205
Feminism:
    and birth control, 225–6; in Britain, 2,
    55, 59–60, 65, 70, 72, 132, 183–6,
    228–9, 256, 259, 262, 266–7,
    269–70, 272, 276, 287, 307–24;
    cartoons of, 230, Plate 12; conser-
    vative potential of, 319–20, 323;
    definition of, 1; and domesticity,
    190, 215, 232, 242–3, 276–7, 317;
    in France, 2, 33–4, 44–5, 48–9, 50,
    51, 53, 105, 124, 168–70, 186–7,
    216, 220–2, 229, 234, 247, 272–3,
    276–7, 277–80, 291–300, 321–3;
    and health reform, 258–9; hostile
    reactions to, 51–2, 66–72, 95–6,
    234–5, 251–3, 295–8, 321; inter-
    national, 320; language of, 3–4,
    42, 64, 231–2, 276–7, 290, 304–5,
    321, 322; and legal reform, 190,
    227–9, 286, 292, 313–14; limita-
    tions of, 321; middle-class nature
    of, 124, 183, 185, 222, 262–3, 277,
    291, 299–300, 304, 312–16, 319–20,
    322–3; and millenarianism, 101;
    and moral reform, 254, 257, 262,
    305, 307; and racial prejudice,
    253, 262–3, 304; and single
    women, 229–30; and suffrage, 43,

Feminism – *continued*
272, 276, 287, 292, 293, 298, 300–2, 306, 307–13, 315–16, 318–20; in the United States, 2, 38–9, 187, 222–3, 227–8, 248–54, 257–9, 262, 270–2, 276, 281–4, 300–7, 320, 322–3; and working-class women, 168–70, 182, 183, 188, 221–3, 242–3, 300; *see also* abolitionism; black women; education; employment; Owenism; philanthropy: Saint-Simonianism: temperance: trade unionism

Femme libre, 105, 220, 262
Ferguson, Adam, 23, 24, 219
Ferrier, Susan, 111, 113
Fildes, Mary, 236
Finney, Charles Grandison, 73, 79, 80, 81–2, 126, 259, 301
Flaxmer, Sarah, 102
Fourier, Charles, 1, 217, 220, 283, 292
Fourierists, 217, 278, 297
Fox, Eliza, 228
Fox, William Johnson, 106, 114, 228, 247, 285, 309
French Revolution:
of 1789, 43–54, 104, 135; of 1830, 163, 232; of 1848, 168–70, 232–3, 277, 291–5
French societies, 161–2, 179, 234
Froebel, Friedrich, 118
Frost, John, 238, 241
Fry, Elizabeth, 267–8
Fuller, Margaret, 277, 280–4

Gardner, John, 264
Garrett, Elizabeth, 135, 314, 319
Garrison, 249, 252, 301
Gaskell, Elizabeth, 206, 211, 228, 230
Gaskell, Dr Peter, 189, 195, 196
Gay (Veret), Desirée, 168, 169, 186, 220–4, 291, 294, 296
Gay, Delphine, 124
Gazette des Femmes, 262
Genlis, Mme de, 17–18, 109
Girardin, Emile de, 297, 298
Girton College, 132
Gisborne, Rev. Thomas, 88, 89–90
Glove-making industry, 158, 159–60, 164
Godwin, William, 55, 56, 64, 70, 216, 282
Goodrich, Samuel, 120

Gouges, Olympe de, 33, 45, 46, 50, 68
Governesses, 5, 125, 129, 130, 131, 133–5:
colleges for, 130, 131, 134; glut of, 134–5, 287; and the Governesses Benevolent Institution, 131
Graham, Isabella, 263
Grand National Consolidated Trades Union, 165
Grant, Zilpah, 42, 126, 127
Grassby, Mary, 204
Greeley, Horace, 182, 306
Gregory, Dr John, 109
Grimké sisters, 249, 251, 252, 253, 304, 305:
Angelina, 83–4, 208, 250, 251; Charlotte Forten, 306; Sarah, 251–2
Grimstone, Mary Leman, 115, 116, 129, 309
Grote, Harriet, 24, 315
Grotius, Hugo, 10
Grubb, Sarah Lynes, 93
Guindorff, Marie-Reine, 220
Guizot, Pauline, 100, 122
Gutman, Herbert, 197

Hale, Sarah, 230
Hall, Catherine, 213
Hall, Samuel Reed, 128
Hamilton, Elizabeth:
as anti-feminist, 71; on domestic life, 206; Plate 5; on education, 109–12, 118, 121, 122; on the 'feminisation of religion', 77
Hanson, Elizabeth, 241
Harney, Julian, 242
Harper, Frances, 306
Harrison, 254, 255
Hartford Female Seminary, 121, 126, 127
Hays, Mary, 59, 64, 65, 70
Hays, Matilda Mary, 318
Health reform, 258–9, 266
Hélvetius, Claude Adrien d', 20, 23
Hemingway, Eliza, 176
Héricourt, Jenny d', 296–8, 320
Hersh, Blanche Glassman, 303
Hertz, Fanny, 144, 145, 185
Hill, Michael, 317
History, women's, 25–8, 30–2, 38, 53–4
Holbach, Baron d', 19–20
Holcombe, Lee, 313
Holcroft, Thomas, 55, 56, 58
Holland, Lady, 243
Holyoake, George Jacob, 242, 308

Home and Colonial Training College, 132
Homoeopathy, 258
Household work:
advice manuals for, 206, 211–2; collective, 218, 219–20; education for, 143; and the family budget, 199, 211–12; for middle-class women, 206–8, 211–13; and 'sanitary reform', 266–7; and the visiting movement, 265–7; among the working classes, 191–3, 214; *see also* domestic service; domesticity
Howitt, Anna Mary, 314
Howitt, Mary, 217, 228, 230, 247, 282, 308, 314
Howitt, William, 217, 228, 247, 282, 308
Hume, David, 13–14, 20, 111
Hunt, Harriot, 258, 304
Hunt, Henry, 235, 236
Hutcheson, Francis, 9, 11–12

Icarians, 217
Illegitimacy, 43, 197–8, 292, 293
Immigration, 146, 153, 190, 197, 200:
feminist view of, 304; German, 146, 182; Irish, 146, 176–7, 182, 190; and stereotypes of sexuality, 197
Infant schools, 116, 123, 124, 132:
and infant teachers, 124, 132–3; and *salles d'asiles*, 123, 272, 274–5
Inchbald, Elizabeth, 55, 56, 57, 70, 71
Infanticide, 226
Inge, Susannah, 241–2
Ipswich Female Seminary, 126–7
Irish, 190:
in the United States, 146, 176–7, 182, 190

James, John Angell, 76
Jameson, Anna, 228:
on the double standard of morality, 262, 316; on employment, 130, 184, 187, 270, 316, 317; Margaret Fuller on, 283–4; on philanthropy and the 'communion of labour', 270, 316
Janet, Paul, 211
Jewsbury, Geraldine, 217, 228
Jex-Blake, Sophia, 132
Jones, David, 238
Jones, Ernest, 238

Journal des Femmes, 124, 221, 222, 291
Kelley, Abby, 253
Kingsley, Charles, 131
Knight, Anne, 247, 293, 308–9, 310
Knowlton, Charles, 225

Labrousse, Suzette, 103
Lacemaking industry, 158, 164, 179
Lacombe, Claire, 33, 51, 69
Ladies National Association for the Repeal of the Contagious Diseases Acts, 315
Lady, ideal of, 214
Lafayette, Marquis de, 222
Lamb, Anne Richelieu, 131, 310, 317
Lamb, Caroline, 129
Lamber (Adam), Juliette, 297
Laqueur, T. W., 140
Lawrence, James, 65–6, 221, 222
Law, Harriet, 309
Le Play, Frédéric, 199
Lee, Ann, 101, 102:
see also Shakers
Lee, Jarena, 85–6
Lemonnier, Elisa, 169, 186, 291
Léon, Pauline, 34, 48, 49, 51, 69
Leroux, Pierre, 292, 298
Lesguillon, Hermance, 297
Levi-Alvarès, David, 117, 138
Lewes, George Henry, 217
Lewis, Sarah, 75, 113, 117, 123
Lille, 98, 190, 192, 194, 196:
middle-class women of, compared to Manchester, 299; women's role in philanthropy in, 274–5
Lily, 257, 303
Literacy, women's:
in Britain, 140, 143; in France, 148; in the United States, 145–6
Livermore, Mary, 307
Locke, John, 7, 8, 9, 10, 12–13, 108, 109:
see also sensational theory of knowledge
'Loi Falloux', 139, 147
London:
City Mission, 194, 260; other missions, 261, 265–6; water supply in, 191; women's work in, 145, 150, 155, 158, 162, 166, 181; World Anti-Slavery Convention at, 247, 252, 320
Lovett, William, 238
Lowell (Massachusetts), 146, 157, 173–7, 182, 277

Lynn (Massachusetts):
   abolitionists lectures at, 251; shoemak-
      ing industry in, 146, 159, 166–7
Lyon, Mary, 126, 127
Lyons, women in:
and the Church, 98; and family life,
   198–9; in the revolution of 1848, 233;
   in the silk industry, 157–8

Macaulay, Catherine, 18, 115, 129, Plate
   2, 263n
McDowell, Anna, 303
Macfarlane, Helen, 241
Mackenzie, Henry, 20–1
McMillan, James, 298
Magnaud, Louise, 222
Maistre, Joseph de, 96
Manchester, women of:
   in the Anti-Corn Law League, 244–5;
      in bread riots, 201; compared to
      Lille, 190, 299; contemporary
      view of, 189; in Female Radical
      Reform Society, 237; literacy of,
      140; in trade unions, 162; and
      water supplies for, 191–2
Marcet, Jane, 225
Marriage:
   contracts of, 227, 229; feminists and,
      190, 217–18, 220–3, 227–9,
      313–15; and free unions, 190,
      194–5; Margaret Fuller on, 282;
      Francis Hutcheson on, 11–12;
      Jacobin radicals on, 58, 59; law of:
      in Britain, 4–5, 194–5, 228–9; in
      France, 4–5, 49, 53, 69, 194, 229;
      in the United States, 4–5, 36–7,
      41, 288–90; John Locke on, 9;
      John Stuart Mill on, 286–9; and
      millenarianism, 103; of the Nairs,
      65; Owenite views of, 217–20;
      Samuel von Pufendorf on, 10;
      Georges Sand on, 216; Mary
      Wollstonecraft on, 59–64
Martin, Caroline, 238, 240
Martin, Emma, 106–7, 219, 226, 259, 309
Martin, Sarah, 267
Martineau, Harriet, 106, 139, 145, 230:
   on the Anti-Corn Law League; on birth
      control, 225, 280, 308; on the
      education of women, 115, 116,
      134; on women's employment,
      134, 184; and legal reform, 228;
      and the suffrage campaign, 315; as
      a Unitarian, 314

Martineau, James, 106
Marx, Karl, 224
Mary, 86, 99
Maternal Associations, 79, 80, 81, 215:
   in Britain, 96; in France, 275
Maternal education:
   see education, for motherhood
Mauchamps, Mme de, 229
Maurice, Frederick Denison, 131
Mayeur, Françoise, 139
Mayhew, Henry, 145, 158, 194
Mazzini, Giuseppe, 217
Meade, Anne Randolph, 84
Mechanics Institutes, 144
Medical profession:
   and midwives, 183; on sexuality, 209;
      women's access to, 135, 186, 187,
      258–9; and women's hospitals,
      271
Melder, Keith, 307
Melun, Armand de, 273
Mère de Famille, 124
Méricourt, Theroigne de, 48, 49, 50, 68
Metal trades, 160–1, 194
Methodism, 77, 83, 85, 88:
   development of, 87; and district visit-
      ing, 264; and millenarianism, 101,
      102; and Primitive Methodism,
      87, 92–3
Michelet, Jules, 98, 296, 297–8
Midwives, 43, 168, 183, 259
Mill, Harriet Taylor, 184, 215, 284–5,
   314:
   and the 'Enfranchisement of Women',
      285, 311, 318, 320
Mill, James, 218, 284
Mill, John Stuart:
   and On Liberty, 289; and Harriet Taylor
      Mill, 284–5, 311; Bessie Rayner
      Parkes on, 318; and the Principles
      of Political Economy, 285, 287, 318,
      359n; and the Subjection of Women,
      2, 185, 190, 225, 284–91, 310, 311
Millenarianism, 101–5
Millar, John, 23, 25–8, 29, 30
Millet, Jean-François, 98, Plate 3
Milne, John Duguid, 184, 185, 287, 359n
Miner, Myrtilla, 147
Mining industry, 171–2, 195
Missions, 78, 81, 82:
   to the American Indians, 86; to the
      'fallen', 259–62; in France, 97, 99,
      100; and the London City Mis-
      sion, 194; and philanthropy, 271;

Missions – *continued*
        to slaves, 84–6: and the visiting
        movement, 265–6: women in, 78,
        95, 96, 259–62: see also Bible
        Societies
Monroe, Sarah, 167
Montesquieu, Charles Secondat, Baron
        de, 15, 21–3, 24, 30, 31
Monthly Repository, 106, 114, 115, 129, 285,
        309
Moral reform, 82, 254, 259–62, 270, 307
More, Hannah:
        conservatism of, 2: and the education
        of girls, 88–9, 112–13, 207: and
        evangelicalism, 75, 88–9: on
        women's role in family life, 88–9:
        and philanthropy, 89, 90, 91: and
        Sunday Schools, 90, 91, 94, 141
Morell, John, 114
Morrison, Frances, 219, 224
Morrison, James, 166
Mossaique Lyonnais, 125
Motherhood:
        Chartists on, 144, 239: Diderot on, 19:
        education for, 17–18, 38–40, 42,
        90, 108, 109–25, 137, 139, 144,
        209, 282: and evangelicalism,
        75–6, 79, 80–1: idealised, 29, 30,
        31, 39, 123: and the law, 4, 53, 227:
        magazines for, 210: John Stuart
        Mill on, 287: republican idea of,
        34, 52, 68, 118: responsibilities of,
        198, 209–11: Benjamin Rush on,
        38–9: Flora Tristan on, 279: Mary
        Wollstonecraft on, 62: *and see also*
        childrearing: family life: Maternal
        Associations
Mott, Lucretia, 227, 252, 253, 301, 302,
        303
Mount Holyoke College, 126, 127
Murray, Amelia, 131
Murray, Judith Sargent, 33, 38–9, 119
Mudie, R., 131
Mylne, Margaret, 116, 117, 309

Nairs, 24, 26, 66–7
Napoleon I, 137, 216
Napoleon III, 233:
        insurrection against, 233–4, 295
Nasmith, David, 260
National Association for the Promotion of
        the Social Sciences, 144, 184, 185,
        266, 267, 269

National Society for Promoting the Edu-
        cation of the Poor, 132, 141–3
National Society for Women's Suffrage,
        319
Natural law, 7–12
Natural rights, 7, 33, 42–3, 48, 49, 50:
        and feminism, 231, 304: of slaves, 250,
        253
Needlewomen, 158, 184, 187, 194, 287
Neeson, Elizabeth, 241
New Moral World, 115, 117–18
New Poor Law, 197–8, 203–5, 238, 268
New York, women of:
        in clothing trades, 156, 159, 170, 176:
        as domestic servants, 182: and
        missionary societies, 81–2: and
        moral reform societies, 82,
        259–60, 261–2: and philanthropy,
        263, 270–1: in temperance work,
        257: and trade unionism, 167
Niboyet, Eugénie, 125, 222, 274, 291,
        293, 294, 296, 299
Nichols, Clarina Howard, 305, 307
Nichols, Mary Gove, 258
Nightingale, Florence, 183, 317:
        and the Nightingale School, 186
Noel, Rev. Baptist, 142, 261
North London Collegiate School for
        Girls, 132
Norton, Caroline, 227
Novels:
        anti-feminist, 70–1: of domestic life,
        206, 230: of education, 111–12,
        113–14: Jacobin, 57–9
Noyes, John Humphrey, 223
Nursing, 184, 186, 214

Oberlin College, 126, 302
O'Connor, 204
Opinion des Femmes, 169, 170, 294
Ossoli, Marchese d', 281
Outwork:
        see domestic manufacture
Owen, Robert, 105, 278:
        on marriage, 218–19, 222: and trade
        unionism, 165: on women's edu-
        cation, 117–18: *see also* Owenism
Owen, Robert Dale, 225, 227
Owen, Sarah, 187
Owenism:
        and feminism, 170, 217–18, 222–4,
        307–8, 309: and marriage, 198,
        217–20: and women's education,
        144, 198

Ozanam, Frédéric, 273

Paine, Thomas, 7, 237
Pape-Carpentier, Marie, 274
Paris, women of:
  in the clothing trades, 158, 166; education of, 136, 137–8; family life in, 199; and free unions, 194; and French Revolutions: of 1789, 44, 46–9, 50–1, 68–9, 104; of 1830, 232; of 1848, 168–70, 292–3; and philanthropy, 272, 273–4; as workers, 150, 163, 164, 168–70, 193
Parker, Theodore, 76, 119, 281, 304
Parkes, Bessie Rayner, 228, 267, 308, 314, 317–18
Parkes, Joseph, 314
Parliamentary reform:
  in 1830–2, 237, 243, 309–10; and the Charter, 238; and Female Reform Societies, 235–6; and Northern Reform Society, 312; and Reform League, 242
Pastoret, Mme de, 274
Peabody sisters, 120, 281
Peabody, Elizabeth, 280, 281
Peasantry:
  declining birth rate of, 224; education of girls of, 123–4, 148; and women in crowd action, 153, 233–4; women's religious life among the, 98, 99
Pease, Louis, 271
Pease, Elizabeth, 247:
  and the Pease family, 315
Peel, Sir Robert, 244
Pendered, Anna Elizabeth, 114, 131
People's Journal, 217, 308
Perfectionists, 217, 223
Perrot, Michelle, 188, 190, 200
Pestalozzi, Johann Heinrich, 108, 117, 118, 120, 124, 137
Phelps, Almira, 120
Philanthropy, women in:
  and evangelicalism, 89, 262–4, 271–2; and female charities, 262–75; and feminism, 266–7, 272–3, 289, 316–17, 322–3; and hospitals, 269, 271, 317; and houses of industry, 271, 317; John Stuart Mill on, 289; and prisons, 267–8, 270; and the state, 274–5; and the visiting

movement, 263, 264, 265–6; and women's employment, 184, 187, 270, 316–18; and workhouses, 268–9
Phillips, Wendell, 306
Physical education, 124
Pierrard, Pierre, 274
Pinchbeck, Ivy, 173
Pioneer and Woman's Advocate, 303
Place, Francis, 225, 284
Pochin, Agnes Davis, 311
Pochin, Henry Davis, 312
Political economy, 318, 359n
Politique des Femmes, 294
Preaching, women's, 78, 85–6, 92–3, 101
Presbyterians, 77, 78, 79, 80, 83
Priestley, Joseph, 55
Primitive Methodism, 87, 92–3, 255
Prince, Lucy Terry, 147
Printing industry, women in, 167, 170:
  and the Lily, 257; and the Victoria Press
Prison visiting, 267, 274, 281
Prochaska, Francis K., 95, 263, 264, 267
Proctor, Adelaide, 132, 314
Prostitution:
  Condorcet on, 42; and the double standard of morality, 259; feminists on, 187, 221, 261–2; Margaret Fuller on, 283; and moral reform movements, 259–62; Flora Tristan on, 278; and women's employment, 187, 196
Protective legislation, 171–2
  and campaigns for, 175–6, 177, 178–9
Protestantism, in France, 100–1, 247, 274:
  and feminism, 299
Proudhon, Pierre-Joseph, 170, 234, 295, 296–8
Public speaking, women's, 2, 218, 223–4, 245, 309, 322:
  and the abolitionist movement, 232, 248–9, 250–2, 253; and female Chartism, 241; and Female Reform Societies, 235–6; and feminism, 2, 301–2, 309, 322; and secularism, 106–7, 236–7, 309; and trade unionism, 175, 176; see also preaching, women's
Public houses, 162, 205, 343n
Pufendorf, Samuel von, 9, 10, 11

Quakers, 91, Plate 4:
  in the abolitionist movement, 247, 249, 250; and feminism, 304, 309, 314, 315, 323; and the temperance movement, 253; women preaching in, 93
Queens College, 131–2, 314, 315

Racial prejudice:
  and feminism, 250, 253, 262–3, 304; among Quakers, 249, 250
Raikes, Robert, 141
Ranyard, Ellen, 96, 265–6, 271
Reddy, William, 232
Reed, Esther de Berdt, 36
Reid, Elizabeth, 131, 228, 253
Reid, Marion, 131, 247, 310, 321
Religious orders, 97:
  Anglican, 261, 317; and the education of girls, 136–7, 139, 148; and philanthropy, 272–5
Remond, Sarah, 253, 306
Remusat, Mme de, 100, 122, 136
Republicanism:
  classical, 3–4, 22–3, 27, 28–9, 31, 54, 288; and feminism, 3–4, 277, 309, 321–2; in France, 29, 42, 52, 53–4, 70, 139, 186, 234–5, 291, 293–4, 296–8; John Stuart Mill on, 288; Montesquieu on, 22–3; and motherhood, 34, 52, 68, 109, 118; Charles Theremin on, 53–4; Antoine Thomas on, 28–9; in the United States, 36, 39–40, 41, 67–8, 118, 174–5; Mary Wollstonecraft on, 64–72; see also American Revolution; citizenship; French Revolution
Revivalism:
  in black churches, 85–6; in Britain, 92–3; decline of, 254; in France, 97, 100; in United States, 77–83, 85–6
Ribbonmaking industry, 159
Richardson, R. J., 198, 239
Richer, Léon, 296
Richomme, Fanny, 124, 221
Ripley, Dorothy, 85
Robertson, William, 23, 24–5, 29, 30
Rodrigues, Olinde, 220, 292
Roland, Pauline, 168, 170, 222, 291, 293, 296, 320
Rosalie, Soeur, 272, 273

Rose, Ernestine, 227
Rossi, Alice, 306
Rousseau, Jean Jacques, 7, 15–17, 19, 31, 298:
  criticisms of, 17–18, 57, 60, 62, 71; influence on women's education, 17–18, 108, 109, 110, 120, 137; and La Nouvelle Héloïse, 15, 16, 17, 21, 63; Mary Wollstonecraft on, 60, 62, 63, 71
Rush, Benjamin, 39–40, 41, 109
Ryan, Mary, 206, 210, 213, 214, 271–2
Rye, Maria, 185, 314

Saint-Gilles, Antonine Andrée de, 291
Saint-Simon, Henri de, 104, 217, 220, 292
Saint-Simonianism, 104–5, 220, 234:
  and collective living, 217–18; and education of women, 124–5; influence on feminism, 105, 125, 169, 217–18, 220–3, 278, 280, 285, 291–2, 297, 298; Jenny d'Héricourt on, 297–8; John Stuart Mill on, 285; Flora Tristan on, 278, 280
Salt, Thomas Clutton, 240
Sand, Georges, 124, 216, 217, 294, 314
'Sanitary reform', 266, 267:
  and feminism, 272, 307; and women's employment, 317
Saussure, Mme Necker de, 100, 120, 122–3, 125, 210:
  Margaret Fuller on, 284
Schools, for girls: 114, 122, 125:
  in Britain, 90–1, 93–4, 108, 114, 125, 129, 131, 132–3, 140–3, 145, 198; charity schools, 42, 49, 140–1, 142, 143, 263; elementary, 108, 123, 126, 131, 132, 137, 139, 140–9, 200; factory, 143; in France, 123–5, 135–9, 147–8, 274–5; industrial, 90, 140–1, 143, 271, 272; infant, 116, 123, 124, 132, 272, 274–5; monitorial, 132, 141–3; ragged, 143, 269; reformatory, 269; secondary, 41–2, 108, 114, 126–39, 140; in the United States, 41–2, 121–2, 125–9, 145–7; Mary Wollstonecraft on, 63; workhouse, 143, 268; see also education: Sunday Schools
Scott, Joan, 173
Secularism, 106–7, 237, 309, 323

Sedgwick, Catherine, 230, 270
Segalen, Martine, 98, 152, 205
Seneca Falls Convention, 176, 227:
   and the Declaration of Sentiments,
      176, 227, 253, 300–1; and the
      temperance movement, 257
Sensational theory of knowledge, 12–13,
   18, 19–20:
   and early education, 108, 109, 111,
      117, 118–19; Mary Wollstonecraft
      on, 60–1; and *see* education, for
      motherhood
Sentimentalism, 21, 56–7
Sewell, Elizabeth Missing, 113
Sexual division of labour, 124, 150–3,
   165, 191–3, 321:
   feminist view of, 186, 267, 282, 290;
      Margaret Fuller on, 282; John
      Stuart Mill on, 287, 290; Jean
      Jacques Rousseau on, 15; and
      'woman's sphere', 175, 282, 290
Sexuality:
   and the double standard of morality,
      209, 262, 315, 316; evangelical
      view of, 208; feminist views of,
      208–9, 217–18, 220–3; and ideal of
      purity, 208–9; middle-class views
      of, 195–7; and millenarianism,
      103, 104, 223; and Owenism,
      216–20; racial stereotypes of,
      196–7; and Saint-Simonianism,
      220–1; and sexual radicalism,
      19–20, 65–6, 67, 71, 215, 223;
      Charles Theremin on, 53–4
Shaftesbury, Earl of, 185
Shakers, 101, 103, 217
Sharp, Granville, 246
Sharples, Elizabeth, 225, 236, 237
Sheffield Female Reform Association,
   308, 320
Shelley, Percy Bysshe, 216, 222
Sheppard, Emma, 261, 268
Shoemaking, 159, 166–7
Shop employment, 187
Shuttleworth, Sir James Kay, 132
Silk industry, *see under* textiles; Lyons
Silliman, Benjamin, 66
Simon, Jules, 139, 186, 189, 196
Sinclair, Catherine, 113
Single women, 4, 229–30
Sirey, Madelaine, 124
Sisterhoods:
   Anglican, 261, 327; of Bible-women,

265; feminists on, 169, 317; *see also*
   religious orders
Slavery:
   and anti-slavery, *see* abolitionist
      movement; black compared to
      white, 246–7; and co-operation, in
      Nashoba, 223–4; family life and
      sexuality under, 197; language of,
      232, 248, 304–5; women's educa-
      tion under, 147; women's labour
      under, 154
Smith, Adam, 23–4
Smith, Barbara Leigh, 132, 134–5, 184,
   228, 308, 314, 319
Smith, Bonnie, 98, 206, 207, 212, 274–5
Smith, Charlotte, 57–8
Smith, Hannah, 201, 203
Smith, James Elishama, 105
Smith, Sydney, 114
Smith-Rosenberg, Carroll, 215
'Société de la morale chrétienne', 125,
   247, 274
Society for the Promotion of the Em-
   ployment of Women, 185
Somerville, Mary, 315
'Sophia', 241–2
Southcott, Joanna, 102, 103, 105
Spencer, Anna, 303
Stanton, Elizabeth Cady, 227, 252, 253,
   257, 301, 302, 306, 321
Stewart, Dugald, 110
Stewart, Maria, 248
Stillman, Mrs, 263
Stodart, M. A., 92
Stone, Huldah, 175
Stone, Lawrence, 113
Stone, Lucy, 227, 302, 304–5
Strawplaiting, 158:
   and hat-making, 158, 160
Sturge, Mrs, 256
Sturge, Eliza, 315
Sturge, Joseph, 247, 315
Suffrage, women's:
   in Britain, 239, 242, 245, 272, 307–13,
      318–20; Chartist view of, 239;
      Condorcet on, 42–3; in France, 48,
      53, 292, 293–4, 295, 298; Jenny
      d'Héricourt on, 298; compared to
      male suffrage, 234, 242, 300,
      309–10, 312–13, 319–20; John
      Stuart Mill on, 287; and the tem-
      perance movement, 257, 315; in
      the United States, 37–8, 67,

Suffrage, women's – *continued*
300–7; Mary Wollstonecraft on, 63; *see also* citizenship; parliamentary reform
Sullerot, Evelyne, 124, 220, 318
Summers, Anne, 214
Sunday Schools, 78, 90, 91, 93–4, 100, 132, 141, 143, 263:
and the temperance movement, 255

Taylor family, of Ongar, 206, 207
Taylor, Barbara, 165, 219, 309
Taylor, Clementia, 319
Teaching profession, for women, 42, 123, 124, 125–39, 148–9, 186:
and academies, 126–7; and *cours*, 137–8; in elementary schools, 127–8, 129, 131; prejudice against, 132, 137, 138; and seminaries, 127–8; and training colleges, 124, 125, 128–9, 130, 132–3, 138; women especially fitted for, 123, 125, 127–8; *see also* education; examinations; governesses
Ten Hours campaigns, *see* protective legislation
Temperance movement:
in Britain, 254–7; and female Chartists, 239, 242, 255; and feminism, 254, 257–8, 306; in the United States, 257–8
Textile industries:
and factory production, 172–80, 323; family life of workers in, 155, 172, 173, 177, 180; and female Chartism, 243; industrialisation of, 150, 154–8; and literacy of the labour force in, 140, 146; married women employed in, 172, 173, 177, 179; and supposed promiscuity of the labour force in, 195–6; and women's trade unionism, 155, 162–4, 173–80
Théot, Catherine, 103
Theremin, Charles, 53–4
Thomas, Antoine, 18, 28–31, 38, 39
Thompson, Dorothy, 188, 200, 205
Thompson, William, 217–18, 225, 276, 284, 307
Tilly, Louise, 173
Tocqueville, Alexis de, 232

Tomes, Nancy, 199
Trade unionism, women's, 161–70:
and domestic service, 181; and factory production, 173–4, 175–8; and feminism (women's rights), 168–70, 174, 175–6; and male trade unionism, 162, 163, 165–8, 170, 177–9, 234, 243; and Owenism, 165–6; and utopian socialism, 168–70, 295; and strikes, 163–4, 166–7, 174–5, 232–3
Trades, for women, 158, 160, 176, 183, 184:
and see domestic manufacture
Transcendentalism, 120, 281–2
Tribune des Femmes, 138, 220–2
Trimmer, Sarah, 90, 91, 94, 141, 264
Tristan, Flora, 229, 277–80, 358n
Troy Seminary, 126
Truth, Sojourner, 253
Twining, Louisa, 268–70, 317

Una, 187, 303
Unitarianism, 91, 106, 114:
and feminism, 106, 304, 314, 315, 323; see also *Monthly Repository*
Universalist's Miscellany, 114
Utica, New York, 80, 81, 206, 207, 208, 210, 271–2
Utopian socialism:
and feminism, 3–4, 168–70, 188, 217, 220, 223–4, 292, 293, 295, 297, 298, 318, 323; and Flora Tristan, 277–80; *see also* Fourierism; Icarians; Owenism; Saint-Simonianism

Vasbenter, Louis, 199, 280
Veret, Désirée, *see under* Gay
Villermé, Louis, 189, 194, 196
Vincent, David, 198
Vincent, Henry, 241
Voice of Industry, 175, 176
Voilquin, Suzanne, 221, 222, 224, 291, 296
Voix des Femmes, 168, 169, 262, 291–4
Voltaire, François Marie Arouet de, 7, 15:
on divorce, 12, 15
Vuigneras, Marie de, 46

Wakefield, Priscilla, 125, 183

Walker, Mary Ann, 241
Walkowitz, Judith, 315, 318
Warren, Mercy Otis, 35
Water supplies, 191–2, 212:
  and washing, 192–3
Wedgwood, Julia, 132
Wesley, John, 76, 87
West, Jane, 71
Westminster Review, 116, 217, 228, 285, 309
Wheeler, Anna, 217, 221, 224, 225, 307
Wheeler, Thomas, 238–9
Whitefield, George, 87, 101
Whitelands College, Putney, 133
Wilberforce, William, 73, 75, 88
Wightman, Julia, 256, 261
Wild, Hortense, 299
Wilderspin, Samuel, 132
Wilkinson, Jemima, 102, 103
Willard, Emma, 120, 126, 301
Williams, Helen Maria, 70, Plate 2, 263n
Willis, May, 236
Wollaston, William, 9, 11
Wollstonecraft, Mary, 7, 33, 39, 55–7,
  59–65, 174, 183, 216, 276, 282:
  on education, 60–1, 63, 109, 125, 129;
    life of, 55–6, 64; opposition to,
    66–7, 70–2; and sexual purity,

208; and the *Vindication of the Rights
  of Woman*, 7, 55, 56–7, 59–64; and
  the *Wrongs of Women*, 59, 64
Woman Messiah, 103, 104, 105, 211:
  Flora Tristan on, 278
Woman's Advocate, 303
Women's Elevation League, 309
Women's nature, 12, 55, 189, 208,
  214–15:
  American feminists on, 305; British
    feminists on, 184, 186, 308, 310,
    316; Enlightenment writers on,
    12–21, 22, 28–9, 30–2 (*see also under
    individual authors*); evangelical
    views of, 74–5, 89; French femin-
    ists on, 297–8; Margaret Fuller
    on, 282–4; Jacobin radicals in Bri-
    tain on, 55–64; John Stuart Mill
    on, 286, 290
Woollen industry, *see under* textile indus-
  tries
Wright, Frances, 222–3, 224, 225
Wright, Richard, 114
Wright, Susannah, 236, 237

Yonge, Charlotte M., 114